W9-CMB-039

Wired Shut

Wired Shut

Copyright and the Shape of Digital Culture

Tarleton Gillespie

The MIT Press
Cambridge, Massachusetts
London, England

MIT Press books may be purchased at special quantity discounts for business or sales promotional use. For information, please email special_sales@mitpress.mit.edu or write to Special Sales Department, The MIT Press, 55 Hayward Street, Cambridge, MA 02142.

This book was set in Stone Sans and Stone Serif by SNP Best-set Typesetter Ltd., Hong Kong. Printed and bound in the United States of America.

Library of Congress Cataloging-in-Publication Data

Gillespie, Tarleton.
Wired shut : copyright and the shape of digital culture / Tarleton Gillespie.
 p. cm.
Includes bibliographical references and index.
ISBN-13: 978-0-262-07282-3 (hardcover : alk. paper)
 1. Copyright—Electronic information resources. 2. Piracy (Copyright) I. Title.
K1447.15.G55 2007
346.04′82—dc22

                                                              2006030129

10 9 8 7 6 5 4 3 2 1

Contents

Acknowledgments

I owe a great debt, one that I suspect I cannot calculate nor ever repay, to all those who offered their help, support, and insights throughout the writing of this book. A special thanks for the guidance of Chandra Mukerji and Robert Horwitz. Many thanks to Geof Bowker, Dan Burk, John Caldwell, Julie Cohen, Shay David, Josh Greenberg, Jeff Hancock, Peter Hirtle, Steve Jackson, Joe Karaganis, Leah Lievrouw, Michael Lynch, Lev Manovich, Helen Nissenbaum, Trevor Pinch, Matt Ratto, Lucy Suchman, and Fred Turner for taking the time to read and improve the manuscript. Thanks to Doug Sery, Valerie Geary, Kathy Caruso, Amanda Nash, and Emily Gutheinz at the MIT Press, as well as the anonymous reviewers for their thorough and helpful critiques. A special thanks to Nat Sims for designing the cover of the book and to Alexa Weinstein for her meticulous proofreading. Thanks to all my colleagues in Communication at UCSD, and in Communication, Science & Technology Studies, and Information Science at Cornell, for providing the rich intellectual environments from which this work sprang. Thanks to the people at Claire de Lune Coffee Lounge in San Diego and at Wownet Cafe and Juna's Cafe in Ithaca for their caffeine and hospitality. And for their endless support, patience, and encouragement, my eternal gratitude to my parents, my family—and most of all to Jenna and Jonas.

Portions of this book were assisted by a grant from the Digital Cultural Institutions Project of the Social Science Research Council, with funds provided by the Rockefeller Foundation. Thanks also to the participants of the "Digital Cultural Institutions and the Future of Access: Social, Legal, and Technical Challenges" workshop at the Center for Science, Technology, and Society, Santa Clara University, October 21–23, 2004, for their advice. Thanks also to the Center for Internet and Society at the Stanford Law School for the support and community provided by its 2005–2007 fellowship award.

Pieces of this research, at various stages of completion, were presented at conferences hosted by the Association of Internet Researchers (AoIR) and the Society for the Social Study of Science (4S), and as colloquia for the department of Science & Technology Studies at Rensselaer Polytechnic Institute, the department of Information Science at Northeastern University, the Information Society Project at Yale School of Law, and the Center for Internet and Society at Stanford Law School. Many thanks to the participants and audiences in all of those places for their attention, questions, and suggestions.

A version of chapter 6 appeared as "Copyright and Commerce: The DMCA, Trusted Systems, and the Stabilization of Distribution," *The Information Society* 20.4 (Sept. 2004): 239–254. Reproduced by permission of Taylor & Francis Group, LLC., http://www.taylorandfrancis.com.

A version of chapter 8 appeared as "Designed to 'Effectively Frustrate': Copyright, Technology, and the Agency of Users," *New Media and Society* 8.4 (Aug. 2006): 651–669. It appears here with the permission of *New Media and Society* and Sage Publications.

A portion of chapter 9 appeared as "Autonomy and Morality in DRM and Anti-Circumvention Law," *Triple C: Cognition, Communication, Cooperation* (2006), co-authored with Dan Burk. It appears here with the permission of *Triple C*, and with gratitude to Dan Burk.

A portion of chapter 9 will also appear as "Price Discrimination, Regional Coding, and the Shape of the Digital Commodity," in Joe Karaganis and Natalie Jeremijenko, eds., *Structures of Participation in Digital Culture* (forthcoming, 2007).

1 | The Technological Fix

It seems like ages, although it's been only a few short decades, since Alvin Weinberg posed the question, "In view of the simplicity of technological engineering and the complexity of social engineering, to what extent can social problems be circumvented by reducing them to technological problems? Can we identify Quick Technological Fixes for profound and almost infinitely complicated social problems, 'fixes' that are within the grasp of modern technology, and which would either eliminate the original social problem without requiring a change in the individual's social attitudes, or would so alter the problem as to make its resolution more feasible?"[1] We may be a bit amused, or perhaps a little shocked, by the naïveté of Weinberg's tragically optimistic question—especially when we discover that his answer was a qualified "yes" pointing to, of all things, the hydrogen bomb as a successful technological fix for the social problem of war.

We can only hope we'll never again be so naïve as to think we can somehow simply and justly resolve social problems with technologies, or so oblivious to their own intricate consequences when we try to do so anyway. But it's a surprisingly elusive lesson. We still search for, and long for, such "technological fixes"—even as we give perfunctory lip service to how they are only stopgap measures or technological add-ons to social policies. As Carolyn Marvin wrote, "People often imagine that, like Michelangelo chipping away at the block of marble, new technologies will make the world more nearly what it was meant to be all along."[2] And the social problems we hope to resolve are as intractable as when Weinberg wrote. We hope trigger locks will reduce violent crime, cameras and facial recognition algorithms will ensure privacy and public safety, smart ID cards will squelch terrorism, the V-chip will protect children from images of sex and violence. These technologies hold out the promise of attaining progressive social goals, and of doing so effectively, fairly, and without discrimination—a promise built upon the persistent sense that technologies exist outside the frailty, inertia, and selfishness of human politics.

This faith in technology as an inherently progressive force is a powerful Western paradigm wrapped tightly into the ethos of American culture. Yet it is an illusion. By itself, technology can never solve the problems its proponents aspire to solve. Imagining that new technology will rescue us from our persistent social ills allows us to momentarily forego the much harder questions: What are the social bases for the problem, how do they work, and why does the problem persist? What forces shaped this technology, what is it supposed to accomplish, and what does it demand of us in order to work? Technological fixes also help abrogate the responsibility of both the people involved in the problem and the designers of the technology themselves. Perhaps this sense of determinism is appealing—don't we want the new dishwasher to scrub our cares away? Rob Kling notes that these "utopian visions" resonate with the public imagination because "their causal simplicity gives them great clarity and makes them easy to grasp, to enjoy or to abhor. They can resonate with our dreams and nightmares."[3] And in a culture bound tightly to an economic and ideological commitment to a never-ending flow of new commodities, planned obsolescence, and the luxurious promises of advertising, the claim that technologies will fix what ails us is an all-too-familiar marketing ploy.

Whenever a new technology arrives, it typically evokes a flurry of questions, hopes, fears, and predictions about what it will do, marked by an underlying faith in social progress through technology. The particular character of the claims about what the technology will accomplish will depend on which of its features are most novel. But, even more, the claims will depend on the particular dilemmas we as a society are facing at that moment. The arrival of a new tool will often get entangled in current tales of social conflict and cultural failings, championed as a long-awaited solution. The printing press would bring forth a new era of learning; electricity would end the tyranny of nighttime over human accomplishment; the radio would unite the nation into a single community; television would bring the world into our living rooms; weapons of mass destruction would banish war.[4] Discourses surrounding new technologies typically "predict a radical discontinuity from history and the present human condition";[5] we expect technologies to intervene in precisely those aspects of society we find most troubling, those we have secretly hoped to finally resolve.

Paul Duguid suggests that these cycles of technological prophecy regularly depend on two principles: supersession, "the idea that each new technological type vanquishes or subsumes its predecessors," and liberation, "the argument or assumption that the pursuit of new information technologies is simultaneously a righteous pursuit of liberty."[6] These make a kind of logical sense together: An old technology imposes constraints on its users, an improved technology resolves those problems and thus replaces its now worthless predecessor. Social limitations (e.g., the stultifying isolation of life in the vast American wilderness) are tied to established technologies (newspapers, which require human proximity to be distributed); the new technology (radio) will fully replace the old because it removes the barrier it imposed.[7] The "pioneer in the wilderness, the farmer on his isolated acres" will have the news of the nation at their fingertips, will find themselves connected to their fellow man despite the miles, and will be free to exercise their democratic rights as citizens in a way that they could not before.[8]

It is a cohesive vision well suited to an Enlightenment idea that history itself is always a tale of broad social progress. It is also well suited to the interests of capital, which must convince consumers that, despite the quality, durability, and initial appeal of the old commodity, the new product is an urgent improvement rather than a frivolous luxury. Most of all, the broader social structure survives intact; the break is not only resolved, it's welcomed, assured somehow by "the paradoxical prediction that freedom from technology can be achieved through technology."[9]

This requires, of course, that tales of a technology's progressive potential must follow, or be paired with, tales of the previous technologies' limits, failings, and dangers. Dystopic worries about technology are the necessary flipside of the coin; faith in the new technology requires that we perennially forget, or ignore, our faith in each technology that preceded it. This deliberate aphasia allows us to map social ills onto the caricatured evolution of our tools, conjuring a reassuring tale of benevolent and unproblematic progress. Discussing an optimistic faith around the coming of electricity, James Carey notes that "electricity promised, so it seemed, the same freedom, decentralization, ecological harmony, and democratic community that had hitherto been guaranteed but left undelivered by mechanization. But electricity also promised the same power, productivity, and economic expansion previously guaranteed and delivered by mechanical industrialization"[10]—the very ills that critics were looking to electricity to cure.[11] Instead of addressing the complexity and specificity of the interaction between technologies and the sociocultural activities in which they are embedded, critics prefer to embrace this compelling fantasy of waves of technological progress.

The Internet and the Question of Copyright

There are certainly better ways to think about the relationship between technological and social change, yet this naïve optimism persists. The Internet brought with it the same rhetoric of supersession and liberation in the whirlwind of hype and hoopla that surrounded its arrival.[12] In a culture fascinated with technological innovation and devoted to the religion of progress, it should come as no surprise that the Internet captured our imagination, spurring the same optimistic predictions as electricity, the automobile, radio, even the hydrogen bomb. According to the Internet's proponents, education would become truly universal as all human knowledge became perfectly and instantly accessible to all. Championed by both the left and the right,[13] the Internet would allow democracy to flourish as citizens went online to debate important issues and politicians spoke directly to the people. Environmentally destructive urban populaces would scatter to the natural idylls once they could work flexible hours from home. The social barriers of race, class, and gender would disintegrate as identity became a virtual plaything, a costume put on with a keystroke. Censorship would fail and wisdom would flourish as those who deserved to be heard could speak freely. Or as *Wired* announced (ironically, in an article about technological disasters), "We think technology is rapidly opening up possibilities and revolutionizing the old order in a way that gives a chance to smaller players. We are unabashed optimists about our collective opportunities as we round the corner into the next century. We are skeptical of anyone's claims (including our own) to know what the future brings, but we look at the glass and see that it is no longer half-full but brimming over."[14]

Yet amid all this promise, the Internet was also being criticized as a grave threat to culture, morality, and society. The earliest legislative attention paid to the new medium concerned the proliferation of pornography online, accessible to anyone in any community at any age. Though these particular worries turned out to be dramatically overstated, we continue to fret about the "promiscuity" of the Internet, facilitating the circulation of not only the loftiest elements of our culture, but also the basest: pornography, hatred, misinformation, unbridled gossip. Concerns also erupted about the "death of privacy" harkened by the Internet: personal information vulnerable to identity thieves, corporate information open to clever hackers, children's personal safety threatened by online stalkers offering virtual candy.[15] Again, the concerns about the Internet's impact on privacy have since shifted. Nevertheless, the fear that the "radical discontinuity" of the Internet would lead to social ills rather than progress persists. So once again we look to technological solutions to seemingly technological problems, now with the Internet as the problem in need of a technical solution so that its liberatory promise can be fulfilled.

Nowhere has this been more visible than in the recent controversies around copyright law in the digital environment. Once the exclusive domain of corporate lawyers and policymakers, copyright spilled into public awareness with the emergence of the Internet. Designed to regulate the movement of culture by making it a market commodity, copyright now faced a technology that dramatically reimagined how and by whom culture is produced, sold, distributed, and consumed. At the same moment, those industries most invested in copyright found themselves scrambling to keep up with the accelerated stakes of the so-called knowledge economy. The game had changed, not only technologically but economically, politically, and culturally. Would the Internet prompt the renovation of copyright law and the proliferation of new techniques of cultural production that could exceed traditional copyright's limited imagination? Or would it require the imposition of even more stringent versions of the law, to compensate for the absence of those material and economic constraints endemic to physical manufacture and exchange?[16] Many have argued that this battle extends well past the definition of copyright to a clash of paradigms about the control of information: Lawrence Lessig describes it as the choice between "free" versus "permission" culture, Siva Vaidhyanathan calls it a struggle between "anarchy" versus "oligarchy."[17]

The rapid rise of Napster and peer-to-peer file trading offered the flashpoint, provoking the major U.S. entertainment corporations to declare a legal war: against Napster, against proponents of an unregulated Internet, and at times against their own customers. Some foretold the death of copyright; others railed against the sin of piracy and called for new laws to save the endangered species known as artists. Record labels found themselves suing their own consumers; movie studios produced expensive trailers lecturing reluctant audiences, some of whom were, at that moment, automatically downloading Hollywood blockbusters on their computers at home. Digital startups looking to take advantage of the ease of distribution the Internet provides found themselves caught in the crossfire, while the major content providers took flak in the press for not pursuing new business models themselves. Some artists proclaimed their support for their publishers, while others looked the other way as their work appeared online, or even helped it get there; Metallica sued Napster to protect its copyright while Chuck D spoke out in Napster's support. Apple courted the middle with an industry-friendly plan to sell content through iTunes, only to find itself in competition with a resuscitated Napster providing authorized digital music by subscription.

For the most part, these battles have taken place in the courts and in the court of public opinion; a legal effort to use copyright to stem the tide of "piracy" faces a cultural movement enamored with the appeal of the new technology. But under cover of this noisy debate, content providers and lawmakers have begun to implement significant changes in the way copyright is applied in a digital culture. At the core of these changes is a fundamental shift in strategy, from regulating the use of technology through law to regulating the design of the technology so as to constrain use.

Such strategies aim to take advantage of the fact that, while digital technology may facilitate a dizzying array of choices and opportunities at blistering speed and with total access, it can also be used to keep close tabs on what is being done and by whom. Technical barriers and rules can be incorporated directly into the communication networks that we increasingly use to participate in community, in commercial exchange, in politics, and in the conversation of culture. What we might call "social engineering" has come full circle back to actual engineering, where the tools and the environment are built to assure that the right practices are facilitated, the wrong are inhibited. These technologies are largely being developed and deployed below our cultural radar, enamored as we are with the thrill of the "information revolution," the faith in progress, and the freedom of individual agency.

Turning to Technology

Consider the court's decision in the lawsuit against the Napster peer-to-peer (p2p) network. While the most important aspect of the decision at the time was the fact that Napster lost the case, it is the particular way in which they lost, at least in the courtroom, that offers an important harbinger of the broader shifts in law, technology, and culture we are now experiencing. Cursory histories of the Napster case may remember only that the courts, finding on behalf of the major record industries, shut down Napster for contributing to massive online copyright infringement. But the Ninth Circuit Court of Appeals actually did no such thing; although it may have been their underlying intention, the court did not mandate that Napster turn off its servers or cease its business operations. Instead, noting that "Napster has both the ability to use its search function to identify infringing musical recordings and the right to bar participation of users who engage in the transmission of infringing files,"[18] they called for a technological fix, one designed to change Napster so it would systematically discern and filter out the unauthorized music the Recording Industry Association of America (RIAA) had complained about.

Set aside for the moment the legal question of whether the maker of a tool should be held accountable for the uses the tool is put to. This effort to deploy a technological artifact as a legal intervention represents a larger strategy that, even in the short time since the Napster decision, has become a full-fledged project on behalf of the major culture industries.[19] Rather than articulating what can and cannot be done legally with a copyrighted work, this approach favors the design of encryption technologies (once reserved for military secrecy) to build the legal standards of copyright directly into the artifact—such that some uses are possible and others are rendered impossible. While the proponents of this approach (most notably the U.S. music and film industries) have taken great pains to maintain that this is simply a practical improvement required to counter the hazards of the Internet, matching copyright law in terms of the ends it will achieve, this use of encryption represents a dramatic new intervention into communication and culture. Once again, we are putting faith in a technical solution to a social problem.

The film and music industries are in some ways following in the footsteps of the software industry, which in the 1980s had to grapple with the ease of unauthorized reproduction and distribution of their content; indeed, they are expanding on some of the solutions the software industry developed in response. But what was once simple password protection is becoming something much more significant. Current encryption techniques allow content owners to decide who gets access to their work according to much more precise, subtle, and modifiable criteria. Today, digital content can include information indicating how, when, and where that content can be used, rules that will be honored automatically by the devices we use to consume it. With these innovations, film and music distributors are going far beyond what the software industry had once imagined, to govern not only whether we copy their work, but also how we buy, share, experience, and interact with it.

The inflated rhetoric of the copyright wars has provided a compelling cover for a sometimes concerted attempt to develop this technological architecture. This intervention aspires to regulate not only copyright but also nearly every dimension of the distribution and consumption of culture. These control strategies have thus far been of limited effectiveness in the face of persistent hackers, the efforts of commercial bootleggers, the powerful appeal of free and accessible entertainment for a generation that has known little else, and the ubiquitous cultures of sharing pervasive to the societies and economies of India, China, and elsewhere. However, regardless of (or even in spite of) its likelihood of success, this strategy warrants critical attention, and not only for its possible consequences for copyright. Enlisting technological design as a way to regulate its users will have significant consequences for the trajectory and cultural life of digital technologies, and for how we get to make use of them.

We don't usually think very explicitly about how the construction of walls subtly regulates our activity. Certainly, some of us are aware of this at moments—prisoners know it is the walls and the guards, and particularly their combination, that restrict their freedom so effectively; the residents of what was once East Berlin, or today's inhabitants of the Gaza Strip or Tijuana, are all too cognizant of the unique power of combining political authority, legal force, and technical barriers to intervene in people's lives. Those of us who are relatively untouched by such dramatic impositions of control are afforded the pleasure of seeing the technologies around us as facilitating rather than limiting, offering opportunities to participate in social life as we please. But this invisibility does not mean these arrangements are any less consequential. Technologies choreograph our social activity, often with political consequences, and can be made to do so in increasingly sophisticated ways with digital technology. And when technological design must be directed so that the technologies will enforce laws, the delicate dynamics of technological innovation can be profoundly disturbed.

Building the rules of copyright into the technologies themselves similarly aims to intervene in human activity while disappearing beneath business as usual. Technical copy protection preempts those activities that copyright law has traditionally prohibited, but the translation of legal rules into code may not prove particularly adept at handling copyright's legal subtleties. At the same time, new possibilities for communication and collaboration encouraged by the particular shape of the Internet may find little space to grow inside restrictions based on traditional copyright, especially as it is understood by those whose business models are most powerfully undercut by these new practices.

Beyond the Technical

The premise of this book is that in order to understand what is happening to digital copyright, we must broaden the question. While important concerns have already been raised about the consequences of these technical control strategies for copyright law,[20] considering these artifacts away from their broader sociopolitical contexts fundamentally misunderstands the kind of controls being developed. We must dare to expand our scrutiny, to see this complex shift in a wider context. The technologies are only the most visible elements of an increasingly cohesive regulatory strategy, sometimes called the "trusted system."

Consider for a moment how most of us are prevented from copying our DVDs. The first line of defense is that the DVD players widely available to consumers do not have a Record button. The act of copying is simply absent from the technological choices offered. This is a powerful barrier, enough to stop most people most of the time from copying the movie they rented. Yet this is only the interface to the underlying system of control, and to stop there begs the question why manufacturers of DVD players, knowing their customers might like to copy their favorite movies, don't design for it.

Manufacturers of DVD players do not offer Record buttons because they are prohibited from doing so by a license arrangement with the movie industry. They assent to this license in order to get the key to unlock the encryption system of DVDs, which is necessary even just to play them; these keys are developed and held by the movie industry and its select technology industry partners. Users simply must abide by the rules built into the technology, even rules that extend well beyond the traditional prohibitions of copyright.

Additionally, any users who might tinker with their DVD players or hack around the protection codes on the DVDs themselves can be criminally prosecuted under new copyright statutes that now strengthen all technical content protection. Such laws are backed by legislators and courts willing to privilege the interests of content providers over the public protections of traditional copyright law, a perspective well fed by the culture industries, which have carefully articulated the problem of Internet piracy as a dire emergency.

An effective version of this system would not be merely a technical achievement. The trusted system relies on more than technology as its primary means of enforcing copyright. It must back that technology with the persuasive force of law and the legitimacy of new political and commercial alignments, and it needs a cultural performance of the risks and rewards sufficient enough to justify it. These elements work in tandem to reshape the movement of culture in ways that cannot be perceived when the elements are considered alone. No one element is sufficient to enforce the rules being applied, yet in combination they impose a surprisingly strict code of conduct on users and manufacturers.

This is now well beyond a question of how copyright should work, in a digital world; it is the construction and legal authorization of socrotechnical systems designed to select out those activities we want to render impossible (and the converse, those we hope to encourage). Critiques that fail to recognize these heterogeneous elements and how they interact not only misunderstand the situation; they inadvertently grant the trusted system greater power by portraying it as merely the sum of its parts. The situation demands the examination of how these legal, political, and cultural elements are produced, and how this complex array of forces is being lashed together in the service of technical content protection. Only that inquiry will effectively demonstrate that these structural alignments are as consequential for the dynamics of digital culture as the technologies they support.

The Shape of Digital Culture

Understanding not only the turn to technology as a regulatory strategy, but also the social, legal, political, and cultural mechanisms by which it is possible, is, at one level, crucial to the ongoing disputes about copyright and the Internet; it is a debate that has significant implications for both the production and circulation of culture, for the digital networks upon which that culture will move, and for the practices and institutions that will accommodate decisions made in the courts and in the marketplace.

Copyright is at the heart of cultural policy[21]—those rules that help to govern what is said, by whom, and with what effect. If we are at all concerned about the power of communication, the dynamics of democracy, the politics of culture, or freedom of expression, copyright must be a fundamental part of our inquiry. Shifts in the design and application of copyright law must be recognized as having consequences in all of these domains as they migrate to the digital realm. To the extent that the Internet, among other technologies, is increasingly designed and legislated to be a medium that not only facilitates communication but also imposes tight controls on it, we are very much shaping what the Internet is, will be, and can be. If the personal computer and the Internet are and will continue to be fundamental tools for cultural participation—the "new media"—then the institutional arrangements bent on pressuring hardware manufacturers to embrace restrictive, technoregulatory control systems warrant significant concern.

Moreover, whether or not this is the right strategy for copyright, what is most striking is that this tightly coupled arrangement of institutions, laws, and technologies is being deployed toward ends well beyond that of copyright protection. It is, in many instances, an effort to rename those rules and radically expand the rights traditionally granted to copyright owners. As I began my investigation into these cases, I expected to find a pull back toward the status quo, what Marvin described as "the process of social adjustment around a new technology, which is an occasion for introducing new rules and procedures around unaccustomed artifacts to bring them within the matrix of social knowledge and disposition."[22] It would go roughly like this: the Internet arrives; a number of critics in different domains, especially those shut out of existing arrangements of power, point to it to suggest the possibility of change; those in power turn to the stability and authority of existing law; using the law, they tame the new technology into submission. Instead, what I found was a story of both stasis *and* change. The maneuvers visible in these cases are not only about reaffirming existing arrangements familiar to copyright, but also about extending them, strengthening them, expanding them, reimagining them. Historically, copyright has privileged not the authors of cultural work but its distributors; the modern media industries are dominated by a select few corporations that have consolidated control over the culture market by asserting their intellectual property rights as a way to govern where work comes from and where it goes and to benefit financially from its circulation. While it appears that, as culture shifts into a digital environment, copyright will continue to give them this economic leverage, and that many of the same distributors will be able to retain this control, what is changing is what it will give them the authority to do.

The trusted system as it is being pursued can certainly prevent copying. More than that, it can also enforce complex pricing schemes and undermine the potential for fair use. In fact, these technological restrictions can make access to digital content dependent on users satisfying any number of obligations, well beyond the simple promise to use it within the strictures of copyright law. These constraints, piggybacked along with technical copy protections, will even more dramatically commodify culture, transforming our every encounter with a cultural work into a financial transaction, slicing up the populace into laser-precise market segments at the whim of industry. To the extent that such technological interventions impact some participants more than others, or normalize certain practices and marginalize others, they are likely to shift the structures of participation in culture and society more generally. They are a revised road map for the movement of information, tightly regimented to ensure that, first and foremost, cultural goods are always and already commodities, and that being commodities trumps all other considerations.

While the debates about copyright law have historically focused on how the law helps or hinders the democratic movement of information, we must recognize that the dynamics of the market can also promote or stifle the production of and access to newsworthy insight, political diatribe, artistic expression, and biting parody. If the trusted system is used to enforce particular market constraints, then the entire arrangement is implicated in this question. The trusted system warrants serious questioning by those interested in the future of digital technology and all the cultural and social interaction that it may or may not host. As Thomas Streeter puts it, "The choices that shape property in media, insofar as they shape what it means to be a speaker and a listener in an electronically mediated environment, and hence subjectivity, may influence the character of social existence. The law of ephemeral property is thus becoming a principal terrain for constructing the contours of contemporary cultures. Ongoing developments in 'information' law and policy will draw boundaries that will undergird the development of social life."[23]

A clearer understanding of not only the relationship between law and technology but also the political and commercial arrangements beneath, will also contribute to the ongoing investigation into the political economy and sociocultural impact of digital cultural institutions. The emerging alignment between the culture industries, hardware and software manufacturers, policymakers, and the courts will have its own consequences. Recognizing this requires moving beyond the overblown hype of "information revolutions," as well as the converse tendency to take such changes for granted. It requires an analysis attuned to the quiet arrangements that are building new patterns and alliances in the industries that produce and distribute culture.[24]

Finally, the implications may extend well beyond the digital circulation of cultural expression. As technology moves from being the object of law to being the means of its implementation, those concerned with the social implications of technologies must prick up their ears. To the extent that we choose to turn to technology to regulate copyright, we are likely to embrace that strategy in other sociopolitical controversies where technology appears to have similarly neutral effects: genetics, nanoscience, public health, education, national security, etc. Be it for the protection of pop music or any other reason, the extent to which lawmakers are willing to regulate and arbitrate over technological design must be made plain, scrutinized, and judged according to the criteria of political transparency, social equity, and cultural freedom.

Chapter by Chapter

These questions are at once legal and philosophical, social and cultural, political and economic. As part of its theoretical engagement with these questions, this book aims to move beyond the standard legal critique of copyright by drawing on recent theories of technology, communication, and culture to consider its broader ramifications. Digital copyright is a perfect domain for examining not only the way we structure cultural expression through the mechanisms of law, technology, and the market, but also the way controversies such as these become sites for powerful and consequential debates about the future of culture to be reframed, for participants in that debate to position themselves as powerful agents in that future, and for provocative questions to be closed. With these insights, we can begin to reveal how political efforts, powerful but by no means determining, work to engineer digital culture both through technological design and through the production of laws, institutional arrangements, and cultural discourses to match.

At the same time, while we must address these questions on a theoretical level, the most useful insights come from an interrogation of real world arrangements, of the character of the alliances and compromises that have been constructed to make them possible, and of the disputes that have arisen around them. This book bases its analysis in this on-the-ground interpretive approach by considering three of the most prominent efforts by the U.S. content industries (one a failure, one largely a success, one still being debated) to impose complex control arrangements through the design of technology, and to build the legal and political infrastructure they would need in order to work.

To understand these controversies, it is important to understand the law of copyright and the forces that have shaped it over three centuries. The law represents the slow accumulation of years of disputes and compromises; cutting it open reveals this legacy just as tree rings reveal seasons of growth and tumult. **Chapter 2** introduces the reader to the workings of copyright law and the premises on which it is based. It is written for readers who are largely unfamiliar with copyright law and the recent controversies, but even those well versed in both will find some new approaches for moving beyond the first wave of concerns. Arguments for why copyright exists and how it should be applied are considered in light of its fundamental contradiction: that it aspires to serve the public good by constructing a property regime premised on private gain. The effort to strike a balance between these often competing interests requires limits and exceptions that are both fundamental to copyright law and, at the same time, revealing of its inherent tensions.

The emergence of new technologies tends to disrupt the balances within this legal regime that manage its structural tensions. Like many technologies before it, the Internet made visible ambiguities that copyright law had not had to deal with before, and afforded an opportunity for those most invested in the workings of copyright law to tip the scales to their benefit. In response, traditional content industries and self-appointed Internet enthusiasts made very different claims for how the distribution of culture would work in a digital age, and how copyright should change to accommodate it. This largely theoretical dispute became all too real with the arrival and astounding popularity of Napster and peer-to-peer file-trading. This chapter offers a quick and dirty history of the music industry's legal attempts to shut down the deluge of unauthorized music sharing, and introduces the technical solutions being proposed: digital rights management (DRM), a means of encrypting digital content in order to limit access to it; and the "trusted system," a scheme whereby hardware and software authorized to access encrypted content will police what can be done with that content. The chapter ends by introducing some of the concerns that have already been raised about this shift to DRM as a copyright solution, particularly around its implications for the fair use doctrine of copyright law.

Using encryption technology to govern cultural distribution is only an example of how we regulate human activity through the built environment. **Chapter 3** attempts to arm the reader for scholarly inquiry into this phenomenon by exploring recent thinking in the fields of communication, science and technology studies, and information studies.[25] Technologies can powerfully shape the social activities in which they intervene, sometimes with significant political consequences; at the same time, technologies are also powerfully shaped by the individuals and institutions that produce them and reshaped in powerful ways by users, suggesting that their impact has a lot to do with the meanings that are negotiated and the cultural contexts in which that negotiation occurs. We can resolve this tension between seeing technology as constructed versus seeing it as consequential by noting that technology is constructed so as to be consequential. In every instance, designing and implementing a technology is an attempt to intervene in social practice. To the extent that designers of technology can agree about how they would like to choreograph the practices of users, this regulatory role of technology is enhanced; to the extent that designers cannot control what happens to the technology after it leaves their hands and cannot entirely predict its consequences, it is diminished. Understanding the complexity of technology as a political artifact is useful as we begin to consider the implications of deliberately using technologies in place of the law.

However, while technologies can have political consequences, and the move to install DRM encryption systems into digital distribution of culture seems to depend only on technology's ability to do so, an exclusive focus on technology would mask the way it requires much more than mere objects to effectively regulate the movement of culture. To the extent that the actors powerful in this negotiation about the meaning and purpose of a technology are also often powerful in other domains, they can appeal to law, policy, and public discourse to buttress and normalize the authority of the tools they build. Alongside the new technologies come new laws to back them, new institutional and commercial arrangements to produce and align them, and new cultural justifications to convince legislators and users to embrace them. This is not engineering culture through technology, but a more heterogeneous effort to regulate through the alignment of political, technical, legal, economic, and cultural elements that must be held in place for a new paradigm of copyright to take hold.

Chapter 4 analyzes the construction of the cultural justifications necessary for the trusted system approach to gain any traction at all with manufacturers, artists, legislators, and users. The regulation of the Internet had, before the copyright wars, been largely hands-off; when it first appeared, Napster was wildly popular not only with music fans but with the press as well. To counter these attitudes and to justify a massive change in the character and enforcement of copyright law required a powerful tale of sin and redemption. This narrative not only reframed the debate, it set the stage for the kind of institutional alignments that content providers needed to establish.

In his role as the director of the Motion Picture Association of America (MPAA), the U.S. film industry's powerful lobbying organization, Jack Valenti was the most powerful and articulate of the storytellers, offering up a narrative arc that went something like this: Movie production is an economic boon to the nation; Internet file-trading is a financial danger to that business; content producers, faced with this threat, will withhold valuable content and the medium in question will suffer; however, with stronger copyright protection and technical measures of self-enforcement, the culture industry will provide a rich consumer experience. The entire chain of assertions was wrapped in a narrative of good beset by evil, coated with dramatic metaphors and salacious scares, and contrasted against a rosy alternative only possible if copyright law were strengthened. Valenti's logic is just one version of the situation, and has been contested on a number of fronts. Nevertheless, it is slowly becoming the standard understanding of how copyright does and should work, and how digital culture depends on the fullest imposition of technical copy protection.

Technologies for the production and distribution of culture have long been designed so as to guide the activity of users, from early printed folios locked to the lecterns on which they sat, to sophisticated password protection systems on consumer software. In order to orchestrate such a system of control, content producers require the cooperation of technology manufacturers, but this turns out to be difficult to achieve: manufacturers are numerous and commercially competitive, and generally see value in offering users as much choice as possible. One attempt to wrangle these interests into agreement, initiated by the record industry, was the Secure Digital Music Initiative (SDMI). The major record labels gathered consumer electronics manufacturers, information technology providers, and fledgling online distributors to produce copy protection for music and the standards for all hardware to honor these protections. **Chapter 5** traces the history of this effort, investigating how the music industry attempted to forge a consensus, and the reasons why it collapsed. SDMI is a reminder that the alignment of technology and content envisioned in such plans cannot be imposed without a matching alignment between the commercial players that produce them, and such an alignment is not so easily achieved.

In stark contrast to the failed SDMI project, the encryption that protects Hollywood DVDs from duplication is a revealing case of how such a trusted system can be produced, and how the necessary institutional alignment can be achieved despite the strategic differences between content and hardware manufacturers. **Chapter 6** reveals how the Content Scramble System (CSS) encryption used to protect DVDs is merely the technical edge of a complex arrangement of content, machines, licenses, and industry partners that together work to contain the activities of users.

In this case, the trusted system also required recourse to the law when that arrangement was breached, as it was when a "crack" called DeCSS was posted online. The industry turned to the Digital Millennium Copyright Act (DMCA), itself a dramatic shift in copyright law produced by the rethinking of copyright around the Internet and, in particular, the powerful "Valenti logic" offered by the content industries. Prohibiting circumvention of technical protections rather than copying itself, the DMCA embodies this shift toward technical solutions, while also revealing that the technology cannot function without support from the law. Rather than regulating users, the DMCA shores up the arrangements imposed by the content industries on the manufacturers, and forms the fourth side of this heterogeneous square of regulation: technical artifact, commercial agreement, cultural justification, legal authority. And it does so in a way that allows these industries to impose new controls on users that were not available under copyright law before this moment. The trusted system, then, is built on a fundamental mistrust—a mistrust of the technology manufacturers, who must be licensed into submission, and a mistrust of users, who are seen as immoral pirates until they can be technologically compelled to be good consumers.

The record industry tried to organize a voluntary agreement with technology manufacturers, and failed; the movie industry got one by holding their content ransom and forcing technology manufacturers to sign away their interests, but found they were still vulnerable to upstart manufacturers who would not agree to their terms. The next step is to seek the authority of the state to make such systems mandatory. Calling on the state promises to more powerfully bind this trusted system together and impose it on users, but it also brings new forces into play. As **chapter 7** describes, the movie studios hoped to impose similar technical controls onto digital television, and called upon the FCC to give their system legitimacy and assure its imposition. An industry coalition proposed the "broadcast flag," a technical means to mark digital TV content as deserving protection, and to set rules for manufacturers for how to treat that content so as to prevent redistribution over the Internet.

Ideological gaps between these industries, and between these industries and the regulators who have jurisdiction over them, have always been narrow; nevertheless, they have been important in preventing an industry view of copyright law from completely dominating other public interests. Now these gaps are closing around technical copyright protection, thanks in part to the efforts of these industries, the increasing sense of the inevitability of this project (and thus the desire of manufacturers to be on the winning side of its commercial consequences), and the persuasive power of the piracy narrative. This suggests that, whether or not such trusted systems are ever installed and ever succeed, the changes in industry alignment being pursued in order to produce them may themselves have consequences for culture and technology. This may extend to the increasingly close ideological partnership of the content industries and legislators. However, as the broadcast flag case reveals, the FCC did make significant adjustments to the plans proposed by the movie industry and its consumer electronics partners. Furthermore, the courts subsequently decided that the FCC did not have the authority to install such a technical control regime, revealing further cracks in the political alignments necessary for a comprehensive trusted system to work.

The attempts thus far to impose technical solutions onto the promiscuity of the Internet have all faced intrepid users who refuse these constraints: from the casual users of peer-to-peer networks to the amateur DJs creating innovative forms of digitally reworked music; from the widespread use of "black market" circumvention technologies to the hackers that take on every new system; from academic critics who challenge these strategies to the campus activists who mobilize against them. This kind of agency with culture and with technology has been the biggest hurdle for content owners' attempt to realign digital culture in more commercially viable terms. In some ways, it is this agency that must be curtailed if the broad and heterogeneous strategy of technolegal control is to succeed. **Chapter 8** turns its attention to the robustness requirements that accompany most DRM systems, which require manufacturers of hardware and software not only to limit what users can and cannot do but also to design their tools to fend off the attacks of hackers, the prying eyes of hardware enthusiasts, the curiosity of tinkerers.

Just as digital rights management threatens the agency we have with the culture we encounter, these robustness rules threaten our sense of agency with the technology itself. Critics of the CSS encryption and the broadcast flag made this point by noting that both systems exclude the possibility of open source innovations in the distribution and consumption of film and television. To prevent users from seeing how content is protected and potentially circumvented, robustness rules require technology designers to "weld the hood shut"—something very much at odds not only with open source design, but with the traditions of user appropriation and innovation. What is clear is that these solutions are not just strategic, they are paradigmatic, embodying and imposing a persistent worldview on what is otherwise a much richer set of options for how we interact with culture and technology.

Chapter 9 attempts to step back from these cases in order to consider the cultural implications of the technology at the heart of these protection schemes. Once a mechanism for ensuring secret communication between confidantes, encryption is being employed here for a very different purpose: extending control over otherwise public materials. In terms of the distribution of culture over the Internet, encryption is the digital means to assure a subtle, complex, and context-sensitive system of regulation. By encoding a film, the owner of the copyright can dictate to an unprecedented degree what can and cannot be done with it. Most importantly from a philosophical perspective, encryption intervenes before an infringement occurs rather than after. Such a preemptive measure not only treats all users as would-be criminals, it makes the imposition of copyright less open to exceptions like fair use, renders unavailable the ability to challenge a law through civil disobedience, and undercuts the individual's sense of moral agency in a way that can undermine the legitimacy of the rule itself.

While this new application of encryption and licensing is justified in terms of a threat to copyright, the system can accomplish much more. The license that DVD manufacturers must sign requires them not only to honor the restrictions on copying demanded by the movie industry, but also to honor a system called "regional coding." Regional coding stipulates that each disc is numbered according to the continent in which it was produced; DVD players must only play discs from their own region. This is in no way a means of protecting copyright; instead, it gives the movie studios a way to slice up the global market, engage in price discrimination, stagger releases, and even ignore markets they do not see as lucrative. If and when the distribution of culture moves entirely to the Internet, this strategy could be extended in any number of ways, not to protect copyright but to maximize profit.

As copyright was traditionally conceived of as a way to regulate the commercial practices of those who don't own a work (so as to protect the interests of those who do), it has rarely had to consider the way the commercial practices of the owners themselves can have the kind of antidemocratic implications copyright was designed to avoid. Such practices, built directly into the technology and using the threat of piracy as rhetorical cover, are now having those problematic consequences, most powerfully by reifying a clean distinction between producer and consumer in a world where communication is always a recursive and productive process. This precludes the use of new communication technologies in ways that could powerfully shift the roles of such cultural production in a more egalitarian direction.

Wired Shut ends there, with a concern well beyond copyright per se, the Internet and its regulation, and the juncture between industry and politics. It reveals a crossroads faced by a society embracing technologies that can both facilitate digital culture and be made to regulate it. The choices we make now will help decide whether we will be active participants in our culture and creative users of our technology, or passive recipients content to quietly embrace what is sold to us and fulfill the roles prescribed for us.

Developing technical solutions to the problem of enforcing copyright is no easy task. Copyright itself is a terrifically complex legal doctrine, built over many years by many hands, full of exceptions and caveats that even legal scholars find "complex, internally inconsistent, wordy, and arcane."[1] Moreover, its central aim may be unattainable, and is at the very least founded on a fundamental contradiction. In offering authors legal property rights over their work so they may enjoy a profit from its circulation, copyright is supposed to ensure the sustenance of art, knowledge, and culture. This precarious balance between public good and private gain, while logical in an ideal sense, may suffer from "the impossibility of serving one of the described objectives without disserving the other."[2] And, in a society in which culture is predominantly delivered through the market, copyright (along with the laws regarding freedom of speech and the regulations attached to broadcast licensing) is one of the central rules that structure culture. As such, its interpretation and implementation have tremendous significance for art, journalism, scholarship, and the health of democracy.

On one level, shifting the locus of control from law to technology means mapping legal doctrines onto technical prohibitions, and risks losing something in the translation. Critics of digital copyright strategies have already pointed out a number of the legal details of copyright that don't fit neatly with what can be built into software. But more than that, the move to a technical copy protection creates an opportunity for practitioners, legislators, and users to subtly reinterpret and redefine the law itself; questions once settled can be reopened, while persistent tensions can be downplayed as if resolved. An existing balance can be undone, using digital technology as the urgent reason for why an old compromise no longer works, while new opportunities afforded by the Internet can be brushed aside as being simply incompatible with the traditions of copyright law. More is at stake than just how pop music will be distributed online; everything about the rights associated with information is once again up for grabs, and the decisions made in this moment will set the terms for how we understand copyright and what it is supposed to accomplish for years to come. It is important, then, to look back at where copyright law came from, how it has been implemented differently over time and toward what ends, and how new challenges posed by digital computing and communication networks are both challenging copyright's balance and serving as a rationale for a new legal and technical framework.

The Aims of Copyright

The language of the U.S. Constitution authorizing Congress to create copyright laws also announces its priorities: "Congress shall have power ... to promote the progress of science and useful arts, by securing for limited times to authors and inventors the exclusive right to their respective writings and discoveries."[3] The book, song, film, painting, or software you create belongs to you by law; you have exclusive rights to duplicate, distribute, or perform that work, and legal recourse against those who attempt to do any of these things without your permission. Important to notice, first and foremost, is that at its foundation, U.S. intellectual property law is a means to an end, not an end in itself. William Fisher has noted that there are several countervailing philosophical justifications for the law of copyright, and these are regularly invoked by jurists and lawmakers, as well as by scholars, often unaware of their potential contradiction.[4] However, while these all play a role in justifying copyright and structuring the complex debates about its application, the philosophical core of U.S. copyright law is that the individual's right of ownership is lashed to a societal aspiration.[5] Rather than justifying this privilege as a "natural" right of authors to enjoy the fruits of their own labor, or as a reward for expending the creative effort itself, copyright is framed in terms of spurring cultural and intellectual progress. As Matt Jackson reminds us, "One cannot overemphasize that the constitutional purpose of copyright is to stimulate content creation for the public's benefit, not to create a private property right based on a moral notion of ownership."[6]

There is an important presumption about the nature of authorship and culture hidden in this constitutional mandate, that authors require financial incentives to motivate them to produce—or at least that ensuring such financial incentives will encourage more authors to produce more work more of the time. Or as Ronald Bettig notes, "The underlying assumption here is that human beings require economic reward to be intellectually or artistically creative. The philosophy of intellectual property reifies economic rationalism as a natural human trait."[7] This may feel like mere common sense: While the idea that art is made "for art's sake" may remain a powerful mythology among painters and punk bands, self-proclaimed realists tend to scoff at the idea that culture can ever be separated from commerce—or should be. The logic of a market economy suggests that authors need an assurance that they'll be able to sell their work; the profits due to them must not be diverted by flagrant piracy. Copyright law attempts to assure this fair and productive arrangement, ensuring authors the ability to seek their just reward in the marketplace. Financial reward provides incentive, which provokes cultural production, which benefits society, QED.

Of course, to justify copyright in this way may be circular logic: It is only with copyright law in place that we have been able to design a cultural sphere premised on the assumption that work will circulate through the market and enjoy financial rewards, and that, by law, authors are owners. As such, we build industries around this "truth," conventionally see culture in these terms, cultivate this expectation in budding creators, and downplay the myriad of other reasons why people create—for creative satisfaction, for the promise of impact, for reputational gain, for ancillary rewards, etc. One need only look at the World Wide Web or at sites like YouTube, MySpace, Wikipedia, or SourceForge to see that financial compensation is not the only, or perhaps even the most compelling, incentive to produce. In fact, it is possible that the development of real alternatives to this strictly commercial arrangement for cultural production is actually inhibited by the self-fulfilling prophecy of copyright law, the stable social and institutional structures that depend on it, and the ideological assumptions on which it depends and thereby reaffirms.[8]

Because our culture generally holds authors in high regard, it is easy to presume that copyright is in some way designed to reward authors because they deserve reward. This seems so obvious to some that it is a difficult proposition to even investigate. The widespread sense is that authors provide a valuable service, that their work is their own, and therefore that they have the right to sell it and reap the financial reward. In this view, authors enjoy legal protection because they create something worth paying for; piracy is taking something that doesn't belong to you. Even as we labor within a corporate industrial system where workers have no rights over the things they help produce, we continue to believe in the principle that we own what we make and we deserve to be paid for what we create.[9] It is important to remember that this is not the case. Rewarding authors has never been the *purpose* of copyright—it is merely its preferred strategy. The law in fact has grander aspirations.

Eager to help their young nation grow but deeply skeptical of the power of monopolies (be they royal or commercial), those who crafted the U.S. Constitution justified copyright in terms of the social and the intellectual—in the name of "progress in science and the useful arts." For them, "progress" may have meant a number of things.[10] As a young nation, the United States hoped to gain its footing as quickly as possible; this required a spirit of cooperation in almost every endeavor: political, commercial, intellectual, artistic.

In each of these fields, there was (and continues to be) benefit in the unhindered circulation of information, knowledge, and culture.[11] Democracy demands that every citizen be well informed, literate about the pressing issues, and capable of making informed decisions. The "marketplace of ideas"[12] should expose citizens to lively, adversarial debate: Multiple and conflicting voices should all be heard; consensus will arise from citizens rationally considering alternative viewpoints. Commerce also depends on its constituents being well informed. The flow of goods and the setting of prices can only attain a fair equilibrium if consumers have "perfect information" about the products they desire, and if sellers know their potential buyers. In academic research, scholars should "stand on the shoulders of giants," learning what the field has accomplished thus far, then contributing to it at its emergent edges. The scientific principle itself depends on past work being available for study and current work being available for scrutiny.[13] Artists similarly learn their craft by being surrounded by the work of others; they emulate great masters and eviscerate mediocre contemporaries; they lift ideas and techniques from the work they encounter.[14]

The challenge, then, was how to build the rules of culture such that individual creators are given rights and responsibilities in a way that will encourage them to make their work available to the public at large. Like the British doctrine it came from, U.S. copyright law turned to the metaphor of property, applying the legal structure of ownership of tangible goods to the more intangible goods of "writings and discoveries." This substitution is so commonplace that it's hard to even recognize it as a choice, or to see that there is any alternative. To facilitate culture, we give every contribution to it the means to be traded on the open market and tie its sale back to its author/owner such that the financial reward returns to them. This is an effort to both encourage and control cultural discourse, to be both its distribution venue and its system of reward. The commodity stands in for the work; allowing the commodity to circulate in the marketplace presumably allows the ideas within to circulate along with it, resulting in a real marketplace built to support the marketplace of ideas. Far from this being a free market strategy, as some copyright owners proclaim, this is very much an artificial regulation of the market—in the business of information, the most logical strategy in purely economic terms is in fact piracy, except for the fact that copyright law makes it illegal.

The Problem with "Property"

To call the story or the song or the image one's "property," while it may now seem intuitive, is an awkward and potentially problematic use of the term. In many ways, intellectual property does not work the way material property does, primarily because of its economic properties as a "public good".[15] First, cultural expression is *nonrivalrous*: Use does not deplete it. When you finish reading your copy of this book for the first time, it will in no way be diminished for a second reading. You can return to the book for years, reading it again and again, to your children and grandchildren. The same cannot be said for a candy bar, a firecracker, or laundry detergent. Of course, this is not a simple dichotomy. Sequential use might be seen as a spectrum, with different kinds of things having different half-lives—a tank of gas is consumed in one trip, but the car is driven many times before it is finally rendered unusable. You may turn the pages of this book so many times that the binding glue softens and the pages fall out, or you may smear the print with your thumbs to the point of illegibility. However, if you memorize the argument, you can continue to "use" it even after the pages are destroyed. A book may be exhaustible, but the "work" itself is not. Culture cannot be consumed.

Second, cultural expression is *nonexcludable*, in that once it is sold to one consumer it is difficult to prevent it from being enjoyed by others. We might think of this as having two dimensions: collective use of the same object, and duplication of one object into many. As noted before, cultural works are particularly susceptible to simultaneous and sequential use by many consumers—the hockey team rents a DVD to watch together in a dorm lounge, or the same magazine is read by every person who comes through the doctor's office waiting room. It was (until recently) difficult to extract any payment from those additional consumers. In addition, intellectual property can be easily duplicated in a way that, say, a sandwich cannot. The fact that it is difficult to exclude those who did not purchase the work from using it, because of both sharing and copying, makes it even more difficult to extract compensation from those additional users—or to impose rules on them. As Lessig notes, this does not mean that the work cannot be guarded in any way; it can depend on the manner of distribution. Before I publish this book, I can exclude people from it by keeping it locked in my office; if I distribute a film via national theaters, I can keep people out who do not buy a ticket; but if I sell a CD, I have much more difficulty keeping people from making copies for their friends.

The fact that cultural expression is (more or less) nonrivalrous and nonexcludable tends to undercut the ability to maximize its value in the market. If the sale of the work to one consumer can lead to it being used endlessly by many, profit will not return as effectively to its producers, no matter how clearly defined their rights are. One sale represents many uses, meaning substantially less compensation returns to the producer. The price of pirate copies can be low, since the original producer bears all the costs of production, whereas the pirate need only cover the miniscule costs of copying.

The market by itself, then, is clearly insufficient for ensuring that suitable compensation returns to authors of cultural expression. The promise of the market, that through competition worthy authors will be paid for their efforts by consumers, is undercut by a competing logic, that producers will find the cheapest way to provide what their customers want—that is, piracy.[16] What is further required is a legal standard that legitimizes the part of the market that compensates authors, and outlaws the part of the market that undercuts them. Copyright does this by making the author the owner of the work and granting exclusive rights of reproduction and distribution to that author/owner. Copyright secures an alliance of legal and commercial mechanisms—the market will serve the interests of the law, and the law will ensure that the market functions such that it can do so.

It is worth noting that these differences also matter for the demands they make on the economics of cultural production and distribution. All production incurs startup costs—hiring employees, building or renting spaces for manufacturing and management, gathering raw materials, designing prototypes. Plenty of money had to be spent before Nike ever sold their first sneaker. However, the cost of producing each additional sneaker also incurs significant costs: more materials, more manufacturing, more labor, more packaging, more display. When a pair of sneakers enters the market, its price must primarily cover the cost of producing that actual pair; the startup costs are spread across all Nike sales, and in the long run end up being a fraction of the price of each individual commodity. There cannot be piracy of sneakers, since a pirate producer incurs the same costs of making each shoe as the original manufacturer, making it much more difficult to undercut their prices and lure away customers. There are no sneaker pirates, only competitors and knock-offs.[17]

The production of creative work, on the other hand, tends to function on an economy of scale: the overwhelming majority of the costs of production are incurred before the very first product is made; the cost of making each additional commodity is tiny by comparison. The cost of making a film is practically the same whether you only produce the master reel or you distribute millions of copies on DVD. With discursive goods, it is the additional cost of each copy that is negligible.

Markets that exhibit an economy of scale tend to privilege large and well-established corporations. They are more likely to have the financial heft to commit significant capital up front and can afford to wait for the returns. Digital technologies of production and distribution may be changing this, as the barriers of entry are in some instances lowered, but this affects different kinds of content differently, and can never completely undo this dynamic. The problem is at its most extreme when the cultural work is most costly—that is, the summer blockbuster, the celebrity biography, the pop phenomenon, the sprawling documentary, the comprehensive database. This means it is those producers best positioned to produce expensive cultural work who will have the most vested interest in protecting and enforcing copyright.

That cultural expression doesn't work like other tangible goods, even in its most tangible forms, is a problem only because we have chosen to embrace the legal metaphor of possession. With the "intellectual property" frame in place, other qualities of cultural expression are systematically ignored. There is no natural reason why we must conceive of it in such terms, but in the Western regulation of discourse, the property metaphor has long been the overwhelming and (for the most part) binding approach.

Striking the Balance

To assume that imposing this metaphor of property and regulating the market for culture will facilitate "progress in the science and useful arts" requires another very particular leap in faith. The fundamental risk with copyright law as it is currently designed is that, for each cultural work, it produces a legally enforced monopoly—I am the only one authorized to sell this book, or by contract the MIT Press is, which means there is no legitimate competition for buyers. Like all monopolies, this arrangement is prone to commercial exploitation. But because the commodity in question is information, abuse of this monopoly position would not merely inflate prices or make a worthwhile product hard to acquire; it might deplete public debate, disable democracy, or starve art and culture. As Julie Cohen notes, "A model that attempts to relate 'property' to 'progress' must consider the public-good nature of creative and informational works, and cannot assume equivalency between private wealth and social gain."[18] The risk of a legally enforced monopoly over information is that publishers may be able to restrict the circulation of expression, which may in turn restrict the circulation of important ideas. In an attempt to avoid this, U.S. lawmakers and courts have built several limitations into copyright law, aiming to restrain the power it gives to authors/owners and pass some of that power back to the public at large.

Perhaps the most important of these conditions is the "limited times" referenced in the constitutional clause. These two words are perhaps the most powerful evidence that, despite relying on the property metaphor, copyright law does not intend to treat cultural expression exactly like property. Over the years, the duration of copyright protection has been dramatically lengthened,[19] but the principle remains that authors may only enjoy their rights over publication and reproduction for a certain number of years. Once this time has elapsed, the work enters the "public domain"[20] and can be freely reproduced by anyone. Unlike material property, this kind of property reverts to public ownership after a certain period of time—we might say it is returned to the original owners, if we think of copyright as a right temporarily granted to authors by the public they serve.

Copyright also protects only an author's particular expression, and not the underlying ideas it conveys. In other words, although I am granted ownership and control over this book about copyright and the Internet, it does not mean that I can prevent others from also writing about copyright and the Internet; I can only prevent their use of my specific words. If copyright privileges extended too broadly around a work, any work that addressed similar topics might be deemed infringement.[21] Without this distinction, copyright could easily become a mechanism for controlling information, depleting the public domain, and chilling free speech. Ideas are free to circulate, and can never be constrained; copyright, as long as it honors this distinction, will then never run afoul of the First Amendment's assurance that no law can prevent me from saying what I please.[22] All that I must avoid is actually using the phrasing or design of existing work. As James Boyle puts it, "The idea/expression division resolves (or at least conceals) the tension between public and private . . . By disaggregating the book into 'idea' and 'expression,' we can give the idea (and the facts on which it is based) to the public world and the expression to the writer, thus apparently mediating the contradiction between public good and private need (or greed)."[23] The problem, of course, is that the distinction between idea and expression is really only a theoretical one; the two always coexist in practice, and the task of distinguishing infringement from works that simply explore similar ideas is left to jurists.

The most important of these limits, especially in light of recent controversies, is the "fair use" doctrine. The greatest risk of an unlimited copyright is that copyright owners might be able to enforce their rights in ways that inhibit the production of new work, squelch the expression of particular opinions, or undermine the health of public discourse. Quoting someone's book requires copying and distributing some of their work; so does making copies of an article for use in a classroom. Both would require asking permission of the owner and, in most cases, compensating them financially. But if quoting someone's work means having to ask permission to do so, the author is in a position to simply say no if they don't like how their work will be used. If teachers cannot afford to pay for the use of works vital to their courses, they might not use them despite their value to the students. This is particularly problematic when either the use is critical of the original (a damning news report or a negative book review, for example) or the sheer cost of seeking permission of the owners and paying for the right to use their work would be prohibitive (amateur documentary filmmaking, for example). Some of these reuses are common to the most important democratic mechanisms of our society: education, scholarship, journalism, and criticism.

In cases like these, fair use allows some breathing room for the reuser by limiting the conditions under which they can be prosecuted for infringement. The fair use exception grants special protection to uses that would otherwise be infringement, that would be unlikely to receive authorization from the copyright holder, and that without fair use would be a violation of the law. The law delineates four factors[24] that courts weigh when determining if an infringing use should be protected: What kind of work is being copied, how much is taken, what financial impact the copying might have on it, and to what use it is put.

Fair use originally focused exclusively on what William Patry calls "productive uses": uses that create a new work by a new author.[25] But in the last half century fair use has been expanded, hesitantly, to include certain "passive uses": uses that duplicate some or all of the copyrighted work without any obvious intellectual contributions, but do so in order to facilitate access to it.[26] The 1976 Copyright Act created a special dispensation for photocopying copyrighted materials under specific circumstances: single copies, for educational purposes, by libraries and public archives.[27] Multiple copies for use in the classroom are also included in the fair use exemption, although subsequent case law has designed very specific restrictions on that activity. The *Sony v. Universal* decision made room for copying television broadcasts onto videotape, again under specific circumstances: for the purposes of limited educational use or "time-shifted" personal use, with restrictions on how long copies can be kept.

There are a number of justifications for such an exception. Fair use serves as a further safety valve between copyright law and the First Amendment. If copyright law permitted authors to restrict how others could speak when using their work to do so, it could limit free expression; fair use offers the second speaker some breathing room, setting limits on how they can be held liable for infringement, and bounding the reach of copyright owners when the use of the work does not directly damage its market value.[28] Fair use also helps mitigate the transaction costs involved; if each and every use required a license, the cost and difficulty of locating the proper copyright holder and negotiating each license might inhibit some uses.[29] Finally, fair use has allowed for some flexibility for technological innovation. New technologies often allow users to do things with information that can look like copyright infringement on first glance (for example, taping television programs using a VCR); fair use allows the courts to first consider, and sometimes indemnify, a new technological practice that could otherwise have been squelched as copyright infringement by existing economic forces.[30]

If ideas both do and do not act like property, then the law of copyright alone cannot fully ensure their circulation. The installation of a property law entails orchestrating a massively complex alliance between law and market, lashing together stubborn and sometimes conflicting cultural rhetorics to justify it. Copyright is imagined to be the best means of circulating ideas and nourishing those aspects of society that rely on them, but even its designers fretted about its consequences and vulnerabilities. Most clearly in the doctrine of fair use, the law itself acknowledges that the commercial exchange of intellectual property is far from an ideal mechanism for the circulation of discourse. Some argue that copyright is sufficient, the best compromise for achieving important cultural goals. Others fear that the premise itself is flawed, and that a mountain of caveats couldn't undo the damage copyright law does.

Accommodating New Technologies

Thanks to a series of technological innovations, copying and distributing cultural works has grown easier over the last century. With the Internet, it has reached unprecedented simplicity. And whereas the casual redistribution of intellectual property was always a problem for the culture industries, the new scope of that distribution is unheralded.

With each information technology, be it the jukebox,[31] radio broadcasting, television,[32] Xerox machines, the VCR, or cable, has come a reappraisal of the copyright balance. Of course, it isn't just technology that stirs up old copyright questions: The logistical compromises of the past can be unraveled by an innovative business model, a new alliance between producers and manufacturers, or a shift in the way culture is consumed. The current debates about copyright have as much to do with the cultural dominance of media content, the increasing concentration of the industries that produce it, and the political climate of market deregulation as they do with the computer and the Internet. The embrace of the global information economy and the shift toward what David Harvey calls "flexible accumulation"[33] models of post-industrial production have not only fueled the development of digital information networks and put personal computers on every desk; they have also encouraged a "digital culture" in which users expect information to be instantly accessible and easily portable, increasingly see themselves as producers and collectors of information as much as consumers of it, and accept the commingling of leisure- and work-related communication activities. All of these changes put pressure on copyright and the traditional forms of information distribution.

But typically it is the technologies that come to herald and stand for the cultural and economic shifts that helped produce them, and as such they become the flashpoints for the legal dispute that follows. The technologies represent both the potential of shifting the balance of copyright to account for new dynamics in the circulation of culture, and the justification for why an older balance must be preserved or regained. Of greater consequence than the new technologies themselves are the decisions—legal, economic, political, cultural—that we make around them.

With the emergence of the Internet as a technological and a sociocultural phenomenon, the already unsteady balance of copyright seemed, quite visibly, to explode. The proclamations were dramatic. Some believed that the law needed to be fortified and expanded to counter the Internet's effects. Some thought copyright could shift from a law of property to a kind of contract law for managing relationships between content providers and consumers.[34] Others believed that copyright could be discarded altogether.[35]

Long before this vox populi eruption of excitement and concern, the Internet was an obscure engineering project commissioned and overseen by the Advanced Research Projects Agency (ARPA), a subsidiary of the U.S. Department of Defense (DoD).[36] Drawing on innovations in digital computing and packet-switching communication networks developed in semi-autonomous research centers (including most notably the RAND Corporation, a nonprofit research group devoted to projects with broad military relevance[37]), researchers at ARPA developed the protocols to allow computers to interface—that is, to exchange digitized information between geographically disparate locations and allow users to access and manipulate remote computers from a distance. Only four computers at first, the ARPANET slowly grew as university computer science departments with military funding established their own nodes fitted with the same shared protocols and logged on to what would eventually become the Internet.[38]

The network's early uses were mostly just efforts to test the system; it was too new to be trusted with important tasks, but too exciting to be left alone. Operators of the system tended to encourage any use at all; according to Janet Abbate, "In the early years the ARPANET was underutilized, and ARPA had little reason to discourage users or activities that might make the network more popular. Increased use of the network would also make it easier for ARPA's computer scientists to evaluate the system's performance."[39] So it was of little concern that some early users, particularly graduate students at the various university research centers, began to use ARPANET to send messages from site to site.

The emergence of these communicative activities ended up broadening the early focus of network research. While the military interest in network technology did include sending messages to remote sites, particularly under adverse conditions of war, researchers had more generally assumed the network would be a way to share computing power over a distance; a user at site A could log onto and run a computer at site B that specialized in crunching data in a way he needed, without having to send that data away to be processed, or having to purchase another costly computer himself. The growing population of users seemed to have a different idea. As Katie Hafner and Matthew Lyon tell it, "In the mind of its inventors, the network was intended for resource-sharing, period. That very little of its capacity was actually ever used for resource-sharing was a fact soon submersed in the tide of electronic mail . . . The ARPANET's creators didn't have a grand vision for the invention of an earth-circling message handling system. But once the first couple of dozen nodes were installed, early users turned the system of linked computers into a personal as well as a professional communications tool. Using the ARPANET as a sophisticated mail system was simply a good hack."[40]

As researchers noticed the activities of ARPANET users, the initial focus on distance computing gradually shifted to include this interest in distributed communication.[41] Both purposes would persist in the further development of the Internet, but much of the Internet's design and deployment would revolve around imagining new forms of *distribution* of cultural expression—by all users. Still, it's worth noticing that the initial premise of the network, computing at a distance, was based on the principle of transmitting exact copies of digital content so that the computer at the remote site could run that program or crunch those numbers and return the result. Though the copyright implications of this may not have been fully anticipated, the idea of transmitting perfect copies of authored work was by no means the invention of peer-to-peer file-traders, but was crucial to the earliest notions of what the network would be for.

With this surge in interest in distributing information across the new network came a particular politics about doing so. Early users were fascinated by the way the network seemed to be almost self-organizing: Data could move without centralized oversight, and users seemed able to share the network without needing a controlling authority to oversee them. Once the shared protocols (the technical language each computer would speak) were established, each user could focus simply on their own contribution to the system. The activity would be patrolled, if at all, by the users themselves; the tool seemed to encourage certain activities without enforcing them as explicit rules. Eventually, when the military began to fret that so many unauthorized users were accessing this system, they chose to split off their own proprietary network that they could control access to, rather than attempt to wrestle this unruly community of ARPANET users into submission.

The Netizen Vision

So perhaps it is no surprise that, as this technology gained public visibility, the prevailing opinion among its early users was that it should be given free rein, rather than being regulated by government. These (self-described) "Netizens" ardently believed in the liberating potential of the new technology, and of technology in general. Many had cut their teeth on the anti-authority counterculture rhetoric of the 1960s.[42] They had been enlisted (ironically, by the military) to design a tool that wouldn't have or need a central mechanism of organization and control. Their solution was a decentralized network designed and maintained by an equally decentralized set of user communities working by association rather than under regimented, official oversight. This produced a network distinctly open in both its technical workings and its cultural ethos.

Part of this community's enthusiasm was a faith that changes in technology have the power to transform the world. The early rhetoric is revealing: Now-familiar platitudes like "the Net treats censorship like damage and routes around it"[43] and "information wants to be free"[44] accord a sense of agency to things and ideas ("the Net *treats*," "information *wants*") and presume that change is nearly inevitable (the same declarative certainty so common to sociopolitical rhetoric). The assumption may in fact be a disempowering one. As Duguid observes, "Freedom of information, once a citizen's right to gain access to information, by a sleight of argument becomes the right of information to move freely, free of material impediment."[45] But the appeal of this notion is undeniable. The Internet represented a complex network on a scale never before envisioned, with much of that complexity managed by the interaction of tools rather than by authorized institutions. In the eyes of these user-designers, the Internet seductively offered a ground for potentially perfect freedom, which, to them, meant free speech, human creativity, unfettered innovation, and robust community.

Much of the early community discussions focused on authorship and the shifting politics of distribution. The Netizen vision held the new technology up as a solution (sometimes characterized as inevitable, sometimes as the best among many) to a fundamental problem of communication— that the division of labor between the production of information and its distribution often affects what can be said and by whom. The system of distribution Netizens wanted to undo (i.e., corporate broadcasting and mass-market print) exaggerates the distinction between producers and the rest of us; they hoped the Internet would up-end that distinction by allowing everyone to be a user, a participant, a citizen of cyberspace. Instead of the "consumer-as-commodity"[46] model common to broadcasting, the Internet would foster a network of users bound by loose social ties; their work would circulate according to a gift economy rather than strictly commercial imperatives.[47] By handing the power of distribution to anyone who wanted it, Netizens hoped to create communication that would be more about open interaction than exclusive publication.

What happens to copyright, a law that grants authors the power of distribution within a market-structured culture (and generally through professionalized media to a mass audience), when a new communication medium reimagines what is distributed, by whom, under what conditions, and to what ends? Some believed that copyright wouldn't work online because the market transactions it supported wouldn't survive in a digital, networked environment. John Perry Barlow, for one, speculated that the immateriality of digital information would undermine the traditional distribution of culture. When information is delivered in a material form— book, CD, film, photo—rules about information can depend on its material dynamics. With the Internet, "digital technology is detaching information from the physical plane, where property law of all sorts has always found definition."[48] The material existence of cultural expression gave the law something to hold onto, just as it gave the market something to assign a price to. Once digitized, information might travel from author to reader without taking any more physical form than an electrical impulse. Would we need copyright at all in such a frictionless environment? Nicholas Negroponte focused on the ease of distribution. With a global, digital network, the process of distributing someone else's work was simpler, and enjoyed a dramatically broader scope. Mass distribution, once the near exclusive domain of institutions, now became available to the individual. Copyright would not need to assure the kind of financial incentives it once did, because the costs of distributing information would so significantly decrease in a digital world as to be negligible. Esther Dyson argued that content providers would do better to forego selling their content and instead recoup costs from ancillary markets or charge for service relationships around the use of the work: maintenance, training, arrangements with businesses that want users to seek them out, and so forth. "Content providers should manage their businesses as if it were free, and then figure out how to set up relationships or develop ancillary products and services that cover the costs of developing content."[49] Copyright, instead of imposing a metaphor of property, could instead oversee the ancillary human interactions such that profit could flow from them.

Some went even further. Weaned on the viral communities developing over the Internet, some believed that the social dynamics of those communities and of the Internet itself would sustain the flow of information. In a Netizen utopia, cyberspace would not only be freed from the limitations of the human body and the impositions of government legislation, but also shed the demands of the market. Ideas would run free across a networked "hive mind"[50] organized around information flows rather than the well-worn routines of real-space commerce. Copyright simply has no place in this vision of the Internet as a gift economy; the changes to information were too dramatic, the risk of its restriction too great. Borrowing the dual rhetorics of technological inevitability and political libertarianism so pervasive in the Netizen discourse, Barlow spoke as if copyright was already rattling its last breath: "It may well be that when the current system of intellectual property law has collapsed, as seems inevitable, that no new legal structure will arise in its place."[51]

The Clinton-Gore Vision

The common Netizen complaint about what happened instead, that this once-free and anarchic cyberspace has been tamed by bureaucrats with little understanding of its potential, is curiously naïve considering the Internet's military ancestry. The U.S. government, via the Department of Defense and later the National Science Foundation (NSF), has always had a guiding hand in the design and implementation of the Internet. As the Netizens were proclaiming their techno-libertarian information policy on websites, in cyber-fetish magazines like *Wired*, and in dotcom consultant manifestos, the federal government was beginning to articulate its own vision of the Internet's future in a series of policy initiatives. The Clinton administration, driven by technophile Vice President Al Gore, appointed a task force to help plan for the financial and infrastructural sustainability of the Internet—or what they dubbed the National Information Infrastructure (NII). Committees and working groups were developed on a number of foreseeable issues: universal service, technological innovation, interoperability, privacy, government use of IT, and intellectual property. The working groups enlisted federal agency directors and representatives from the private sector to together develop a policy agenda for supporting and expanding the Internet into an "information superhighway"—and one particularly amenable to U.S. interests.[52]

The language of this NII plan makes claims about the Internet and its potential ramifications as bold as the Netizens' starry-eyed predictions, serving up the same assumption—that technologies spur radical change—to both defend the urgency of this effort and rationalize its cost.

All Americans have a stake in the construction of an advanced National Information Infrastructure (NII), a seamless web of communications networks, computers, databases, and consumer electronics that will put vast amounts of information at users' fingertips. Development of the NII can help unleash an information revolution that will change forever the way people live, work, and interact with each other . . . the NII can transform the lives of the American people—ameliorating the constraints of geography, disability, and economic status—giving all Americans a fair opportunity to go as far as their talents and ambitions will take them.[53]

This information revolution could only happen, in the NII model, when cyberspace was rendered hospitable to investment and commerce. The sense of liberation and possibility—geographic, educational, bureaucratic, physical, economic—provided a utopian justification for a policy committed to, first and foremost, encouraging private investment in the infrastructure and content of the Internet.

The Clinton-Gore vision of the Internet as a vibrant new marketplace for information provided the perfect contrast to the dystopian concerns about copyright that emerged from the NII Task Force's working group on intellectual property issues. The group was led by Bruce Lehman, then Assistant Secretary of Commerce and Commissioner of Patents and Trademarks, and at one time a lobbyist for the software industry.[54] Lehman's policy suggestions, released in July 1994 as the Green Paper draft and updated in September 1995 as the official White Paper, began with the NII assumption that the Internet could and should be a vibrant marketplace for information. If this marketplace were made safe for vendors to ply their wares, they would naturally choose to fill it with the best and widest array of cultural goods. Without adequate protection, however, those content providers would be reluctant to bring their goods to that marketplace:

The full potential of the NII will not be realized if the education, information, and entertainment products protected by intellectual property laws are not protected effectively when disseminated via the NII. Creators and other owners of intellectual property rights will not be willing to put their interests at risk if appropriate systems—both in the U.S. and internationally—are not in place to permit them to set and enforce the terms and conditions under which their works are made available in the NII environment. Likewise, the public will not use the services available on the NII and generate the market necessary for its success unless a wide variety of works are available under equitable and reasonable terms and conditions, and the integrity of those works is assured. All the computers, telephones, fax machines, scanners, cameras, keyboards, televisions, monitors, printers, switches, routers, wires, cables, networks and satellites in the world will not create a successful NII, if there is no content. What will drive the NII is the content moving through it.[55]

On the other hand, this marketplace would be undercut by the Internet's capacity for unauthorized reproduction and distribution of information:

Advances in digital technology and the rapid development of electronic networks and other communications technologies raise the stakes considerably. Any two-dimensional work can readily be "digitized"—i.e., translated into a digital code (usually a series of zeros and ones). The work can then be stored and used in that digital form. This dramatically increases: the ease and speed with which a work can be reproduced; the quality of the copies (both the first and the hundredth "generation" are virtually identical); the ability to manipulate and change the work; and the speed with which copies (authorized and unauthorized) can be "delivered" to the public.[56]

The ease of network distribution and the exactitude of digital reproduction offered by the Internet meant that copyright restrictions would need to be even broader and more rigorously enforced.[57]

This is merely the latest instantiation of the incentive logic of copyright, matched with the belief that content provides an incentive to technological adoption—a commonplace assumption as old as the adoption of radio. But the particular metaphor being used here is an insidious one: While Lehman may or may not have meant "market" literally in the sense that every bit of information provided online would come with a price tag attached, it is increasingly difficult now to think outside of the market analogy when describing the character of the Internet. The metaphor paves the way for an Internet that is more or less (or only) a vehicle for commerce, including both intellectual property and more tangible goods. This makes property-based laws of distribution the most relevant framework and gives them a rhetorical high ground: Within the incentive logic, allowing publishers to charge for every use "would better fulfill the constitutional purpose of copyright, because the greater the financial return to them, the greater will be their incentive to make works available to the public."[58] In place of the copyright "balance" that recognizes that a monopoly intended to serve the public might also limit it, the incentive logic tends to see stronger copyright protection as precisely what will ensure the public good—in other words, more is always better.[59]

The working group's perspective replaces the information playground imagined by the Netizens with a dichotomy between the legitimate distribution of content and the rampant piracy always ready to undercut it. To do so requires neatly equating communication with commerce, but this is a logical and unproblematic leap if you believe the best way to spur the growth of the Internet is to allow private investment to transform it into a marketplace. The metaphor becomes its own justification:

The absence on the NII of copyrighted works for which authors do wish to exercise their rights—fully or to some limited extent—under the copyright law, of course, would not necessarily result in its demise. The Internet, for instance, could continue to serve as a communications tool and resource for Government, public domain and works of willing authors. However, unless the framework for legitimate commerce is preserved and adequate protection for copyrighted works is ensured, the vast communications network will not reach its full potential as a true, global marketplace. Copyright protection is not an obstacle in the way of the success of the NII; it is an essential component. Effective copyright protection is a fundamental way to promote the availability of works to the public.[60]

It should come as no surprise that this perspective was in near-perfect alignment with the view of the major content industries. The efforts of the working group were motivated in large part by the major record labels and movie studios, who were already vigorously lobbying for stronger protections, and who certainly hoped to play a part in the global, digital marketplace envisioned in the NII initiative.[61] (The White Paper would also become the foundation for the Digital Millennium Copyright Act of 1998. This is discussed further in chapter 6.)

The Netizens dreamed of a new relationship between authorship and distribution; authors could distribute their own work, reaching interested readers without having to enter into the commodified and increasingly mega-corporate system of distribution that characterized existing forms of cultural discourse. The Internet would provide a forum where individuals could have a presence, and would provide the building blocks for innovative distribution schemes to develop in the future. Copying, now made perfect by digital technology, would be the foundation of this distribution system, and should be embraced. The system of distribution common to traditional media, which depended on copyright, would enjoy no strategic advantage on the Net; its failings would be overcome in the new medium. The Clinton-Gore vision, on the other hand, looked to conventional media producers and traditional copyright law as precisely the means for supporting the Internet. Concerned that, as a medium of information distribution, the new technology would fail unless it could be filled with viable content, this group planned to assure existing content producers a protected and profitable means of distribution. This meant both embracing the logic justifying copyright and the distribution system it helped spawn and ensuring that the traditional media system would enjoy a strategic advantage on the Internet, with the law's help. Copyright would have its work cut out for it, and should probably be strengthened, because the Internet seemed to copy so perfectly and promiscuously that the worst pirate tendencies would be facilitated.

What all of this initial rhetoric tended to overlook was that the technology itself was, and is, still up for grabs; each side of the dispute treated the Internet as a given thing, a fixed and stable object around which to make claims. This may have been error, or it may have been strategy; rhetorical claims often hold the material object still in order to build on something known, to make some outcomes appear inevitable. Regardless, technology refuses to hold still, because it too is entangled in the same social dynamics. The cadre of technologies that together form the Internet were and still are very much in development. Moreover, their development has continued within the context of these evolving disputes, and has been shaped by them. Those with the power to intervene can use and even adjust the technology to leverage particular goals. Even the earliest claims about what the new technology was for—distance computing, or networked communication, or information distribution, for example— were not merely technological facts. They resulted from research priorities and design decisions, which were already shaped by debates about the needs of military control, academic research, and social communication, and by the values of the designers and institutions involved in those decisions.

As the Internet took root in public life, these arguments about copyright emerged and developed as a tangled mess of claims and uses, rules and tools. Applications of the technology by users would be countered in legal arguments for their prohibition; technological limitations established and supported by law would be challenged by statements undermining those limitations; political claims criticizing legal rules would be embodied in technological innovations that changed the way people would make rhetorical arguments. It would be inside those controversies that these concerns about law and technology, design and use, private and public, commerce and communication, and authorship and distribution would be negotiated. The biggest of those controversies arrived in 1999 with the introduction of a little software application called Napster.

The Cultural Politics of Peer-to-Peer

As the National Research Council noted in its influential 2000 report, music has been the "canary in the coal mine"[62] for the digital copyright wars. Millions of copies of digital music in an unprotected format were already in the hands of consumers (in the form of CDs); in this encoded form, songs could be further compressed to relatively small file sizes, meaning download times were reasonably fast; music sharing, along more informal networks of friends, was already commonplace and largely overlooked by the industry. Together these conditions made music the first form of commercial culture to begin circulating widely online, and the first case to spark the dilemmas anticipated by Netizens and the NII.

Well before the arrival of Napster, the dimensions of that dispute were already taking shape around digital music.[63] As artists, fans, entrepreneurs, and hardware manufacturers approached the new technology, each began to envision ways in which the Internet might serve as a vehicle for music distribution, perhaps even offer it new form, wider reach, and greater consequence. As these ideas were put into practice the record labels, themselves just beginning to work out what the Internet might offer, decided to counter these visions with a hard-line legal stance against what they characterized as piracy. As these competing discourses came into conflict, each began to articulate the technological affordances, the economic dynamics, and the legal principles they hoped would justify their aim.

It was back in 1987 that Italian researcher Leonardo Chiariglione petitioned the International Organization for Standardization in Switzerland to lead the development of standards for digital audio and video. With the official sanction of the IOS, his Motion Picture Experts Group (MPEG) sought out like-minded research teams; one response came from German researchers at the Institute for Integrated Circuits of the Fraunhofer Gesellschaft, who proposed a codec[64] that shrank the size of sound files at an 11:1 ratio by removing elements of the recording the human ear cannot register. The standard was designed to be open, meaning both that it included no protection mechanism or encryption and that anyone could have access to the standard in order to design software to work with it. Chiariglione's group dubbed the German codec "Level 3," and incorporated it into its first proposed standard, "MPEG-1."[65] The IOS approved the MPEG formats as the new standards in 1992, but some time during their deliberation, a hacker named SoloH slipped unnoticed into Chiariglione's university server and lifted the codec.[66] The new format, dubbed "mp3," quickly spread online and was embraced as the de facto audio format by hackers and online music aficionados. Within two years, high-quality music files were circulating online by the thousands on newsgroups and fan websites.[67]

Some artists began posting their own music in mp3 format, especially those without major label contracts, hoping the Internet might help loosen the corporate stranglehold over popular music and forge a more direct connection between artist and fan. A number of new websites, like MP3.com, began hosting authorized copies of music from unsigned artists and, in the process, began experimenting with different models of distribution, and different models of copyright and contract arrangements. But not everyone was quite so scrupulous. There was a burgeoning black market for mp3 versions of popular, copyrighted music. Software for "ripping" a CD into mp3 format was free and quickly becoming ubiquitous. Some of this digital music was made available for download on personal websites, more was traded person-to-person via e-mail and in Internet Relay Chat exchanges, and even more was collected on semi-private, password-accessible file servers. As Jonathan Sterne notes, the very design of the mp3 format put a high priority on portability; users quickly found it well suited to casual distribution of music online.[68]

Despite a few early efforts to make songs available on the Internet as promotional vehicles, the major labels remained reticent to use the web without some certainty that they could control what happened to their product. The protected formats they preferred, such as Liquid Audio and a2b, were incompatible and clumsy, and consumers seemed generally uninterested. But mp3 posed a dilemma; it was widely embraced by precisely the consumers they hoped to keep, but it afforded no protection—with it, copyrighted music could proliferate widely across the Internet, with no financial compensation to label or artist. The record industry wanted very much to curtail what they saw as widespread piracy, and they began deliberately speaking of it in those terms. But they also did not want to seem behind the curve in terms of what the Internet could offer.

So as music fans went online to share mp3s, and dotcom startups challenged the major labels by building clearinghouses for digital downloads, the major labels felt it necessary to contain these challenges, both by articulating their place as the natural patrons of a shift to digital music, and by outlawing the alternatives. The record industry began exploring a number of different strategies: educational, legal, commercial, technological. At the start, copyright law was the most powerful tool in their arsenal: As early as 1997, some of the major labels were sending out "friendly warnings" to the hosts of FTP servers and websites that were posting their music.[69] By early 1998, the RIAA had three full-time staff whose job was simply to search the web for mp3s of copyrighted music and, as a stopgap measure, send cease and desist letters to the individuals who had posted them and to their Internet service providers.[70] Soon they began developing automatic applications to scan the web for unauthorized mp3 files and churn out cease and desist e-mails. The industry similarly challenged upstart labels and manufacturers with the threat of lawsuits. They failed to stop Diamond Multimedia from releasing the first portable mp3 player; they enjoyed more success in their lawsuit against MP3.com for the personal music storage service they tried to introduce in 2000.

As Richard Barbrook predicted, "The greatest threat to the commercial music corporations comes from the flexibility and spontaneity of the high-tech gift economy."[71] This was most apparently true with the meteoric popularity of Napster and the peer-to-peer (p2p) applications that accompanied it. With Napster, the record labels faced a more dramatic problem than before. Certainly, the software made it substantially easier to redistribute copyrighted music casually and on a much wider scale. But Napster also threatened to change the balance of power of who did the distributing. Rather than using a clearinghouse model like MP3.com, peer-to-peer lets users be distributors as well. This does more than widen the scope of distribution. It challenges the very assumptions the music industry relies on for profit and longevity: the privileged place of artists and their designated patrons; the assumption that cultural expression moves in one direction, from the few producers to the many consumers; the relentless commodification of that cultural expression; and the management of those commodities by established corporate interests through copyright.[72]

In some sense, Napster was itself the product of the simmering copyright battle already underway. In 1998 Shawn Fanning, a computer science student at Northeastern University, would surf the Internet with his friends for mp3 files, which meant trawling through massive archives of unknown bands at sites like MP3.com, and more likely skipping through "warez"[73] sites in search of an unauthorized copy of a more popular song. In part because of the efforts of the RIAA and in part because of the limits of search engine technology at the time, finding these files was an arduous, though not impossible, task. A website blatantly offering copyrighted music would draw the attention of RIAA lawyers, eliciting at least a cease and desist letter, or a call to the ISP, maybe even a NET Act[74] lawsuit. So mp3 sites were fleeting, buried, dilapidated, outdated. Fanning decided to design an application himself that would allow users to make their personal collections of mp3 files available without having to post them to the web, and to peek directly into others' collections, searching by song title or band name rather than from site to site. And, though the application he designed was first posted online in July 1999, its popularity didn't spike until 2000, after the lawsuit brought by the RIAA drew the attention of the press, and with it a massive population of eager users and their music.

It is important to understand how Napster and peer-to-peer applications actually work, if only because they have been somewhat caricatured in the subsequent argument for technical copy protection. While trading copyrighted music may not be a bold, political act, the cultural potential of the peer-to-peer architecture does pose a more conceptual challenge to the ways in which we commonly distribute information. Napster was not just an economic threat to the corporations that traffic in culture, it was an ideological challenge to the very legal and economic principles on which they depend, and it did make plain some of the limitations of that system (however crudely those limitations were then exploited).

Amid all the excitement for the peer-to-peer phenomenon,[75] stirred by supporters and detractors alike, it was easy to misrepresent it as a dramatic new innovation. The gleam of the new can be a powerful tool for anyone debating the impact of a technology—change is a more compelling call-to-arms than continuity, regardless of whether it is benevolent or disastrous. The applications that appeared and proliferated alongside Napster were not new; they merely expanded on the architecture of the Internet, building on the same logic as a host of applications that preceded them,[76] and drawing on models of information distribution with a long, if often marginalized, history. The more important story here is one of continuity; the link between these tools and a longer tradition of how culture moves is too often lost in the debates about their legality—in many cases, deliberately. That said, there are two features of peer-to-peer tools that are, if not radically innovative, then at least worth noting, because they reveal how the design of these tools invokes alternative traditions for how information can be distributed. In his expert testimony in the Napster case (where he carefully described Napster as an "*evolution* in Internet technologies") Lessig noted, "Neither of these two components alone represents a radical advance in Internet technology . . . but Napster does combine these two functionalities in an innovative way."[77]

The first is that, unlike Internet applications like the web browser, peer-to-peer tools allow the user to be both client and server simultaneously. When you logged onto the Napster network by getting online and running the program, you joined a large group of current Napster users. You could request files from a designated folder on their hard drives, and other users could request files they found in yours. Napster helped negotiate the protocols so that one user could provide the requested file directly to the other. No intervening server was necessary for the actual exchange to be made.

While the Internet opens up access and participation much more widely than more centralized systems—many-to-many rather than one-to-many or few-to-many—it has never actually been an all-to-all communication network. The web retains a distribution hierarchy in the distinction between client and server. Individual computer users—clients—can request files from servers (surfing the web); they can provide specific kinds of information when asked (filling out an online form, adding to an online shopping cart); they can provide their files via certain servers under certain conditions (posting a website, contributing to a newsgroup); and they can send specific files to known addresses (e-mail, file transfer). But they could not, until Napster, automatically field requests from users for files stored on their computer. Being a server requires special (and somewhat less user-friendly) software applications, as well as the resources to effectively field requests (a fast and reliable connection, a terminal that's on and connected all the time, protection against hackers and viruses, etc.). These special conditions mean that, although anyone with a computer and the requisite skills can be connected to the Internet, only a subset of those people can actually be two-way information providers in the fullest sense. The rest have only limited means to provide information to others, and are beholden to service providers for the wide distribution of their documents.[78]

The promise that the Internet "revolution" would allow anyone to be a multimedia producer, and would erase the barriers to cultural expression posed by centralized authority, was not so much wrong as it was overstated. The dynamics of production and consumption are always tied to the particular politics of how information is *distributed*, and the Internet as a system of information distribution has a particular political character. While the Netizen rhetoric tended to emphasize free and equal access to the network, a system of control, dispersed and fractured but not evaporated, remained in place; the power relationship in the client-server relationship is parallel to the traditional distinction between information providers and information recipients. This nodal design is not inconsequential; gaining space on a server and thus visibility on the Internet costs money and resources, and is limited by time, server space, and the rules of use that webmasters establish. Most important, this system can be exploited; the way the RIAA pressured universities in their role as providers of Internet service into policing their users, for example, reveals how this client-server relationship can be used to reassert control over the many by the few. The experience for a user of being both client and server simultaneously, then, is significantly different from, say, browsing the web.[79]

The second of Napster's important innovations helped make this breadth of information distribution more feasible. Peer-to-peer applications include a way to search for a particular file across a constantly fluctuating network of users in real time. The system can accommodate users logging on and off the network at their whim, and the files they offer changing from moment to moment. Napster did this by storing a regularly updated list of files made available by all users currently logged on. A request for a specific file would be sent to Napster's server; Napster's server delivered a list of files currently available from logged-on users, including their IP addresses (although they are invisible to the user); selecting a file initiated a direct file transfer. Logging off Napster removed your files from the central list; a search request "pinged" users to see if they were still available to the network. The fact that this search function was centralized made Napster more efficient than some competing peer-to-peer applications, but also made it easier to control; this technical choice made Napster both the most popular of the file-trading tools and the most obvious target of an RIAA legal challenge.

A more decentralized model, used by Gnutella and others, depended instead on a series of requests spreading from the user to others, in a branching tree pattern. A user requested a file; that request was sent to a few users; each user sent it to a few more; and each of those sent it to a few more, and so on. If anyone who received the request had the requested file, they responded to the initial user and a download began. This made Gnutella less susceptible to legal challenge, since there was no central server to shut down. But it also posed a problem of scalability as the service grew; the more people connected, the more of these requests were propagating across the Internet, increasing traffic and slowing responses. Regardless of the drawbacks, the ability to search in real time allows peer-to-peer applications to enjoy the benefits of decentralization— lack of control, wide range of voices and texts, easy access, cheap distribution—while minimizing some of the disadvantages in terms of the organization and availability that usually follow.[80]

These innovations, regardless of whether we characterize them as massively transformative or historically continuous, mark peer-to-peer applications as a different way of structuring and exploiting the Internet—a difference that is not only material, but symbolic. Together they organize users and materials in ways particular to a decentralized network, but they have also come to symbolize the system's value and purpose: a cultural politics of decentralization. Peer-to-peer applications, like the Internet itself but to a greater degree, can shift the power of distribution into the hands of a much wider population of users than can traditional media systems. They pose a conceptual challenge to our ideas about how information should be produced, organized, distributed, and consumed—and most important, by whom—and to the economic actors whose business models depend on being the exclusive distributors of information to a dependent public.

In everyday practice, technologies can never be separated from social claims of their purpose, significance, and value. Public debates about peer-to-peer applications invoked these technological features as proof of the cultural agendas they purportedly represent; when the software was redesigned, it was improved not only technically, but also to better embody a political stance or duck a legal obligation; designers explained those changes by invoking claims about the technology's social impact. Thus the record industry faced not only a new system for the unauthorized circulation of their work but also a nascent political movement that justified file-trading in terms of new models of the distribution of culture, with a vocabulary of technologies that seemed to support them.

Killing Napster

In December 1999, only five months after the first version of the Napster application was posted online, eighteen of the largest record labels brought suit against the company in Northern California U.S. District Court. They alleged that Napster was guilty of promoting the unauthorized distribution of their copyrighted music recordings, and sought an injunction and damages on the order of $100,000 per copyrighted recording infringed. Separate suits from Metallica, Dr. Dre, and independent label TVT Records followed. Napster came under an attack that was at once legal and discursive—an effort to shut it down, to squelch the commercial and legal aspirations of peer-to-peer, and to stabilize what counts as authorized and unauthorized, legal and illegal, and ethical and unethical distribution of cultural expression. Copyright's presumption that authored work is best distributed as a purchasable commodity would be put to the test, against not only the individual pleasure of getting something for free, but also the powerful counterideologies being articulated around Napster and peer-to-peer: freedom of information, the value of the public domain, the corruption of the music industry, the rights of fans, and the significance of culture.

The initial complaint attempted to articulate a natural alliance between the principles of copyright, our hopes for technology, and the interests of the record industry. Notice how the RIAA tries to take back the promise of the Internet from peer-to-peer boosters, although with an implicitly different future in mind for it: "Napster has thus misused and is misusing the remarkable potential of the Internet, essentially running an online bazaar devoted to the pirating of music."[81] The "remarkable potential" they refer to is, of course, not the vibrant public forum prophesied by the Netizens, but the digital marketplace that both the record labels and the Clinton-Gore administration imagined. The RIAA also began the work of demonizing Napster as a threat (and a particularly deliberate, snide, adolescent one) to culture as they understood it—which, of course, it was.

Napster's defense depended primarily on the 1984 *Sony v. Universal* "Betamax" case, in which the film industry similarly targeted a technology that it claimed encouraged copyright violation and undercut the legitimate market for cultural work: in that case, the VCR. They sued Sony for contributing to and financially benefiting from copyright infringement, hoping to either shut down the market for the new device or compel Sony to work with them to better protect their copyrights. The court narrowly decided that the VCR, while it could be used to copy copyrighted movies, was also useful for other purposes—for instance, what Sony had termed "time-shifting" (the practice of taping a television program to watch later). Because the device was "capable of substantial non-infringing uses," the courts decided it could not be held liable for when users did use it to violate copyright. Napster similarly argued that, because users could trade non-copyrighted music just as easily as they could copyrighted material, and could "space-shift" their own music rather than carrying around CDs, Napster also had noninfringing uses.[82]

In July 2000, Judge Marilyn Patel granted the RIAA the injunction it had requested, ordering Napster to find a way to prevent the circulation of copyrighted music through its service. Considering the circumstances, it was probably the judicious thing to do—if we are reflexive about exactly what we mean by "justice" when we say justice was served. Napster users *were* directly infringing the copyrights of the major labels, Napster *was* facilitating their behavior and would eventually gain from it financially. As such, they should be found liable for contributing to copyright infringement. Justice here is a finding that fits with and confirms existing legal doctrine and judicial precedent; in terms of the specifically legal vision of the situation, Napster *is* liable. In terms of the *Sony* defense, Napster was arguably being used overwhelmingly for copyright violation; more important, although the court agreed that some uses of the system might be "fair," this was irrelevant because Napster could prevent infringing uses in a way that Sony could not.

What this overlooks, of course, is whether the existing copyright law could accommodate, or even comprehend, how different the arrangements of distribution offered by peer-to-peer networks were, in comparison to traditional material and commercial means. What was at stake here was a powerful paradigm, a commercial system of distribution based on a powerful confluence of legal and economic values, facing an alternative paradigm that worked on substantially different terms. It was the same challenge posed by early peer-to-peer boosters: that the very hierarchy of provider/consumer would be replaced with something like a network of *peers.* People would trade cultural expression rather than purchase it, would see it in terms of experiential and social value rather than exclusively in the commercial terms that have come to stand in for those values.[83] If price is treated as the ultimate marker of value, then free goods are worthless; but in the absence of price, the industry feared that their consumers would come to recognize other forms of value, ones that could not be translated into dollars, or didn't need to be. Copyright law, however, is both premised on and the basis of the commercial logic being challenged, and does not have much space to accommodate this alternative paradigm.

Napster died an ignominious death in 2001, after some legal wrangling with the RIAA about how to comply with the court's decision, a dramatic drop in users once the copyrighted music became largely unavailable, and a surprising last-minute influx of capital from music giant Bertelsmann, who broke ranks with its RIAA partners in the hope of transforming Napster into a legitimate music platform. However, a series of peer-to-peer alternatives emerged in its wake, each one designed specifically to avoid the kind of legal threats the RIAA could impose: a more decentralized architecture offering no point at which legal consequences can be imposed, and corporate headquarters located overseas where U.S. law cannot reach. Networks such as Morpheus and Kazaa rapidly exceeded the user base enjoyed by Napster even at the height of its popularity, and file-trading has become commonplace for music fans, especially with younger generations for whom digital music is not a novelty, but the only format they've ever known.

The major music and film companies continued to seek lawsuits against these technologies, most recently in *MGM v. Grokster.*[84] The industry was shocked when the appeals court found in favor of the peer-to-peer companies, under the same *Sony* defense Napster had attempted to use, and appealed to the Supreme Court. Many guessed that their decision would not only signal the fate of peer-to-peer technology, but would also finally clarify how the *Sony* defense should translate to the digital realm. In 2005, the Supreme Court found for the entertainment industries, but added an unexpected twist. The court could not agree on how the *Sony* standard applied. They did agree that defendants Kazaa and Morpheus should be held liable for facilitating copyright infringement, but according to a new standard: not only whether they knew of and materially aided the infringement of their users, but also whether they had actively encouraged users to violate copyright. The court pointed to how the two companies had marketed their services, the deliberate absence of technological features designed to prevent infringement, internal e-mail and corporate documents that revealed their intentions, even the fact that the name "Grokster" was meant to remind users of Napster. This "inducement" standard, similar to the "Inducing Infringement of Copyrights Act" proposed by the Senate the previous year, now stands beside (or perhaps against) the *Sony* "substantial noninfringing uses" standard in determining how digital distribution technologies will fare in copyright liability cases.

For the biggest distributors in the music and film industries in particular, the threat of widespread copyright infringement posed by Napster, Grokster, and peer-to-peer tools appears to be a real and substantial danger. Putting aside for the moment whether they're correct, and whether this view may also be opportunistic, file-sharing is perceived to be undermining the very foundation of the music business. Songs are certainly being downloaded by potential customers at a bewildering rate, and traditional CD sales are taking a dive that has coincided with the rise of networks, although evidence of a causal link is inconclusive.[85] But the record labels are even more frightened by the possibility that whole generations will come to perceive music as a free resource. Not only would sales be lost today, but the very idea that music must be bought might also vanish. As Richard Parsons, president of Time Warner, warned, "It's a reality. An increasing number of young people don't buy albums, so we are not only losing that immediate revenue. They are also growing up with a notion that music is free and ought to be free."[86]

Napster and peer-to-peer file-trading provided the necessary justification for the entertainment industries to declare war; the court's decision in the Napster case was a portent of that war's future. While the music and film industries have continued to pursue the legal avenue of suing both individuals and the institutions and technologies that aid them, they have increasingly turned toward technological solutions in the hope that the clean intervention of technology might succeed where the messier mechanisms of the law have not.

Digital Rights Management and the "Trusted System"

Just as digital technology seems to facilitate the reproduction and distribution of cultural work, it also facilitates new forms of technological intervention that are more specific, flexible, and invisible. Even as they slowly began to seek new ways to deliver content, the major music labels and Hollywood studios were also seeking technological roadblocks to the easy redistribution of intellectual property, should the legal ones fail. What they want is something more vast than just stronger statutes, copy protection systems, and watermarks; they are slowly building the material infrastructure and digital standards, as well as the social, commercial, and legal preconditions, for the rise of "digital rights management." DRM is an umbrella term for a family of technical applications, and for the legal and commercial arrangements they require. Some are already being experimented with and used; others are mere proposals being considered and researched.[87]

Most DRM systems begin with the kind of copy protection already commonplace in the sale of software and the delivery of television through cable and satellite, which depends on the use of encryption. Encryption is a security technique that takes advantage of the ease with which information, stored digitally, can be mathematically altered (but not destroyed) according to complex algorithms. With a key that precisely reverses the mathematical distortions, the original data can be retrieved; without the key, the data is meaningless. Once a technique used almost exclusively for sending secret messages, primarily for military or criminal purposes, encryption has been incorporated into the commercial distribution of information in order to distribute work widely and yet ensure that only authorized users can access it. The key to a particular encryption algorithm may be built into a device (cable television is scrambled according to an algorithm whose key is built into the decoder cable box given to subscribers); it may also be delivered along with the content and triggered by a particular piece of information possessed by the receiver (some software applications can only be accessed by entering a password, serial number, etc., which the consumer receives at the moment of purchase or after subsequent registration); it may also be delivered separately, triggered only when the work is used in a particular way.[88] Content providers may have only a single key that all consumers will use, may deploy a range of keys so as to distinguish different devices or contexts in which they can be used, or may even assign a single key to each and every user or each and every device.[89]

Such encryption schemes have been experimented with by the culture industries for nearly three decades, and often serve well as a "curb-high"[90] protection by discouraging casual infringers. But taken by themselves they are insufficient for the kind of airtight copyright protection to which many producers aspire. Encryption schemes can be cracked and circumvented, inasmuch as any system built can be unbuilt. Most important, encryption does not actually prevent copying. While these systems may stop unauthorized users (i.e., a television viewer without the requisite cable box cannot access the encrypted signal), encryption by itself cannot prevent authorized users from making unauthorized copies, nor can it prevent unauthorized users from making exact copies of the encrypted data.

So, increasingly, these encryption schemes are being paired with a second level of control, in which the receiving device not only decodes the encrypted content, but also obeys a series of rules about the content's subsequent reproduction and redistribution of it, ensuring that such functions are made impossible for the average user. This set of arrangements, sometimes called a "trusted system"[91] or "trusted computing," greatly expands the complexity of DRM, but offers copyright owners at least the promise of a great deal more, and more precise, control.

Imagine that your stereo is a small, handheld device. It stores, organizes, and plays songs you have purchased in digital form. (Perhaps it is an all-purpose media device: DVD and mp3 player, e-book display, cell phone, wireless web browser, PDA, portable game console, everything but the virtual kitchen sink.) It interfaces with your home entertainment system to play music through your expensive speakers, snaps into your dashboard to play in your car, and pumps tunes through your titanium headphones. To purchase music, you link it to your personal computer to download from your favorite website, or to a kiosk at the mall, or even to a friend's player. This device would offer the ultimate in convenience, audio fidelity . . . and digital commerce.

The "trusted" part of this system is that this device obeys rules established by the copyright owner when they first make the song available—the "digital rights." These policies can be built into the device itself, embedded along with the delivered file, or sent separately by a licensing authority (typically, the producer of the content) whenever the user initiates a function that requires authorization.[92] In one model the music is encrypted, and the digital file is marked with tags that indicate not only its title and artist and such, but also its legal owner, its fee to play or to transfer, its duration of usability, and the account to which fees are to be paid. These tags can provide almost any kind of information, including any kind of rearticulated copyright specifications; they can also be flexibly redesigned as producers come up with new ways to carve up the distribution and use of their product. Trusted devices would "precisely interpret"[93] these digital tags and act accordingly.

Let me quote at length the description of one such system. The comments toward the end of the passage come from George Freidman, CEO of InfraWorks, and one-time intelligence and security expert for the U.S. military during Operation Desert Storm:

The InTether system consists of a packager, used by the originator of a file, and a receiver, used by the recipient. The packager enables a publisher, record label, movie studio—or, for that matter, a law firm, doctor's office, bank or anyone else who wants information security—to impose a set of restrictions on almost any digital file. . . .

Using the packaging software, the originator can determine how many times the recipient can view or play the file; whether the recipient can alter it and send it to others; the identity of permissible recipients (determined by ID numbers and passwords); whether the file can be printed freely, once, or never; how long the file can be viewed or played (in hours and minutes); the date on which the file can first be opened; and the date on which, if the originator wishes, the file will self-destruct and vanish from the recipient's hard drive. . . .

. . . From the perspective of the user, the Infraworks software is almost invisible, except that when viewing or playing an InTethered document the consumer will not be able to use certain commands—typically, the "copy," "print," "cut," "paste" and "save as" commands.

. . . The receiver is anchored to the C drive, where it cannot be moved or copied, and it is "cloaked" to render it invisible to the Windows operating system. . . . Although the InTether system does involve cryptography—InTethered files are encrypted, and the receiver contains the key to decrypt them—the receiver does much more than that. It places "system-level controls on what you can do that are persistent," Friedman says, effectively overriding the operating system. . . .

"We're fairly deep in the operating system," he says, "so we see what's going on and we either permit or deny it from happening in relation . . . to the files under our control."[94]

The rhetoric is classic command-and-control, a far cry from the delicate balance of copyright; it should come as no surprise that the design of this technology has been developed by military security experts. The device, and the entire system, aspires to be a "black box" in the way Bruno Latour intended: The "assembly of disorderly and unreliable allies is thus slowly turned into something that closely resembles an organized whole . . . It is made up of many *more* parts and it is handled by a much *more* complex commercial network, but it acts as one piece."[95] The user would, ideally, be completely unaware of, and completely regulated by, this system.

A number of restrictions are likely to be common to all DRM-based trusted systems. First and foremost, the device must in some way forbid unregulated copying—and not only duplication inside of that device, but also the output of the data in any form that could then be recorded by an attached device. Devices would refuse to output to other devices that were not compliant with these protocols and rules, that were deemed "untrustworthy." You try to load the file from computer to stereo, or stereo to computer, but your request is rejected, the copy function disabled.

This, Lessig argues, is a fundamentally different way to enforce law: "What copyright seeks to do using the threat of law and the push of norms, trusted systems do through the code. Copyright orders others to respect the rights of the copyright holder before using his property. Trusted systems give access only if rights are respected in the first place."[96] Such a system would not require a monolithic system of authority to oversee the production of every device; it would, like the Internet, depend only on shared or translatable protocols, so that a network of networks could function as a system and together ensure that the rules are comprehensive and inviolate.

This raises the question, of course, of how a cable box, DVD player, or computer can know what an attached device is capable of. One solution is to restrict the kinds of formats in which a signal may be delivered; the DVD player could output in analog (i.e., to a TV) but not in digital format (i.e., to a computer, which would presumably make it more vulnerable to unauthorized duplication and distribution). In more ambitious versions of the trusted system plan, *all* devices that handle digital information of any kind would either honor the rules embedded in the trusted system, or have a compartmentalized portion of the device that does so. Inside a computer, this would mean that authorized applications could be loaded within a bounded set of trusted processes, only inside of which the digital work could be decrypted and manipulated.[97] Then these applications and devices could interact freely, after a "handshake" assures the first device that the second device will honor the same copyright restrictions.[98]

In a basic version of DRM, the fact that the material is encrypted could be the signal that indicates to a trusted device that the work should not be copied; or the work could be accompanied by a simple "copy/do not copy" mark. But, if such a trusted system could be established, in which all consumer hardware honored a set of matching copyright rules when dealing with materials protected by DRM encryption, then the particulars of these obligations could be designed in increasingly precise ways. Instructions to the trusted device could indicate that a work may only be copied a certain number of times, or under certain conditions, or for certain additional fees. Already, the popular online music services (iTunes, Napster 2, Pressplay, Rhapsody) limit the use of downloaded files by tethering each file to one or more computers, preventing users from burning songs to CD or changing their file format, and limiting how many portable devices the song can be ported to.[99]

Some have suggested that trusted systems could eventually be matched up with a micropayment scheme, when a workable one is developed, such that fees are billed at the moment the user decides to play or copy a work, at prescribed costs and according to encoded arrangements. These arrangements could be included in the encoded instructions, and automatically obeyed by the trusted device.[100] Each use of a file or transfer between trusted devices would accrue charges, which would find their way back to the copyright owner through an "always online" network. This system of exchange could extend well past the original point of sale. You might buy a copy of a song from me, the fee returning to the copyright holder; or you might pay a smaller fee to "borrow" it from me, at which point the copy on my device would be disabled temporarily as long as you "had" it. Sales could be for a limited duration, an extended music rental, or for a set number of plays; the device could erase the song after the authorized period, unless you agreed to pay more. The "accountant inside"[101] would log all sales and transfers, and accumulate them into a monthly bill payable to the content owner. With such a system in place, "digital property can be anywhere on the planet without the knowledge of its creators and still make money for them whenever it is used or copied."[102] As long as the interconnected system of devices that handle the digital content and its accompanying instructions were all designed to comprehend and obey the same instructional language, these copyright rules could be infinitely and precisely specified for uses, conditions, and even different users.

The trusted system, though regularly justified as a specific response to the threat of online copyright infringement, is much more. It allows for an incredibly subtle and complex parsing of the use of information so as to be sold; and it provides a tool that will act as clerk, distributor, broker, police, and judge, all in one. Geoffrey Nunberg has remarked how commercial industries, looking to best transform culture into commodity, often work toward the greater "morselization"[103] of culture; the flow of ideas and expression is endlessly subdivided into discrete portions—books, chapters, albums, singles, movies, clips, sequences—so that they may be monetized in various ways for individual purchases. This, he argues, is not a cultural logic, but rather a strictly commercial one; it is not what is best for public discourse, but for the market. The trusted system is a morselizer of unprecedented depth; it can divide the same materials into all manner of discrete packages (song, album, sample, playlist, number of listens, time period), offering multiple forms of commercial transaction to suit the liking of the user and the precise price discrimination between users.

All of these forms move us closer to a "pay-per-view society," where digital technology offers ever more subtle and specific means of commodifying every bit of expression, and every practice involved with it. According to Vincent Mosco, "Though information has been a commodity from the earliest days of capitalism, the new technology deepens and extends opportunities for selling information by transcending the boundaries that space and time impose on the packaging and repackaging of information in a marketable form."[104] A more recent embrace of a subscription-based model by Napster 2 and its major label partners may signal a move away from the more classically pay-per- arrangement adopted by iTunes in its à la carte pricing, and there is an argument to be made that these particular pricing models urge different kinds of consumption practices and different orientations towards culture.[105] For the moment, the fact that we have both subscription-based and pay-per- arrangements only supports Nunberg's notion that culture is being further morselized—not only in more precise ways, but along multiple and overlapping dimensions. To the extent that such commercial arrangements can, in certain cases, offer economically equitable services to more people, they may have some benefit; however, when a pay-per-view arrangement is pursued solely for its commercial value and efficiency, and other cultural needs are overlooked, we risk leaving to the market precisely those aspects of public life we already know are badly served by it.

It is worth noting that my description thus far has focused exclusively on the use of DRM for entertainment media, and will continue to do so. There are a number of reasons for this. First, the major U.S. music and film industries have been the most active and visible proponents of DRM arrangements, and the technologists experimenting with DRM techniques are doing so largely on their behalf, or at least with the recognition that entertainment is the most obvious and lucrative use of their tools. Second, it is the media companies that have been most successful in shifting the debate about copyright and framing technological solutions as an imperative. But the questions about DRM as a tactic are not exclusive to entertainment. DRM encryption techniques are increasingly being used in the circulation of all types of digital information, from satellite maps to distance learning materials to preservational archives to intracorporate documents—anywhere that someone wants to retain control over what users do with their information. The same tools being designed for the sale of movies online can easily be fitted to the protection of any digital content, and for whatever end the owner of that information desires, be it copyright protection or otherwise. In some ways, how we implement technical copy protections on pop music will have ramifications for how we circulate information more broadly—just as the interests of entertainment providers have long directed the shape and interpretation of copyright law, though the law applies to information of all kinds.

Fair Use in an Encrypted World

Most of the commercial distributors of media content have looked eagerly to DRM encryption and the trusted system, both as the answer to their fears of piracy and as a new mechanism for commodifying their goods in unprecedented ways. And some scholars agree that DRM is the most promising solution to the problem of managing copyright on digital networks, perhaps the only viable choice.[106] But others have taken DRM to task for altering the character and consequence of copyright. Most prominent among them is Lessig, who notes that while the "West Coast code" of software is quite similar to the "East Coast code" of law in that both can be used to regulate human activity, they differ in *how* they regulate in important ways. These differences have material, economic, cultural, and, most important, democratic consequences.

Part of the problem is where decisions are made as to which rules are built into technological systems, how they are built in, and to what ends. The law, at least in principle, is the product of public deliberation by elected representatives. The goals pursued are supposed to be those of the public interest, the health of the nation and its economy, and the aspirations of the Constitution and American democracy as understood in the modern context. Of course, whether these goals are regularly achieved or even pursued is a separate question. As Jessica Litman has noted, copyright laws have historically been written by a conference of representatives from "relevant" or "aggrieved" organizations, which has overwhelmingly meant commercial publishers and producers.[107] Still, the public interest remains the principle according to which the law is written and adjudicated. The regulations in code, on the other hand, are designed inside of private, typically corporate contexts. There is no guarantee, indeed no expectation, that these rules will be designed in any way other than in the designer's best interests. Even private law in the form of contracts must remain beholden to the public; as Lessig describes it, "Private law creates private rights to the extent that these private rights serve some collective good. If a private right is harmful to a collective good, then the state has no reason to create it. The state's interests are general, not particular."[108] Technological code designed outside of this system is under no such obligation.

Joel Reidenberg points to the increasingly central role of standard-setting organizations as warranting similar concern: "The shift in focus toward technical standards as a source of policy rules emphasizes technical fora whose institutions are not normally associated with governance. The Internet Engineering Task Force, the Internet Society, the World Wide Web Consortium, and traditional standards organizations like ISO, ETSI, and committees like T1 are the real political centers."[109] These consortia are often not strictly governmental organizations, and are often populated by representatives from relevant industries. But at least these coalitions attempt to represent multiple interests, even if they are all one sort of interest and not another. The kind of private organization Lessig worries about is not an IETF, but a Microsoft. In their software development, they end up setting many of the ground rules for how computing will occur in a variety of places. Their market dominance[110] allows them to set standards that have implications for a majority of computer users, because their standards are likely to be built into third party applications and systems so as to be interoperable with Microsoft's platform. The threat Microsoft made in the late days of the Napster dispute—that they might redesign their Windows Media Player (an application built into their Windows OS and widely used) so it would artificially degrade the sound quality of mp3 files—revealed the kind of power they have to technologically regulate behavior in systematic ways.[111]

Lessig's concern is that the code designed by private corporations will be designed according to private agendas. While Congress is supposed to serve the public interests and the existing laws of the land, Microsoft and other corporations serve the interests of the consumer—specifically their consumers, and specifically in ways that serve the interests of their investors—bound only by the pursuit of continued profit and the dynamics of the market. These, Lessig worries, are far from ideal priorities, since standards can have consequences for a wide range of human activity: commercial, organizational, political, expressive, creative. A trusted system takes this to an extreme. As Mark Stefik argues, in a trusted system the copyright owners could determine the rights they wanted assigned to their particular work, creating a kind of "shrink-wrap license" specific to each work and each user. The nature of these assigned and restricted rights, and even the categories of rights, would be determined in the private and commercial contexts of the publishing house, movie studio, and record label, rather than on the floor of Congress, and in these private companies' interests, rather than the public's. "Trusted systems give the producer maximum control—admittedly at a cheaper cost, thus permitting many more authors to publish. But they give authors more control (either to charge for or limit use) in an area where the law gave less than perfect control."[112]

The most obvious way in which privatized technical copy protection can distort the subtle balance built into copyright law is with fair use. As noted previously, fair use was designed to allow some breathing room for the reuse or redistribution of copyrighted work that would otherwise be considered infringement. The exception applies when the use serves a valuable social purpose—quotation, classroom copies, criticism, journalism, parody. This exception was designed to be purposefully ambiguous and context-dependent. The four factors to be weighed in each case are vague, and the law refuses to indicate exactly how they should be applied. Fair use leaves to the discretion of a judge the task of determining how a particular use of someone's work is affecting its market, to what use it is being put, etc. This gives judges leeway in protecting users against the restrictions copyright owners might hope to impose, building in a grey area where users can dare to experiment and copyright owners may choose not to litigate.[113]

Whether it is a deliberate strategy or simply the function of limited resources in the face of nearly infinite possibilities, law typically does not specify exact regulations for every possible behavior in every possible context. Instead, the law attempts to articulate a broad regulatory principle, accounting only for the most obvious factors and the most likely conditions; subsequent decisions in the courtroom apply the law to specific circumstances; those decisions become precedents, enriching the law for the next dispute. Determining when fair use is applicable is a messy business, best left to judges who can consider the character of the works and the context of the use.

This ambiguity is a positive feature, not a failing. When we engage in a specific behavior, we make an educated guess as to whether it is legal or not—some seem very likely so, like ordering dinner at a restaurant; others are very likely not, like shooting someone in the head. (Even in these simple cases there is ambiguity in both the moral context and in the law itself: ordering dinner while your child is choking might be depraved indifference, while shooting someone in the head as they are attacking you might be self-defense—and each of these general exceptions themselves come with their own murky edges.) Between such extremes there are activities that may or may not be legal, depending on an interpretation of the law. Those practices that are not neatly described in the explicit language of the law and have not yet come up in court, which means almost all of them, remain in an ambiguous but productive purgatory between legality and criminality. This grey area is expanded by the fact that copyright owners often overlook some practices that they either do not see at all, see as possibly beneficial, worry might be bad publicity to attack, or simply see as not worth the financial cost of pursuing. Private copying and trading music among friends have long fallen into these categories.

As Cohen notes, there may be real cultural and democratic value in this grey area: "One could also conceive the noncommodified 'breathing space' the current system allows citizens for browsing, public domain use, and fair use to be a public good worth preserving—notwithstanding the fact that most consumers do not plan to reverse engineer software or publish a parody or critical essay directed at a literary work and would see no need to bargain in the market for the right to do so."[114] This "noncommodified breathing space" has allowed for, among other things, ingenious uses of content that the original owners did not anticipate or foresee as commercially valuable (e.g., sampling in hip-hop music), the possibility of unexpected technological innovation (the VCR, the web browser, Napster, etc.), and the development of informal networks of culture sharing that, while perhaps qualifying as infringement in technical terms, arguably also serve a wide, robust public discourse.

To code such rules into a technological device or software application, on the other hand, would require much more precise rules than the law provides, and the resulting system would be fundamentally less capable of judging ambiguous and contextual situations than a human. Even if we wanted to develop a DRM system that does allow for fair uses, how would we encode the same ambiguity that is encoded in the law? While a trusted system would be more precise in exacting fees along finer and finer distinctions, it could never assess the intent of its users or the consequences of use. Edward Felten has noted that this ambiguity and flexibility is nearly anathema to computer scientists, who necessarily design mathematically precise tools: "The legal definition of fair use is, by computer scientists' standards, maddeningly vague. No enumeration of fair uses is provided. There is not even a precise algorithm for deciding whether a particular use is fair . . . To a computer scientist, such imprecision is a bug; to lawyers it is a feature, since it allows judges to take into account the unique circumstances of each case . . . The vagueness of the fair use test makes it essentially impossible to create a DRM system that allows all fair uses."[115] In a DRM system, "only those policies that can be reliably reduced to yes/no decisions can be automated successfully."[116]

This is not just a question of the different mindsets of lawmakers and programmers. Technological systems, unlike laws, are designed to fully iterate every possible activity. They do not do so by anticipating each possible action in each possible context. Instead, they articulate all the categories of possibility such that activity can only happen within those discursive boundaries, they describe a series of available actions within each category such that activity becomes choices from a preset menu,[117] and they set a default action for anything that does not fall within the anticipated parameters. No activity goes unnoticed, since the technology is present at every encounter. Within this system, there is no room left for ambiguously permissible behavior; every use is either allowed or refused, free or priced, at the moment it is attempted, with no exceptions.

As Lessig puts it, we are then faced with a choice: "The architectures of property will change; they will allow for greater protection for intellectual property than real-space architectures allowed; and this greater protection will force a choice on us that we do not need to make in real space. Should the architecture allow perfect control of intellectual property, or should we build into the architecture an incompleteness that guarantees a certain aspect of public use? Or a certain space for individual freedom?"[118] And if a device cannot distinguish between copying that is fair and copying that is infringement, the worldview of copy protection is better safe than sorry. Were someone interested in making a traditional fair use of the work— using a clip in a satirical montage, or in an online news report—it is not clear how such a system could allow it, if allowing that also meant allowing analogous uses that were infringing.

Because fair use is so antithetical to the design of technologically enforced rules, some worry that it will simply be discarded. The Napster filter could not tell what you intended to do with the song you downloaded, so it simply prevented the song from being downloaded at all. It could not distinguish between pirates and parodists and professors, so it restricted all equally. We have judges because we know the case will always be more complex than a law can anticipate, and we count on their judgment. Instead of using law's ex post assessment of intent and consequence, technology prepares for the worst and lives by it: Every unauthorized use is the first open door to a swelling wave of piracy; every tool is an epidemic.

Perhaps, though fair use might shrink, use more generally might actually grow. Some have argued that digital tools might facilitate the simple and affordable licensing of routine uses in ways that could not be managed before. Digital databases would make it easier to find and negotiate with owners, and easier for owners to establish collective licensing organizations; even more, DRM would allow these licenses to be automatically achieved: it could provide, for instance, a pop-up window that offers, "For another 25 cents, you can clip and save ten still images." Tom Bell, calling this "fared use," suggests that an array of new and beneficial licensing arrangements simply await exploration: "As copyright owners and consumers contract around the default rules for fared use, they will experiment with a wide variety of methods for managing information in the digital intermedia. A full assessment of this exploratory and entrepreneurial process must await our observations of actual results. We can assume, however, that copyright owners and consumers will modify fared use's reciprocal quasi-compulsory license only when they find it mutually beneficial to do so."[119] Such a system would be flexible, not only in charging micropayments for use, but in charging differently for different kinds of use: "usage rights could provide for different kinds of uses and fees, distinguishing between copying rights, loan rights, transfer rights, play rights, broadcast rights, print rights, extract rights, embed rights, editing rights, and several others."[120] Within this paradigm, DRM represents for some the long-awaited renovation of an imperfect system: Until now, it was not feasible for the law to intervene at every moment in an appropriate way.

There are, however, some problems with this notion. Unless the federal government intervenes to ensure that DRM accommodates fair use, it will rarely be included voluntarily. "Privately negotiated DRM mandates are unlikely to accommodate fair uses, and once industry groups have agreed upon a DRM standard, the public will have little leverage for demanding fair use accommodations."[121] What incentive does a content provider have to choose a DRM system that allows for the transformative use of their work? Presumably, they would only incorporate such options if there were a likely economic benefit—that is, only if those who could pay for it will pay, and only if they can anticipate the value of untested uses. "Fared use" prefers established users (entertainment companies, private libraries, established academics) and the uses they would likely make, while those who cannot afford such licensing fees will either not be granted the right, or will be unable to pay for it. This would tip the scales of creativity toward established institutions and away from amateur, homegrown production, privileging Time Warner's musical innovations over the innovations grown on the streets of the Bronx.

Further, nontransformative fair use accommodations may be easier to encode than transformative ones. Time-shifting the movie you recorded may make the cut, as it is technically simple to both discern and allow, and economically more desirable to producers; cutting-and-pasting may be harder to code for and less appealing to content owners. If nontransformative fair uses are the only ones that can be built in, they are the only ones that will be available, and over time they may come to replace the richer set of possibilities users now enjoy.[122] The question of whether there is a public interest in ensuring a right to make transformative use would essentially be deleted.

Finally, part of the premise of fair use was that such uses should not require asking permission of the owner. Ensuring the free speech rights of the reuser requires making use free not only in terms of financial compensation but also in terms of the freedom from having to ask for the right to speak, or even to alert an owner beforehand that the (potentially critical) speech is on its way. The Supreme Court has gone so far as to note that even asking for permission and being denied should not affect a fair use defense; fair use should apply even when the owner has explicitly said the use would not be allowed.[123] An automated licensing mechanism may make some reuses more affordable, but it also subjects all use to a permission regime that runs counter to the notion of fair use as a First Amendment safety valve for copyright.

What is clear is that, in the translation of law into the technical code of circuitry and software, the subtle dynamics of the rules are bound to change. We must take great care with this translation—we may lose more than we gain, or find that some kinds of authors and some kinds of authorship are more constrained than others. A more precise regime of control may not always be a better one. With the imperfections and potential abuses of any system of control, room for adjustment, even if it allows some illegal deeds to go unpunished or some distributions to go uncompensated, allows the system to stay healthier and be applied in a more just manner.

Most important, as this system is being designed by industries that currently enjoy a great deal of economic and political power, we must be skeptical of claims that this shift is for anything other than opportunistic reasons. The curious balance designed into copyright law, and the various caveats and limitations created to sustain that balance, were themselves the result of disputes like this, often spurred by the arrival of new technologies that seemed to offer new opportunities and new risks for the distribution of culture. But in the move toward a DRM version of copyright, we are witnessing not just the articulation of a new balance, but a radical reworking of the law and its implementation, based on a seductive retelling of the purposes for which copyright was intended.

There are real questions to be asked about copyright and DRM—how well the technology can substitute for the law, whose interests are best being served, and whose are being overlooked. However, there are bigger issues to tackle. And they begin with the recognition that a trusted system based on DRM encryption is just that: a system. It is more than just the technologies themselves. When we begin to discuss the political consequences of technological content protection for copyright and communication, we must be aware that we're really referring to a complex array of elements—some technical, some human, some legal, some institutional—that together produce a matrix of restrictions and guidelines shaping what can be done with digital culture. This is an important insight for analyzing the DRM technologies that this system deploys and how they really regulate people's activity. But it is also crucial to notice that the very process by which these elements are brought into alignment may have its own consequences, consequences that could occur whether DRM systems work or not, whether they are eventually embraced or not. To begin this analysis, we need to understand how technology works as a social phenomenon, and what we really mean when we say technology has consequences for social activity.

Much of why the debates around digital copyright remain so intractable is that our commonplace ideas about technology and its consequences are similarly polarized: either technologies change the world, or technologies are neutral. If the first is true, then the most radical predictions, utopian and nightmarish alike, can seem imperative enough to overwhelm more careful consideration. If the second is true, then we can "stop worrying and love the bomb," overlooking the subtle ways in which the practices, policies, and expectations are changing around us. To fully investigate these disputes and their implications for digital culture requires more nuanced insights into the social embeddedness of technology, as well as an attention to how the political and social spaces from which technologies emerge shape their design and use.

Certainly, the effort to design technological fixes like DRM points to what sociologists of technology have been saying for some time: The material world regulates human activity, sometimes deliberately so. Human-made things are inserted into social contexts and organize both the practices that happen in and around them and the relations between the people involved. Walls and gates physically direct the movement of people who stand behind or pass through them. Prisons and asylums keep the inmates from the rest of the world and carefully choreograph their day-to-day lives. Industrial assembly lines draw people's hands and eyes into a precisely choreographed dance with machines. Lenses and screens urge people to gather in front of them. Voting machines mediate the conversation between citizen and government, and ensure (or sometimes undermine) the reliability and credibility of that communication. Technologies shape their use; architecture choreographs what's done amid it.

To return to Lessig, the way we design the manmade world in which we act means that "spaces have values. They express these values through the practices or lives that they enable or disable. Differently constituted spaces enable and disable differently."[1] His point is simply to remind law scholars, judges, and software designers that, like the law, the construction and implementation of technology can be used productively as a way to regulate. And like law, technologies are the product of political choices and have political consequences that must be recognized and acknowledged. Another way to put this is that law is a technology too, an artificial apparatus designed by man to intervene in and organize human activity in a way that (ideally) produces more equitable human arrangements by prohibiting behaviors that its designers wish to prevent.

However, the consequences of a technology are complex, fluid, and hard to pin down. While our culture remains enamored with the promise of digital technologies and communication networks to offer interactivity, choice, speed, convenience, and freedom—the tools of our intellectual liberation—critics have noted a flipside of this optimism. These same technologies also offer more powerful ways to track and surveil, to direct and regulate the social and economic practices that depend on them. Moreover, technologies always intervene alongside the social and political dynamics that designed, implemented, and depended on them, so it is particularly difficult to separate out their particular impact—perhaps what we think of as the impact of the automobile is more the impact of the suburbanization that called it forth and fed off its use. We are drawn to these technologies as potential solutions to the crises we face, the levers that might move us toward some beneficial ends, whether that benefit is individual gain or social equity. And digital technologies seem to have a special capacity for regulating their own use, in more subtle ways than analog and non-informational tools ever could. In order to begin an analysis of the particular push toward technological solutions for the management of copyright, we must consider how technologies can more generally shape and restrict the practices to which they are put, and what made them that way. Lessig's concerns are of a piece with these broader inquiries into the relationship between technology and social activity.

What follows is a brief encounter with some of the scholarship concerning the sociology of technology and the cultural study of media and communication technologies, as a way to gather tools both for the consideration of technical copyright protection in particular, and for the study of communication and information technologies more generally. Drawing on the arguments and examples of Langdon Winner, Bruno Latour, Weibe Bijker, Trevor Pinch, and John Law offers useful insights about the complex relationship between technology and society, a relationship that is prone to oversimplification in social science more broadly. We must avoid the claim that the design of a technology wholly determines what is done with it, while also recognizing that the shape of a tool can have real, political consequence; we must recognize that technology is shaped by its designers and its users in material and symbolic ways, while not also assuming that it is infinitely malleable and therefore of little concern.

If the major media industries and the U.S. Congress are in fact pursuing a shift in copyright that asks technology to serve as its leading edge, then it is essential that we draw on all available resources for thinking about the impact of technology. We must understand how the design of such technologies is a political and contested process, how the implementation of a technology can have consequences for its use, and how what looks like a technological fix in fact depends on more than just technology being put into place. In the end, I hope to demonstrate that this strategy depends not just on choosing the "right" technology for the job; it depends on the political mobilization of various partners and allies to hold this sociotechnical apparatus in place, and it requires the cultural legitimation of the strategy in order to convince the rest of us that it is a worthwhile and viable project to undertake.

Thinking about Technology

For centuries, philosophers, historians, and sociologists have struggled to characterize the relationship between technology and society. Too often, these inquiries have posited a neat, causal connection between new technologies and the social changes that followed, usually on a grand scale. Using the history of technological innovation as a timeline for broad historical changes—the era of print, the industrial age, the information revolution—has proven an all-too-compelling shorthand. Historians and social scientists, especially those interested in communication, have often chosen to explain grand societal shifts—the rise of agrarianism, the exploration of the New World, the Scientific Revolution, the Enlightenment, the Protestant Reformation, the post-industrial service economy—by linking them to the technologies that apparently made them possible.[2] Important technologies develop and proliferate, the logic goes, and the world changes in their wake.

This paradigm has a powerful corollary outside academia. The claim that technologies can alter the course of history, especially in its most utopian gloss, is a powerful tale for those who sell those technologies to us. What better ad campaign than one that suggests that a product is going to change the world. Typically, these promotional claims are focused on the individual and interpersonal: Cell phones and e-mail will keep parents happily in touch with their college-bound kids, the new car will give the middle-aged man a sense of freedom—not unlike the claims that the latest kitchen appliance would finally end the suburban housewife's endless drudgery, and that the atomic bomb would end war. This same techno-optimism can be found in the work of futurists such as Alvin Toffler and George Gilder, and in *Wired*'s breathless coverage of the cyberspace revolution—which, in their own ways, are also linked to the marketing of new technologies and the improved forms of life they hope to provide.

The dystopian version has proven just as compelling. Politicians rail against the Internet for corrupting the fragile innocence of children; the press points to video games as the likely trigger of brutal school shootings; the medical journals warn of "Internet addiction." The power that both kinds of claims offer to the person making them—here's a tool that will dramatically change your world, here's the single cause responsible for a messy social phenomenon—is compelling enough that we're regularly tempted to overlook the way such claims simplify the technology itself, the social fabric in which it is embedded, and the complex give-and-take that occurs between tools, people, and events.

This perspective has been criticized as "technological determinism" by increasingly vocal scholars from a number of fields, including communication, sociology, history, and cultural studies. Their concerns are numerous.[3] The historical examples that "prove" these claims are often sketchy, simplified, or mischaracterized, and they sometimes overlook the inconvenient fact that the changes "caused" by the technology had actually begun to develop long before its invention. The periodization schemes that emerge from such thinking are, by necessity, oversimplified.[4] Similar inventions in different cultures are followed by very different social arrangements, suggesting that the technology does not have a single, universal outcome. Sometimes the "better" of two technologies loses out, suggesting that the adoption of technologies is never determined wholly by objective criteria of quality or efficiency, but can be driven by social practicalities that emerge around them.[5] Technologies change over time, often in response to these apparent consequences, such that a simple cause-and-effect explanation is necessarily incomplete. People experience technologies differently in different contexts, to the extent that they are almost different things for different people. Not least, the fact that such stories of causality fit so neatly into marketing discourse raises some suspicion as to their validity as social analysis.

However, as critics have challenged these determinist arguments, it can sometimes seem as if the only alternative is that technologies have no consequences at all, as if they are neutral tools that people put to whatever use they choose, for good or ill.[6] This position also has a familiar version outside academic arguments, the most well known perhaps being the NRA slogan, "Guns don't kill people, people kill people."[7] In other words, the atom bomb was bound to be invented, a neutral scientific act; the people who weaponized it and dropped two on Japan caused the destruction, not the bomb itself; the political decision to design a national defense policy around the threat of using those bombs caused the Cold War, not the bomb itself. Faith in technological progress, so endemic to Western society, requires its proponents to assert the neutrality of tools, laying blame instead on users for whatever direct or even structural consequences follow. Just as the claim that technologies have consequences can be compelling to a politician or activist looking to assign responsibility, the claim that technologies are neutral also has power, to the extent that it can deflect responsibility.

To carve out a space between these two conceptual poles, we need to hold onto the notion that technologies can be consequential, while asking something more specific than whether technologies can wholly explain epic societal upheavals. As Leah Lievrouw put it, we must avoid the either/or of social and technological determinism, focusing instead on the "dynamic relationship between determination and contingency."[8] We must look at how technologies subtly urge certain uses, how debates around their design concern how they should intervene into social activity, and how users orient themselves and their worldviews so as to best use the technologies. We need to question whether small pressures, applied regularly to many people over many moments, can end up having consequences not just for individuals but in the aggregate for the community and the culture. And we need to ask: If a technology renders certain tasks more or less feasible, giving some users more or less capacity to act, does this matter in ways that are culturally or politically significant? If so, should we say that the technologies themselves have a political valence in their design and implementation beyond the politics of their users? We need to inquire into the politics of design—who gets to design a technology and under what circumstances; why is a technology designed in a certain way; what do the designers hope to accomplish with it; and how do users find that these design choices both facilitate and constrain their practices? And we need to examine the continued negotiations that surround a technology as it enters into the world of users, how the technology is taken up in meaningful ways, and how it is built into a sociotechnical matrix of practices, meanings, and institutions.[9]

Concrete Politics

Let's begin with the speed bump.[10] It is one of the simplest tools, a mere lump of concrete, strategically placed across a road such that it is inconvenient and uncomfortable for drivers to pass over it at otherwise normal speeds. A similar outcome could be achieved by posting a police officer at that particular point in the road, holding up a sign that says "slow down" and ticketing those who ignore his stern look. But this would be costly (the officer's salary, the costs of the judicial process of collecting fines and dealing with appeals, etc.) and far from perfect, as the officer might fall asleep on the job or be called away to handle a more pressing emergency. The speed bump, laid down once, applies to all drivers fairly, requires little upkeep, and simply and effectively regulates the behavior of all who pass. In fact, as Latour reminds us, it is common in the British vernacular to call speed bumps "sleeping policemen" even though, except for being prone, they're quite alert in their duties.[11] Most drivers obey not because slowing down at that point in the road strikes them as the right thing to do, necessarily, but because taking the bump at high speed could damage their car's suspension and will certainly rattle old bones. Yet the result is slower traffic and, hopefully, improved safety for pedestrians and other drivers.

This technological obstacle is not perfect, though neither are legal ones. Drivers can speed over the bump if they don't mind the consequences, and they're unlikely to be caught or punished for their minor crime. (In fact it's not a crime at all, unless the speed bump is accompanied by a posted speed limit to match.) Nevertheless, speed bumps are effective deterrents to speeding at the particular points in the road at which they're placed, because they render the unwanted behavior unlikely, if not impossible.

To begin to understand not only the effectiveness of technological regulations, but also their potential consequences, we must look at how such material artifacts are designed to intervene, and according to what criteria. Langdon Winner's insights, most explicitly articulated in the article "Do Artifacts Have Politics?" are a useful starting point. In answering yes to his own question, Winner reminds us that a technology could have been designed many different ways, even within the various material, economic, and physical constraints. The way the technology did end up being designed was the result of a series of deliberate choices, if not always with the benefit of foresight. Some of these choices were made to design the technology to intervene in the world in particular, deliberate, and thus political ways. Winner is challenging both the belief that technologies are neutral and the belief that technologies cause social change: "Rather than insist that we immediately reduce everything to the interplay of social forces, the theory of technological politics suggests that we pay attention to the characteristics of technical objects and the meaning of those characteristics. A necessary complement to, rather than a replacement for, theories of the social determination of technology, this approach identifies certain technologies as political phenomena in their own right. It points us back, to borrow Edmund Husserl's philosophical injunction, *to the things themselves.*"[12]

Winner argues that these technological politics operate on two levels. First, a technology can be designed in order to close off certain options for its users and open others. A wall is designed to prohibit movement in a particular direction, while a door is designed to facilitate it. In this most general sense, nearly all technologies in some way choreograph human activity, though this in itself does not mean that the results are political. This should come as no surprise to, for instance, architects, who are constantly being asked to design spaces so as to choreograph the location and proximity of people to facilitate certain activity within: One floor is full of windowed offices for executives to have well-appointed, private spaces in which to conduct their business, another floor has modular cubicles and wheeled desks so that project teams can flexibly self-organize ad hoc collaborations—and, of course, the executive floor is built on top of the project floor, to symbolically represent the corporate hierarchy within which all of the employees are required to function. "All works of architecture imply a worldview, which means that all architecture is in some deeper sense political. 'To imagine a language,' Ludwig Wittgenstein famously wrote, 'is to imagine a way of life.' The same is true of buildings, parks, cities—anything conjured up by the human imagination and then cast into stone. The way we choose to organize our space says an enormous amount about the society we live in—perhaps more than any other component of our cultural habits."[13]

It certainly should come as no surprise that the design and implementation of certain material artifacts are decidedly political: Prisons, for example, are explicitly for enforcing incarceration, and have the political consequences of substantially restricting the freedom of their inmates and enacting the condemnation of society upon them.[14] But Winner also wants to point out the subtle consequences of technologies that their users don't recognize as doing political work. To do this, he focuses on the bridges that pass over the Long Island Parkway, designed by notorious city planner Robert Moses. These bridges are substantially lower than bridges on most other New York highways, with what Winner suggests is a very particular result: While cars can easily pass beneath them, buses cannot. This technological restriction, he argues, has political consequences: The bridges prohibit buses from passing, and therefore discriminate against the working class and predominantly African American passengers who cannot afford cars. The suburbs and beaches of Long Island, largely the playground of a wealthier and whiter subset of New York's residents, enjoy a kind of quiet segregation, imposed not by law or force but by the design of the bridges themselves.

Winner finds these politics not only reprehensible, in that they may have exacerbated the racial and class tensions of twentieth-century New York City, but also insidious, because they took the form of brick and mortar. Because the political consequence of these bridges was submerged in a seemingly neutral material fact—the buses simply can't pass underneath—it is difficult to hold anyone accountable for the injustice. In fact, the very intervention is difficult to recognize, and the impact difficult to notice. "Not only (do) artifacts have politics, but it's the most perverse of all since they hide their biases under the appearance of objectivity, efficiency or mere expediency."[15] It is these stealth politics that separate Winner's bridges from a prison, whose politics are more transparent, and deliberately so.

It is important to note that several critics have raised concerns about Winner's particular example, though not necessarily about his underlying point. Bernward Joerges notes that while the story is compelling, it overlooks some extenuating factors—that commercial traffic, which would include buses, was restricted on parkways anyway, and that there are other routes for getting to the beaches Winner says were rendered inaccessible. Steve Woolgar and Geoff Cooper even challenge Winner's story at its most fundamental point, having heard from several sources that public buses in fact did travel the Long Island parkways.[16] We're left with the bridges not so much as evidence, but as a parable of the possible consequences of seemingly innocuous technologies—though since this particular example may be more urban legend than fact, we should tread carefully with this argument.

However, others have provided examples that also suggest that technologies can be designed to subtly intervene in the practices of users.[17] Batya Friedman and Helen Nissenbaum describe, for example, the way the

Sabre and Apollo airline ticketing and reservation databases (run by American and United Airlines) were challenged as antitrust violations in the 1980s for subtly privileging flights that were handled by one carrier, which put domestic carriers above foreign ones for international flights.[18] Similar ranking issues arose with search engines, which initially permitted commercial sites to pay to boost their ranking for a certain search term.[19] This practice was disliked by users, and although it still continues it is generally made explicit by demarcating those results as "sponsored links." Richard Dyer argues that photographic technology tends to represent Caucasian faces in a more naturalistic way than darker faces. This troubling fact, he suggests, stems from the early development of the chemistry of emulsive photographic paper; designers, seeing the popularity of portraiture, assumed that the human face would be the most common object of photography, and decided to use skin tone, which meant Caucasian skin tone, as their de facto reference point.[20] Rachel Weber makes a similar point about the design of cockpits in military jets, where an ergonomic layout based on the average pilot's body, assumed to be a male body, has worked against accommodating the smaller frames of female aviators.[21]

Beyond technologies that directly exclude or enforce, Winner also notes that some technologies are simply more compatible with certain forms of social organization. As we adopt and deploy a technology, we find ourselves persuaded or compelled to also adopt and deploy the social arrangement that best suits it at that moment. For example, unlike coal, oil, and solar power, nuclear energy involves the manipulation of decidedly hazardous materials, materials that could easily cause an environmental catastrophe if mishandled, or be built into weapons if they fell into the wrong hands. So, unlike its alternatives, nuclear power requires stricter security measures—more laws, harsher punishments, barbed wire, armed guards, training, public education, and so forth. In its current instantiation it is better suited to centralized energy production (i.e., we aren't likely to ever have consumer-grade nuclear generators in our garages) and to military-industrial states that already have the resources and cultural justification for the security infrastructure its volatile materials demand.

However, this link between a technology and the sociopolitical arrangements it requires is not natural or inevitable, but depends itself on the particulars of social context. For example, if the United States were to perilously drain its resources and find itself dependent on a desperate few hydroelectric power generators, these technologies might become targets of sabotage by political insurgents, and therefore also require a degree of security they do not require today.[22]

Technologies can have political consequences, then, both in the choice to adopt them at all and in the secondary arrangements they tend to require. Technical copyright protections certainly have both kinds of consequences. DRM systems are designed in particular ways to intervene in and regulate user behavior, a political choice legitimating some actions and rendering others impossible. This is both a political intervention into human activity and a means to intervene through the technology in a social dispute—that is, the battle over ownership and culture waged around the Internet, peer-to-peer technology, and popular entertainment, and more broadly around knowledge production and the circulation of information. But it is also a system that, if embraced, "requires the creation and maintenance of a particular set of social conditions as the operating environment of that system"[23]—conditions that are social, political, and economic. At the same time, it is crucial to note that while DRM makes demands of our political infrastructure, these demands can also be overstated. The presumption that DRM needs legal backing in the form of anti-circumvention rules says little about how those rules should be crafted, what penalties should be imposed, or what exceptions should be allowed.

The resolve of this argument has been (and must be) regularly tested, since the claim can so easily slip into the very caricature it aims to challenge. The argument that artifacts have politics can sound, in less sure hands than Winner's, like a more adept version of technological determinism. Perhaps it was the tyranny of the automobile rather than specific bridges that had racially inflected political consequences for New Yorkers, and the design of the bridges, while embracing that arrangement, did not itself make it so. If we take into account the rise of the automobile and the massive expansion of the highway system, and beyond that the design and proliferation of the suburb, we might reveal a more complex but perhaps also more compelling sense of the ways in which material technologies intervene into social dynamics, often to the political benefit of some and the detriment of others. Perhaps Moses, although a powerful player in the construction of specific pieces of this matrix, was himself bound by the broader paradigm of the automobile and interstate road system, an instrument of a broader social politics of space and movement that had its own racial dimensions.

Further, the exclusive focus on a single technology and its impact may overlook the way technological systems, rather than individual artifacts, often have more dramatic and subtle consequences. While poor, black New Yorkers may have been materially blocked from Long Island beaches by a bridge, it would be more accurate to say that it was the combination of bridge, road, and bus that did so. A speed bump is a meaningless obstacle without a curb to keep drivers from going around it, and is impotent without an automobile design that conveys the impact of significantly large bumps back to the driver. This may be a particularly important observation as we bring these insights to the study of digital technology and culture. As the technology we are most interested in, the Internet, is itself a "network of networks," a self-proclaimed technological system, we might use it as inspiration to pursue this insight, looking not only at the entire network and the system of artifacts it represents, but at the structure beneath the structures: The pathways, connections, standards, and boundaries built into the network itself that define the way the technologies interact.[24]

This attention to systems, however, opens up a subsequent question: What should we include in the definition of the "technology" as we look to uncover its consequences?[25] Once the circle is drawn more broadly than the single artifact, it can potentially be drawn anywhere; if it is not just the speed bump but also the road, the curb, the shock absorber, the bus, the suburb . . . why not include the mechanics of fuel and its extraction, refinement, and delivery, which now links our hapless Long Island bus passengers to the global geopolitical battle over oil? In a very important sense, the implications of a technological system depend on how that system is defined; as such, the choice of how to define it is itself political. To critique the U.S. reliance on automobiles and not talk about the infrastructure of fuel production is a political choice, as much of a choice as linking the two. These characterizations come not only from scholars, but from designers. Builders of these systems also build them in the rhetorical sense, drawing linguistic boundaries around them to indicate what is part of the system and what is not, shaping how the relationship between elements can and will be characterized.[26]

The Subtle Consequences of Mundane Things

Despite the hesitations, Winner's parable is a compelling one, in part because of the sense of real injustice involved—these bridges may have been steadfast bastions of a racist agenda in a time when racial equity was (at least nominally) a vital societal goal. Not only have white faces been overrepresented in U.S. media since its invention, but if Dyer is correct, even the black faces that did make it to the screen didn't look quite "right" to black audiences longing to see a glimmer of themselves somewhere in the cultural landscape. The feminist movement has worked tirelessly to open up opportunities for women where once only men were permitted, even in male bastions like the Air Force, but it may not have counted on the way the jets retained the legacy of gender discrimination in their very design. The consequences, if indeed we can attribute them to the bridges and the film stock and the cockpit, are of a particularly political stripe, political in the classic sense of the rights of citizens and the equity by which those rights are assured.

The politics of copy protection technologies may be just as significant, but they need not be. Latour reminds us that any intervention into human activity enacts a kind of discrimination, allowing some uses and users and dissuading others. The result is a more mundane politics that is at play during nearly every moment humans interact with their built environment—less reprehensible, but much more pervasive.[27] Latour considers a more quotidian technology, the hydraulic door-closer at the top of many institutional doors, designed to gather up a small amount of energy from each person who opens the door and use that energy to return the door slowly to its closed position. While we may go through our entire lives without contemplating this nearly invisible object, Latour insists that it reveals the regular interchange between human and nonhuman fundamental to our manufactured and mediated world. He takes us along a mental exercise, imagining the underlying logic behind the installation of a hydraulic door-closer on the entrance of his building. Architects could have built only a wall, which would require patrons to destroy and rebuild it every time they came and went. The building owners could then either hire someone to regularly rebuild it, or could cut a hole and block it with a movable slab of wood or metal. Now residents would have a convenient opening, but a heavy object to remove and put back into place every time they passed; at that point, they could either hire a "door replacer" to stand there day in and day out, or they could add hinges. Then they'd have a door that swings open easily, but stays open after forgetful users pass through. Here the architects again may choose to delegate the task of closing the door to a human, or they may choose to install a mechanism like the hydraulic door-closer. Like the speed bump, this seemingly insignificant object is actually the latest decision in a massive chain of functions, some allocated to people and some to things, to accomplish a task together in a reasonable way.

Designers choose on a regular basis what combination of people and things a particular task will fall to, weighing the relative costs and benefits of every choice.[28] Though each new problem is solved at each stage of this decision process, it is by no means without its trade-offs. The hydraulic door-closer is no exception: As Latour notes, "Neither my little nephews nor my grandmother could get in unaided because our groom needed the form of an able-bodied person to accumulate enough energy to close the door. . . . because of their prescriptions these doors discriminate against very little and very old persons. Also, if there is no way to keep them open for good, they discriminate against furniture removers and in general everyone with packages, which usually means, in our late capitalist society, working or lower-middle class employees."[29] At every step, decisions were made about who to help and who to discriminate against. Even a technology designed merely to make something possible must always render other actions less so. And "if, in our societies, there are thousands of such lieutenants to which we have delegated competencies, it means that what defines our social relations is, for the most part, prescribed back to us by nonhumans. Knowledge, morality, craft, force, sociability are not properties of humans but of humans *accompanied* by their retinue of delegated characters."[30]

While our speed bump may not have the kind of racially charged impact that Winner's bridges may, it also discriminates, and in potentially consequential ways. It imposes more impact (literally) on those with lower-quality shock absorbers, which may mean those who can't afford expensive cars or costly repairs when their axles crack. It discriminates against bicycle riders, who are not speeding yet are forced to endure a more visceral impact than drivers who are. In a culture that has a deep love for cars and a matching disregard for public transportation, the fact that our chosen method of slowing down drivers also works against bicyclists could be seen as politically and economically significant. These discriminations may be minor, not rising to the level at which the technology itself needs to be reconsidered. But the speed bump also discriminates against those who have an urgent need, and legal permission, to exceed the speed limit: the ambulance rushing a sick patient to the hospital, the fire engine racing to a burning building. These uses are as constrained as all other forms of speeding, but they are of far greater consequence; here the speed bump actually works against a legal right and a societal need we would otherwise want to protect.

Furthermore, technologies have a particular kind of permanence, or obduracy, which means they can impose these discriminations long after they are initially installed. Or as Latour puts it, "Technology is society made durable."[31] Of course, laws have a kind of permanence as well, designed to persist until they are changed, setting precedent for court decisions and future laws that extend their influence. But it takes few additional resources to undo a law beyond making the decision to do so, whereas speed bumps must be physically removed. Combined with the stealth of their political intervention, this inertia can be significant. As Winner notes, "For generations after Moses has gone and the alliances he forged have fallen apart, his public works, especially the highways and bridges he built to favor the use of the automobile over the development of mass transit, will continue to shape that city. Many of his monumental structures of concrete and steel embody a systematic social inequality, a way of engineering relationships among people that, after a time, became just another part of the landscape."[32]

This notion of permanence is tricky business, though. Certainly, technologies and even material infrastructures do change, both physically and culturally. Their seeming permanence may be as much an illusion as the belief that laws can so be easily adjusted. Speaking of buildings, Thomas Gieryn argues, "Brick and mortar resist intervention and permutation, as they accomplish a measure of order. And yet, buildings stabilize *imperfectly*. Some fall into ruin, others are destroyed naturally or by human hand, and most are unendingly renovated into something they were not originally. Buildings don't just sit there imposing themselves. They are forever objects of (re)interpretation, narration and representation—and meanings or stories are sometimes more pliable than the walls and floors they depict. We deconstruct buildings materially and semiotically, all the time."[33] Conversely, the permanence of a technology can also impose its politics onto new populations, or impose unimagined politics long after design is complete. Latour notes that in his Parisian apartment building, the primary residents have a spacious elevator whereas the students living in the back apartments are relegated to climbing a cramped stairwell.[34] This discrimination is not ugly university politics exposed; the arrangement was designed to separate servants from residents in a building long ago used for very different purposes. (Of course, the fact that professors earn enough for the fancy apartments while students can only scrape together enough for the servants' quarters suggests that the current inequity is not entirely coincidental.) The speed bump may remain, but the community activity around it that once made its presence worthwhile may shift in ways the speed bump cannot adjust to. As we look at the politics of digital technologies, it would serve us well to remember that technologies may have politics, but those politics are not easily imposed, and time, use, and subsequent innovation can wreak havoc on even the best laid plans.

Anticipating the User

The most powerful way in which technologies regulate, then, involves rendering some actions impossible and, by extension, privileging others. If it is nearly impossible to avoid the speed bump with your car and nearly unbearable to go over it at high speed, then speeding is quite effectively sanctioned by this mere slab of cleverly placed concrete. Designing systems such that certain functions are simply unavailable is the primary way in which DRM hopes to regulate users. However, if we dig deeper into the politics of technology, we might also consider subtler ways in which technologies choreograph human activity; these will necessarily work alongside a system such as DRM to more thoroughly regulate users.

First, technologies "speak" in a number of ways, announcing what they do and who they're for. The most obvious examples of this are product names, symbolic elements, the claims made in promotional material, the ways in which they are offered. The packaging of a consumer technology is generally a glossy parable of and for its intended uses.[35] The symbols associated with a technology speak in coded ways about its purpose: The Nike swoosh is a significant cultural emblem not only because it is widely recognized but also because it symbolically suggests speed, reminding us of aerodynamic wings, racing stripes, even the winged shoes of the Greek goddess herself.

The purpose and value of a technology are also articulated in accompanying materials—instructions and technical support, examples offered, and the design of the artifact. This is not exclusive to digital tools, though the range of opportunities in which to make such suggestions, and the depth to which they may be articulated, may be expanding. Only retired photographers or newspaper editors are likely to understand the icon for the "crop" function in Adobe's Photoshop image software, which looks vaguely like the tool once found on drafting tables. The "desktop" and "files" and "trash can" icons of the PC and Mac operating systems metaphorically invoke a very particular idea of what is to be done with these tools; Microsoft's failed "Bob" interface attempted to appeal to home users by giving the desktop a more domestic look they might be more familiar with, but the office metaphors were simply too well established.[36]

These coded claims about what the tool is for can extend into the support materials that accompany the software; in help documents or user tutorials, evocative examples hint at the kinds of projects the designers expect users to undertake.[37] Roger Silverstone notes that, with media and communication technologies, this articulation of the tool and its proper use occurs on two levels: Not only does the tool itself make oblique claims for its purpose and value, but the content can also comment on the proper use of the technology—from the sitcom family sitting in front of a television together to online web design tutorials, media content can often include subtle or explicit ideas about the manner in which it should be consumed.[38] This "double articulation" suggests that the semantics of technology, if not literally prohibiting certain uses, certainly map the terrain of possible uses in persuasive and subtle terms.

Technologies also anticipate and choreograph the actions of their users, building in roles for users to play and paths for them to follow. It can appear at first glance that the tool is simply moving the user toward a goal. But as with Latour's door-closer, facilitating some uses always means restricting others. And while we generally feel ourselves to be the masters of our own tools, we are usually quite willing to adapt what we do to what the tool does, rather than the other way around—especially to the extent that we desire the promised results. Of course, the cell phone has made it easier to call and be called at any hour of the day and in any place. At the same time, to best enjoy these benefits we are generally willing to accept not only the cost of the device and the burden of being reachable, but also the changing social rules about boisterous ring tones and loud conversations in public spaces, the prioritizing of incoming phone calls over ongoing face-to-face conversations, the abandonment of making and sticking to plans in exchange for the last-minute game of phone tag. Cell phones urge us to store our numbers on the device, making it both more handy for calling and at the same time more likely that we'll lose all of that accumulated information when the phone slips from our pockets. These trade-offs happen with every technology and are usually deemed worthwhile in light of the benefits they offer. But they always reorganize social activity to suit the features and requirements of the technology, often with oblique consequences.

This set of rewards and sanctions for appropriate use stems from a built-in vision of the users, their purposes, and their social world. Speed bumps expect drivers—and not just drivers, but drivers going about a set of predictable tasks, drivers who are generally law-abiding but have a tendency to hurry. Madeleine Akrich calls these "scripts" to indicate that they narrate the user's world as the designer imagines it: "When technologists define the characteristics of their objects, they necessarily make hypotheses about the entities that make up the world into which the object is inserted. Designers thus define actors with specific tastes, competences, motives, aspirations, political prejudices, and the rest, and they assume that morality, technology, science, and economy will evolve in particular ways."[39] Users are by no means bound by these characterizations, and can reject or modify them, but the invitation to inhabit these anticipated roles and contexts is a powerful one, as it comes with built-in as well as societal rewards and sanctions. As Woolgar observed, "Ways of using the software other than those the designers had in mind are possible, but they turn out to be prohibitively costly (since alternative sets of material resources will be needed to counter or offset the effects of the technology) and/or heavily socially sanctioned. The social relations confronting the user of technology are therefore relatively durable because they are not easily disrupted and repackaged."[40] In some sense the user is constructed inside of the technology.

This process is a powerful part of the design process; as Woolgar notes, the spaces in which technologies are designed depend themselves on a powerful distinction between the designer and user. Most designers take great pride in being unlike mere users, as a result of their technical expertise; when they build for users, they reenact this distinction. Explicit points of contact such as focus groups and beta testing, despite being moments where designers claim to want to know users better, are mapped over with presumptions about the user as a distinct category, defined in opposition to themselves. These moments of contact are many; thus designers encounter a multiplicity of user representations, all of which are incomplete, stylized, and dismissible.[41] The technology itself ends up negotiating and stabilizing the distinction between designer and user, assigning certain characteristics to the user (technically novice, result-oriented, easily confused) and "speaking" to the user in those terms.[42] Of course, considering all of the ways these roles can be articulated, from the interface to the advertising to the accompanying materials to the corporate symbology, it is not just designers doing the articulating, but also marketers, technicians, and retailers.[43]

The power of this kind of "inscription"[44] of anticipated roles for the user is different than the political impact of design described by Winner. Winner's bridges selectively exclude people from use; poor African Americans who could only rely on the bus for transportation simply would not get to the beaches beyond. This is the politics of walls, of locks, of turnstiles, of gates: the capacity to reject some users and thus forbid them from the benefits of use. It is the politics of the outer wall of the prison, but not the politics of its internal layout. A more powerful politics is to persuade a user to adopt the technology, but on specific terms. For the speed bump, the persuasive power is the value of wherever the road leads, paired with the relatively minor inconvenience imposed, such that few drivers will look for alternate routes just to avoid it. Other technologies persuade by promising to facilitate a desirable and compelling task, to make possible an appealing activity, to get the job done. And sometimes, as in the prison, persuasion is compulsion through brute force, that is, dragging people there in shackles and chains.

Once use of the technology is assured, the technology's material and discursive arrangement can create provisions to urge the user to use it in particular ways, on particular terms. Because technologies that are not obligatory need the active consent of the user, they can rarely have the kind of comprehensive power of high walls and low bridges, since we can opt to do without them—although refusing a technology is not always simple if those around us have embraced it and built it into everyday practice, as cell phone holdouts have discovered. But even when it is entirely optional, the offer of a technology that will lead to a desirable outcome is also always an invitation to reach that outcome on the technology's terms. Digital technology in particular expands both the ability to attach provisions to the use of a technology (clickthrough licenses, limited function menus, etc.) and the ability to more richly "inscribe" the user and the world the designer predicted for them inside the technology itself—making possible technologies that regulate in both senses, through persuasion and obligation.

Things Made and Unmade

A rich understanding of technology cannot end with the realization that technologies may have political consequences. We must also consider the social and political valences that shape the technology itself. Technologies are not autonomous inventions. The particular trajectory of technological innovation is not the inevitable outcome of exclusively material or economic forces; according to John Law, "Artifacts and practices are underdetermined by the natural world."[45] They are built and deployed inside of social and political contexts that shape what gets designed, by whom, and to what ends. As Silverstone put it, "Technologies are themselves effects. They are the effects of social, economic and political circumstances and structures, decisions and actions. These in turn define, in their development, their implementation and their use, technologies' meaning and power."[46] Technologies also have different consequences in different settings; changes a tool can seem to cause by itself are more often a product of the social dynamics in which it is being incorporated. And the influence of a technology can never be separated from the social and political factors that surround its use, such that pointing to consequences as evidence of the technology's inherent character is a tremendously difficult task.

Let's return to our speed bump. For the moment, things are going well: Drivers are slowing down to the recommended speed as they pass over it, and the chicken is feeling safer as it crosses the road. Now let's imagine two incidents that might complicate the politics of this technology. First, a group of teenagers from the local high school take to what they're calling "bumpjumping," a game in which they race over a speed bump to see who can endure the jolt at the fastest speed possible. A few of them, having actually paid attention in shop class, are designing new "extreme" shock absorbers that will allow them to pass over the bump at high speeds without feeling much physical impact inside the car. Second, a young man rushing his pregnant wife to the hospital is forced to slow down to pass over the speed bump that interrupts his only route. His wife almost loses the baby due to complications that, their doctor suggests, could have been avoided if they had reached the hospital sooner. Now the couple is petitioning the city council to redesign all the local speed bumps to include small, tire-width portions made of Nerf foam, such that those with a legitimate need to speed can aim their car for those sections and pass over the bump quickly and comfortably.

Here we have efforts, along both authorized and unauthorized lines, to redefine the artifact. The bump may still have the same literal result, making the cars that go over it bump up and down, but it will no longer have the same experiential or political consequence, or the same meaning. For the teenagers, the speed bump has come to mean something different: a challenge, part of a game, a meeting place—a treasured object rather than a vaguely irritating one. For the young couple and their supporters the speed bump has also changed: It is now a nuisance, a liability, a menace— a disruption of civic life rather than a benefit to it. Technologies ancillary to the speed bump, but that helped it regulate, are being changed: The regulatory impact of the speed bump could be undone by changing the way shock absorbers work. And the grassroots movement to redesign the speed bump itself, fueled by the way it was redefined as a liability, could change the artifact materially.

Trying to pinpoint the political consequences of an artifact can often lead us to overemphasize a linear, singular, or intended purpose, overlooking not only the way a technology's impact is often diffuse and context-dependent, but also the fact that the thing, once embedded in cultural activity, is never simply that which was designed. In a very real sense, the technology we encounter is the outcome of a cultural negotiation over not only how it should be designed but also what it should be and what it should be for. This negotiation dosen't end when the technology is built or deployed, but continues on through its use. That technologies are socially constructed, argued most forcefully by Trevor Pinch and Wiebe Bijker,[47] has opened up a new set of questions that, on first glance, seem to run counter to, or at least complicate, the claim that technologies have politics.

Pinch and Bijker suggest that the negotiation around the design, implementation, and use of a technology is a debate about what the thing is and what role it should play. This negotiation does not stop at alternative design plans and practical solutions; it includes questions about the meaning of the technology itself and the character of the society in which it is involved. We may think a bicycle is a bicycle, but during the device's early days a number of designs competed for public embrace, and did so not only by being built and sold, but also by being offered up as cultural possibilities: a way to get to work, a means to get exercise, a vehicle for "proper" ladies, an exciting new sport, etc. Not only were different design proposals contesting for dominance; different ideas of what was needed and what problem was to be solved by the bicycle were up for grabs. As these different forms of the bicycle became objects of public consideration, different groups of people characterized bicycles in ways that shaped how they would be received, used, and even rebuilt: the bicycle that is a danger to its rider, the bicycle that is for competition, the bicycle that is disrupting the tranquility of public parks. The bicycle as we know it now did not succeed because it was the obvious or best idea in human transportation, but because enough designers and users were convinced to see it as a viable addition to human society. This consensus overcame the critics, resulting in a coherent set of things and meanings we now label "bicycle."

Constructivists use this insight to revisit the question of users, especially in light of digital technologies. While technologies inscribe subject positions for their users and offer rewards for inhabiting them, these scripts are very much negotiable. Different groups of users choose what tools to use, they reimagine the purpose and function of the tools, they change them materially when they have the skill to do so,[48] and they incorporate the tools into their social experience as meaningful objects in ways unanticipated by designers. As Roger Silverstone and Leslie Haddon noted, the particular process of bringing media and information technologies into the home is a powerful process of interpretation, one in which the technology must be "domesticated" to fit into the dynamics of home and family, while those dynamics must also shift to accommodate and mesh with the technology.[49] And designers in some ways want this process to occur. As Woolgar notes, "The production of all cultural artifacts involves a continual struggle, on the one hand to freeze and embody social relations and, on the other, to render sets of social relations manipulable and manageable."[50]

This attention to the "interpretive flexibility"[51] of a technology does not simply point out the way the initial design of a technology is contested, but recognizes that technologies are always both material and semiotic accomplishments, perpetually being made and remade, named and renamed. Users never encounter a technology apart from the contested cultural meanings that swirl around it; to the extent that they also give it meaning, they too have helped articulate the tool and its political valence. As Streeter put it, "when people describe a distant planet as a wandering god, their guesses about the unknown object do not change the planet itself. But if people describe television alternately as an artwork or a commodity, in the right circumstances their talk can help shape it."[52]

A speed bump is more than just concrete. We treat it with a respect we do not afford to other slabs of concrete, because it speaks its own significance. It is laden with a general sense of authority bestowed upon it by the institutions that put it there. As Keith Grint and Steve Woolgar note, discussing Hiroshima, "What the nuclear bombs did—and what they can do—is not a reflection of the actual technical characteristics of the bombs but the result of various agencies' (scientists, military experts, historians, victims, and so on) constructions . . . Our 'knowledge' of what bombs can do is not based simply on our looking at them or watching them go off. It depends, instead, on a complicated variety of factors, including our reading or listening to the accounts of others, our susceptibility to persuasion by authoritative sources, our willingness to credit claims of expertise, and so on."[53] These meanings often enjoy a kind of stability, not as the inevitable byproducts of the workings of the machinery, but as the result of a set of technical and societal compromises that steer the course, and of the slow sedimentation of time and use.[54]

However, this set of cultural meanings is always in flux, and can be reopened by particular events, political challenges, or shifting attitudes. If we choose to disrespect or ignore the speed bump, we have already changed it. Whatever the consequences of a technology, then, they are as much a result of the social processes by which that technology was named, characterized, justified, and stabilized as by the material design and political implementation. They cannot exert influence over human activity without being accompanied by a set of meanings that justify and support that influence. Enough disagreement about its purpose and value, and the speed bump loses its political heft, even as it keeps pushing tires up off the ground as they pass over it.

Technology as Mediation

This recognition complicates our original concern, about how technologies regulate human activity, as well as Winner's question of whether technologies have politics. However, social constructivism can easily be overstated, until it appears that there is nothing to technologies but their interpretation, as if one could simply evade the consequences of a technology by characterizing it as something else—that's not a wall, it's a butterfly. The best work on the social construction of technology avoids this pitfall. First, we must remain aware that materials do have "affordances,"[55] things that by its design a tool allows users to do and, by extension, things a user simply cannot materially do with that tool. No matter how imaginative you may be, you will never use a hammer to clean up spilled milk. Still, we never encounter these affordances apart from their meanings; as we choose to pound nails into boards, we are being guided not only by the hammer's firmness and its flat pounding surface, but also by a culture that understands that hammer to be for certain things, builds nails to suit it, and provides training for how to apply the one to the other. Second, interpretation of our tools is primarily a social rather than an individual activity. Not all interpretations of a technology will be embraced by enough people to grant them any real political significance. I can try to interact with the wall as if it were a butterfly, but few are likely to join me, and I risk that others will take my bizarre interpretation as evidence of my deteriorating sanity. However, should enough teenagers or activists successfully enlist enough support for their view, the speed bump will in fact change, at the very least in a cultural way, and possibly in a material one.

How do we discuss the politics of the speed bump when its purposeful design and material longevity do not ensure a consistent meaning? The literature on the social construction of technology does not offer much guidance in this regard. As critics have noted, the constructivist perspective tends to focus on how technologies came to mean something, how they were negotiated and stabilized; it expends less attention on what consequence these contested technologies may then have "for people's sense of self, for the texture of human communities, for qualities of everyday living, and for the broader distribution of power in society."[56] In other words, one line of inquiry (Winner and Latour) emphasizes the control that technologies can impose; the other (Pinch and Bijker) emphasizes the contingency in the process of their development.

The fact that the speed bump can become a teenager's plaything or a rallying cry for a grassroots organization is the first clue to how we might reconcile these two concerns. The desire on the part of users to rearticulate the technology for their own agendas can powerfully limit how directly a designer's intent can be imposed. After these two challenges, the speed bump is no longer what it once was. But this should remind us that "what it once was" was itself already the result of a process of interpretation and negotiation, rather than some natural fact. Just as the activist couple work hard to represent the speed bump as a menace, the makers of the speed bump worked hard to represent it as a valuable safety measure. Both intended for their speed bump, in material and in meaning, to direct the activity of others. Both attempted to anticipate the social context into which their speed bump would enter and have consequence.

When Winner or Latour asks the question of what happens to people who interact with the low Long Island bridges or the automatic door closers, they ask a question of how human agency exists amidst the constraints of technical structure. When Pinch and Bijker ask how the bicycle came to be what it is, they ask a question of how human agency produces what ends up as technical structure. Putting these two insights together means we can avoid privileging either: The structure we live in is the product of human agency, which itself exists within structures, which were the product of human agency, and so forth.

Perhaps the most useful way to, if not resolve this tension, then at least draw productively from both perspectives, is to think of technologies as not causal at all, but as *mediational*.[57] Technology is a means for someone to intervene in human activity, at a distance, with specific consequence. When social actors, embedded in institutional, political, and ideological contexts, attempt to shape the social practices of others, which are also complexly embedded, they sometimes turn to technological artifacts as a way to insert their interests and subtly organize that activity. In other words, we often talk about "political leverage," but we rarely think about the materiality of that metaphor—in some cases, it is literally a lever that we seek, to move, direct, or prod someone else into action. Rather than focusing on how the technological shapes the social, or the social shapes the technological, we can look at how social actors in one context (designers) aim to shape the social activity in another context (users), using the technology as a means to do so, and how users then not only work with the tools for their own purposes, but find they must sometimes work against them.

As users, we rarely have reason to think about the designers of our technologies and what they have in mind for us, at least not until they break. In fact, we are discouraged from doing so in many ways. We live in an industrialized consumer economy that puts both geographic and conceptual distance between us and the makers of our things, then offers as a substitute brands and symbols to which we might instead feel connected. Nevertheless, designers do reach out to us through the technologies they make, offering us meaning through the material. The design of a technology is not unlike the act of communication, albeit communication that is asynchronous, remote, one-to-many, and difficult to respond to.

Engineers are not neutral tool-makers, although they may enjoy seeing themselves in this light, and may benefit from appearing so.[58] They're well aware that the tools they design will migrate into a new social context and intervene in human activity there. Knowing this, they design tools to intervene in ways that speak to that context and to particular ends, in ways that also make sense to them. "Every design is a blueprint for human behavior and social structure, as well as a schematic for the 'thing' itself," Gieryn observed.[59] Engineers craft their technology as they might formulate an argument, and they put it into circulation hoping someone will receive it and find it persuasive. We might even think of each technology as a coded claim: "Here's a way to do things," or, more important, "This is the way things are, such that you'd want to do this, so do it this way." As Bryan Pfaffenberger put it, "The technology is designed not only to perform a material function but also to express and coercively reinforce beliefs about the differential allocation of power, prestige, and wealth in society."[60] The material dynamics of the technology will have consequence within this mediation, and were assembled in hopes of having such consequence, but they cannot determine, or be determined, in any direct way.

This coded claim is by no means a designer's individual message, however, just as a story or film is never just its main point. Whatever underlying values shape the social context in which a technology is produced also imprint themselves on that technology—through the choices made by the designers, the dynamics and sources of funding for such projects, and the worldview driving the project. Military research projects embody a militarized worldview not just because of why and by whom they were designed, but because of the principles and priorities, the social hierarchies, and the criteria for success by which they were built. "In this way of thinking," Woolgar argued, "technology can be regarded as 'congealed social relations'—a frozen assemblage of the practices, assumptions, beliefs, language, and other factors involved in its design and manufacture."[61] Pfaffenberger seems to think that the way designers' worldviews get embedded in what they design is precisely what makes technology a political phenomenon: "Technological innovation provides an opportunity to inscribe political values in technological production process and artifacts, which then diffuse throughout society."[62] When that vision of a technology's purpose and use is contested, it is in some way the politics of the artifact and the values it obeys that are at issue.

However, Latour reminds us, "to detect politics in artifacts is always tricky because of the exact opposite of what is implied by Winner's argument: the lack of mastery exerted over [those politics] by engineers."[63] Users, embedded in their own social context, which the designer may or may not have accurately predicted, take this materialized claim just as a listener might take an argument spoken in words. They must somehow comprehend it and, if they choose, incorporate it into their own actions in a meaningful way. Just as with communication, this is a process in which they have some power to interpret, challenge, reject, and modify the claim being made, though it is not unlimited.[64] Of course, the statement made by the designer and built into the technology can be a forceful one. There are powerful rewards for adopting the technology as it was articulated. Use it as intended, and you will enjoy the benefit of the completed task the tool was made to offer; use it in other ways and you risk failing at your task, violating warranties, nullifying offers of technical support, and running up against a pervasive but quiet set of social expectations of "how things are done."

Still, this process is never complete or determining. To overstate the consequences of a technology independent of how users engage with and remake it is to make the same mistake made in the old "hypodermic needle" theory of media effects.[65] Movies don't tell us how to think. Just as the viewer can refuse the implied meanings and implicit worldviews in a film, choosing to see things in a different way, a user may refuse the implied arrangement of their activity the tool proposes. And this cycle continues, just as conversation does: As noted by Gieryn, "We mold buildings, they mold us, we mold them anew."[66] Sometimes an unexpected use can upend what designers intended, but never entirely, since it can no more escape the intended consequences than one can reject a political argument without making reference to it. Every use creates yet another context in which this negotiation will continue.

Technologies, then, are socially constructed, but they are socially constructed so as to have consequences. The fact that technologies are negotiated and renamed and undone does not mean they have no impact. But sometimes they succeed in being consequential in the intended ways, and sometimes they end up having very different results. Users have a great deal to do with this. The construction of a technology, both material and social, is always purposeful, and the contestation around it is a symbolic battle to see whose idea of the proper choreography of user activity will triumph. Understanding this in terms of mediation allows us to see both sides as agents negotiating a contested collaboration, and both efforts as being forceful without being determining—a give-and-take with quite a bit of latitude, but not on a level playing field.

That this mediated "conversation" is never conducted on a level playing field may help explain why some technologies do have consistent politics despite the room for negotiation. The bridge and the speed bump are produced and deployed by institutions that are in a powerful position from which to insist on their proper use. The makers of consumer technologies must convince users to use them, which means the negotiation must be a substantively open one. Things built by the state, on the other hand, though they too have to gain the consensus of citizens to some extent, come with built-in authority and with real consequences for those who contest them. It is difficult for users to negotiate the meaning of state-sanctioned artifacts on a level that could alter their political imposition of control. (DRM, we will see, is both a consumer technology and, at the same time, sanctioned by the state.)

Like an argument, a technology puts its authors/designers and their social context into contact with its listeners/users and their social context, and attempts to convince them of a particular way to understand the world. The technology mediates between these communities by bringing them into meaningful, if coded, conversation, and the political implications of that technology emerge from that conversation—a conversation about possible implications. Of course, as recent communication scholarship reminds us, the act of communication is never only about getting your point across, getting the listener to understand or be persuaded. Communication is simultaneously transmission and ritual.[67] The very act of communicating is a coded claim designed to bring into existence a world as the speaker sees it; the conversation around that act of communication is a negotiation about the world as it stands and as it could become—"not toward the extension of messages in space but toward the maintenance of society in time; not the act of imparting information but the representation of shared beliefs," according to Carey.[68] The point of contact manifest in the act of communication unites people as belonging to and participating in the same project, helping to confirm or occasionally interrogate ways of being, creating a collaborative site for negotiating our shared reality. Using a sophisticated understanding of communication along both of these dimensions, we can bring the same insight to technology. Designing a tool is not only an attempt to facilitate (or inhibit) a behavior in an existing world; it's also an attempt to bring about an imagined world, and align human activity according to its logic. As Silverstone argued, "Technology, in this view, is the site of an (albeit often unequal) struggle for control: for the control of its meanings and for the control of its potency."[69]

But in the end, this comparison between technology and communication breaks down. In the case of communication, encountering the work is the entire interaction. I may read your story, and even be inspired to subsequently write my own, but the negotiation around the meaning of your story has ended. The same may apply to the bridge or the speed bump, in that I encounter the technology, decide in what way I will act within the constraints it imposes, and then move on. But with tools, particularly information technologies, I not only engage with the technology, I also then use it to produce something of my own, which often means bringing it to a second social context and imposing its implicit values on others. I may dislike Microsoft Word; I may cleverly add macros and shortcuts to struggle with the constraints it imposes upon me. But when I produce my manuscript in Word and send it to others in Word format, my renegotiation of its constraints is invisible to the next user. They only see that I have chosen Microsoft Word myself and have made it necessary for them to use it too; my reluctant use nevertheless extends and stabilizes its presence and influence in the world.

By Design

When it comes to law, we have no problem with authorized agents developing and imposing a set of rules, involving themselves in the activities of others, allowing some activities and prohibiting others, and sometimes imposing severe consequences. While we may not always love or admire every detail of that system in every instance, we generally consent to it. As it becomes clear that technology can be a similar means of intervention with similar consequences, it should come as no surprise that those charged with enforcing the law, and those with a legally legitimate interest in the activities of others, have turned to the power of technology. This puts our question in a slightly different light, because what makes our speed bump different from the Long Island bridges is that it is officially designed and authorized to regulate by government fiat. The fact that an artifact regulates on behalf of the state raises specific questions, which are crucial to our analysis of technical copy protection and digital culture. We must wonder not only whether technologies have political consequences, but also whether they can be made to have them, and whether there are ramifications for using technologies in this way.

It may be somewhat simpler, though I would argue that it is just as important, to explain the political valence of technologies explicitly designed to regulate. A useful philosophical example here is the Panopticon, a prison imagined by philosopher Jeremy Bentham but never built. In a jail built as a cylinder of cells surrounding a central guard tower, with light from outside the jail shining through each cell, many prisoners could be watched by a single jailer. Even more powerfully, the prisoners could not see the jailer in his darkened tower, but would know that he could see them. According to Michel Foucault, this means that prisoners would experience surveillance whether or not anyone was even watching—internalizing the system of control and making it vastly more effective.[70] The particular design of the prison would serve political ends because it would force prisoners' bodies into lines of sight that would effectively discourage misbehavior, and would do so with very little force or ongoing human intervention.

Lessig points to more mundane examples to demonstrate not only that architecture governs behavior, but also that we regularly turn to the design of the material world as a regulatory mechanism, especially when other avenues such as the law are ineffective or prohibitively expensive. We may regulate driving by enforcing speed limits, arresting drunk drivers, and posting traffic cops at busy intersections. But we also install guardrails to orient drivers into lanes and keep them on the road; we put disruptive bumpers between highway lanes to keep them awake; and we lower and raise barriers to ensure that no one drives in front of an oncoming train, or leaves a parking lot without paying. Lessig's concern, as he tracks a shift already underway from "East Coast code" (law, as designed in Washington DC) to "West Coast code" (software and technical protocols, as designed in Silicon Valley), is that the technology of law and the technology of software regulate in different ways and with different implications. And the law will not merely give way to West Coast code; according to Lessig, it increasingly "sees how it might interact with West Coast code to induce it to regulate differently."[71]

The copy protection technologies being used or imagined for digital media are designed to work in similar ways. Certain practices, such as purchasing and playing digital content, will be facilitated and thereby encouraged; these technologies might even benefit users by offering more works in more settings at the touch of a button. But, at the moment of empowerment, the technology will also decisively regulate behavior. The restrictions on copying will be absolute, and blind to intention; this neutrality has distinctly political consequences, in that it blocks uses that have regularly been defended as crucially democratic, but that do not interest the corporate owners of the works being used.

Legal regulation, in both its articulation and its enforcement, is visible. If you want to know the details of a law, you can go to the library, state house, or Internet to read it. It may be in a difficult language for some, but not one so impenetrable as C++ or Javascript source code. The enforcement and adjudication of the law also happens in plain sight: police arrests and judicial decisions are all open to the press and to concerned citizens. These information flows are certainly far from perfect. But the public-ness of these processes is important because they adhere to an underlying democratic principle of transparency: The possibility of public scrutiny helps to ensure accountability. If there is a mistake in the law, someone will spot it. If a law seems unfair, someone will question it. If a law is being abused, those who are wronged can take action against it. Public agents like journalists and legislators are devoted not only to identifying problems and writing laws to solve them, but also to assessing how well a law is working and with what unintended consequences. This is the principle of a court of appeals: While district courts handle questions of fact, a case may be appealed if a participant believes there is a question of law to be resolved. Our legal system admits that rules are imperfect, open to interpretation, and vulnerable to misuse; it demands that the system regularly and skeptically reassess the imposition of control by scrutinizing the laws themselves.

Software code, on the other hand, is much less visible than law. These tools are generally designed in a language that is only comprehensible by a very small community. It is much more difficult for an interested citizen, who does not have the necessary programming expertise, to raise a subtle concern about the way a certain application or protocol organizes activity. Furthermore, most applications do not reveal their code even to those who might understand it. While Internet protocols are, for the most part, openly shared and publicly available, the protocols built into proprietary intranets are not, especially not to the employees governed by them. The majority of consumer software is "closed," in that you purchase the tool but do not gain access to the underlying code in doing so.[72] A user concerned with the implications of Microsoft's word processor or AOL's browser literally cannot read the code that establishes and enforces those regulations. As Gieryn pointed out, "Once sealed shut, machines are capable of steering social action in ways not always meaningfully apprehended by actors or necessarily congruent with their interests or values."[73] For technical copy protection, this closed design includes the trusted system itself: The security of a trusted system depends on keeping its workings absolutely secret from its users.

While law speaks about what is and is not allowed, and intervenes after activity violates those conditions, technological regulation "allows for automated and self-executing rule enforcement,"[74] exerting control by making certain possibilities unavailable or nonexistent. What is not there cannot be done. After the court ordered Napster to impose a filter on its peer-to-peer network, copyrighted works available on one user's computer simply did not appear on the list when another user searched for them. A search for a particular song would turn up no hits—without explaining whether that was because no one had it, or because it had been filtered out. It was simply rendered invisible, as was any possibility of downloading it.

What we're talking about here is not a concrete speed bump, but a magnetic field that imperceptibly slows the car, and that the government makes both mandatory to obey and impossible to investigate. In fact, one of the purported appeals of a fully instituted trusted system is that the complexity of obeying the assigned digital rights would be buried inside the device. No longer will people have to know, or risk not understanding, the arcane intricacies of copyright law; the rules can be more complex and more sophisticatedly applied, while all users will see will be clean interfaces and gently rebuked requests—the perfect absence of a function, or a civil "Sorry, this file cannot be transferred" message, or, perhaps more likely, "Would you like to initiate the transfer? Only $1.75!"

The contest between law and its subjects, visible and messy but also accountable and improvable, is invisible in technological controls. Enforcement comes in the form of an absence of possibility rather than a prohibition; abuses, flaws, and injustices in the system are themselves encrypted. It is not clear that users will even know exactly what it is they cannot do, which makes it exceedingly difficult to criticize an unfair system. And much of this technological regulation is an indirect form of government regulation, which means the legal intervention it enacts is also obscured. As Lessig frets, "indirection misdirects responsibility. When a government uses other structures of constraint to effect a constraint it could impose directly, it muddies the responsibility for that constraint and so undermines political accountability. If transparency is a value in constitutional government, indirection is its enemy."[75]

Heterogeneous Engineering

The speed bump, once an unassuming slab of concrete, is revealed to be a complex sociocultural artifact, an object of contestation struggled over by designers, legislators, critics, and users. It regulates, quite effectively, though not with anything like the simplicity we imagined, and it can be unbuilt and rebuilt as users come to it, reconstruct it as meaningful artifact, and convince others to see it as such. It is one element in a complex "sociotechnical ensemble,"[76] as it connects with curbs and bicyclists and shock absorbers and pavers and pedestrians and political slogans. Together all these elements form a relatively stable array that best suits the desired activities of a great many people sharing a single space, and imposes some regulatory consequence on some of them when they drive too fast.

Yet even this complex and interlocking matrix of elements is insufficient to achieve the results necessary. The speed bump cannot work alone. We regularly overlook this; in fact, we may even be impressed that the speed bump seems to function without any help, whereas any alternative would require the messy combination of police officers, speed limits, jurisdictions, exceptions, courts, and prisons. This is a mirage, though not a surprising one in a culture that holds such great faith in the way technologies can cleanly intervene and solve messy social problems. In a way, Winner is seduced by this idea too, marveling at how the bridges, by themselves, discriminate between car and bus passengers with political effect, and do so with such subtlety and apparent disconnection from human politics that they are overlooked by the very people being discriminated against.

Low bridges may regulate the passage of people in buses. But it is easy to overlook, as Winner does, that this is both because it is difficult to get under them *and* because it is illegal for the driver to blow them up. No bridge, low or otherwise, could stop a bus whose driver was equipped with and willing to use a small charge of dynamite. No speed bump can regulate drivers who choose to take a sledgehammer to it. No prison can incarcerate people who have not been shackled and forcibly dragged there and stripped of the tools necessary to escape. These observations may seem slightly absurd or obvious, but this is only because they are so contrary to our foundational set of laws prohibiting the destruction of public property, because we rarely dare to act outside of those baseline rules.[77]

What Winner's argument overlooks is that, just as technologies are constructed in ways that serve systems of power, systems of power are constructed along with the technology, so as to regulate human activity together. The power of the artifact as an accidental or deliberate constraint depends in part on a set of rules, and on the social and institutional mechanisms behind those rules, guaranteeing that the artifact will remain in place and continue to intervene in human activity as it was designed to, and that trying to avoid or change it will have consequences. These mechanisms also lend the artifact additional authority: As Joerges writes, "The power represented in built and other technical devices is not to be found in *the formal attributes of these things themselves*. Only their *authorization*, their legitimate representation, gives shape to the definitive effects they may have . . . In this view, it is the processes by which authorizations are built, maintained, contested and changed which are at issue in any social study of built spaces and technology."[78]

The permanence of material artifacts, then, is a sociopolitical accomplishment, not a natural fact. We could imagine, though it's not easy, a world in which there were no rule against destroying public property and no compunction not to—where the moment someone built a speed bump, someone else came along and smashed it to bits. As Chandra Mukerji reminds us, New Yorkers experienced this for a cruel moment in September 2001, when terrorists destroyed the World Trade Center. Part of the shock of that act, beyond the criminal and moral violation of mass murder and destruction, was the political violation of bringing down a technological monument that until that moment represented a vision of national and commercial power—that spoke for most Americans of efficiency, progress, and benevolent growth—and bringing it down by violently slamming another legitimate technological system against it.[79] The speed bump cannot have force outside of a legal environment that distinguishes between public and private property and criminalizes the destruction of that which is not your own, and it is that political regime that is reified when we build a speed bump or impose technical copy protections, engineering the material world in order to embody and impose its ideals.

These political frameworks may be in place not just to support the artifact itself, but to pursue the same goal alongside it. Technical design is one, but certainly not the only, avenue for choreographing human activity.

Even when it is relatively unimportant to do so, designers attempt to guide users in ways other than the technical. Stickers warn users away from tampering with certain parts, manuals describe appropriate use, training demonstrates the proper ends to which the technology should be put. When the technology must regulate, especially in an explicitly legal way, it is always, and must be, one piece of a multi-pronged strategy. Though speed bumps need not be accompanied by a reduced speed limit, they almost always are. Curbs and sidewalks are accompanied by community regulations articulating what a sidewalk is for, who is authorized to use it, and under what conditions. What technical regulations do is merely move the point of intervention. This may mask the force of the state in the way Winner suggests, but it certainly does not remove it from the equation altogether.

Thomas Hughes addresses this multipronged approach when he reminds us that all engineers are "system builders,"[80] designing not only material artifacts but also the economic, political, social, and cultural arrangements that will best suit those technologies. Designing the speed bump to the right height such that users tend to slow down to the desired speed is one way to choreograph human activity, but it is not the only way: The same local officials who installed the speed bump may also mandate speed limits, impose financial penalties, shift cultural attitudes about speeding, and tax the sale of fast cars to reinforce the behavior. Furthermore, designers may work to shift material elements of this "seamless web"[81] of things, people, and rules to ensure the speed bump does its job: lobbying for higher curbs, calling for bans on extreme shock absorbers, designing movable speed bumps to encourage their deployment in a context-dependent way, etc.

John Law, discussing the efforts of explorers to develop reliable oceanic trade routes down the coast of Africa, offers us a useful way of thinking even more broadly about this feature of technological regulation. For him, technology is a combination of heterogeneous forces and elements, some material and some not, that is designed to intervene in a social and material environment to some end. "Let me, then, define technology as a family of methods for associating and channeling other entities and forces, both human and nonhuman. It is a method, one method, for the conduct of heterogeneous engineering, for the construction of a relatively stable system of related bits and pieces with emergent properties in a hostile or indifferent environment."[82]

To say that European sailors built stronger ships better suited to the African journey is to overlook the wide variety of other tactics they used to solve the problems posed by the harsh Atlantic currents. Sturdier ships drew more power from the wind, which meant fewer crew and therefore more room for supplies, which meant the routes could move away from the coast; magnetic compasses meant they could reliably find their way back from the open sea; this made possible new routes that went out into the open ocean and used the strong currents of the Atlantic to return, which proved better than slowly tacking up the coast. The solution was not exclusively technical, although technical innovations were important. The effort of the explorers required lashing together heterogeneous elements (natural, manmade, social, intellectual) into a stable array that together could overcome the forces of a hostile environment determined to pull them apart. This is "the fundamental problem faced by system-builders: how to juxtapose and relate heterogeneous elements together such that they stay in place and are not disassociated by other actors in the environment in the course of the inevitable struggles—whether those are social or physical or some combination of the two."[83]

The speed bump may be the most visible element intervening in the road traffic on our hypothetical street. But if we share Law's commitment to noticing the heterogeneous engineering at work, we can see how city authorities brought together the speed bump and its tendency to not give when vehicles pass over it, the curb and its capacity to keep cars channeled into the roadway, shock absorbers and their tendency to transmit rough terrain to the body of the driver, yellow paint that draws the human eye and has come to signify a warning, speed limits and the mechanisms of law and order to impose consequences for speeders, pervasive cultural attitudes that privilege the safety of pedestrians over the desire to hurry, and the legal and intellectual regime of property that discourages and penalizes the destruction of a public artifact like a speed bump. The laws of physics, the design of automobiles, the rights of ownership, and the cultural mores of human liberties are bound together in a concerted strategy to compel drivers to slow down along that particular stretch of road. The hypothetical challenges faced by our speed bump suggest some of the ways in which forces hostile to this project work to disassociate these elements: The teenagers adamantly embrace the bumpy ride as an entertaining sign of youthful endurance rather than an unpleasant shock worth avoiding, and the young couple works to separate the speed bump from its cultural justification by posing a different right that's potentially worth more protection. We could even imagine the steps that might follow in an effort to maintain the utility of the speed bump: laws outlawing the super shock absorbers, the removal of speed bumps on routes near hospitals, a public campaign heralding the importance of pedestrian safety, and so on.

To understand the regulation of human activity imposed by a bridge, a speed bump, or a DRM encryption system, we need to look not simply at the technological edge of that regulation and what its political consequences may be, but at the heterogeneous network of elements it represents, how they together regulate activity (more than the technology could ever do by itself), and, most important, how these elements are being held together, by whom, and against what challenges. As Law notes, "Successful large-scale heterogeneous engineering is difficult. Elements in the network prove difficult to tame or difficult to hold in place. Vigilance and surveillance have to be maintained, or else the elements will fall out of line and the network will crumble. The network approach stresses this by noting there is almost always some degree of divergence between what the elements of a network would do if left to their own devices and what they are obliged, encouraged, or forced to do when they are enrolled within a network."[84] These efforts are the real force that either successfully regulates users, or fails to do so. The crucial point of analysis is the set of tactics particular individuals or institutions use to assemble this heterogeneous network of elements, justify each of them in isolation and together, and work to vigilantly bind them together against the onslaught of those who remain unconvinced. And, to fully appreciate the power of this heterogeneous approach to regulation, we must also recognize that the heterogeneity itself can help obscure the machinations of power at work here. No one element (technological, legal, economic, political, cultural) by itself could sufficiently regulate the activity in question. As it is only when all elements are deployed in concert that they have the consequences they do, it is much more difficult to identify and assign responsibility for those consequences.

Technological regulation, then, is never merely regulation by technology; it is the prominent inclusion of technical elements into an aligned set of efforts, partnerships, and laws that together arrange people and activities into a coherent system. DRM as a technology draws our attention and criticism, but it is only a part of what is going on in the enforcement of copyright in the digital age. Legal, institutional, and cultural interventions are also being designed to work alongside DRM, and even to make it possible for it to do what it claims to do. These interventions may be of the greatest consequence. If we take Law's perspective, technology has always been a part of the project to regulate users in their copying and redistribution of culture: For example, music distributors long relied on the fact that cassette tapes lost a generation of quality with every subsequent copy, thus curbing some piracy and requiring somewhat less stringent legal enforcement. What may be new here is only the relative importance of the technical elements, or the fact that the technology is now the first line of defense, or that "technology" as a neutral and comprehensive arbiter is being held up as a new symbol of fairness. Or, perhaps what we're seeing is that digital technology, because it can be designed to intervene in particularly sophisticated ways, is serving two purposes here: as a mechanism for guiding user activity and closing off certain options, but also as the means to hold all the elements of this regulatory regime together.

A Regime of Alignment

In the most recent battles over copyright, content owners have been turning to technological strategies, but the ability to successfully intervene cannot rely on the technologies alone. As Law's analysis suggests, it involves the careful deployment of technological artifacts, social institutions, and discursive justifications, in a sociotechnical arrangement of material and ideological resources that facilitates some behaviors and shuts down alternatives. DRM and the trusted system architecture make this most apparent. What's necessary to make a trusted system work? Certainly the technological apparatus and the necessary protocols must be designed, and this is no small task. Further, the public must be convinced and/or required to adopt it. This technology has not only a number of parts but also a number of supplemental components, each of which has technical and institutional kinks still to be worked out. But the technology itself, robust as it might be, cannot regulate by itself. Complex technological systems require the simultaneous reworking of not only technical artifacts, but also legal, economic, and cultural arrangements to match.

A different way to pose this question is to ask again: Why, unlike your VCR, does your DVD player have no Record button? At one level, it is the simple fact that there is no Record button that prevents you from making unauthorized copies of Hollywood movies. But this speed bump is only the leading edge of a sociotechnical ensemble designed to regulate your consumption and use of your movies. Your DVD player does not have a Record button because the manufacturer signed a license with the major movie studios; this license stipulates a series of technical mandates about the device, the purpose of which is to protect the content of DVDs from being duplicated. These mandates include the absence of a Record button.

The reason you can't easily buy a different DVD player that has a Record button is that all major manufacturers have signed this same license. The reason they all sign and honor this license is that every Hollywood DVD is encrypted, meaning that any DVD player must include one of a set of decryption keys—keys they can only get from the studios upon signing the license. The DVD is encrypted not in order to prevent users from making copies (traditional pirating operations that simply stamp exact copies of the DVD are not frustrated by encryption) but to ensure that DVD manufacturers consent to the terms of these licenses, giving the studios the ability to dictate what DVD players will and will not allow. So while it is the device that specifically prevents copying, and it is the DRM encryption technology that makes the disc unreadable, it is all of these elements working in concert that render some activities possible and others impossible. In fact, the technological innovation is not copy protection, but a more powerful assurance that this complex arrangement will be necessary and enforceable—a trusted system.

The death knell of the trusted system is, of course, the ability to circumvent the built-in rules: As Stefik warns, "The physical integrity, communications integrity, and the behavioral integrity of a repository are the foundations of a trusted system."[85] The system must therefore also be designed to withstand attack, technologically and legally. If the user can break the encryption, or trick the system into dumping unprotected copies onto their computer, or pry open and re-wire the device, or reprogram the system to not charge fees, the system will be leaky. And if a hacker can develop a tool to do these things and pass it around on the Internet, the entire system will disintegrate. So the seamless web of heterogeneous elements must grow. The reason people don't simply build their own DVD players with Record buttons is because they cannot get a decryption key without signing a license; either they would have to sign the license and then violate it, risking a lawsuit, or they would have to devise another way to build that recording DVD player—one that does not need a decryption key because it circumvents the encryption altogether. This is certainly possible, but it is also a violation of the law: The Digital Millennium Copyright Act (DMCA), a law the content industries vigorously lobbied for, prohibits circumvention of copyright encryption schemes.

Using the specter of Internet piracy as a powerful and persuasive scare tactic, the music and movie industries are actually pursuing a four-pronged strategy to control use of their content: legal efforts to prosecute users who share and download, and to also criminalize the production of tools and networks that facilitate these users; technological efforts to make their content, and the devices used to experience it, more resilient to casual copying; contract arrangements between industries to ensure that the guidelines imposed through law and technology are followed; and political efforts to convince legislators to make such systems mandatory.[86] It is not DRM but the sociotechnical ensemble in its entirety, including the political, institutional, and cultural efforts that ensure its presence and its legitimacy, that has consequences for users' engagement with digital culture.

Mark Rose called modern copyright a shift from a "regime of regulation" to a "regime of property";[87] I'll call this new approach a "regime of alignment": the alignment of distribution systems through material and legal constraints, the alignment of allied institutions through technologically enforced licenses and ideological linkages, and the alignment of access, use, and consumption through a network of restrictions and facilitations. Even if hardware manufacturers, in order to appeal to their consumers, might want to reject the content restrictions preferred by copyright owners, they will find themselves compelled by encryption systems to either accept the terms of the arrangement or get out of the game altogether. This is not a mere imposition of code, not just a speed bump, but the interlocking of the technological, the legal, the institutional, and the discursive to carefully direct user activity according to particular agendas. And more often than not, it is not law designing these regimes. Instead, the legislators and courts assent to play a support role to privately organized arrangements that, while they may pretend to be in the service of public goals, were not designed for those ends.

The way the media industries are intervening into the practices of their consumers, both to regulate copying and to extract payment, requires the careful and systematic alignment of resources around the use of digital content. If the content industries cannot get hardware manufacturers to agree to install the technological limits they desire, or if lawmakers will not use the prohibition of circumvention to stop designers from evading the industry agreements, the entire system collapses. As Joerges observes, "The power of things does not lie in themselves. It lies in their associations; it is the product of the way they are put together and distributed."[88] DRM cannot work without this regime of alignment.

It is this set of associations, this heterogeneous engineering, that we must examine. Looking only at the DRM technologies, or strictly at the law of copyright and its application, or exclusively at the economic dynamics of the entertainment industry, we will always come up short. The efforts to regulate depend on their intersection, on their combination. This complex alignment of technologies, rules, institutions, markets, and people is by no means simple or inevitable, but it thrives in part because our scrutiny so often sees only its components in isolation, like the blind men unable to describe the elephant.

The remainder of the book will consider this particular regime of alignment in terms of four components: (1) the effort to give this strategy cultural legitimacy, (2) the political mobilization necessary to bring into economic and ideological alignment the institutions that could produce the trusted system, (3) the particular effort to grant this arrangement the authority of the state, and (4) attempts to build the system to resist the agency of its own users. By scrutinizing this heterogeneous system of associations, we may not only reveal the more subtle elements of the copyright debates that so often disappear from view. We may also recognize how this process of legitimation and mobilization, regardless of whether the particular implementation succeeds, can have its own consequences for the movement and regulation of digital culture.

We must begin this analysis by understanding how such a complex set of alignments was invoked and justified. In a world in which doing nothing is easier than doing something, and "staying the course" is a legitimate political position, radically revising copyright law and installing a menagerie of new technologies designed to restrict uses that are becoming massively popular is much harder than not doing so. In order to pull together all of the pieces of this strategy, the proponents of the trusted system would need a provocative call to arms, a compelling rhetorical justification that offered a clear articulation of right and wrong, a dramatic narrative that could persuade a number of reluctant elements to coincide. The first step in producing this regime of alignment is cultural legitimation.

| # A Heroic Tale of Devilish Piracy and Glorious Progress, by Jack Valenti

The turn to digital encryption and hardware constraints to regulate copyright is no small undertaking, and is in some ways a drastic shift of purpose, tactics, and authority. It is a shift that Congress and the courts might have initially resisted as too interventionist, far from the spirit of the original doctrine. Modern copyright law is premised on a careful balance between the interests of content providers and the interests of the public. In the language of the Constitution, the very rights offered to copyright owners are intended as a means to eventually serve that public good. But this balance has been reinterpreted over the last century, most dramatically in response to the arrival of new technologies and the changing demands of increasingly powerful media industries. Each shift requires these proponents to offer some justification for why the balance should be shifted, or, more typically, to claim that new technologies have already tipped the balance, then propose that the law must change to restore equilibrium. To the music and movie industries, the Internet looked precisely like the kind of shift that would unbalance the copyright bargain and threaten their livelihood if it was not addressed.

Market leaders in any industry, facing the "waves of creative destruction"[1] brought on by technological innovation that threaten to upend their existing business models, often turn to reactionary economic and legal strategies to stem the tide. It seems safer to preserve an existing business model than to be forced into the riskier alternative, that is, having to renovate that business model, with no guarantee that it will succeed, in order to compete against more innovative challengers. Attempts to improve their product, usually along existing trajectories of development—a "bells and whistles" approach—are often paired with (sometimes collective) efforts to guard their market position by seeking legal restrictions against the new challenge.[2] The embrace of DRM and the trusted system is precisely this kind of effort. Moreover, it may provide an opportunity. If the traditional media companies can carefully and powerfully characterize the Internet as a threat to culture, they may be able to gain some advantage in the midst of the repair—in Pamela Samuelson's terms, a "copyright grab"[3] disguised as a return to the status quo.

Engineering a technopolitical shift of this magnitude requires a number of elements—economic, political, legal—to fall into place, which includes aligning various institutions' interests and coordinating the strategies by which those interests are pursued. This is the grunt work of diplomacy—concerted lobbying efforts to bring about this law and that partnership—which means it's a primarily discursive effort. The challenge is to convince those in a position to act that a problem exists, that something must be done, and that the best something to be done is the plan being proposed. But this does not depend only on literally convincing one party to help out another. A crucial kind of rhetorical work necessarily precedes and paves the way for such a request. As Pfaffenberger observes, "It is by no means sufficient merely to project the artifact into the fabricated social context . . . the artifact must be discursively regulated by surrounding it with symbolic media that mystify and therefore constitute the political aims."[4] In some ways, this is precisely the kind of discursive negotiation Pinch and Bijker had in mind when they talked about the "interpretive flexibility" of technology; DRM as a technology could end up meaning a number of things, some of which would not serve the interests of the industry: illegal intervention into culture, technical boondoggle, pain in the ass, unconstitutional. To improve the likelihood not only that this technology would be embraced by the public, but also that the institutions crucial to making it work would embrace the paradigm it served, its story would have to be told, and told powerfully.

In the case of technical copy protection, the aim of this cultural legitimation was to construct the problem in semantic terms such that it appeared urgent with potentially dire consequences, had a particular response that was certain to be beneficial to everyone involved, and fit within a clear moral framework that posited those deploying it as the good guys, beset on all sides by enemies. According to Debora Halbert, "The power to define the villains and heroes, appropriate and inappropriate, ethical and unethical behavior, constitutes control over the story. By changing the terminology used to describe computer-related actions, copyright owners control the discourse. Thus, sharing becomes stealing. Creative work becomes private property. Corporations become victims of piracy."[5] The "heterogeneous engineering" behind copyright's turn to technology required framing the controversy in terms that would make it both a legal and a cultural imperative, and providing a convenient and logical paradigm for understanding the solution in terms most amenable to the corporate content owners.

This was not as simple as it sounds. Language is messy and fraught with pitfalls; persuasion is arduous and the resources to act are scarce: The government and commercial actors being addressed are marked by inertia and political reticence. Furthermore, the argument that the media industries needed to make when it came to justifying DRM faced an uphill battle on two fronts. First, with the bewildering success and popularity of the Internet, the U.S. government had made it clear that it was opting for a generally hands-off approach to regulation. With a few exceptions, such as the issue of pornography, the U.S. government hoped to sweep away the barriers that could inhibit the growth of the network, innovation in the technology, and most of all e-commerce. Hardware manufacturers in the IT sector welcomed this hands-off approach, seduced by the sheer range of opportunities for them to market this new technology and its ever-widening range of applications.

Second, both the Internet and, more specifically, peer-to-peer networks had captured the public imagination. In less than a year Napster grew from a college student's plaything to a pulsing network of seventy million users at the peak of its popularity; dozens of similar peer-to-peer applications followed in its wake. Press coverage of the phenomenon was widespread, and tended to weigh equally the potential legal implications with the populist enthusiasm for music, digital technology, and online community that it seemed to reveal. Scholars championed the Internet for the way it made the tools for the production and distribution of culture cheaply available to amateurs and thus lowered the barriers to entry for public expression. Critics of the existing music industry championed Napster as a way for music fans to break the major labels' stranglehold on artist development, control of CD prices, and manufacture of pop culture trends. Some suggested that, because artists could distribute work themselves and fans could set the agenda for what was popular, there was less need for copyright protection to ensure reasonable and fair compensation.[6]

To overcome both the wild popularity of peer-to-peer networks and the reticence to intervene legislatively in the development of the Internet and e-commerce, the music and film industries needed more than just the eternal Western faith in technological progress to help justify the changes in copyright law they sought, as well as the massive shift they would demand in attitudes toward copyright, culture, and technology. This required not just a distress call, but a rhetorical intervention that could turn this phenomenon on its head, portraying with stark and dramatic clarity the dire emergency file-trading represented, and the glorious potential that could be lost if it was allowed to spread.

Over the past decade, this justification has been effectively constructed by the U.S. film and music industries. From public education campaigns to congressional testimony to behind-the-scenes lobbying, the Recording Industry Association of America (RIAA) and the Motion Picture Association of America (MPAA) in particular worked hard to frame the Internet as a specific danger to both commerce and culture. Even before Napster, these industries were testifying to Congress that computer networks would wither if artists and producers were hesitant to make their work available, and that this fear would only be assuaged by stricter copyright laws.[7] After the rise of peer-to-peer networks, they railed against file-trading as piracy, theft, conspiracy, and sin. Richard Parsons, CEO of Time Warner, fretted that music would come to be seen as free, then backed that fear with doomsday rhetoric: "This isn't just about a bunch of kids stealing music. It's about an assault on everything that constitutes the cultural expression of our society. If we fail to protect and preserve our intellectual property system, the culture will atrophy. And corporations won't be the only ones hurt. Artists will have no incentive to create. Worst-case scenario: The country will end up in a sort of cultural Dark Ages."[8] Over the course of ten years, as early as the Clinton-Gore plans to support the National Information Infrastructure, through the early popularity of the mp3 format, in the lawsuit brought against Napster, and into the discussion of the regulation of digital television, representatives of these industries have constructed a powerfully compelling imperative: the massive threat to their business posed by Internet piracy.

Leading this rhetorical charge has been Jack Valenti, who until his retirement in 2004 was the president and CEO of the MPAA, the industry lobbying organization that represents the major Hollywood studios. Valenti, perhaps the most powerful and articulate of those defending megacorporate entertainment content against the threat of peer-to-peer, offered up a compelling tale of sin and redemption in order to reframe the public discourse about the Internet. In his vision, the Internet's great potential is beset by marauding pirates determined to steal all they can get their hands on; this threat is too great for content producers, who can only respond by withholding their content. Their reticence to make music and movies vulnerable to digital thieves means artists suffer, the Internet withers, the culture runs dry, the American economy falters in the eyes of the world. He paired this dire prediction with a rosy alternative: With stronger copyright protection and technical self-enforcement measures, the culture industry will be able to provide the rich consumer experience the Internet has always promised. This tale of bad pirates and good consumers, law and lawlessness, villain and victim, cause and effect, was backed with contentious evidence and laced with incendiary allegations (the link between peer-to-peer networks and child pornography being only the most lurid).

Valenti's vision was, of course, just one take on the issue, and a distinctly interested one at that. His tale was a precarious chain of logical presumptions, each of which could be challenged on its own merits. In later chapters we will see a number of ways in which Valenti's perspective, if not plain wrong, was certainly not the only viable interpretation of what has happened. Furthermore, his tale was cloaked in a dramatic rhetoric that painted a complex legal and economic controversy in stark moral terms of virtue and vice, overstating the problem and working against substantive deliberation over possible solutions.[9] Nevertheless, it was put forth so powerfully and persuasively that it is slowly becoming the standard for understanding how copyright does and should work, and how it must be renovated for a digital age. This persuasive tale helped to reorient the early excitement about a file-trading revolution in music into a story of a wronged industry seeking justice. As a framework for understanding the copyright wars, it has proven persuasive to government regulators, justifying the construction of technical solutions and the legal regimes they require. Valenti's prose, easy to mock, proved a powerful element in granting the proposed solution the kind of cultural and normative legitimacy it needed to actually bring together the political and institutional elements that could make it a reality. The effort to lash all these elements together in the service of a particular social goal, and to fortify it against the unruly elements and unexpected circumstances that might unravel this precarious alignment, was not simply material, social, or political, but also discursive.

Jack

Since 1966, Valenti has helped lead the movie industry through a series of challenges and opportunities, including calling for the replacement of the old Hays Code rating system with the current voluntary one, steering his industry through the globalization of the mass culture market, responding to recurring concerns at home about Hollywood's moral values and advertising practices, and articulating the studios' response to the various new technologies that have altered the distribution and display of their films.

The statement released by the MPAA announcing his retirement in 2004 iterated his sense of the MPAA's fundamental goals and how they have shifted toward the technological in recent years:

Valenti has often remarked that the mandate of the MPAA can be summed up briefly: "To make sure the American movie and TV program can move freely and competitively around the world." In recent years, he has added, "and [be] protected from theft in the digital environment." . . . Valenti and his colleagues direct a planet-wide strategy whose objective it is to keep markets open, lessen discrimination, conciliate and/or resist attempts to exile, shrink or hinder American participation in the world marketplace of cinema, television, cable, satellite delivery, pay-per-view, and soon-to-be Internet delivery, which has demanded a vigilance to combat the theft of valuable creative works throughout the world.[10]

While the rest of the film industry typically prefers to emphasize the creative goals of their act over base economic imperatives, Valenti unapologetically sought to ensure the ideal political, economic, and legal climate for a stable and profitable movie business. This meant seeking support from Congress and the courts when he needed it (e.g., trying to outlaw the VCR) and demanding they stay out of the way when he didn't (e.g., championing industry self-censorship over government rules on content); it meant loosening trade arrangements amenable to the global circulation of American films, and tightening trade barriers when other nations refused to comply with copyright crackdowns or imposed nationalist restrictions on American cultural imports.

When it came to the Internet, Valenti's job was to normalize the Internet as a place of commerce—not just to squelch file-trading, but to establish the conditions in which the Internet can be a viable distribution system for Hollywood films. Those who wonder how the popularization of the Internet, once a military and research network over which commercial exchange was prohibited,[11] became synonymous with the commercialization of the Internet need only look at the efforts of men like Valenti, who told Congress that "the Internet is the wave, perhaps tidal, of commerce in cyberspace"[12]—making the Internet and the market one and the same while retaining the dream that the one would revolutionize the other. So it should come as no surprise that, as peer-to-peer file-trading spread, Valenti also took the lead in calling on Congress and industry to regulate that market, and gave them a compelling explanation for why they should do so.

Valenti was certainly not alone in this regard; there were many other representatives of the content industries making the case against file-trading, both publicly and behind the scenes. I am singling out Valenti's rhetoric here for two reasons. First, because of his prominent position, he played a unique role in representing the content industries' concerns on this issue. His access to the upper echelons of legislative power and his flair for the dramatic single him out as the most compelling voice from that side of the table. Second, his goals and his argument are parts of a surprisingly coherent (if not necessarily coordinated) discourse with many sources, which frames the transition of media online in stark and morally charged terms. Valenti stands out as the most provocative, and perhaps the most listened to, representative of a broader discourse emanating from the major U.S. film and music companies.

One of Valenti's primary tasks was to deliver the opinion of the major Hollywood studios on any new technologies they feared would undercut their business, and to do so using rich, vivid sound bites that would prove persuasive. In testimony given to Congress in 1982, he famously compared the VCR to the Boston strangler,[13] implying that, like the notorious killer, the new device would sneak up in the night and choke the life out of American filmmaking. Valenti brought similar rhetoric to bear on the Internet and especially on peer-to-peer file-trading networks. But this was not just overdramatization, or a stylistic flourish for the sake of the press. Valenti's rhetoric was a carefully and deliberately constructed narrative designed to characterize the new technology as both an economic threat and a moral one—indeed, to equate the two. His proclamations took a complex legal and social dilemma and painted it in the broad brushstrokes so familiar to his industry: promise and peril, sin and redemption, good and evil—and, matched to that, conflict and resolution. This narrative was accomplished by drawing stark contrasts between the sacred and the profane, carefully framing the debate so that the outcomes appeared as binary choices between light and dark paths, and linking the representation of that threat to a series of other cultural fears that bring with them a nearly absolute moral sense of right and wrong.

Through a series of public statements and congressional appearances[14] that have since been circulated to the press by the public relations arm of the MPAA and made available online, Valenti worked first and foremost to frame the file-trading phenomenon as an indisputable case of theft, massaging what was rapidly becoming a popular and populist phenomenon back into legal terms so that the MPAA might retain the upper hand. Second, he directly appealed to Congress to provide the legal help to counter this criminal behavior, which meant giving this "theft" an urgency requiring that real and symbolic capital be expended on curtailing it. He did this by demonstrating an array of dire consequences including, perhaps most important, economic ones. Finally, he attempted to enlist the help of an array of other institutions in this battle: not just Congress, but also the manufacturers of consumer electronics and information technologies, the community of artists and producers both inside the film industry and out, and international allies in both the legal and commercial realms. This last goal required not only that Valenti and his colleagues narrate this threat as a "clear and present danger,"[15] but also that they implicate these others, portraying these risks and rewards as their own—that is, if Hollywood sinks under the weight of digital piracy, everyone else goes down with the ship. In working to accomplish all of these goals with a single narrative, Valenti constructed the rhetorical justification necessary to draw these allies into alignment, and to pitch the digital battle such that their economic survival not only lined up with the MPAA's but also seemed morally just.

Though the rhetorical approach taken by Valenti shifted over the course of the peer-to-peer controversy, and his preferred imagery was regularly retooled to best resonate with the particular cultural and political moment, the underlying structure of his narrative was remarkably consistent. The logic it represented went something like this: (1) we are in a time of great promise (be that promise economic, technological, cultural, or political); (2) copyright theft made possible by the Internet is a threat to that great promise and to all who might benefit from it (again, be that artists, consumers, or the nation itself); (3) widespread piracy will convince the film industry to withhold its content or be reluctant to build online distribution systems; (4) if this happens, consumers, the Internet, and the culture will suffer; (5) with the proper countermeasures (be they technological, legal, or legislative), this threat will be diminished and the Internet will meet its promise, which is (6) a digital cornucopia of multimedia entertainment that gives American consumers exactly what they want, when they want it, for a reasonable price. This was by no means a simple narrative logic to establish, and these were not necessarily easy audiences to convince. Valenti had to carefully build his story and repeat it endlessly, link it to a series of related tales of threats faced and potentials realized, and coat it in a language that made abundantly clear the moral foundations of this issue and the urgency with which it must be faced.

Lobbyist-Slash-Screenwriter

Like any good Hollywood screenplay, Valenti's opening scene established a stable world in which things were as they should be and the future looked bright, then quickly punctured that world with an impending threat that could bring it all crashing down. Sometimes this happy universe was the creative space of Hollywood, sometimes it was the promise of digital technologies. But Valenti was certainly attuned to what would appeal to his typical audience; most often, he began with the economic strength of the film industry as a national asset:

The copyright industries are responsible for over five percent of the GDP of the nation. Over the past quarter century, these industries' share of GDP grew more than twice as fast as the remainder of the economy. They earn more international revenues than automobiles and auto parts, more than aircraft, more than agriculture. The copyright industries have been creating new jobs at three times the rate of the rest of the economy. The movie industry alone has a surplus balance of trade with every single country in the world. No other American industry can make that statement. And all this comes at a time when the U.S. is suffering from some $400 billion in trade deficits.[16]

This economic bounty, of course, was in impending danger. While Valenti's typical villains were "digital thieves"[17] and "Internet pirates"[18] bent on undercutting this economically and politically appealing equilibrium, in some ways the bad guy in his story was the Internet itself. Valenti gave his narrative arc some depth as he introduced the foil to his hero (Hollywood); this villain had two sides, offering both "the opportunity and the threat,"[19] both "the promise and the pain."[20] Janus-faced, the promise and peril of the Internet were two sides of the same coin: "Like Emerson's doctrine that 'for every gain there is a loss and for every loss there is a gain,' within the glittering potential of the Internet lies the darker forms of thieves who, armed with magical new technology, are capable of breaking-and-entering conventional barriers to steal copyrighted material borne to the Internet by just about anybody with a working computer."[21]

Valenti was careful not to sound like the Luddite that his job often required him to be. He tapped into all of the available late-1990s hyperbole surrounding the Internet, from the familiar frontier iconography[22] to the recurring trope of technological revolution, to reassure his audience that he too saw its grand potential: "There is little doubt that [the] Internet is one of the most inventive adventures to which the human society has borne personal witness, ranking with Gutenberg's design for movable type, jet transportation, and the appearance of television."[23] Nevertheless, the peril the Internet brings with it was surely coming: There were dark clouds on the horizon, a "nightmare scenario."[24] Despite the promise of the Internet, or perhaps in order to salvage that promise, "we have to confront a problem which both vexes us and haunts us as well. It is Internet piracy."[25]

Before Valenti could further narrate this promise and peril, it was crucial that he firmly establish that file-trading is theft. At the start of his rhetorical crusade, this was by no means a foregone conclusion; it wasn't until the 2001 *Napster* decision[26] that a court affirmatively declared that downloading and uploading music over a peer-to-peer network was a direct infringement of the reproduction and distribution rights of copyright protection. The issue is still not entirely settled.[27] Valenti worked to establish this as fact not by making a particular legal argument for why it should be the case, but by treating it as though it already were, and using the terms interchangeably: "A plague of piracy—theft of intellectual property— threatens to blight this new marketplace."[28] To simply and unproblematically equate file-trading and theft cemented a specifically legal set of meanings and assumptions onto the new practice. Since peer-to-peer technologies have been under vehement legal attack by the culture industries from almost the very start, it is difficult to recall moments when the discussion was free from (that is, neither aligned with nor reacting to) the effort to put the issue in legal terms. The compelling power and cultural authority of legal discourse is precisely why the industry chose copyright law as its first line of defense against peer-to-peer.

Even when the metaphoric characterization of these technologies was not so florid and the politics were not quite so explicit, the choice of words to even name the phenomenon was a contest over the purpose and value of information distribution itself. Most powerful for this task is the term "piracy," which has proven particularly effective in colonizing the debate and framing it in terms that are particularly amenable to an MPAA legal victory.[29] The term does a great deal of work in this regard. It builds the semantic bridge between file-trading intellectual property and the theft of material property, lacing it with legal connotations, suggesting a bright-line distinction between self-evidently ethical and unethical practices. "Piracy" is a term that has long been part of the copyright lexicon—though before the Internet, it represented something dramatically different in scope and consequence. Importing "piracy" from traditional copyright debates not only assures the relevance of copyright law, it implies that the response to classic piracy logically pertains to the new kind.[30] As Litman notes, the content industries have "succeeded in persuading a lot of people that any behavior that has the same effect as piracy must *be* piracy, and must therefore reflect the same moral turpitude we attach to piracy, even if it is the same behavior that we all called legitimate before"[31]—that is, unlicensed but personal, noncommercial copying.

Finally, "piracy" is a historically rich term that exceeds its specific use in copyright law. Its kinship to oceanic crime dramatizes the current conflict as a tale of noble captains and marauding thieves. With its broad, good-vs.-evil brushstrokes it leaves little room to consider the complicity of those being pirated, no room to speculate as to the social value the act of piracy might have. The semantic ambiguity keeps these older connotations alive, so that legal disapproval of peer-to-peer file-trading is culturally loaded. The metaphor is not accidental, and often was played up explicitly, as in the RIAA's description of the issue:

No black flags with skull and crossbones, no cutlasses, cannons, or daggers identify today's pirates. You can't see them coming; there's no warning shot across your bow. Yet rest assured the pirates are out there because today there is plenty of gold (and platinum and diamonds) to be had. Today's pirates operate not on the high seas but on the Internet, in illegal CD factories, distribution centers, and on the street. The pirate's credo is still the same—why pay for it when it's so easy to steal? The credo is as wrong as it ever was. Stealing is still illegal, unethical, and all too frequent in today's digital age. That is why RIAA continues to fight music piracy.[32]

Of course it is worth noting that although the term asserts a clear distinction between good and evil, its semantic richness may tend to undermine this value; tales of piracy also have a romanticized quality in Western culture, often with our sympathies firmly on the side of the pirates—a mythology partially produced by the very same film industry that now feels it is being forced to walk the plank. Moreover, the term may also remind us that the current dispute, like its oceanic predecessor, is fundamentally about commerce. This could undercut those moments when the record industry portrays itself as the noble defender of artists who, history can attest, have more often been exploited by it.

This discursive strategy, deployed by the RIAA when facing Napster in the courts and in the court of public opinion, could potentially have held much less gravitas in the case of Hollywood, since the sheer quantity of file-trading of movies was dramatically less than what the music industry faced. To address this, Valenti extended this tale of certain peril into the uncertain future, depending on the presumption of technological progress to foresee a pending danger—the widespread adoption of broadband Internet access, clearly near at hand: "The moat that has slowed a wide-spreading assault on movies in digital form is the languor with which American computer-homes have valued broadband access . . . But that moat will gradually be drained as broadband grows, both in its speed-power and in the deployment of broadband to homes. Once that happens, the moat will flatten, and all barriers to high-speed takedowns of movies will collapse. The avalanche will have begun. It is the certainty of that scenario which concerns every movie maker and distributor in the land."[33] Now it's barbarians at the gates. Of course, he was almost certainly right about the growth of bandwidth and digital storage. In fact, this technological growth is precisely what Valenti and the Hollywood studios were eagerly hoping for; the Internet will only become a viable commercial distribution system for their films when connection speeds improve. But the threat of these fast pipes could also be used rhetorically to help justify a pre-emptive strike before the damage was done.

Next in his narrative logic, Valenti needed to put someone in the path of the grave danger posed by the Internet, a damsel in distress tied to the rails and facing impending doom. He had a number of noble figures to choose from, and he managed to endanger them all. His first victim was the creator whose work was being violated. Valenti pointed to filmmakers and screenwriters as those most endangered by the promiscuity of the Internet: "Whence comes a superior film or TV program? It starts in the brain pan of a creative artist, and springs forth to search for life and endurance."[34] Of course, the noble author has been an "ideologically-charged,"[35] and potentially misleading trope in copyright disputes since its inception; in practice, copyright law structurally benefits distributors much more than the authors they represent. As Halbert notes, "The division of original author from copyright is rarely addressed, yet the author is pulled out of the bag when a defense of intellectual property rights and the incentive they provide for creation is needed."[36]

Beyond the authors currently in the employ of the major Hollywood studios, Valenti further extended the threat to all those employed by the industry: "We have to stem the tide of film theft online before it is too late, before it puts to peril the creative energy of the industry and the jobs of the nearly one million Americans who work within the movie industry."[37] What's more, the artists' loss was also a loss for the entire culture: "The future of movie entertainment springs from the human condition's grand simplicity. It is this: People, no matter their culture, creed or country, want to be entertained. That human desire has never shrunk or faltered in over 2,500 years."[38]

Beyond those who make films and the culture they enrich, Valenti pushed a few more victims in front of the oncoming train of Internet piracy. Quite often, his opinion was being solicited in the context of how to best regulate the Internet; so it was often the Internet itself, sometimes the source of peril, that might also be in peril. To a Senate subcommittee

Valenti posed the question, "What incentive will companies have to create, nourish and market digital movies online when they are kidnapped and flung around the world? Can high value, legitimate creative works live in an environment of abundant theft unchecked and growing?"[39] To that question he assured his listeners that there was only one answer. Owners and producers of valuable intellectual property would inevitably do the rational thing when faced with this threat: They would withhold their work from this unprotected market, at least until protection was assured. In this scenario, the Internet would wither without the valuable content provided by the film industry (and its brethren in music and publishing), killing off the digital revolution he had already so dramatically celebrated. As online file-trading proved resilient, and the call from industry critics to develop a legitimate alternative model of online distribution grew louder, this warning morphed into the suggestion that content providers would not experiment with such distribution models so long as piracy continued to run rampant. With this reluctance, it would be the consumers who would suffer, "ordinary citizens who will soon find the reservoir of creative works diminishing,"[40] and the market itself: "When piracy flourishes, commerce shrivels."[41]

However, Valenti was savvy enough to know that his real audience was Congress and the hardware industries he was trying to implicate, and his best tactic for persuading them was economic. Not only does peer-to-peer threaten art and artist, he argued, it threatens the financial health of the film industry, and with it, the entire content industry, the consumer electronics industries, and the nation itself. Valenti exaggerated when he said, "I do not exaggerate when I say that the future of America's greatest trade asset, its copyright industries, is truly at stake,"[42] positing Hollywood not only as America's economic powerhouse but also as its cultural missionary to the world: "The most important economic asset of the United States is the ever-mounting worth of Copyright and Creativity, from which springs America's greatest trade export. The Copyright Industries of the U.S. produce what is called Intellectual Property which reaches to every crevice and corner of this wracked and sometimes weary planet and is welcomed in every country with a hospitable embrace."[43] Smoothed over here was the longstanding worry that it is precisely the U.S. culture industries' push to colonize international markets that makes their product so culturally problematic for the rest of the world, and not always so hospitably embraced.[44] In Valenti's narrative, Hollywood's role in the world was a force of good abroad and a foundation at home, and must be protected from being undercut by an Internet that cared little for geopolitical niceties.

Copyright as a Moral Imperative

It is important to note that, already, this narrative has established a precariously long series of logical steps, each of which could be challenged on its own merits, and some of which could be argued to be contradictory. The economic strength of the United States depends on a healthy and protected market for film as orchestrated by the major Hollywood studios; the Internet as a distribution technology will usher in a great digital revolution; the Internet as a distribution technology will certainly undercut the legitimate goals of the film industry; the act of file-trading is illegal and immoral; file-trading hurts artists and others who work in Hollywood's creative community; if file-trading goes unchecked, content producers will withhold their intellectual property or will be reluctant to develop alternative models of legitimate and commercial online distribution; without that content, the Internet will wither; the invention and adoption of faster broadband connections will expand the problem and especially harm the film industry; stronger copyright protection will support the movement of cultural work over the Internet.

All of these observations are only arguably true depending on how the question is asked, and more important, by whom. But Valenti and his lobbying organization need all of them to appear to be not just true, but transparently obvious. The film and music industries have spent a great deal of time and money on other ventures supporting these claims: research to prove that file-trading means lost sales, public statements linking the rise of peer-to-peer networks with various economic downturns experienced by the industry, etc. None of these claims went undisputed. So, perhaps to shore up this house of cards, Valenti also paired his argument with some more familiar, more compelling, and more visceral "nightmare scenarios,"[45] loading what is fundamentally an economic concern with a rhetoric of fear designed to associate online file-traders with a host of cultural monsters, and to paint file-trading in the stark, black-and-white palette of a "moral imperative."[46]

In his book *Fear: The History of a Political Idea*, Corey Robin reminds us that, even in a liberal democratic society that prides itself on having rejected totalitarian rule through intimidation and violence, much of our political discourse is still laced with powerful fears. We continue to debate even about whether fear is good for us: does it stir political activity, calling us to act, or does it paralyze us, urging us to seek reassuring solutions rather than delve into more complex intellectual discussion? Fears, be they political or cultural, of threats internal or foreign, are often represented as being beneath or beyond politics, in the domain of psychology and/or morality. In fact, Robin argues, fear is fundamentally a political phenomenon, produced sometimes by activists but more often by elites, to push a specific agenda or lend support to a more general goal.[47] This is fundamentally discursive work, in that political elites

can define what is or should be the public's chief object of fear. Political fear of this sort almost always preys upon some real threat—it seldom, if ever, is created out of nothing—but since the harms of life are as various as its pleasures, politicians and other leaders have much leeway in deciding which threats are worthy of political attention and which are not. It is they who identify a threat to a population's well being, who interpret the nature and origins of that threat, and who propose a method for meeting that threat. It is they who make particular fears items of civic discussion and public mobilization. This does not mean that each member of the public actually fears the chosen object; not every American citizen, for instance, is actively afraid today of terrorism. It merely means that the object dominates the political agenda, crowding out other possible objects of fear and concern. In choosing, interpreting, and responding to these objects of fear, leaders are influenced by their ideological assumptions and strategic goals. They view danger through a prism of ideas, which shapes whether they see a particular danger as threatening or not, and a lens of political opportunity, which shapes whether they see that danger as helpful or not.[48]

Though such fears are not false, they are also manufactured; though they can be of cultural and political benefit, they are also strategic.

In the politics of culture, many have noted the recurring impact of "moral panics," a politics of fear focused on particular shocking events or cultural practices proclaimed to be harbingers of the disintegrating moral fiber of modern society.[49] Often provoked by political leaders and fueled by breathless media coverage, these panics frequently focus on the content and sometimes the distribution of popular culture—comic books, Saturday morning cartoons, violent video games, Internet pornography. While the panic may be provoked by particular incidents and may revolve around the specifics of that phenomenon, it draws on and extends deeper cultural anxieties. Arnold Hunt argues that "the underlying cause of the moral panic was the 'cultural strain and ambiguity' caused by social change."[50] Still, these panics can be politically strategic for those invested in the moderation and restriction of popular culture.

The construction of a moral crisis is very much a discursive project. If problems themselves are socially constructed, then, according to Malcolm Spector and John Kitsuse, we must "describe and explain the definitional process in which morally objectionable conditions or behaviors are asserted to exist and the collective activities which become organized around those assertions."[51] But to the extent that such words are carefully constructed for real audiences who have real political power, they are fundamentally a mechanism of legitimation and mobilization. The concerns must be made both believable and palpable, and given both urgency and legitimacy as issues worth addressing. To the extent that they appear to warrant action, they work to mobilize those who can take such action. While the rhetoric of fear can be, and often appears to be, a call for change, it is more often a means to resist change, to stabilize the status quo by demonizing proposed alternatives. As Angela McRobbie and Sarah Thornton argue, these strategies use "moral panics as acting on behalf of the dominant social order. They are a means of orchestrating consent by actively intervening in the space of public opinion and social consciousness through the use of highly emotive and rhetorical language which has the effect of requiring that 'something be done about it.' "[52] Such outbursts often direct attention away from the structural conditions that are in fact the foundation for the phenomenon being decried.

As the peer-to-peer debate emerged, and early successes in the courts to shut down Napster and the like did not stem the tide of online file-trading, the music and movie industries returned to public education efforts as a part of their strategy. This was especially important when the music industry began suing individual users, and needed a positive move to balance the negative publicity produced by doing so. Particularly (but not exclusively) when speaking to public audiences, Valenti began framing his discussion of Internet piracy not just in economic terms, but in moral ones. This rhetorical strategy went well beyond saying file-trading was wrong, or constantly attaching the term "piracy" to it in order to cast the practice in a legal framework. Valenti also linked the file-trading question to the very moral structure of a democratic society. At a gathering of students at Duke University he turned their moral relativism against them as future citizens and, more important, as future employers:

No free, democratic nation can lay claim to greatness unless it has constructed a platform from which springs a moral compact that guides the daily conduct of the society and inspires the society to believe in civic trust. That "moral imperative" connects to every family, to every business, every university, every profession and to government as well. . . . There is no larger objective in this country than the reassembling of civic trust, the reaffirmation of honorable conduct by the most powerful among us; in short, holding fast to the sustenance of civic trust. . . . If choices chosen by young people early in their learning environment are infected with a moral decay, how then can they ever develop the judgment to take the right fork in the road? How will you, when many of you are in leadership roles in the future, deal with younger employees who have learned as students that, if you have the power to take what doesn't belong to [you], you do it?[53]

The comfortable equation here of legal, economic, and moral values cleanses each argument of any challenge, rendering invisible such questions as: Is downloading music the same as theft of material property? Are the rights elaborated in intellectual property doctrine the same as the work "belonging" to the copyright holder? Are the solutions Valenti and his colleagues proposed economically viable in this new context? And at what point does the sheer number of people breaking this law suggest the law should be reconsidered? Valenti's rhetoric mapped these complex questions into a "moral imperative" that has only one answer, and leaned on the powerful tenets of private property for ideological support.

But Valenti went much further in his language, to give this moral imperative not only ethical clarity, but also visceral connotations and shadowy partners, dipping deep into the well of cultural fears to demonize online file-trading. As his "Boston strangler" comment suggests, Valenti was, if nothing else, a master of metaphors. His vivid and almost comically exaggerated language often frustrated critics who wanted the conversation to stay on the ground. But, though any one comment may have seemed outlandish, overall he managed to lump file-trading in with some of the most unnerving cultural horrors of this decade and frame the issue in terms we reserve for the most insidious threats our world faces. Valenti constructed a new moral panic by drawing on already established and widely available ones, invoking a moral judgment about one horror in order to apply it to another.

In early statements, Valenti drew on some classic tropes to portray both the Internet and the more specific issue of peer-to-peer file-trading as something to be feared rather than understood. If honoring the inviolability of personal property is the bedrock of civic trust and democratic society, society must be purged of those mysterious forces that could undermine it. A favorite metaphor of Valenti's was magic: Even as he marveled at the promise of the Internet, he described its power the way one might have in the days of witch trials—the "digital and satellite sorcery"[54] and the "as yet undefined new technical witchcraft."[55] While this metaphor might seem to fit with the utopian hyperbole of technological progress, the "revolutionary technological magic"[56] he and many others promised, it was soon made clear that this was a magic that could be put to heathen and unnatural ends. Those that made music and movies available on peer-to-peer networks were not just "thieves," they were "zealots."[57] Discussing what he saw as a new mythology developing on the Internet—that anything posted online is free for the taking—he warned, that "this mindset grazes the outer edges of both the rule of law and the moral covenant which governs a stable society."[58] This precarious ideology would lead not only to "near perfect anarchy"[59] but also to cultural and moral relativism: "Perhaps this pagan philosophy was most famously expressed by one of Dostoyevsky's characters in Notes From the [sic] Underground, who said 'I agree that two plus two equals four is an excellent thing. But two plus two equals five is also an excellent thing.'"[60] The only solution to this black magic and the lure of paganism is the law, which offers not just an economic corrective but a near religious ritual of salvation, leaving us two choices: "the dark underside of Internet piracy as well as the possibility of a cleansing redemption."[61]

When Valenti was not portraying the circulation of movies online as a struggle between pagan sorcery and civilized spirituality, he leaned on a language of invasion and defense more familiar to modern political rhetoric. Whether it is fighting the war on drugs or calling the school shootings the cancer of our society, American politics relies heavily on the metaphorical framing of sociopolitical issues as external threats invading an otherwise stable and idyllic body. For Valenti, this invasion was sometimes of a military sort, where "copyright is under siege,"[62] movies can be "ambushed,"[63] and "as legitimate businesses emerge on the Internet, illegitimate intruders find the Internet a haven."[64] Borrowing from his industry's preferred mythologies, this "invasion of the copyright snatchers"[65] was a violent one, where "illegal copying can lacerate our future"[66] and "disfigure and shred the future of American films."[67] With this threat, we faced monstrous consequences: "our mutual aim is to shield the digital future from intruders, to give it nourishment and zest by making sure it doesn't eat its young."[68] At other moments the metaphor was one of disease, not invasion but infection: "the cancer in the belly of our global business is piracy,"[69] "a plague"[70] or "disfiguring fungus"[71] in which, "without protective sinews in place, without rules of the game enforced by law, America's largest economic asset would be put to peril, blighted by new technology so beneficial, and yet so corrosive if copyright owners are unable to protect their private property."[72]

Without being explicit about it, Valenti's rhetoric incorporated newly available cultural fears after the events of September 11, 2001. Occasionally, this dangerous world served as a subtle justification for the power of movies: "Those few moments of detachment from daily anxieties are quite valuable and, perhaps, quite necessary, particularly in these scrambling and unquiet times."[73] But beginning in 2003, Valenti began lining up peer-to-peer file-trading alongside the threats that this unquiet world poses—not just equating them through metaphoric language, but suggesting explicitly that one can be the doorway to another.

The most consistently compelling association was to pornography, an Internet issue with a long history in congressional and judicial discourse. Here, copyright protection would somehow help with the fact that peer-to-peer networks make pornography available alongside music and movies, although it's unlikely that Valenti would defend the copyright of the pornographers themselves. Instead, file-trading is guilty by association, an association with the filthiest of smut:

We know that the infestation of p2p not only threatens the well-being of the copyright industries but consumers and their families as well. As hearings in the House and Senate have conclusively established, downloading Kazaa, Gnutella, Morpheus, Grokster, etc., . . . can bring into your home and expose your children to pornography of the most vile and depraved character imaginable. Most insidious of all, the pornography finds its way to your children disguised as wholesome material: your son or daughter may "search" for "Harry Potter" or "Britney Spears," and be confronted with files that contain bestiality or child pornography . . . the business model that current p2p networks celebrate as "the digital democracy" is built on the fetid foundation of pornography and pilfered copyrighted works.[74]

The risk of stumbling across "the most throat-choking child porn"[75] "on a scale so squalid it will shake the very core of your being"[76] was combined with a series of other threats already associated with the Internet: peer-to-peer "can lay bare your most private financial and personal information to identity thieves"[77] and expose computers to "computer viruses" and "spyware."[78] With this link, peer-to-peer file-trading was placed in the alliterative legacy of Internet panics: porn, privacy, and now piracy.

It is important to note here that stronger copyright laws would have no consequences for these other digital scourges, unless of course (contrary to claims made in the Napster case and elsewhere) the goal was not just to protect copyright, but to shut down peer-to-peer networks altogether. This conflation of evils was designed not only to encourage stronger copyright rules, but also to work against the entire system of amateur distribution that could challenge the existing arrangements preferred by the movie studios.

Most important, considering the political ethos of the moment, was the association of peer-to-peer file-trading with the darkest of bogeymen, global terrorism. In testimony given to a subcommittee of the U.S. House of Representatives, Valenti linked copyright infringement to organized crime and international terrorism, quoting an article from *U.S. Customs Today*: "A lucrative trafficking in counterfeit and pirate products—music, movies, seed patents, software, tee-shirts, Nikes, knock-off CDs and 'fake drugs' accounts for much of the money the international terrorist network depends on to feed its operations."[79] In a later statement made to the Committee on Foreign Relations of the U.S. Senate, Valenti warned that "Interpol believes there is a significant link between counterfeiting and terrorism in locations where there are entrenched terrorist groups. How much of the revenues flow to terrorists is hard to measure, but doubtless it is there."[80]

To make this association stick required a set of additional rhetorical moves; notice that both statements above were not about online peer-to-peer file trading, but about the more the traditional "hard" piracy of VHS tapes and DVDs, which is a much more widespread problem than peer-to-peer file-trading has ever posed. The line between hard and "soft" (i.e., online) piracy was regularly blurred in Valenti's statements, helping both to equate them and to suggest that the justification for government intervention already in place to stop the one should justify efforts to stop the other. The elision was subtle. Sometimes they were simply treated as two parts of a single problem: "Brooding over the global reach of the American movie and its persistent success in attracting consumers of every creed, culture, and country is thievery, the theft of our movies in both the analog and digital formats."[81] At other moments, it was an elision from one to the other over the course of an argument. Consider the move in his September 30, 2003, statement to a Senate subcommittee. First, he addresses online file-trading: "Can anyone deny that when one can upload and download movies in seconds or minutes the rush to illegally obtain films will reach the pandemic stage? Can anyone deny the degrading impact this will have on the movie industry? And can anyone deny that limitless stealing of creative works will have a soiling impact on the national economy?"[82] Then the very next paragraph begins, "Not only is this piracy endemic in the United States, it flourishes abroad, though most of the pilfering is in the analog format: videocassettes and optical discs, as well as counterfeiting of DVDs. A good part of that thievery springs from organized criminal organizations."[83] In the course of four sentences, peer-to-peer file-trading becomes black-market DVD piracy becomes organized crime. The tenuous links are again built rhetorically, by laying each threat atop the other and mapping all onto a single and unquestionable moral dichotomy.

The semantic associations of witchcraft / anarchy / invasion / disease painted file-trading as a monstrous violation, while the associations of child pornography / identity theft / computer virus / organized crime / terrorism linked file-trading to a gang of established villains. This kind of rhetorical strategy replaces rational debate with the politics of fear, and replaces discussion with a flight-or-flight response. As Robin warns, "Looking to political fear as the ground for our public life, we refuse to see the grievances and controversies that underlie it. We blind ourselves to the real-world conflicts that make fear an instrument of political rule and advance, deny ourselves the tools that might mitigate those conflicts, and ultimately ensure that we stay in the thrall of fear."[84] Fear offers compelling rationalizations to those looking for ways to align with the political and economic aims of the film industry, and helps to build a high moral barrier against those who might want to argue against them. Critics are left in the untenable position of seeming to defend pornography and terrorism, while neglecting children, families, and the basic moral values of democratic society.

Introducing . . . the Celestial Jukebox

The virtuoso flair of Valenti's proclamations was certainly compelling, and the structure of his narrative logic was nearly airtight. Nevertheless, his was not an entirely unproblematic discursive strategy. In particular, it could easily have put Hollywood on the wrong side of two issues. First, the rhetorical thrust of Valenti's position required him to characterize file-traders as pirates, willful violators of both legal and moral standards, a corrosive scourge to be cleansed. Yet these miscreants were also legitimate consumers of their products. Without some care, his characterization of this problem could have come off as anticonsumer—a problem the major record labels ran into when they started to sue individuals for trading music over peer-to-peer networks. Second, his depiction of the Internet as a dangerous technology and of cyberspace as lawless and amoral came at a moment when many saw the Internet as the pinnacle of innovation and the savior of U.S. business. His position could also have been construed as anti-Internet, which could easily have resonated as antitechnology and antiprogress.

Valenti solved both problems with a final rhetorical gambit. He suggested that, while digital technology and networked distribution were facilitating copyright infringement, they were also the key to a radically new consumer experience with culture: instant access, infinite choice, pristine quality, interactive possibilities. This "celestial jukebox"[85] would be Hollywood's greatest accomplishment—provided that copyright be extended to and strengthened for the Internet.

Describing this digital cornucopia was an opportunity for Valenti to give the battle a positive spin, or at least give some sign of good faith that the MPAA was not just after backward-looking protectionism against any and all challengers. It was important that he make this clear, especially as critics began taking the film and music industries that he task for dragging their feet in designing legitimate alternatives for online distribution. But this was also a chance for him to continue to discursively frame the controversy in terms most amenable to the film industry's corporate agenda, now with a careful portrayal of the population of cyberspace and their goals.

First, it was imperative that Valenti describe Internet users as consumers, replacing the active connotations of use with the more passive terminology associated with buying. Yochai Benkler notes a general move in the opposite direction—the rhetoric of digital culture tends to address people as users of tools, rather than as consumers of goods, who actively engage with information rather than passively receiving it. He has urged that Internet policy recognize and support this important shift in subject positions.[86] Valenti's industry would be best served by resisting this trend and continuing to equate Internet use with media consumptions, renaming interactivity as consumer choice. "All this," Valenti argued, would be "to the ultimate benefit of American consumers, 99.9 percent of whom are not hackers, who have moral standards which inhabit their daily conduct. Consumers would readily rent or buy movies on the Net—at fair prices. They would have an additional choice, how they want to watch movies, when they want to watch them."[87]

Valenti populated this normalized category of consumers with a series of subject positions, all of which are traditionally sacred figures in regulatory policy: "families,"[88] "parents,"[89] "children,"[90] "students."[91] These are consumers who traditionally require protection from the aforementioned horrors of the unregulated market: pornography, spyware, terrorism, etc. He then contrasted these virtuous and vulnerable consumers with their opposite: "digital thieves,"[92] "hackers,"[93] "pirates."[94] He drew this contrast as a bright-line distinction; there was no room in his rhetoric for people who inhabit several of these categories simultaneously. As these distinctions were elaborated and reaffirmed in speech after speech, Valenti positioned his industry as the champion of both the consumer and the

Internet, working desperately to ensure that the Internet reaches its commercial potential, under constant threat from the forces that will lead it to anarchy:

The movie industry is eager to use the Internet to deploy our movies, thousands of titles of every genre, to homes in this country and around the world. We want to give American families additional options for watching movies. They can make their choices easily, as well, when they want to see a movie. All at fair and reasonable prices, a phrase to be defined by the consumer and no one else. . . . There is only one barrier to expand [sic] this immense bounty of movies and other entertainment for consumers. It is a forest thickly crowded with outlaws whose mission in life is to hijack movies and upload them to the Internet; then the feeding begins with illegal downloads. Once we defeat this illegitimacy, the consumers of America will be the cheerful beneficiaries of a never-ending source of high-value entertainment in a lawful environment.[95]

Digital technology, in this characterization, would be enhanced by the legal and technological protection of the industry's product, and individuals would be consumers, not pirates, satisfied by the appealing digital environment that the industry promised to produce. Dystopian scaremongering was served up alongside its sparkling alternative: Should the copyright wars end in the defeat of the industry, piracy will undermine culture and kill the Internet; should the threat be successfully curtailed, the industry will lead cultural production to a digital, consumer paradise. It is this promise that has continued to provide the rhetorical cover for the recent efforts to impose DRM and trusted computing.

The last step in the logic, then, was to make clear what would allow this promise to be delivered, what would ensure that we all make the moral choice to be consumers rather than thieves. For Valenti, technological solutions held a special place in his narrative, offering the very same kind of magic that his industry finds so threatening: "If technology breeds an unwholesome felicitous ease for illegitimate downloads—and it does—then technology with all its alluring legerdemain can be the salvation for the protection of valuable creative works—and it will."[96] The DRM arrangements he obliquely proposed here promised to act as the "shield"[97] against the corrosive influence of peer-to-peer piracy. Discursively, it was a neat fit with the spatialized metaphors of invasion and infection Valenti deployed. Technology promised not only to be the cure to this ill, but also to be a simple, fair, and comprehensive cure—a far cry from the ambiguity and partiality of legal and economic measures.

Still, while technology continued to hold a coveted place in Valenti's argument, offering a sheen of novelty that suggested new days were ahead, more often than not, technology was only a part of his proposed plan. Extending the battle metaphor, Valenti proposed to "attack this problem on a number of fronts,"[98] offering a litany of legal and institutional interventions that must be brought together to collectively overcome this threat. On the technological side of this "multi-faceted approach,"[99] he called for "a digital environment that offers the security necessary to attract high value content."[100] On the legal side, "strong legal protection must be adopted and, more importantly, vigorously enforced worldwide if sufficient intellectual property incentives for creative effort are to be preserved."[101] This included suing websites that made decryption tools available, bringing injunctions against ISPs that refused to hand over the names of their customers, proposing new laws criminalizing peer-to-peer networks and digital music hardware, spearheading international treaty efforts that would extend these laws to partner nations and encourage their enforcement, and initiating individual lawsuits against those customers caught downloading films. Valenti also regularly spotlighted his industry's educational campaigns, which strove to instill a respect for copyrights in viewers and make clear the legal danger of doing otherwise.[102] He referenced the MPAA's pursuit of partnerships with universities to further educate college students, seen as the most prolific downloaders, and to impose bandwidth regulations when threats of punitive action proved insufficient. He noted new ways to track the circulation of material and the IP addresses of those who circulate it. And, in later speeches, he pointed insistently to the development of legitimate alternatives for the regulated distribution of digital movies—"keep in mind that movie producers and distributors are filled with optimism over the prospect of the Internet as another new delivery system to dispatch their movies to consumers, at a fair and reasonable price."[103] In other words, Valenti called, step by step, for the construction of a regime of alignment; together, his statements laid out a map of the heterogeneous elements required to produce it.

Most important, perhaps, in this array of possible solutions, was the number and variety of institutions that would have to cooperate to put these plans into action: not just the studios and Congress, but consumer electronics manufacturers, IT hardware manufacturers, software designers, ISPs, universities, libraries, artists, producers, the other content industries (his "kinsmen in the copyright arena"[104]), and international governments. To establish these partnerships meant instilling in each a palpable sense that both faced this threat, and both should face it together. Many of Valenti's speeches were to these communities directly; those that were not still attempted to normalize the perception that all of these institutional actors were in the same boat.

In Valenti's rhetoric, the effort to implicate all these actors did not take the form of specific arguments for how peer-to-peer file-trading would impact this business model or that trade partnership. His goal was a deeper one—the invocation of kinship, a dedication to a common purpose, and the call to join him in a great crusade—one that promised spiritual and economic glory. To the Consumer Electronics Manufacturers Association, Valenti began by stating his mission,

to talk to you about that ill-lit future and why your industry and mine are bound together, lashed to the bow of the same vessel guided by the same compass course, riding the same tidal trajectory. That which your industry makes and markets represents miracle delivery systems which transport to consumers whatever it is they find alluring and attractive. That which my industry creates and distributes is the allure, the attraction. Neither of us can find our way alone to that imprecise bewitchery which we call "the future". We have had our moments in the past where we circled each other in an uneasy state of antagonism, sometimes quarreling in confusion and doubt. But now, we are partners, welded in common purpose. For no matter how the future will finally be defined, there is one constant which if we treat casually will one day enfeeble us. That constant is the sanctity of copyright ownership. We are pledged to honor and protect it, thereby making forever certain that the new digital magic will rise to the highest point to which it can soar, without soiling the protective embrace of copyright or narrowing your own reach.[105]

Importantly, the project requires both the "attraction" of film and the "miracle" of its technological delivery. This symbiosis has been the basis of every partnership between content and hardware industries. But it is also its structural weakness, in that this partnership is always vulnerable to a scenario in which one partner refuses to go along with the crusade.

Setting the Terms

Whether or not Valenti's speeches were elements of a grand plan, and whether or not his statements were coordinated with others coming from the major content corporations in any deliberate way, together they articulated an approaching peril and a possible redemption that has proven a particularly effective rhetorical strategy. First, online copyright infringement and the emergent peer-to-peer file-trading networks were portrayed as threats to not only the Hollywood studios, but also the entire industry (which implicated and rallied manufacturers and distributors), artists (which conveniently lent the industry's commercial imperatives a more noble sheen), and consumers. It was also described as corrosive to the Internet itself in order to enlist cyberspace enthusiasts eager to build virtual community with progressive possibilities, as well as legislators eager to fortify a global telecommunication network beneficial to U.S. commercial and political aspirations. Peer-to-peer was framed not merely as a private economic liability but as a public danger—in the specific terms of copyright, and also in terms of ambiguous links to everything from child pornography to cyberterrorism—and highlighted as a reasonable object of federal legislation. And the music and film industries were careful to always frame the threat in implicitly or explicitly legal terms, helping pave the way for court challenges to follow.

The perceived threat the Internet posed to producers, and the language of copyright in which it was wrapped, offered a rich ideological vocabulary with which these industries could pursue what was to their particular commercial advantage. Justified in compelling terms such as progress, culture, art, and democracy, copyright granted the music and film industries one kind of moral high ground. This contrasted quite neatly with the perceived lawlessness of the Internet "frontier,"[106] which seemed in dire need of lawmen so that homesteaders might risk the journey. Each step of this logic can be challenged, of course, as a particular gloss on a much more complex issue. But it effectively drew on and reinforced a familiar sense of how things work, linked to other issues with similar frameworks that have rhetorical pull at this cultural moment.

As Chas Crichter observes, "Moral crusades are initiated by moral entrepreneurs, using the issue as a vehicle for their own interests. To become a moral panic, a crusade has to mobilize a wider constituency with a variety of interests. The crusade is an organized agitation, the moral panic a contingent alliance of interests."[107] This tale of digital piracy has become a moral panic, in that its claims have been embraced by these wider, and politically consequential, communities. Though not yet taken as incontrovertible fact, the story proffered by Valenti and his fellow industry representatives has proven persuasive in the courts, in the halls of Congress, and among related industry partners. To some extent, it has become an available commonsense proposition in the court of public opinion as well, one self-evident way of understanding digital technology and its impact on culture.

To demonstrate the impact of Valenti's rhetoric does not require finding his particular metaphors in the mouths of others. In some ways, his slightly absurdist overstatements and rhetorical flourishes carve out an extreme position precisely so that others can take more "reasonable" stances that nevertheless embrace his underlying view of things. Of course, it's not hard to find places where the factoids and bullet points offered by Valenti's speeches find their way into the hands of legislators. For example, California Representative Howard Berman introduced his "P2P Piracy Prevention Act" to the House in 2002 with the following statement:

The massive scale of P2P piracy and its growing breadth represents a direct threat to the livelihoods of U.S. copyright creators, including songwriters, recording artists, musicians, directors, photographers, graphic artists, journalists, novelists, and software programmers. It also threatens the survival of the industries in which these creators work, and the seamstresses, actors, Foley artists, carpenters, cameramen, administrative assistants, and sound engineers these industries employ. As these creators and their industries contribute greatly both to the cultural and economic vitality of the U.S., their livelihoods and survival must be protected.[108]

It's not just that Berman's district is the Los Angeles basin. The curiously film-specific jobs populating his second sentence should probably prompt us to reflect back on both the opening paragraph of Valenti's stock speech, and the 2004-5 MPAA publicity campaign that put "trailers" in movie theaters in which actual camera operators and set designers explained how piracy threatens their livelihood.

To look for specific words to travel from Valenti to lawmaker to journalist to user would be to subscribe to a simplistic understanding of the dynamics of political discourse. Instead, we must look for the circulation and acceptance of particular paradigms—not claims that copyright infringement is a "disease" per se, but the creeping embrace of the idea of file-traders as pirates, the comfortable positioning of them as generally bad figures in contrast to generally good consumers and generally noble artists and producers. Nissenbaum, discussing the way the public characterization of "hacker" has shifted from misfit programmer to dangerous criminal, observes that "the transformation has been achieved not through direct public debate over conflicting ideals and interests but through an ontological shift mediated by supportive agents of key societal institutions: legislative bodies, the courts, and the popular media."[109] Such is the case here. This kind of shift in meaning does not simply happen. It must be produced, through the articulation and rearticulation of the technologies, people, and activities involved, until one view becomes commonplace, dominant, unassailable. The normalization of cyberspace through the articulation of deviance[110] is precisely what Valenti had in mind when he spoke of emerging civilizations threatened by unseemly hordes and villains. The consequences of these paradigm shifts can be profound, if not always easy to pinpoint.

Halbert noticed one such shift in the consideration of the Internet as a threat to property, one that predates Valenti's speeches discussed here but not his involvement in the effort to frame these issues. She points to two characterizations of the Internet and its implications for copyright, in reports issued by the (now defunct) Office of Technology Assessment, one in 1985 and one in 1994. The 1994 report depicted the Internet as a threat to intellectual property holders, in much the same terms as the IITF White Paper did just a year later. The earlier document from the same organization was much more circumspect, suggesting that the Internet was largely a positive transformation that could usher in new forms of authorship and new structures of economic compensation. The OTA argued that the Internet should be nurtured, and recommended holding off on instituting any changes to copyright law. According to Halboert, "Perhaps the greatest difference between the 1985 report and the 1994 report is that in 1985 the new dimensions of authorship were not billed as threats to property and ownership, but seen as challenges and opportunities."[111] Momentarily visible in the first report is a network that seems to encourage users to produce, and to do so according to new priorities; by the second, the assumption that content owners will be unwilling to put their content online without new copyright assurances has taken hold.

To be sure, Valenti and his colleagues have not achieved some sort of perfect consensus. There is not even consensus within the music and movie industries, or among producers and artists, and there are certainly still vocal critics of Valenti's stance. Instead, what is significant is the way in which some details, once contested, have been taken off the table. Even among those who regularly use peer-to-peer file-trading networks and have little sympathy for the economic imperatives of the music and movie industries, most accept that peer-to-peer is hurting those industries, and even that their actions are in some sense immoral. The effort to render Valenti's views ubiquitous, and to marginalize alternative ways of looking at the issue, may be even more powerful than the political lobbying that Valenti's rhetoric accompanies.

This is also not to suggest that Valenti and his corporate colleagues were the only ones trying to win this battle discursively. I could just as well have told the story of the efforts to characterize peer-to-peer use as "sharing," mp3s as a "revolution," or the more recent, organizing efforts of the "free culture" movement or the "creative commons" project to give name to these activities and credit to their principles. Just as this dispute has been fought in the courts and in Congress, it has been a competition of discursive paradigms, each viewpoint seeking a foothold in the public consciousness, each looking to debunk or, ideally, erase the other. In its earliest days, Napster got as much positive press as negative. File-trading was legitimately described as "sharing" as often as it was called "piracy." Those who hoped peer-to-peer technologies would succeed chose words that, while casting peer-to-peer use in a more favorable light, also evoked systems of communication and society that they hoped to encourage. Dubbing the use of Napster "file-sharing" (or "file-swapping") situated it in both a model of exchange based on gifts rather than commodities, and an ethic of altruism, selflessness, and equality; the term lent the new practices a useful cover against the charge of piracy. The contrast between the two perspectives offered journalists a conveniently two-sided controversy; a *U.S. News and World Report* article at the time asked, "Is It Sharing or Stealing?"[112] and was genuinely open to it being either. "Sharing" is a compelling trope; it not only depends on a kind of kindergarten fairness, it calls upon specific discourses about the shape and purpose of the Internet that had quite a bit of cultural currency at the time.

The major entertainment corporations attempted to defuse this language directly by explicitly redefining it, as in their original complaint when they stated that "Napster has created a fully integrated system that enables users to "share" (i.e., illegally download or permit the downloading of) the MP3 music files on their hard drives."[113] This attempted to reveal the word "share" as code for behavior they hoped the courts would condemn. But the more powerful response was to deploy a counterdiscourse to replace it—to offer this up in front of not just the courts, but the public, as the natural explanation of present circumstances. This required language that was not merely legal, but that carried powerful cultural connotations to further authorize its legal consequences.

We might ask why one worldview seems to have championed the other, though it's important to keep in mind that while Valenti's tale may be compelling in some contexts, the other may be more widely embraced by the less powerful but more populous group of young music fans. The discussion of Napster changed, not only with the legal judgment clarifying the court's opinion on the subject, but with persistent lobbying by Valenti, the RIAA, and others. This lobbying, not just to congressional subcommittees, but on college campuses and even in industry-produced educational materials designed for schoolchildren, pitched copyright protection as an overwhelming good and infringement as a violation of the golden rule. The industry's persistence in framing the story in these terms, backed by its immense resources, helped stabilize their version of the story, casting content owners as the victims and technical copy protection as the valiant hero destined to protect helpless consumers and vanquish the villain of piracy. And the linkage between a moral fable and a legal one gave this characterization the full weight and authority of the courts, something peer-to-peer boosters did not have for their argument.

"The Earth is flat" is a powerful statement, but in its demonstrative confidence as a declaration, it makes itself available for scrutiny and refutation. As a claim, it necessarily remains open to dispute. What may be more compelling are characterizations of the world inside of comments that do not announce themselves as such. As Todd Gitlin argues, one of the most powerful dimensions of the coverage of a news event is its "framing"[114]— that is, what the report presumes to be significant, how it certifies the relevant players, how it narrates the conflict. Each statement renders others invisible. The frame is most powerful not for what it includes, but for what it leaves out as either insignificant or obvious. The acceptance of terms like "pirate" and "consumer" accepts their implicit assertions of right and wrong, of what the Internet should be for, of what ends copyright should serve. This carves the world into social categories that preempt debate by defining the harder questions away.[115] This sleight of hand is not that of the magician; it is the more human trickery of three-card monte: the art of distraction, the small gesture behind the grand one, the ability to play on the expectations of the crowd, all in an attempt to hide the object and slip away with a few extra dollars.

Copyright law offers content owners ways to distract the public, to cloak economic self-interest in apparently noble, just, or obvious terms. The valorization of authorship has always been a rhetorical flourish for masking how often the rights reside not with authors but with publishers. Another is the incentive argument, which is regularly invoked to justify stronger and stronger copyright protection. It is not so much a falsehood as it is an illusion: Authors may very well thrive from incentives of some kind, but the incentives that corporate distributors proclaim in the name of authors rarely actually reach them, while other motives for cultural production are overshadowed. Similarly, Valenti's rhetoric aimed to articulate the concerns about copyright protection and online infringement in a way that—knowingly or otherwise, or somewhere in between—would draw our cultural attention away from the economic strategies it was designed to pursue. These claims, which have proven a strikingly compelling way to enlist legal and legislative resources, are increasingly a cover for building not better copy protection but better mechanisms of commerce.

Valenti's narrative of sin and redemption utilized the specter of Internet piracy to provide a cultural justification for technical copy protection and the legal foundations it would require. His tale was a call to arms to put together the pieces of a regime of alignment, and to give it both moral and economic imperative as justification. In the process, this narrative masked the other reasons for pursuing such a system, reasons that extend well beyond those copyright was historically designed to serve. But for this sociotechnical ensemble to take shape, it would require more than just a grand tale; it would require persuading the major players in related industries, especially the makers of consumer electronics and computing technologies, to align politically and economically with the content industries in this complex endeavor. For these industries to join forces, despite their sometimes quite divergent aims and worldviews, would require more than a compelling drama about the threat of piracy. It would require institutional agreement to work toward particular standards and technologies that would together form a trusted system.

Copyright law attempts to ease a fundamental tension inherent in the act of publication: how authors can control their work after handing it to the public. How do you give someone a valuable resource and then prevent them from exploiting it? Until recently, copyright law was the primary means for imposing rules on the user of culture. Copyright owners can call upon the courts to intervene after someone has violated their rights by duplicating or distributing their work without authorization. This depends first and foremost on the legal authority to intervene where creators otherwise could not.

There is a second means for content owners to regulate what people do with a work: by limiting and regulating access to it. This strategy has (until now) not been part of copyright law, but is a common way for owners and distributors to regulate use of their work themselves. It is the strategy of the "velvet rope." Although copyright law applies to movies, the *main* way in which we are prevented from copying movies when they appear in the theater is that we can only get in to view them once, and getting in comes with rules, including not bringing in video cameras. As long as the work is kept in a particular place, and access to that place is regulated and monitored, use of that work can also be regulated. This strategy relies in important ways on technological barriers, be they material or, more recently, digital. Before the days of the printing press, in the days when books were laboriously transcribed by monks, some expensive and sacred texts were bound with iron chains built into the spine. The scribes would keep the book physically locked to a lectern, so that readers who were granted access would not walk away with the valuable manuscript or otherwise mistreat it. Museums, historical libraries, and art galleries regularly place the works they display behind closed doors, Plexiglas, security guards, and metal detectors, using the architecture of the building to help them carefully regulate who gets in, what they can do there, and how long they are permitted to stay.

DRM is designed according to this second logic—not putting the work in a walled physical space, but locking it inside a digital encryption algorithm such that, even as the work is distributed far and wide, access requires permission. DRM regulates use indirectly, by governing access to the work under agreed-upon conditions that describe appropriate use. That this strategy is being given legal teeth in the law marks a shift in the logic of copyright, which is embracing access restrictions for the first time.

Technical constraints offer a number of benefits over traditional law enforcement. Enforcing copyright law depends on locating and prosecuting pirates, a haphazard and costly project. Most users slip quietly under the radar. Technological measures, on the other hand, can be imposed on every single user and enforced automatically. Legal measures can only punish those who have already violated a copyright, often well after the financial damage is done. With technological constraints, infringements can be anticipated and preempted. Turning to the law to protect copyright means involving the bureaucratic machinery of law enforcement and the courts in every instance. Technological measures, while by no means simple to install, involve little institutional effort to see them through. In addition, particularly with digital technology, the regulations imposed by technology may be much more precise than legal measures can be— meaning the intervention made by or on behalf of copyright owners may be as intricate as they see fit.

There are two things to notice about this alternative (or perhaps complementary) approach. First, it shifts the point of control such that it is simultaneous with the moment of sale. It is convenient, and not coincidental, that access controls mesh with the mechanisms for purchasing that content: a nickel for a peep, a ticket for entry, a subscription fee for a month of digital access. P. T. Barnum even duped his audiences into buying only access and nothing more: "This way to the egress." The technological control is both a barrier and a tollgate; use follows access, access requires payment. In fact, the fantasy of DRM is the perfect merger of these two functions: a system that perfectly regulates access, both to protect content from unauthorized copying and to automate perfect commercial transactions for that content, one solution for both ends.

Second, to regulate access rather than punish misuse requires the mobilization of very different resources. It requires the general agreement, voluntary or otherwise, of a series of actors who must together manage access to the work at various points. This kind of access control is easiest to enforce when the owner of the work is also its distributor, as with the sacred text chained to the lectern. In modern media culture, we rarely expect content owners to also act as distributors anymore. It is nearly impossible to distribute work on a mass scale without the help of industrial-strength third parties. Now, to the extent that producers hope to regulate the use of their work through access controls, they must somehow convince or compel distributors and hardware manufacturers to adopt, honor, and sometimes help enforce their system. These entities may have quite different economic and ideological viewpoints on how the content should move, yet these alliances are still possible. For example, though movie studios at one time owned the theaters where their films screened, now they contract with independent theater chains to distribute their movies. Yet this contract includes an obligation on the theater owner's part to have employees patrol audiences in search of illicit video cameras, a burden that does not in any direct way improve the theater's bottom line.

This kind of symbiosis may be getting easier, as the recent deregulation and concentration of the culture industries increasingly allows corporations to own the content, distribution, and hardware. Once again, organizations like Sony and Time Warner find themselves with the means to set the technological access rules for their own content if they so choose. But beyond such cases, access control strategies still require (relatively) independent organizations to be drawn into alignment, through contract, legal obligation, shared sense of purpose, or government intervention.

This kind of political mobilization is what may hold together the regime of alignment that could support DRM, or may prove insufficient against the unruly forces that do not share its political and economic goal. The success of DRM will not be a technological feat, but a political project in which the content industries try to bring together allies that can collude to enforce their rules on users. As these industries explore the possibility of building a trusted system, it is crucial that we examine the techniques by which they attempt to forge such alignment. The history of DRM and technical copyright mechanisms will be the story of these attempts to mobilize institutional alignment, and of the consequences of these mobilization efforts, as much as it will be a story about the particular implications of DRM itself.

Industry Standards

Despite the obvious symbiosis of entertainment and technology companies, as we will see, such alliances are not easy to accomplish. Left to their own devices, companies that produce entertainment often have significantly different world views and business plans than those that produce technology. Yet such alliances are crucial, not just for regulatory strategies such as DRM, but also for agreeing on the increasingly complex engineering terms by which content and hardware will interoperate. Much of this collaboration occurs inside of interindustry consortia, an increasingly common means of setting technical standards outside of government authorized standard-setting organizations (SSOs). It is worth considering these curious formations, in that nearly all of the important forms of DRM have sprung from them—or were actually designed by them. These consortia typically aspire to voluntary agreement of their members, although the practical realities of negotiation between powerful actors means that what is said to be voluntary may in truth not be quite so. This emphasis on voluntary consensus has posed a particular challenge for the development of DRM.

Setting technical standards of interoperability is an especially important aspect of the business of information technology, particularly in light of the infrastructure of networks and the economic imperatives they impose. Communication networks tend to experience "network effects" or "positive network externalities," meaning that the value of being part of the network increases the more users adopt it. The paradigmatic example of this is the fax machine: The first one sold was worthless; only when a second was bought did the first fax machine owner have anyone to communicate with. According to Michael Katz and Carl Shapiro, this is the first level of network effects: The value of the network is in some ways its users, so adoption of the network increases the value of the network for all. Second, as a common platform is increasingly embraced, third-party vendors tend to gravitate toward it, building more services or software for it, further increasing its value. Part of the value of owning a Windows PC is the relative wealth of software written for the Windows environment, as compared to competing operating systems. Third, service and maintenance may be more available for more commonly adopted platforms, further increasing their value to each user—the dearth of mechanics trained to repair Ferraris is a prohibitive factor that does not apply to Fords and Toyotas.[1]

For each of these reasons, network infrastructures experience an acute pressure to move toward interoperability. Networks are produced by many providers, each of whom would like to be the sole source of what they provide; but because the value of the network as a whole depends on its uniformity and interoperability, there's an economic pressure to collaborate with those who provide other components of the network, even with direct competitors.[2] Since growing the network benefits all the firms involved, it is generally in their best interest to agree on standards for interconnection. Further, there is societal benefit to doing so: users would much prefer one standard for cell phones that allows everyone to call each other regardless of what service provider they've chosen or what brand of phone they're using. This extends to the content provided for networks: An agreed-upon format for CDs means anyone can press a CD that any user can listen to on any CD player. The "standards war" between VHS and Betamax in the 1980s reminds us how problematic incompatible formats can be. Technical standards setting has therefore become a site of strategic importance for manufacturers, service providers, and content producers, as well as a site of political importance to the extent that the way we design technologies has consequence for what users do with them.

Establishing standards for technology is not a new phenomenon, though it is only in the twentieth century that manufacturers and governments have taken them seriously enough to move beyond casually organized gatherings of engineers. This has resulted in the emergence of standards-setting organizations (SSOs) such as the National Institute of Standards and Technology (NIST), the International Telecommunications Union (ITU), and the Internet Engineering Task Force (IETF). The institutional cultures of these organizations tend to value openness in participation and process, balancing the interests of their participants with broader public concerns. As a consequence, they tend to work slowly. Some critics worry that these public organizations cannot keep up with the fast pace of innovation in information technology, and that their neutral veneer often masks a kind of industrial capture by the powerful companies that dominate the industry in question.

But increasingly, standards are also being negotiated inside an array of trade associations and intra- and cross-industry consortia that, while often careful not to present themselves as standards organizations, regularly develop "technical working groups" within which to pursue shared technical arrangements. Organizations such as the DVD Forum, SDMI, and the Copy Protection Technology Working Group (which will play a vital role in the next two chapters) allow content producers to meet with consumer electronics and information technology manufacturers to discuss technical formats, as well as the economic and political arrangements that will accompany them. Some may have open membership and procedures, but more often these groups limit membership by imposing large fees and establishing their own rules for informal discussion and agreement.[3] In the digital media industries and in other telecommunication and IT industries, these consortia are increasingly seen as a more effective way to reach technical coordination than the official SSOs.[4] However, it is important to note that this shift in the locus of standards setting has important implications for what standards are chosen, how they are chosen, and why.

The existing literature on these industry consortia is scant. Some attention has been paid to whether such organizations are more effective than SSOs in developing standards, whether the standards they produce are better, and how independent firms manage to cooperate within such consortia even when they are competitors in the market. There has also been discussion regarding the role of intellectual property in such coordination; often the standards being debated include technologies whose patents are held by members of the discussion, giving them a special interest in the outcome.[5] Finally, some discussion has addressed the antitrust concerns that might surround such consortia. That these gatherings of competitors can even exist is an artifact of antitrust law: While collusion and price fixing is illegal, the law recognizes that competing manufacturers must often cooperate to set standards such that their products interoperate, or such that quality and safety across the industries is preserved.[6] There are guidelines for what can and cannot be discussed in such gatherings so that antitrust violations do not occur, but within those guidelines there seems to be a great deal of breathing room, largely because standardization is seen as generally supporting competition rather than squelching it.[7]

The important question being overlooked here is not whether the consortia afford competitors the opportunity to engage in price fixing, but whether standards themselves can be a form of collusion, a means not to fix prices or achieve monopoly, but to preserve both oligopoly control over a market and, more importantly, to stabilize a particular business paradigm, within which the participants can then continue to compete. In some instances, standards can quietly offer market benefits to some players more than others. Certainly, if one participant already owns patents on the technology or technique being adopted, they can benefit financially by the arrangement. But even if this is not the case, members of a consortium can agree upon a way of doing business, bound to the technology they standardize, that benefits them all by excluding competitors who might develop not a new technology, but a new paradigm. The entire industry then becomes a cartel joined not through conspiracy but through a commitment to a particular technology. In a market that exhibits network effects, the traditional dynamics of market competition do not apply: since incremental advantages in the market can magnify into a de facto standard, it benefits firms not only to interconnect but also to stabilize the market as it is currently carved up, to avoid being squeezed out of existence by a Microsoft or an Intel. What looks like self-regulation may work to block upstarts that might offer better alternatives.[8]

The apparent neutrality of technical standards always cloaks their politics. Choosing the "best" standard is always a coded embrace of the logic by which one determines what is "best," including the implied goals (economic or otherwise), the acceptable risks, and the strategy for achieving those goals. What the industry consortia responsible for implementing DRM have been after is not just choosing *which* DRM system to embrace, but establishing that DRM is necessary in the first place. This does not just lock in a standard, it locks in a paradigm. The standard presumes particular legal and economic arrangements, which themselves become standardized.

Recognizing the role of these industry consortia sheds new light on the previous chapter's discussion of the amplified rhetoric around digital copyright. Adopting a DRM standard benefits the content industries involved only if one accepts the premise put forth by Valenti and his colleagues. To present the Internet as an imperative for all industries provides a rationale, besides pure economic self-interest, for developing the industry consortia themselves. DRM becomes the premise that precedes the consortia discussion, rather than the question it must answer. In other words, according to Richard Hawkins, "The assumption is that membership in the consortium implies agreement with its technical objectives and that lack of agreement can be expressed without penalty by leaving the consortium."[9] What this excludes are firms that might not embrace the DRM at all, might pursue distribution arrangements and consumer technologies that don't accept the underlying premise, and might accept unprotected music formats and peer-to-peer file-trading as a marketplace reality that can be turned to their benefit. The result is a "tipping" not toward one firm, but toward the DRM strategy itself, such that all the firms that embrace it enjoy protection of their own business models, as well as the chance to exploit new pricing structures offered by that arrangement, safe from competitors who might make technologies with less restriction.

Most important is the way that such private standard setting can work against the interests of the public. As Hawkins notes, "Although in principle the aim of voluntary standardization is to produce standards that will be available on a non-discriminatory basis for 'public' use . . . the voluntary-consensus process does not guarantee that the resulting standard will provide benefits in any truly 'public' sense. A voluntary standard may only serve to legitimize the consensus of a limited group, and its application may prejudice technological environments in favour of vested interests."[10] Official standard-setting organizations, while they may come under pressure or sometimes be captured by the industry players with the most to gain and lose, generally retain some commitment to developing open standards with some public benefit, however that benefit may be understood. Some have even begun to embrace the participatory design movement, gradually including users and user groups directly in the decisionmaking process.[11] Industry consortia need not consider public benefits or include users, and are likely only to do so when such inclusion is itself strategically beneficial to them.[12]

Robert Merges observes that these industry consortia are not unlike medieval guilds; both are "appropriability institutions" that advance collective innovation.[13] In their careful distinction between insiders and outsiders and their reliance on professional norms of conduct, both strike a balance between cooperation and competition that usually facilitates technical invention and progress. But the comparison can be taken further; medieval printing guilds also helped stabilize the market they served, collectively bargaining with suppliers and distributors, lobbying government for national privileges to compete against foreign printers, and generally working toward a kind of contained competition among themselves—in part by lobbying for copyright law to be adopted.[14] And as Adrian Johns, Michel Foucault, and others have noted, printers guilds were mechanisms of censorship as well.[15] Industry consortia similarly can regulate their market by standardizing technical protection formats and, in doing so, standardizing the economic and political paradigms they represent, depend on, and advance.

The Birth of SDMI . . .

Even within an industry consortium that agrees on some of the basic premises about what they're after, the balance between cooperation and competition is a precarious one. Too much collusion, and the industrial partnerships can run afoul of regulatory guidelines on monopolies and trusts. Regulation of communication and information industries has developed a bright-line distinction between content and conduit (those who produce information and those who deliver it) as a way to protect free speech in a world of mass communication; hybrid partnerships that cross that line can quickly raise eyebrows. On the other hand, too little cooperation and the fragile partnership can crumble as soon as one player decides it is economically savvy to break ranks. Any plan that gives the consumer less is likely to be undercut by a competitor who thinks they can give the consumer more.

The first large-scale attempt to build a multi-industry consensus behind a DRM strategy came from the U.S. record industry. As participants in the DVD Forum, a consortium formed to help work out standards for the nascent movie format, representatives from the major U.S. record labels were encouraged by the cooperation they saw there between the MPAA and the major consumer electronics manufacturers. They soon decided that they should develop their own forum for meeting representatives from the consumer electronics and information technology manufacturers, in order to pursue protection strategies for their music. The RIAA reached out to the major players in the electronics, hardware, networking, and digital content industries, from AOL to Matsushita to IBM to RealNetworks to AT&T.

In December 1998 the RIAA announced the Secure Digital Music Initiative (SDMI), promising "a framework to work with the technology community to create a voluntary digital music security specification . . . [that] will protect copyrighted music in all existing and emerging digital formats and through all delivery channels."[16] The SDMI was, for the record industry, a response to a number of concerns. The first was the dramatic popularity of the mp3 format for distributing digital music. The mp3 was quickly being embraced by both fans and artists eager to post music online and trade it across Internet communication networks and, like the "aiff" format used on CDs, it included no copy protection. The RIAA was increasingly finding their copyrighted work posted on personal websites and ftp servers, and began to anticipate the deluge of amateur file-trading that would follow. Napster had not yet been released; when it appeared a year later, it gave the RIAA member corporations even more motivation.

A second concern was the recent introduction and growing popularity of mp3 players. Diamond Multimedia had released its Rio PMP300 only two months before. Until that point, mp3 files were largely restricted to the computer. CD burners were still uncommon and expensive, and many stereos couldn't play the CD-Rs they produced. This had the side effect of limiting the popularity of mp3s to the technologically literate and quarantining it from the broader arena of music consumption. The record industry worried that the Rio might enjoy the explosive popularity of the Sony Walkman cassette player and Discman CD player, and solidify the mp3 format the way each of those devices had helped cement their fledgling formats. That October the RIAA had appealed to the courts, claiming

Diamond's device violated the Audio Home Recording Act;[17] they were quickly awarded the injunction, only to have it rescinded ten days later by a court of appeals.[18] With the portable digital music player quickly becoming a reality, the RIAA felt it needed to act fast to ensure that these devices would help fortify copyright rather than undermine it.

Finally, the music industry was concerned that early developers of proprietary digital protection formats were pursuing contracts with individual labels. While any one record company might find it tempting to quickly adopt a workable encryption format from Microsoft or AT&T and try to be first to offer digital music sales online, together they recognized that this could lead to incompatibility problems for consumers. The major labels know that their brands don't mean much to consumers; most fans seek out music by artist, not by label. If private license agreements meant that a consumer had to use one application to buy and listen to Warner music and another to listen to Universal, the entire industry might face a consumer revolt. Such a move might also vault the first label with a workable system into an enviable position of market dominance, a game everyone wanted to win but no one wanted to lose. SDMI could save the labels from a format war by establishing standards that would allow each proprietary format to follow matching guidelines, and in the process would stabilize the economic position of all the major labels in relation to each other.[19]

The technical aspirations of the SDMI coalition, which first met in February 1999, were audacious. Cary Sherman of the RIAA, speaking to representatives of over one hundred companies (membership would eventually swell to over two hundred), announced these aims in a plenary at that first meeting:

Imagine, if you will, that every computer and consumer electronics device knew how to respond to an instruction set included in any stream of music or music file. That's what SDMI would like to achieve—a specification for how music can be marked at the source, identified and labeled with rights management information that is embedded in the music or carried with it in such a way that it remains with that piece of music no matter what. No matter what system, network, or device it passes through—whether the Internet or a wireless network in the home, a set-top box or a cable modem, a CD or a new DVD-Audio disc. And any device in which it is recorded, stored, or played on will know how and where to look for and act upon that data. Whether a CD or DVD drive, a portable flash-memory device, or any of the innumerable technologies that are just over the horizon.[20]

Critics suggested that the labels were simply hoping to kill off mp3 by building devices that would refuse to play it. Sherman and other representatives of the RIAA attempted to assure critics that their aim was not to replace mp3, but rather to create a standard for how anyone could voluntarily mark music as protected. These devices would play mp3 files, but would assure artists and labels who wanted their music protected that the hardware would honor such marks. In fact, SDMI was actually after something even more clever. The goal was to build a hardware standard that would be adopted across the consumer music market, then use that market penetration to choke off mp3 by attrition, convincing users to switch to proprietary formats of their own accord through a combination of reward and disincentive.

It is important to understand the difference between watermarks and encryption; SDMI's strategy depended on both to accomplish the plan Sherman had announced. A digital watermark, like the watermark imprinted in expensive paper, is simply a mark embedded in the work that gives some information about its origin or ownership. Some are designed to withstand copying, like the watermark scrawled across a Hollywood script—copies of the work would retain information about where they came from. These marks can be used to track copying and punish those responsible. Others are designed to not survive copying and to be difficult to recreate, such as the watermarks in most paper currency, in order to show that a copy is not an original.

In digital data, a watermark can be some small bit of information, a sequence of digits, that does not affect or disrupt the use of that work but can be located by anyone who knows how to find it. This bit of code by itself does not prevent copying or affect user behavior directly; rather, it allows copying to be tracked to the source or helps distinguish copies from originals. Importantly, a digital watermark can act as a trigger, directing any technology that can detect it to act in certain ways. The plan that SDMI would develop depended on both kinds of watermarks combined with encryption. Together, they would accomplish something more than mere copy protection.

SDMI attempted to deliver its technical specifications in two phases. The first would be the open standards for portable devices, the second for a "screening" mechanism that would allow the SDMI application to spot illicit copies of once-protected music. This two-phase plan mirrored the way they hoped SDMI would be adopted by users. In the first phase, they hoped, consumers would be encouraged to purchase SDMI-compliant devices because the restrictions were minimal. The device would play music marked with the SDMI watermark and honor whatever rules it expressed (most likely, "do not copy"). It would also play unprotected mp3s without imposing rules on them. The SDMI watermark would be the "robust" kind, difficult to remove, to indicate new music from legacy music (i.e., music released before SDMI was deployed) and to articulate rules for the device to follow. Phase II would conveniently follow the adoption of many of these devices, they hoped; the appearance of music with a Phase II watermark would "trigger" the device to prompt the user to upgrade the software. The upgraded version of the device would not only honor SDMI rules but also check every recording for a "fragile" watermark. If the robust watermark were intact and the fragile one were missing, it would mean the file was an illicit copy of what was once SDMI-protected content; the device would refuse to play the file. Not only could this protect against users stripping SDMI rules from their digital downloads, but it could also curtail CD ripping, by imposing SDMI watermarks on the discs themselves.

What SDMI hoped to accomplish was to put piracy-sniffing technologies in the hands of music consumers, which they would use of their own volition. Devices would enter the market with only the slightest hint of limitation; adoption of the technologies would lodge these devices solidly in common use; the release of appealing major label content with the SDMI protection would encourage users to adopt the new format; and all of these together would persuade users to "upgrade" their devices to monitor their own illicit behavior for them.

Most important, the plan was designed to work without any binding force on its various participants. Using the specs or the watermark would be completely voluntary. Manufacturers could make non-SDMI devices if they wanted, and artists could choose to release music without the SDMI mark. But devices that did not adopt the SDMI specs would be unable to play the marked music and therefore be less desirable than their more restrictive counterparts; artists releasing unmarked music would nevertheless be drawn into the protection scheme for users who had chosen the SDMI upgrade. Brand loyalty, the lure of valuable content, and consumer inertia would move the critical mass of devices and music inexorably toward an SDMI universe, and bring users along with it.

It was a bold plan, and one that would require a deft touch and speedy resolve to get all the necessary participants in line. But it was not clear whether the record labels and the technology manufacturers could agree, given their significantly different business plans. Could record labels, who wanted as much technical copy protection and control over the use of their music as possible, reach a compromise with consumer electronics manufacturers, who wanted to give customers maximum functionality and saw the nascent mp3 player market as a potential boon? Could this compromise also entice information technology manufacturers and digital software designers to join in? Both were only beginning to contemplate the market for digital content, and generally embraced a very different model than the record labels for how to provide and profit from information—one in which copying data is fundamental to the tool and should be encouraged rather than prohibited.

In order to corral these varied institutional agendas, in February 1999 the SDMI selected as its executive director someone they thought had both the technical and managerial expertise to handle a project of this magnitude, and who was neutral in terms of the industries involved: Leonardo Chiariglione—ironically, the person most responsible for the mp3 format causing the RIAA so much grief. Head of the Fraunhofer Institute in Italy, he had been in charge of the Moving Picture Experts Group (MPEG) when it designed and released the mp3 format seven years before.

The first six months of the SDMI project were marked by a series of public statements proclaiming unanimity among the partners, coupled with hints of internecine fighting between the different industry interests. While the group tried to hammer out hardware specifications (Phase I of their plan), insiders spoke anonymously of brewing tensions. The technologists were frustrated by the record labels' ignorance of the Internet and the open standards it favored. Companies who provided security solutions were jockeying to have their proprietary formats anointed as SDMI-authorized solutions. Consumer electronics makers were holding back to see if the mp3 player market would take off on its own, and companies like Sony, who had a finger in each of these pies, found themselves stuck in the middle.[21] Side deals between individual labels and DRM providers were announced, through the spring, suggesting that those involved were hedging their bets.

But in June 1999, as scheduled, the group announced that they had settled on specifications for portable digital music devices. Devices that incorporated this spec would play protected as well as unprotected digital music; the device would prohibit the user from copying files containing the SDMI watermark. In addition, it would watch for a trigger that indicated that the device should upgrade to its Phase II functionality, yet to be specified, and that would also watch for and refuse to play pirated music.

It wouldn't be a major technical accomplishment to incorporate the means for the device to respond to a watermark that had not yet been developed. But it was a significant accomplishment to align the goals of these disparate commercial interests, at least for the moment. It required them all to embrace at least the general outline of the plan that presumably would follow: a watermark in all digital music, a set of rules for usage encoded in the watermarked files, a system to honor those rules and protect against such files being moved out of trusted space or duplicated without permission. Jack Lacy, a scientist at AT&T Laboratories and chair of the Portable Device Working Group within SDMI, praised the success of Phase I in these terms: "Through this cooperative effort each industry segment has gained a broader understanding of and appreciation for issues important to the others. This alone is a very significant achievement that is necessary to move forward and develop comprehensive specifications for the digital distribution of music."[22]

. . . And Its Ignominious Death

Following the announcement of Phase I, SDMI turned its attention to the technically more difficult task of Phase II—to turn the portable music player into a self-policing device to spot and refuse music that had been copied illicitly. Many critics suggested that this was a project foisted onto SDMI by the record industry, as a way of not only protecting voluntarily marked music (as Sherman had proclaimed) but also prohibiting unauthorized copying by designing the device to prevent playback of such copies.

At this point, substantial cracks in the institutional coalition began to appear, generally (though not always) at the fault lines between industries. In September 1999, an e-mail from Sony VP Geoffrey Anderson to Chiariglione was leaked to *CNet News* in which Anderson complained that both the sluggish bureaucracy of the consortium and the foot-dragging of other members were keeping his company from marketing SDMI devices during the upcoming holiday season.[23] Sony was the only manufacturer at this point to have developed a digital music player, the Sony Vaio Clip, that met the Phase I specifications. *CNet* theorized that the conflict was not between industries, but between competitors; Diamond, having gotten the jump on the mp3 player market, may have been slowing the process in order to better compete against Sony, who could easily overtake them. It is also possible, however, that Diamond was benefiting from the sales of unprotected mp3 players, and preferred to slow the process rather than have SDMI succeed, at which point it would likely have incorporated SDMI's standards. In April 2000, with no Phase II in sight and deadlines coming and going, Chiariglione publicly admonished the group for slowing the process and letting competing interests get in the way of moving forward. *Wired* suggested that the consensus model of decision making adopted by SDMI was to blame: A single member could stall decisions when they didn't support that member's economic interests. An unidentified source from the meetings reported, "The executive director is very concerned by the veto power that some industries in SDMI exert in SDMI because it enables some business models and disenables others, [and] considers this behavior against the terms of participation, which explicitly say that the purpose of the SDMI specification is to enable multiple business models."[24]

Other technology manufacturers may have also been hedging their bets. One member was quoted as saying, "Everyone will say, 'We support SDMI,' but in our back rooms, we are saying, 'And we are going to do things that will work in the non-SDMI world.' I'm not going out in the marketplace with a product that is tied to SDMI and not have an alternative for all of my competitors who are out there without SDMI products that are being purchased and used."[25] Moreover, with the appearance of Napster in late 1999, it became clear that the genie was very much out of the bottle, and it wasn't the fault of hardware mp3 players, as some had predicted. Users were growing accustomed not only to getting their music online but also to burning CDs or listening to it on their computers. In response to these grassroots peer-to-peer networks, all of the major record labels began preparations for digital music services of their own—Sony's Bitmusic in Japan, Sony and Universal's joint PressPlay venture, and Bertelsmann, EMI, and Warner's MusicNet service—joining a growing field of smaller startups such as MP3.com, eMusic, and Rhapsody. And each major label service would need to secure its own DRM encryption format if it hoped to distribute music while still controlling its redistribution; this meant embracing those proprietary systems being offered by Microsoft, AT&T, Intertrust, and Verance—side deals that undermined the possibility of finding a common standard.

Still, by September 2000, the group had whittled fourteen third-party submissions for Phase II down to four watermarks and two non-watermark supplements they felt could serve to identify files, discern whether they had been compressed, and do so without interfering with the experiential quality of the music. In what could only be characterized as a moment of sheer bravado, the SDMI group then issued a public challenge to hackers. They posted six copies of a song, each with one of the watermarks embedded in it, and anyone so inclined was invited to try removing the watermark without degrading the quality of the music. Chiariglione publicly announced the challenge in the form of a contest. "We are now in the process of testing the technologies that will allow these protections. The proposed technologies must pass several stringent tests: They must be inaudible, robust, and run efficiently on various platforms, including PCs.

They should also be tested by *you*. So here's the invitation: Attack the proposed technologies. Crack them."[26] Anyone who felt they had successfully removed one or more of the watermarks could submit the cracked file and an explanation of how it was done. If the cracked file no longer had the watermark, and passed the demanding criteria of "golden ears" listeners as having maintained its audio fidelity, the challenger could win up to $10,000 in prize money.

The programmer community was divided over its response to the "Hack SDMI" contest. Many wanted to embarrass the record industry. They hoped that a swift crack of all the watermarks would deliver the RIAA a public humiliation at the hands of the Netizens they had been persecuting. There was no lack of animosity for an industry long seen as undervaluing artists and strong-arming technology manufacturers, who had sued Internet users and pushed for new laws criminalizing their behavior in new ways, and who were now attempting to build a secure music delivery service that was anathema to the online culture of openness. Others, with perhaps no less sympathy for the record labels, urged hackers to hold off: to enter the contest would be to give away their labor to the enemy and would only help them develop better watermarks that would be harder to circumvent. Better to let them go to market with a flimsy watermark that could be cracked later, with greater economic harm and more public humiliation. The Electronic Frontier Foundation officially called for a boycott that was already being informally discussed; in their call they linked the hackers' concern to the fair use implications of the SDMI system, were it to work: "The Digital Music Access Technology, or DMAT, format is intended to put an encryption-based shell around digital audio content that prevents unauthorized copying or playback . . . The RIAA is mischaracterizing all 'unauthorized' access or duplication—no matter how well protected by fair use and other rights—to be copyright piracy."[27] The EFF also noted that their group, despite representing users with interests relevant to the SDMI project, had been excluded from joining the organization because they did not have a strictly commercial interest. Chiariglione was forced to open dialogue with the EFF in response to the criticism, but could not convince them to withdraw the boycott.[28]

In the end, the results of the Hack SDMI contest were themselves in dispute. Four hundred forty-seven attempted hacks were submitted. Rumors quickly circulated that all of the watermarks had been successfully removed; SDMI initially refused to comment on stories in *Salon* that quoted an anonymous insider who confirmed this. *Salon's* source even suggested that the SDMI group was itself divided in its support of these watermarks. Representatives of some of the technology manufacturers, increasingly convinced that watermarking was a dead end and eager to get on with their own proprietary arrangements, may have quietly been hoping for the watermarks to fail. "Some of SDMI's geekier members are actually *rooting* for the hackers to bust all the different watermarks. They *want* to return to square one—and possibly be forced to come up with new models for music distribution that would be both consumer and artist friendly."[29]

In November 2000, the group finally acknowledged that two of the watermarks had been successfully broken, but claimed that the others had withstood the attacks (i.e., they had been removed, but the quality of the music had been degraded in the process). But the community of hackers did not retreat quietly. Instead, they rallied around Edward Felten, a professor of computer science at Princeton University. He and his students, using the Hack SDMI challenge as a class project, believed they had successfully removed all of the watermarks. Rather than submitting their results for the prize money, they authored an academic paper about the watermarks for an upcoming conference.[30]

SDMI, its coalition already crumbling, looked to hold itself together by turning to the law to prevent this new challenge. Felten received a cease and desist letter threatening a lawsuit against him, his colleagues, the conference organizers, and his university if his team presented their paper. The charge was that, in downloading the watermarked files and assenting to the click-through license agreement, Felten had agreed to the conditions of the contest, including a confidentiality agreement. Violating this agreement might make him liable under federal contract law, as well as under the new Digital Millennium Copyright Act, for revealing how to circumvent a technological protection measure. Felten and his team pulled the conference presentation, which gave critics of the record industry and of the DMCA ample ammunition to suggest that DRM advocates wanted to squelch academic speech and computer systems research. SDMI later backed off its legal threat; Felten subsequently sued the RIAA, asking the court to guarantee his right to publish his work.[31] Meanwhile, the article in question had been posted online and quickly made the rounds.

After Hack SDMI and its subsequent controversy, the SDMI organization lurched to a quiet end. The group would meet only three times in the following year, and would deliver only further news suggesting the consortium was closing up shop. In January 2001, Chiariglione announced that he would step down over the following few months, citing increased responsibilities as head of the corporate research center at Telecom Italia

Group. News reports after Chiariglione's announcement suggested that the group had agreed to a scaled-back set of new goals, perhaps falling back on the Phase I specifications as a way to include copying rules in each digital file. Finally, in May 2001, the group announced that it had completed its assessment of the submitted security technologies, and that "based on all of the factors considered by the SDMI plenary, it was determined that there is currently no consensus for adoption of any combination of the proposed technologies."[32]

The Challenges of Alignment

SDMI was put on hiatus, and has not since been revived. Work of a similar nature has been taken up by other coalitions, many of whose members were part of SDMI. A recent announcement, for instance, marked the formation of the Coral Consortium, a group that plans to "create a common technology framework for content, device and service providers, regardless of the DRM technologies they use,"[33] the intention being to establish interoperability between the proprietary encryption technologies that are now in use in the market. The group was started by HP, Intertrust, Philips, Panasonic, Samsung, Sony, and Twentieth Century Fox; their president is Jack Lacy, who chaired the Portable Device Working Group in SDMI, became acting CEO after Chiariglione's departure, and is now senior vice-president at Intertrust, a DRM provider that was itself recently acquired by Sony and Philips through a third company.[34] The group has already announced its own Phase I specification and now includes all four major record labels among its members.

Alongside such voluntary efforts to build consensus around a technical protection scheme, music producers have also attempted to pursue protection schemes on their own. Sony made one such attempt in 2005, hoping to render its music CDs "unrippable" by preventing the user from even making the first copy onto their computer, whether that copy was for unauthorized distribution or just for use on an iPod. The new CD would drop a small copy protection application on the computer that would direct all programs on that computer to refuse to copy it; in order to make this application hard for intrepid users to locate and remove, the CD also installed a "rootkit" application that told the computer at its deepest level to hide this copy protection mechanism. Sony soon found itself in a public relations fiasco when critics discovered that their method also rendered that computer vulnerable to viruses and malware that could exploit the rootkit access it provided. The discs were recalled.[35]

With similar kinds of interindustry consortia still being formed, it is important to ask why SDMI failed. Lessons drawn from SDMI may not only help activists and policymakers anticipate the success or failure of similar efforts, they may also point more conceptually to the challenges that copyright interests face as they arduously pursue the "regime of alignment" necessary for such technological protection schemes to work. For scholars interested in how a technology like the Internet comes to take the form it does, it is vital to examine heterogeneous efforts to align the economic and political actors necessary to institute this or that sociotechnical arrangement, as well as the kinds of forces and situations that challenge those arrangements when they pose troubling implications.

So many elements needed to come together into lockstep in order for the SDMI plan to work, one could argue, that it is simply unlikely that such a precarious arrangement could be achieved in the real world. We have yet to see if this is true, though I suspect we are beginning to see projects that could more reasonably be deemed successful, depending on our criteria. But SDMI failed for a number of specific reasons, all of which could be considered problems inherent to the political mobilization of the necessary actors, both willing and unwilling.

Throughout the life of the SDMI coalition, critics inside and outside the group regularly harped on the organization's sluggish pace; deadlines came and went, months turned into years. Both technological innovation and the market's enthusiasm for it are, as conventional wisdom suggests, relentless. It's possible either that SDMI in particular was too slow, or that any coalition trying to represent the interests of multiple industries will likely be too slow to keep up with the lightning pace of technology.

Technological innovation did outpace SDMI, but it was innovation not in consumer electronics but in emerging networks of music distribution. By the time SDMI had officially formed, the mp3 format already had a devoted following. While it had not quite reached the general public, among those who were trading files online, mp3 had no equal. It did a decent job compressing the music to a manageable size without giving up much in the way of audio fidelity, and it offered a simple solution to storage and transmission without any limitations on the user—the very limitations that SDMI would have to impose and justify. But what really outpaced the SDMI project was Napster. Released only a few months before the SDMI consortium assembled, Napster had reached a peak of 70 million registered users, had been successfully sued by the RIAA, and had been shut down by the time SDMI had been put on hiatus. A number of more decentralized peer-to-peer network applications were already taking its place, some surpassing its massive user base. (Apple's iPod was not introduced until the following October; it too would bolster the popularity of mp3, but it would also usher in the iTunes store and its proprietary DRM format).

Napster represented not just a flood of unauthorized copyright infringement, or the technical infrastructure that facilitated it, but the constitution of its own coalition, involving different actors, organized according to very different principles. The technological network was quickly aligning a network of users, designers, software, and budding political principles.[36] SDMI, therefore, was not simply attempting to build a political coalition out of nothing, a difficult task in and of itself; it was trying to build it in the face of a powerful alternative, one that had a persuasive cultural and political rhetoric of its own and intense support from its members. And, while the principles of this Napster-world may have been anathema to some of the SDMI members, the major record labels in particular, it was not without a certain appeal to others; manufacturers of mp3 players, for example, would benefit from the wide circulation of music in any form and saw Napster as a welcome boon to their bottom line.

Perhaps the most damaging impact of Napster on the SDMI effort was that while mp3 players continued to grow in popularity, the availability of mp3 files over the Internet helped shift music consumption to the computer. Specifications limiting what portable music devices could and could not do would be meaningless if users simply gave up on such devices altogether and used the computer as their stereo. A sign of this was the failure of Sony's Vaio Music Clip mp3 player, the only portable device to be released with the SDMI Phase I specifications built in. Reviewers criticized the device, often for the SDMI restrictions, even though the Phase I watermark by itself imposed no limit on use, since no protected music was being released. Sales were soft, and Sony eventually pulled the device, reintroducing it soon after without the SDMI watermark system. The mere possibility of restriction was enough to undercut the sale of a device when alternatives were available that explicitly offered limitlessness.

With the migration of music consumption to the computer, the game had changed. SDMI hoped to build its limits into portable music devices, assuming that these devices would always be a necessary component of the use of digital music. But peer-to-peer users had successfully incorporated new technologies in their arsenal: CD burners, computer hard drives, desktop speakers, and peer-to-peer distribution software. Now SDMI-compliant devices would have to compete not just against other portable players, but against the computers that many music fans increasingly already had on their desks and the array of software that could play mp3 music and, more importantly, locate and distribute it across peer-to-peer networks. The RIAA in turn would have to mobilize a much broader coalition of independent actors, particularly the computer and software industries, who had a different business plan and worldview than the consumer electronics manufacturers, and had less experience with or interest in partnering with the record labels. If SDMI represented an effort at heterogeneous engineering, the embrace of the computer as a music device by users helped undo the alignment of those elements by simply turning to (technical) actors well outside its reach.

SDMI also had to keep pace with the economic interests of its own members. Industry consortia can only hold together to the extent that all of the members perceive participation to be in their self-interest.[37] For digital music, this was not the case. Companies whose primary revenue came from the manufacture of consumer electronics devices were salivating at the possible market for mp3 players that Diamond had begun to serve, that Napster was helping to expand, and that Apple would come to dominate soon after. While they wanted to be part of the SDMI project if it turned out to be successful, they didn't want to have missed opportunities in the interim. Those who primarily manufactured computers and information applications could see the broader advantages of peer-to-peer networks for information distribution, the ancillary economic impact of all this digital music on computer sales, and the opportunities for developing related tools for data organization and storage this would require. Many of the independent music labels saw digital distribution as a way to crack the oligopoly of the major labels, using it to play to their own strengths (like marketing more directly to the music subcultures they served).

A number of critics suggested that as much as the record companies may have wanted SDMI to succeed, the technology manufacturers either were less convinced it could be done, were unwilling to do it the record companies' way, or were simply there to ensure that the worst possible outcomes would not be embraced in their absence. One participant reported that "the only people who like SDMI are the record labels and the companies trying to sell them technology . . . [The rest of us are] mainly there to prevent bad things from happening; I would say this is most of the participating computer and consumer electronics companies, if not all of them."[38] Meetings were said to be tense and sometimes acrimonious, suggesting perhaps that the various interests were never sufficiently aligned to begin with. As Janelle Brown reported in *Salon*, quoting an SDMI member from the computer industry, "'We would have preferred to have a more serious discussion with the record industry about what rationally can and can't be done to limit unauthorized copying of music. But they wanted to create this huge forum with all these participants, and Leonardo the Great leading it.' The picture attendees paint of the past 18 months of SDMI meetings isn't pretty. Bickering was rife, thanks to rooms full of representatives of companies with competing products and interests and executives who displayed what one observer called a high 'blowhard factor.'"[39] It is important to note that the group's major success—agreeing on the Phase I specifications—was a hollow victory; it imposed no regulations of its own, and left the hard decisions to be made in Phase II. The ability to achieve consensus on this first stage was only a sign of an early commitment among the members to the project itself. As soon as the real issues had to be worked out—how the watermark would work, what it would prohibit, who would be responsible for its implementation—the group failed to achieve the same kind of consensus.

Even the major labels, who had most adamantly called for these technical restrictions to be pursued, were themselves considering whether digital distribution might be more cost effective than propping up CD sales with additional security. The same companies that were collaborating in this consortium were also competing to be the first to take a digital music store to market, and were striking side deals with proprietary DRM providers to do so. Had one of these partnerships reached the market first and successfully achieved market prominence (which they did not), their proprietary format could establish its own market presence, and would hardly need SDMI at all. To mobilize the kind of political alignment first envisioned by the SDMI group required forging consensus between a wildly disparate array of economic actors amid a rapidly changing economic landscape.

To suggest that the economic and political interests of the various members were at odds is not to imply that there were simple divisions among record labels, consumer electronics manufacturers, and information technology providers, although it is a convenient shorthand that the press coverage often adopted. While companies certainly self-identified in public with one or another industry in particular moments and contexts, and formed industry-specific lobbying organizations such as the RIAA to push for their shared agenda, the picture is certainly more complicated. Some companies involved drew most of their revenue from a particular product and matured as organizations in that mindset, while others had fingers in each market pie, and faced the challenge of brokering between those goals, both internally and in industry coalitions such as SDMI.

These economic orientations also shift, as companies reach for new markets and through interindustry partnerships. The digital music market was an open question, both a potential risk and a potential blessing, and while record labels had a kind of obvious claim on it, many companies were considering entering on the distribution side. In the later days of the SDMI project, many of the companies joining the organization were coming from the wireless telecommunication industry, where established players like AT&T saw opportunities not only to design encryption technologies but also to deliver content themselves. Some participants suggested that this "mission creep"[40] dissolved an early consensus between the initial members, but it is also a reminder that consensus was already conditional at best, and was vulnerable to the fluid business strategies that the member companies were exploring.

For this heterogeneous network to form and hold against the challenge of peer-to-peer, it would need more than just economic actors to come into alignment; it would need cooperative technologies as well. The most unwilling actor in this case may have been digital copy protection itself. Many critics, especially among the programmers who took pleasure in hacking the SDMI watermarks, argued that digital security of any kind will simply never work, at least not in the way the content industries want. To develop a leakproof trusted system, where no content ever gets decrypted and all rules are followed, requires an unbreakable protection system. This may be either impossible, in that anything made can be unmade, or so complex and unwieldy that it would be cost-prohibitive to even attempt. Even if the goal is not to provide total protection but only to discourage the average consumer, the Internet undercuts that strategy. As Charles Mann (quoting security expert Bruce Schneier) notes, "'You always have two kinds of attackers, Joe Average and Jane Hacker. Many systems in the real world only have to be secure against Joe Average.' Door locks are an example: they're vulnerable to expert thieves, but the chance that any one door will encounter an expert thief is small. 'But if I am Jane Hacker, the best online,' Schneier says, 'I can write a program that does what I do and put it up on the Web—click here to defeat the system. Suddenly Joe Average is just as good as Jane Hacker.'"[41] Hackers don't just circumvent, they also make tools that help others do it without the technical know-how. And one unprotected copy of a song or movie becomes a million with the help of peer-to-peer networks.

A second flaw in the logic of technical protection is known as the "analog hole." Technical copy protection of this sort aspires to regulate content by keeping it within a bounded set of devices and networks that all follow the rules. This is itself a massive undertaking, but even if it is successfully installed, it by definition has a fundamental weakness. Devices like mp3 players that can be designed to prohibit the output of unprotected digital music still have to play that music, sending it as an analog signal to a speaker so it can be heard. That analog signal can be recorded, creating a digital file without protection where none existed. As Felten notes, "Unbreakable codes, whether theoretically impregnable or practically untouchable, do not imply that DRM is possible. To understand why, imagine that you can build an impregnable armored truck. This truck can carry bags of money anywhere; and as long as you keep the doors closed nobody can rob the truck. The problem is that the truck is useless unless you open its doors."[42] It's the fundamental conundrum of communication that began this chapter: To make the work public, you necessarily make it vulnerable to public exploitation. SDMI hoped that its watermark could survive the transition to analog and the transition back to digital, meaning that the digital copy would still obey SDMI rules. This kind of watermark, however, has proven extremely difficult to design.[43]

Others fretted that watermarking was a particularly unlikely candidate for successfully stopping the circulation of copyrighted digital content. Watermarks need to be undetectable to the listener, which means they cannot significantly alter the digital file; they must be detectable by the device, which means they must be recognizable if you know where to look. The content would be freely available to those who wanted to examine it and discover how it worked—not just one example, as the Hack SDMI participants were given, but millions floating around, offering clues to their own deconstruction. Encryption experts have a number of tools at their disposal for discovering and stripping watermarks, and their expertise keeps pace with that of the industry. Even without access to many of those tools, hackers were able to strip all four of the SDMI Phase II watermarks, the best technologies the major digital security providers had to offer, in under three weeks.

What may undermine all such DRM projects is the fundamental tension between the secrecy necessary for encryption or watermarking to work, and the publicity required by contemporary technological design. One of the techniques by which Felten and his team removed the SDMI watermarks was to cursorily examine the digital file and then compare what they saw to the record of public patents. In one case, they found a patent held by Aris Technologies, which had since become Verance, which was known to be one of the companies submitting watermarks to SDMI; the information in this patent helped them come up with methods of removing the watermark.[44] While the technical requirements of DRM require its design to be kept secret, our current legal apparatus requires such designs to be made public if they are to enjoy the protection of intellectual property law themselves. But this could change, as watermark and encryption providers might forego patents, favoring instead trade secret protection because it has no such publicity requirement.[45]

Finally, the SDMI project was intended not to select and impose one proprietary security system, but to design a set of open technology specifications that would provide the underlying standard for any copy protection system to use. They hoped that the new devices would honor legacy music formats as well as those yet to be invented. Such an architecture may simply not exist, or may by necessity be so broad that it cannot offer the kind of tight control content owners hope for.

The network of elements envisioned by SDMI to regulate music consumers would require economic actors, watermark technologies, laws, and cultural norms to come into alignment. Much of the work necessary involved the political mobilization of these economic actors. But technical design is also a kind of political mobilization: How could the coalition "convince" the watermark to do what they wanted it to? Just as the SDMI plan may have been unconvincing to a company like Diamond, it may have also proven unconvincing to the technology itself. My saying that the technology needed convincing is not a grammatical accident; nor is it intended in the manner of a trite little quip, as in "remember, technologies have feelings too." Rather, I mean to acknowledge that the work of producing a heterogeneous coalition like SDMI requires bringing an array of incongruous elements together for the same purpose, and the challenge is in overcoming their resistance (whatever that resistance may be) to the arrangement proposed. Such mobilization may be impossible, or may involve compromises that alter the arrangement in politically significant ways. These alterations are just as often forced by the material and socio-economic dynamics of the technologies and their designers as by the political and socio-economic agendas of the institutions and their representatives.[46]

Of course, while the Hack SDMI contest did torpedo at least some, and probably all, of the proposed watermarks, and may have made clear that the proposed technologies weren't quite up to the task, it certainly didn't mean SDMI had to give up at that point. The SDMI members could have passed along the insights gathered from the hacks to the watermark designers, announced a second call for submissions, and sought out better watermarks. The contest was not the immediate end of the project, nor was it clear whether the technical aims were impossible or just not yet achieved. However, the painful visibility of SDMI's defeat in the press and among technology enthusiasts, combined with the legal wrangling with Felten and the EFF, may have brought enough public relations damage that the project itself could not hope to win over consumers even if it did produce a robust watermark.

The coalition of people, institutions, and things imagined by SDMI (and endemic to all DRM strategies) faced a monumental final obstacle: convincing consumers to adopt restricted technologies over their unrestricted counterparts. Many music consumers are potentially pirates when faced with frustrating choices; some of them are potential hackers when those choices are technical. But in all of them is the potential to reject music altogether and turn their interest, and their dollars, elsewhere. The plan envisioned by SDMI could not be imposed upon users; it would have had to earn their support. The embarrassment of the Hack SDMI challenge and the strong arm tactics that followed certainly undercut that possibility.

The entire Hack SDMI challenge was a curious exercise for such a group to undertake. Typically, interindustry coalitions and standards-setting entities prefer to work outside of the public spotlight, using industry secrecy and the sheer dullness of the topic at hand as gentle cover for their efforts, then announcing their accomplishments as a fait accompli. Most producers, whether of music, electronics, computers, or software, generally share the business logic that you work out the kinks behind closed doors before you announce your product to your consumers. Companies and coalitions may sometimes seek out beta testers and focus groups to get early feedback, but even this is carefully controlled and kept as private as possible. The Hack SDMI contest, on the other hand, was made public, trumpeted as a challenge, and handed to a community of users who not only had specific skills, but may have also harbored more disregard for the SDMI members than they anticipated.

Perhaps the contest represented a new paradigm, embraced by some of the SDMI members and drawn from the dynamics of the Internet and digital culture, where the ethos of software design is "publish early and often." Perhaps the information technology manufacturers wanted the kind of real-world test that could prove that a watermark could survive, hoping to legitimize their efforts in the eyes of their own members, other manufacturers, even Congress and the courts. Perhaps, as was suggested above, some SDMI members actually hoped the watermarks would fail, to either bring SDMI to a halt or turn its attention toward more viable strategies. Regardless, the coalition discovered that the optimistic and committed participation common to open source design projects is not as forthcoming when the project is overseen by industries that the community of programmers disdains. And when your product fails in this world, it does not fail quietly.

In the attempt to construct this heterogeneous regime of alignment, SDMI may have overreached by trying to include hackers and academics. In bringing together record labels, consumer electronics manufacturers, and information technology providers, the group was already attempting to align a quite disparate set of actors and aspirations. Nevertheless, it was not unreasonable to imagine that they would all share some of the same commercial and technical goals. Hackers, amateur software designers, and computer scientists shared fewer of these goals, and would likely see much less advantage in joining this coalition. In fact, the broader SDMI project had already framed them as the enemy: those who would copy, and those who would circumvent and help others copy. It was curious to expect them to also play ally in the design process. The various ways in which such alignment is usually produced—shared interest, commercial bargaining, nondisclosure agreements—could not pull these groups into the same orbit. They instead pursued their own goals—a combination of technical curiosity and vengeance that did not fit with SDMI's project. In the "regime of alignment" approach to regulation, a coalition may often come upon unwilling actors that it simply cannot persuade or compel to fall into lockstep.

Binding Force

Under pressure from the rapid popularity of peer-to-peer file-trading and the emerging market for digital music and devices, and torn by the wildly divergent economic interests of its constituents, SDMI could not sustain the kind of consensus necessary to see the project past the technical hurdles and initial public missteps. The member participants, a population that was itself fluctuating and that held a complex and evolving set of economic aspirations, could not find common ground amidst perceived economic opportunities that were themselves changing. The technologies necessary proved to be unruly, unwilling to go along with the plan. This unstable coalition faced a burgeoning alternative arrangement that was gaining ground—more successfully tapping into shared worldviews of open computing, cultural traditions of music sharing, and anti–record industry sentiment to better align its participants toward a common purpose. The attempt to invite some of those groups and technologies into orbit around SDMI proved to be a mobilization effort that could not hold.

Underlying all of these obstacles was the decision of the SDMI that its protection system would be voluntary. This posed three problems. First, SDMI members could walk away from negotiations if they felt their interests weren't being adequately served, both from negotiations inside of SDMI working groups and from SDMI itself. Had the SDMI project included some binding obligation—a contractual agreement to reach some conclusion, or a regulatory agency breathing down their necks—it is likely that the effort would have continued longer than it did. Shared economic interest is not a sufficient glue to bind such groups when the market opportunities are unclear, unexplored, and rapidly evolving. That anyone could walk away from the project, and perhaps render it obsolete by winning the market for digital music with its own proprietary encryption, meant that any alignment was certain to be precarious.

Second, manufacturers and content providers who did not agree to the arrangement could forego any agreed-upon standard, sell alternatives that would not include copy protection restrictions, and even use that as their selling point. Of course, this voluntary choice would not be without consequences, as manufacturers who passed on SDMI would eventually be selling devices that could not play major label content released with SDMI watermarks. It was in this way that the SDMI coalition hoped to ensure cooperation, with the record label content serving as the lure in this "voluntary" system. As we will see in the next chapter, the movie industry had more success than the music industry with this strategy, though they also pushed it further. But while such a tease might work once the system were in place, getting it into place meant convincing manufacturers to adopt it and consumers to buy it, in the face of competing options that had no restrictions. As John Borland puts it, "A key problem is that partial measures aren't particularly useful. Security locks are foolproof only when all brands of stereos, computers, and mp3 players use the same anti-piracy technology, leaving consumers little choice but to accept it. When products with no protections have been left on the market, consumers have purchased those instead."[47]

Finally, as SDMI's specifications were imagined, users could choose whether or not to adopt the SDMI restrictions. While refusing them would have consequences, that is, rendering their device unable to play SDMI-marked music, the fact that this choice even existed meant there would be room for two worlds of music distribution. Clearly, of these two worlds, the unrestricted one was gaining strength faster than SDMI's protected one could. As we will see, the content industries most interested in pursuing such DRM strategies, both as copy protection mechanisms and as new ways to further commodify their product, would soon discover they needed to bind the members in their coalition and to somehow compel users to adopt the arrangements they produced.

SDMI is a reminder that the alignment of technology and content, of hardware and software necessary for the trusted system to work, cannot be imposed without a matching alignment between the commercial institutions that produce them, and such an alignment is not easily achieved. The content industries would need a more effective means to align these institutions, through persuasion or compulsion. In the case of the DVD, the movie studios cleverly used encryption itself and the economic value of its content as the carrot, along with contractual licenses as the stick, and found the combination quite powerful for gaining the consent of manufacturers to their technical protection scheme. They found, however, that technical copy protection systems do not do away with the law. They continued to need the law to provide the teeth to this arrangement, as the unruly and unwilling participants included not only technology manufacturers but, in a world of free software, skilled users as well. The Digital Millennium Copyright Act (DMCA) they helped design, and to which they turned when their DVD protection system was breached, is as much about regulating upstart manufacturers as it is about constraining users, by providing the backing not for the technical copy protection but for the contractual license upon which it depends.

The music industry's failure to convince technology manufacturers to support their Secure Digital Music Initiative should not suggest that such a project is impossible. But it certainly does suggest that pulling that many unwilling participants into line is a Herculean task. More than just good will, a shared sense of purpose, and a glimpse of a common and profitable future was needed to keep these unruly elements in line. In more recent efforts to establish a trusted system based on encryption and hardware restrictions, content providers have had to find more powerful ways to compel everyone to play along.

This has required a shift in perspective. Although it is the users making unauthorized copies of copyrighted content who are the bad guys in the rhetoric of the entertainment industries, the industry strategy focuses primarily on regulating the manufacturers of the technologies the users need to make the copies. And if the makers of mp3 players are in a position to impose digital content protection but do not necessarily see an economic benefit in doing so, a voluntary arrangement is less likely to succeed than one in which some obligation requires them to participate. This strategic two-step—regulate the manufacturers so that the devices they make regulate users—is both a way to intervene at a more viable point (there are fewer manufacturers than users, they have deeper pockets, and their public profile can be exploited) and a powerful conceptual shift inside the heterogeneous arrangement of the technical protection of intellectual property.

In the case of DVDs, the movie industry discovered that the very content they were trying to protect offered its own political leverage for imposing obligations on their consumer electronics partners. Rather than begin by trying to convince manufacturers to agree to a DRM standard, the studios could simply encrypt their films. Any manufacturer wanting to produce a DVD player, for whatever purpose, would need to build the appropriate decryption key into their device. This meant the studios had power over how those devices would be designed. Holding the films hostage in this way meant that manufacturers had little choice but to agree to the design rules the studios demanded, despite their ideological and financial differences. It also meant that the established manufacturers who did support the studios' strategy could rest easy, as there was little risk that an upstart competitor would offer a less restrictive alternative. Technical protection in fact ensures them a more stable grip on the market, which provides further economic incentive to embrace this plan. While in the SDMI effort the watermarking technology may have been one of the most unruly elements, encryption is not only more amenable, it serves as a powerful lever for bringing other participants into alignment.

While this shift, from trying to mobilize a voluntary coalition to using encryption to compel manufacturers to participate, is a powerful strategic move, it too is insufficient by itself to bring about the trusted system the movie studios desire. But it does change what else must be done to develop a more complete system of control. While it seemed as if this combination of licenses and industry cooperation would be a way to install a system of technical control without requiring the involvement of the state, the film industry quickly discovered that they would nevertheless need the law as recourse if (or in this case, when) the encryption system was breached. Encryption may have forced manufacturers to accept a contractual obligation to build the locks, but it did not prevent the locks from being picked.

When a tool for circumventing DVD encryption was designed in late 1999 and circulated on the web, the major studios turned to a new law they had helped craft, the Digital Millennium Copyright Act (DMCA), to support their protection scheme by criminalizing its circumvention. On one level, the DMCA prevents users from circumventing technical copy protection measures and from designing tools to help others do the same. But a closer look at the law and its application in this case reveals that, more than regulating users directly, the DMCA regulates them through technological proxy: It regulates manufacturers through a license, uses the law to discern authorized manufacturers who accepted the license from criminal "manufacturers" who did not, then lets the technology mandated in the license regulate users. Close consideration of the DMCA and how it works reveals not only its role as an enforcer of the new standard of technical copyright, but also the way it hands the content industries the power to secure the alignment between their own interests and those of the manufacturers.

This system of regulation depends on lashing together many heterogeneous elements: people and technologies, institutions from different domains, rules of different cadence and authority, and, increasingly, the aims and practices of law and those who craft, enforce, and adjudicate it. If it can be assembled, it can potentially produce an environment in which some actions simply cannot be taken. And the fact that no single element of this arrangement is solely responsible for its consequences, or for its missteps, helps deflects criticism. As a legal and a commercial architecture, this heterogeneous approach produces a "regime of alignment"; this is the crucial outcome of the copy protection efforts of the major movie and music industries. Like all good systems of control, it regulates not through force, but by carefully writing alternatives out of existence within a comprehensive paradigm that has its own inherent logic—the regulation of access to content rather than the adjudication of what you do with it. Other frameworks for organizing the circulation of information—for example, the balance offered by fair use—simply have no conceptual place in this regulatory jigsaw puzzle.

Most important, the concern goes well beyond whether this DRM strategy ends up actually curbing peer-to-peer file-trading or not. Whether or not it successfully produces a trusted system, this alignment will have its own consequences for the trajectory of copyright law and the production and use of communication technologies. Historically, there has been a distinct social and political benefit to the fact that content and technology industries do not always share a market strategy or a cultural worldview or assumptions about the interests of their customers.[1] As these gaps narrow, a trusted system may be only the first of many consequences, and these consequences may extend well beyond questions of copyright.

Scrambling and Unscrambling

The home video market provided the major movie studios with a decade-long boom, despite their early efforts to sue VCR manufacturers into oblivion.[2] By the early 1990s, both Hollywood and the consumer electronics industry hoped to expand and transform that market using the power of digital technology. The goal was, at least at first, to improve on the image and sound quality of VHS and add the durability and navigational ease of the disc format. After the laserdisc failed to extend its appeal beyond gadget nuts and cinephiles, consumer electronics manufacturers[3] combined the popular five-inch CD disc and the newly developed MPEG-2 compression format to produce the DVD.[4] Launched in March of 1997, the

DVD format has enjoyed unprecedented success, and is often described as the most successful consumer electronics product ever; within six years of its introduction, 250 million households had a DVD player, DVD-capable PC, or game console.[5] But the long-term aspiration of the film industry was not just digital movies, but the digital distribution of those movies. The industry hoped they could colonize the pay-per-view services pioneered by the cable industry by delivering their films directly to consumers over the Internet.

However, the simple distribution of the Internet and near-perfect reproduction afforded by digital computing were more than sufficient to reawaken the now-familiar fears of copyright infringement. Hollywood didn't want to repeat the music industry's mistake of releasing digital content before establishing a technical line of defense, so they delayed the DVD until they had settled on one. In 1996, a coalition of the major movie studios, consumer electronics manufacturers, and information technology providers formed the Copy Protection Technical Working Group (CPTWG) to consider how to protect digital media content from being duplicated and redistributed over the Internet, using strategies already familiar to the software industry. Protecting the DVD format was their first and most important task.[6]

The CPTWG recommended a series of solutions, a Content Protection System Architecture (CPSA) comprised of protocols for managing a range of more specific restrictions. These included Macrovision's hardware protection against duplicating DVDs to analog video, a protection mechanism meant to regulate serial copying in digital format, an encryption system and watermark specifically for DVD-Audio, and, most important, the Content Scramble System (CSS).[7] CSS, developed by Matsushita (now part of Panasonic) and Toshiba, is a forty-bit encryption algorithm that scatters the digital data of the film around the surface of the DVD. Playing the disc requires the algorithm decryption key, which is built into authorized DVD players, to match two keys on the disc itself. When this match is assured, the player can access the encrypted disc, recover the scattered data bit by bit, and display the film.

It is important to recognize that CSS is a lock rather than a block, part of the broader shift from regulating use to regulating access upon which DRM solutions depend. So, for example, the Macrovision copy protection used in DVDs and VHS tapes performs one function: When the device is instructed to send the movie out a wire, and that wire is connected to another recording device, the Macrovision copy protection distorts the image so that the copy is unwatchable. It's the same protection that has kept users from duplicating purchased videotapes to a second VCR. It imposes no obstacle to doing anything else with the film, but by itself it dissuades copying by degrading the copy. CSS, on the other hand, renders the entire film inaccessible, to all uses legitimate or otherwise, unless the device used to read it includes the appropriate key. Instead of recognizing that a copy is being made and disrupting that act, as Macrovision protection does, CSS prohibits access until it can be granted under controlled circumstances. But, and this is the key to DRM, controlling access can regulate whatever use follows: According to Jane Ginsburg, "Every act of perception or of materialization of a digital copy requires a prior act of access. And if the copyright owner can control access, she can condition how a user apprehends the work, and whether a user may make any further copy."[8]

The difference is an important one. Encryption is not itself a copy protection, at least not directly; CSS does not render the data uncopyable. If someone wanted to duplicate Hollywood DVDs on a massive scale and sell them cheaply, CSS would not stop them; they could merely reproduce the DVD verbatim and press it onto a new disc, using the same equipment the studios use to make them in the first place. The pirated copy would still be encrypted, exactly as the original is; anyone who bought this black market disc could watch it on their licensed DVD player. What CSS does is prevent consumers from watching the DVD using the wrong device—that is, one that hasn't been certified by the movie studios. Control of copying and redistribution is imposed by ensuring that authorized DVD players themselves do not allow copying; CSS ensures that consumers will only use these authorized machines.

In a sense, this has been the control strategy of the movie industry since its inception. While the music industry sells its music once, and uses copyright law to control unauthorized redistribution, the movie industry prefers to control distribution through access barriers: the ticket counter, the velvet rope, the theater door.[9] This depends as much on contractual arrangements with associated industries as on the law. Studios prevent copyright infringement from happening in the theater, both by prosecuting those who sell bootlegs and by delegating responsibility to theater owners to patrol their ticketed audiences for smuggled-in video cameras.[10]

Latour should remind us that just as we can either attach a hydraulic piston to a door to help close it or hire a doorman to do the same, the movie studios have an array of tactics, some human and some mechanical, by which they can keep that "door" closed. Just as building managers regularly choose between the different tactics, Hollywood prefers to control

DVD use via CSS encryption and the regulation of DVD players rather than by prosecuting violators after the fact—although they are willing to do both. Technical protection offers a consistency that cannot be matched by the vagaries of human intervention, the functional limits of the legal system, or, importantly, the limitations of copyright law itself, with its focus on use and subsequent punishment.[11]

Furthermore, access control is not just a way to stop users from copying. By controlling access to the movie itself rather than prohibiting its duplication, the movie industry can monetize each viewing experience rather than charging only for possession. Seeing a film in the theater requires purchasing a ticket for each viewing; seeing it again requires a second payment. Under this arrangement, ancillary markets can be based on layers of access (second-run theaters, screening on airplanes, hotel pay-per-view, video rental, video purchase, subscription cable, commercial television broadcast), with fewer restrictions and cheaper prices at each level. Controlling copying only protects future sales. Controlling access also manages the initial sale in potentially intricate and profitable ways.

The challenge to this encryption solution, as many expected, first appeared online. DeCSS, an application so tiny it can be written in as few as 434 characters and printed on a T-shirt,[12] removes or decrypts ("De") the protective encryption ("CSS") from a DVD and saves the film as a new file in its linear, unprotected form. DeCSS does not work by cracking the CSS algorithm. It is simply a digital key ring that opens the DVDs the way they were supposed to be opened, but with a tool that is not authorized to do so.

When the story of DeCSS is told, the starting point is typically Jon Johansen, part of a team of Norwegian hackers called the "Masters of Reverse Engineering" (MoRE), who designed DeCSS and first posted it online. But the story might just as easily begin with XingDVD Player, an authorized DVD player designed by RealNetworks. RealNetworks failed to sufficiently hide the key that opens CSS inside their application, as they were contractually required to do. When Johansen's crew discovered this, they were able to extract the key; once they had the one, they were able to make educated guesses and identify 170 more.[13] The film industry would subsequently portray them as relentless and immoral hacker pirates hell-bent on stealing their valuable intellectual property and trading it Napster-style with the masses, in line with the story about the Internet that the movie and music industries had been constructing already for several years. But it is important to note that while this story is not false per se, it is a particular and motivated version of what happened. Another version is that the film industry compelled hardware designers to collude with them, to keep users from enjoying certain uses of their works; when one of their partners mistakenly violated the agreement, some users with the technical know-how found the opportunity and created a tool that permitted the uses they desired.

In November 1999, the Motion Picture Association of America (MPAA) demanded that Johansen remove the application from his website, which he did.[14] But DeCSS had already been mirrored on sites around the world. Despite the studios' best efforts at forcibly mobilizing a coalition of institutions and technologies into producing devices only to the specifications imposed by the movie studios, the world now had two kinds of DVD players: some that played DVDs and refused to allow them to be duplicated, and others that imposed no such restriction. To squelch the distribution of this tool the studios turned to a law they had helped to create, hoping to give their technical restrictions legal teeth and re-certify the "good" DVD players by outlawing the "bad". In January 2000, the MPAA sued three of the more prominent websites that distributed DeCSS,[15] requesting an injunction prohibiting them from posting the application, and charging them with violating the DMCA.[16] The argument made by the movie studios, which proved persuasive in court, was straightforward: DeCSS was a device designed to circumvent a technological protection, and posting it on a website was "providing" it. Doing so is illegal under the DMCA. The defendants found they had to challenge the law itself, first by claiming that they fit into one of its exceptions, then by questioning the law's implications and thus its constitutionality. In dispute was whether this law, designed to enhance copyright in its digital context, had perverted copyright in shifting its attention from use to access.

Legal Teeth

In 1976, when copyright law was most recently overhauled, the Internet was not an issue. The ARPANET was only a research project run by the military and a few universities, and the traditional supporters of copyright (publishers, studios, producers, and the like) had not yet discovered why they would eventually care about its copyright implications. Congress was only beginning to tackle the question of whether computer software should be granted the same copyright protections enjoyed by print and other analog works. There was no need to deal with the nascent question of online distribution. Later, when the Internet did appear as a public and potentially commercial medium, legislators began feeling pressure to revise the rules they had written back in the 1970s, to once again keep pace with new technology. When the U.S. government began to consider how copyright law should apply to the new information medium,[17] it not only embraced the view of the major movie studios—that the relentless piracy made possible by the Internet meant that copyright law would need to be stronger and more rigorously enforced—it also introduced a startling new twist.

As discussed in chapter 2, under the aegis of the Clinton-sponsored "National Information Infrastructure Task Force," a working group was formed to help determine what changes to intellectual property law, if any, would be necessary in light of this new medium. Curiously, this was the only NII working group to recommend significant government intervention. According to Litman, "Most documents emanating from the IITF cautioned against undue haste, suggesting that the value of permitting the private sector to thrash things out and work toward consensus could not be overemphasized."[18] The other working groups generally suggested fitting the new medium under existing laws to ensure the continuation of their underlying principles, and taking a wait-and-see attitude on whether new dynamics required new legislation. The copyright working group, on the other hand, was much more eager for the government to take an activist role, arguing that content providers who might be willing to make their products available online needed new protections in order to do so. As Bruce Lehman, the group's director, put it, "While it is not advisable to propose amendment of the law with every technological step forward, neither is it appropriate to blindly cling to the status quo when the market has been altered."[19] Still, the tone of these suggestions should not come as a surprise, since the policy statement was drafted after a public hearing at which leaders of the major content industries (film, music, publishing) were asked what they would want in order to convince them to make their wares available over the Internet—which is the same way all major copyright legislation has been designed over the past century.[20]

The Working Group on Intellectual Property Rights' White Paper[21] proposed what it claimed were minor adjustments, sufficient to protect content owners and make the Internet a safe place to release their work without fear of piracy. But these minor adjustments were in actuality a major redefinition of the scope of copyright, in anticipation of a digital marketplace for cultural expression.[22] Most prominent among the proposals was an anti-circumvention statute: If a copyright owner were to distribute a digital work with some kind of technological barrier built in (password security, watermarking, encryption, anticopying codes, etc.), it would be illegal for a user to gain unauthorized access by breaching that barrier. Furthermore, it would be illegal to make or distribute any tool that helped others do so. This was justified as preparation for an impending arms race between beleaguered copyright owners and determined hackers, as described in the NII White Paper:

The ease of infringement and the difficulty of detection and enforcement will cause copyright owners to look to technology, as well as the law, for protection of their works. However, it is clear that technology can be used to defeat any protection that technology may provide. The Working Group finds that legal protection alone will not be adequate to provide incentive to authors to create and to disseminate works to the public. Similarly, technological protection likely will not be effective unless the law also provides some protection for the technological processes and systems used to prevent or restrict unauthorized uses of copyrighted works.[23]

Note that the conventional wisdom—that technology tends to outpace the law—breaks down here. Lehman and his group were preparing a legal foundation to make it possible to deliver information in encrypted form before such technologies had been widely adopted. This was not a rule for those materials that were already being delivered online; it was an invitation to culture industries to shift their distribution arrangements to the Internet, by paving the way for a world in which digital downloads could be wrapped in encryption. The movie industry knew this. Their public announcement introducing the CSS encryption made clear that the legal constructs needed to be deployed along with the technology:

The multi-industry Copyright Protection Technical Working Group (CPTWG) today announced that its subcommittee on DVD technology has taken an important step forward in the search for an effective system to prevent unauthorized copying of motion pictures and other filmed entertainment on prerecorded DVD-video. Controls will be achieved through a scrambling scheme based on encryption [sic] the content on the discs, and licensing the technology for decryption. The industries intend to ask Congress to adopt legislation to prohibit the circumvention of this copy control technology, and other technologies as they are developed and implemented.[24]

For this encryption system to work, the technology and the law needed to coincide, and were in fact conceived together.

The NII White Paper was delivered to Congress and, in September of 1995, the "National Information Infrastructure Copyright Act" was introduced on the floor of both the Senate and the House.[25] Joint hearings were held through the end of the year and into the next, looking primarily to representatives of the film, publishing, and computer industries for advice.

Library associations as well as newly formed digital activist groups like the Digital Future Coalition (DFC) and the Home Recording Rights Coalition (HRRC) appealed to Congress to reject the law, worried about its implications for fair use.[26] Internet service providers fought for limitations on their liability for copyright violations. Eventually, the bills stalled in Congress and were junked.

While these bills were still in committee, Lehman turned to the United Nations' World Intellectual Property Organization (WIPO), hoping to draft an international treaty that would reflect the new American legislation. After the bills stalled, the international negotiations ended up providing a second opportunity to turn the NII White Paper's proposals into law. WIPO passed a treaty that included versions of Lehman's suggestions. In particular, the language prohibiting circumvention devices was toned down slightly, not prohibiting circumvention devices outright as Lehman had proposed, but requiring only that each signatory nation "provide adequate legal protection and effective legal remedies against the circumvention of effective technological measures that are used by authors in connection with the exercise of their rights."[27]

Arguably, existing U.S. copyright law already did just that, since any infringement, including those that required circumvention, could be prosecuted as a violation of existing copyright law.[28] But content owners, with Lehman as their point man, used the treaty as justification to revive the discarded bills. With the treaty that would ensure American-style protection of American cultural goods everywhere in the world, the old legislation now had powerful new justifications, in terms that simply could not imagine copyright questions outside of the market paradigm. Now it was about more than just encouraging the growth of the Internet; it was about the future economic success of the U.S. culture industries and, by extension, of the nation itself. As the House Committee on Commerce put it,

The debate on this legislation highlighted two important priorities: promoting the continued growth and development of electronic commerce; and protecting intellectual property rights. *These goals are mutually supportive.* A thriving electronic marketplace provides new and powerful ways for the creators of intellectual property to make their works available to legitimate consumers in the digital environment. And a plentiful supply of intellectual property . . . drives the demand for a more flexible and efficient electronic marketplace."[29]

In order to "provide adequate legal protection and effective legal remedies," without unduly restricting the kinds of uses that copyright had traditionally allowed, the congressional bills updated the language of the new circumvention clause from their discarded predecessors. The law would criminalize circumventing a technological protection designed to prevent unauthorized access, and make it illegal to make or provide tools that helped others circumvent technological protections.[30] As David Nimmer described it, its "strictures target not only bad acts (the activity of copying itself), but also bad machines (devices that facilitate copying) and bad services (conduct that enables copying)."[31]

Congress was aware that American law was for the first time adding rules about technology to a copyright doctrine that had long prided itself on being "technology neutral." Nimmer again, quoting the same House Committee on Commerce report, argued that historically, Congress has achieved the objectives of the Constitution's Copyright Clause "by regulating the use of information—not the devices or means by which the information is delivered or used by information consumers."[32] Copyright law had always restricted certain activities and ensured certain rights, without regard to the techniques and tools with which they were accomplished.[33] But, as Congress saw it, the Internet called for a qualitative change.

The Digital Millennium Copyright Act became law on October 28, 1998,[34] and arguably represents the most dramatic change in the history of U.S. copyright law. However, it is not without precedent. Scrambling content has been the primary means to protect cable and satellite broadcasts from being pirated (here "pirated" means gaining access without subscribing, rather than copying, though the logic of DRM is to link these two together). The law protects against the theft of cable television service not only by making the act of theft illegal but also by making it criminal to "assist" by producing or distributing the devices that unscramble the signal.[35] The DMCA also harkens back to old techniques for protecting computer software using encryption, and borrows from "shrinkwrap" licenses, which grant the owner technical control of both the software in the abstract and the particular copy purchased, dictating largely at the owner's whim what the user is and is not permitted to do. All of these help shift copyright law from its traditional attention to delimiting copying to a new emphasis on regulating access.[36]

Some in the legal community have described the DMCA as "paracopyright," to emphasize that it is not so much an alteration or expansion of the copyright doctrine, but rather a companion law that straddles it, staking claim on different though overlapping legal territory.[37] But even this is misleading, for the DMCA shares neither the logic nor the strategy of copyright. It anticipates a new technological regime, where control depends on the tight coupling of technology, law, and license, which share the task of regulating not just copying, but access, use, and purchase. The DMCA is the guardian at the gates of the trusted system, not only patrolling this massive control mechanism but also helping to lash its various elements together. This collaboration of technology and law was revealed when the film industry looked to the DMCA to exterminate DeCSS, in *Universal v. Reimerdes*.

Fair Use and Access Control

The defendants in the case, three website operators who had posted the DeCSS application, faced the task of challenging what is nominally a "copyright" statute for the way it interferes with the rights of fair use.[38] They would have to argue that important and protected uses were being rendered technologically unavailable by CSS encryption, that DeCSS could be used for exactly the kinds of activities protected by the fair use doctrine, and that the DMCA was being deployed to stifle them by making the application illegal. But because the DMCA is a law of access and commerce masquerading as a copyright law, this counterargument failed, in revealing ways.

The most prominent critique of DRM is that the rights ensured to the user by the doctrine of copyright, particularly fair use, will be lost if copying is restricted technologically. Fair use was made explicit in 1976 as a specific (though deliberately vague) shield to a charge of copyright infringement. It asserts that, under certain circumstances and determined by certain factors, copying a portion of a protected work may be allowed without permission from or compensation to its owner. If DRM were commonplace, activities permitted under fair use could be prohibited. The cut-and-paste techniques now possible with digital tools offer the potential for users to clip and recombine not just text, but images, sounds, and other multimedia. Were these materials enclosed in technical boundaries, cutting-and-pasting could be rendered technically unavailable except at the whim of copyright owners.

The legislators who developed the DMCA struggled with this dilemma,[39] and tried to mitigate the concern by including in the statute the phrase: "Nothing in this section shall affect rights, remedies, limitations, or defenses to copyright infringement, including fair use, under this title."[40] They believed, since the DMCA applied only to circumvention of access, that the rules and the exceptions of traditional copyright could coexist with the new statute because they applied only to the use that followed.[41] Kathleen Sullivan, dean of Stanford Law School and a lawyer for the defense in the DeCSS case, challenged this with a hypothetical scenario: A professor wants to excerpt key scenes from different films onto a single CD-ROM to use in a film production class. Copying the film clips would likely be allowed under fair use, but the DMCA would prohibit the tool that professor would need. Here was a situation clearly included in the Section 107 copyright protections—classroom use for the purposes of critical pedagogy—that needed actual quotation to make its point and was explicitly not commercial.

Could access controls protected by an anticircumvention law end up stifling the uses that traditional copyright might call fair? The answer hinges on the two-dimensional structure of the DMCA's prohibition of circumvention. First, the law distinguishes between the *act* of circumventing and the *tools* that facilitate it; second, the law distinguishes between circumventing a technical barrier that regulates *access* and one that regulates *copying*. Within the scope of the DMCA, circumventing an access control is illegal, but circumventing a copy control is not. Unauthorized copying would already violate existing copyright law, and lawmakers did not want the DMCA to impose an additional penalty. However, when it comes to restricting tools, the DMCA does not distinguish according to purpose. Therefore, three of four circumvention behaviors envisioned by the law are rendered illegal by the DMCA, as indicated in table 6.1.

The problem is obvious. Copying is illegal, except when it is fair. But if the content is protected with encryption, circumvention tools are illegal no matter how their user might have intended to use them. The fair user who wants to reproduce part of a work that is encrypted, and who doesn't happen to be a skilled hacker, is out of luck. Those of us who cannot do

Table 6.1
The two dimensions of anticircumvention rules in the DMCA

	PURPOSE	
Act vs. Tool	*Circumvention* of an *access* control measure: **ILLEGAL**	*Circumvention* of a *copy* control measure: **LEGAL**
	Tools that aid in circumvention of *access* protections: **ILLEGAL**	*Tools* that aid in circumvention of *copy* protections: **ILLEGAL**

it ourselves are walled off from our half of the copyright balance. And the restriction on copying is invisible, a lack of technical capability built into the tool rather than a prohibition of an activity built into law. The court even admitted that the law grants the technically proficient a right it withholds from the rest of us: "The fact that Congress elected to leave technologically unsophisticated persons who wish to make fair use of encrypted copyrighted works without the technical means of doing so is a matter for Congress, unless Congress's decision contravenes the Constitution."[42] Which, the court decided, it did not.

So what about the film professor? In oral arguments Judge Jon Newman scoffed at Sullivan's hypothetical example, saying the professor could simply use VHS tapes instead: "Have we ever said as to fair use that you not only get to make fair use of the copyrighted work, but you get to make your fair use in the most technologically modern way? Have we ever said that?"[43] This "let them eat cake" response was disingenuous in two ways. First, purchased VHS tapes have Macrovision copy protection on them as well. There is even a blink-and-you'll-miss-it clause in the DMCA that requires all new VCRs to include mechanisms to conform to this "automatic gain control" technology; that is, VCRs that "circumvent" this measure are prohibited.[44] So, the hypothetical professor could not in fact use VHS copies to produce his teaching tool. More important, DVDs are rapidly replacing VHS, and the film industry already intended to move to online distribution as a replacement for both. It was precisely the DMCA that let them do so, that they had been waiting for. Judge Newman's comment only made sense at the moment it was uttered, when a low-fi and less restrictive alternative to the DVD was still common; this will not be the case in the near future, when all films come in digital form and with digital protections. If the DMCA is the legal assurance the film industry needed before it could kill off analog formats, Newman's suggestion becomes meaningless precisely with his decision in this case.

In the DMCA and in the court's interpretation of it, access and use are treated as distinct. Copying for fair reasons can in theory still be allowed, even though technical barriers and access controls might preempt copying altogether. Rules can be applied to access without seeming to affect use; protections in one are presumably not compromised by restrictions in another. But the DRM strategy depends on the fact that use always follows access and that rules about access therefore have ramifications for use. Access controls channel users into a technical realm where only some uses are possible and copying can be eliminated, leaving fair use nothing to shield.

Beyond Copyright

With the DMCA in place, digital encryption like CSS enjoys the force of law; it is now not only a turnstile, it is a turnstile that's illegal to jump. Most film viewers are not also hackers, of course, which means they would not know how to circumvent it anyway, but the tools that might make it easy to do so are also illegal and scarce. It is this limit on the tools for circumvention that is much more important in moving us toward a comprehensive technolegal copyright strategy. But the DMCA does more than just make it hard for users to find hacking tools like DeCSS. It also helps the movie industry intervene in the design of legitimate DVD players. If regulation by the trusted system is a two-step process, that is, controlling access and then also limiting the functions of the devices that grant access, then the content industries need both steps to hold. The restriction on anticircumvention tools, which may seem at first glance to be about eliminating black-market hacker apps, is really the way in which the studios hold DVD manufacturers to the terms of the trusted system arrangement—the gun to the head that forces them to sign on the dotted line.

CSS encryption is a proprietary lock that forces manufacturers to license the key. Since there's only one place to get this key, the studios can demand that manufacturers enforce whatever limits they desire—a king's ransom for their own films, which they themselves hold hostage, to be paid by the public. Again, CSS does not by itself prevent copying, but it assures that the only technologies that can play the film are authorized ones. It is this authorization that allows the movie studios to dictate the terms for what the technologies allow or prohibit. Encryption serves as a yoke, built by the movie studios and those consumer electronics manufacturers who partnered with them, with which to rein in all manufacturers of DVD players and DVD software and enforce on them the terms of the CSS license.

The CSS license, implemented and overseen by the DVD Copy Control Association (DVD-CCA), maps out the terms that any manufacturer of DVD players must accept.[45] It is overwhelmingly about proper hardware copy control, the structural blueprint for a trusted system device. Section 6.2, which takes up four-fifths of the forty-three-page agreement, spells out what designers of DVD players or applications must do in order to ensure that (1) the device does not copy films itself, (2) the film cannot be transmitted to other devices in a format that would facilitate duplication, and (3) the device will not play illicitly copied discs.[46] Devices must

• incorporate copy control signals, such as automatic gain control, in any analog output signal (to, say, a television);

• not deliver a high definition analog signal unless the DVD was already encoded as such;

• only deliver a digital output in one of three authorized formats (IEEE 1394, USB, and DVI), each of which is equipped with "digital transmission copy protection";

• not play recorded media that indicates that it was not to be copied, or CSS scrambled material stored on a consumer-grade DVD-R;

• scramble the CSS key inside the software as it is passed from portions of the system that authenticate to portions that decrypt, to avoid its discovery by hackers;

• actively frustrate attempts to defeat the copy protection, to discover the CSS keys, or to discover CSS algorithm info, by encrypting this information, building it into physical architecture, protecting the flow of information between parts of the machine or application, and self-monitoring the integrity of the system so that modifications will make the entire system fail.[47]

Licensees must agree to all of these terms and agree to make any further changes the DVD-CCA requests in light of new circumstances. Manufacturers must even submit to surprise spot checks to ensure compliance.

This technologically enforced licensing scheme is an egregious intervention into the distribution of cultural expression. By locking up their movies, the studios can ask almost anything of hardware manufacturers. The manufacturers can only obtain the key if they agree to every demand. And let's remember, nothing in the DMCA says that it applies only to barriers that allow access on a yes or no basis. There's nothing to prevent the major studios from imposing micro-limitations on film, including (but not limited to) pricing schemes, repeat access, access to different portions, access by different types of users. One example already in place is the restriction on skipping trailers, ads, and copyright messages at the start of the DVD. Circumvention of these restrictions has no copyright implications, but could nevertheless be construed as a violation of the DMCA.

It is important to see the impact of this CSS license in the context of the broader role of licenses and contracts in the current execution of copyright. To the extent that copyright articulates the rights of owners and users of cultural works in the midst of a (typically commercial) transaction, the law itself is like a contract between owner and user, though one that is the same for everyone. Historically, licenses have also been used to further specify how the ownership or use rights are transferred within those broader legal guidelines. For example, copyright law says that the MIT Press owns this book and therefore has exclusive rights to publish it; but inside of that rule, you may be able to convince them to give you the right to reprint a chapter in your anthology, an agreement that will be governed by a contract. Particularly because copyright in the U.S. is a divisible and transferable bundle of rights, "ownership and exploitation of copyright are structured at every turn by contract."[48]

Typically, there has been no explicit licensing agreement between copyright holder and consumer. I buy your song on CD and am thus bound by the laws of commerce, and my use of it is restricted by copyright law because, although I own the disc, you retain ownership of the music it contains. Increasingly, however, and especially with digital information, owners are including licenses with their work that further articulate what consumers can and cannot do. In that case, when I download your song, I am bound by a complex agreement that lays out the particular permissible uses I can make of that work, in much more specificity than copyright law ever could—and I remain bound by copyright law as well. Known as "shrinkwrap licenses," these now commonly appear as click-through agreements that pop up before we download or use software, or sometimes upon first arriving at a commercial website. These licenses are binding contracts to which we agree when we click, whether we read them or not, whether we're in a position to define their terms or not.

Mark Lemley worries that the prevalence of these shrinkwrap licenses could tip the copyright balance in the favor of copyright owners:

Giving the parties unlimited power under contract law to vary the rules of intellectual property creates considerable tension with this balanced incentive structure. And permitting the parties to alter intellectual property law with a standard-form, unsigned "shrinkwrap license," in which even the fiction of "agreement" is stretched to the vanishing point, exalts the (standard) form of contract law over the substance of intellectual property.[49]

It is easy to imagine the owner of a work attempting to use the power of a license to distort the typical balance of rights assured by copyright. As I download my music file purchased from iTunes, a licensing agreement could pop up that says "you may not distribute this work without permission of the owner" (merely restating their copyright, although downplaying important exceptions), or "you may only play this file on Thursdays" (a term unrelated to copyright), or "you may not parody this work"—an attempt to prohibit a freedom promised to me by the fair use doctrine.[50]

The mechanism meant to assure that such contracts do not extend past what copyright law allows is the "preemption doctrine."[51] It asserts that the conditions of copyright law trump any other legal arrangement that horns in on its legal territory. But there are those who argue that preemption is a limited and clumsy tool, and that the embrace of the shrinkwrap license, especially in the addition of Article 2B to the Uniform Commercial Code granting digital contracts the force of law, has allowed owners to dramatically contract away users' rights. Lessig noted a particularly poignant example of this when he discovered that the Adobe e-book version of his own book *The Future of Ideas*, about the technical restriction of copyright, demanded particularly strict usage rules inside its encoded user's license—it even prohibited the consumer from using the device's "read aloud" function.[52]

These concerns are further exacerbated by the way DRM works, in that the rights and restrictions are not only imposed without the negotiation or assent of the user, but also built into the technology such that they enact themselves. If I believe the terms of a shrinkwrap license violate copyright law or are unethical, I can defy them. I risk a lawsuit, but a lawsuit would at least provide the opportunity for my grievances to be heard, and to have the contract ruled void. On the other hand, if my hardware simply will not perform the action I would like to perform, I can only reject the DRM-enforced license by not participating at all. Lessig's e-book simply prevents the book from being read aloud by the device; he couldn't defy these rules if he wanted to. It's their terms, or nothing. And the particulars of the restriction can be so embedded in the software code as to leave the typical user incapable of critiquing them.

It is now technologically possible to license and track a wide array of practices for an immense number of users, and to build the terms of a licensing agreement directly into digital files or into the tools necessary to use them. And the current tendency in U.S. jurisprudence is to defer to private contracts as a more precise instrument for managing commercial transactions than the law (especially in cyberspace, which some economists see as more closely matching the ideal of the frictionless market).[53] Now with the DMCA, circumvention is prohibited, meaning that the technologies that automatically enforce these licenses are further assured by the force of law.

This combination suggests that the conceptual relationship between copyright and contract needs to be reexamined. One way copyright law can be thought of is as the default rules for when there is no other articulated agreement. This would suggest that two parties should be allowed to draw up any contract they want that differs from that, and if the buyer signs, the terms are accepted, period. A different way to think about copyright is that it establishes a set of rights for owners and users that should always apply. In this case, licenses should only be for specifying details that are either within, or separate from, those elaborated by copyright. Shrinkwrap licenses raise the key problem with the first paradigm: I am certainly not on equal standing with Time Warner or Microsoft when I "negotiate" this contract, I can only take it or leave it. Entertainment companies are in a powerful position to set the terms by which cultural work is disseminated, with consumers as well as artists. There is nothing to prevent these providers from using DRM-enforced licenses to grab for more copyright control, in order to maximize the value of their work and restrict fair uses that might undermine it.

The DVD-CCA license represents a different problem. DRM-enforced shrinkwrap licenses articulate the rules and responsibilities of content provider and end-user. To the extent that these rights can overlap with copyright, the preemption doctrine can help ensure that content owners don't contractually overreach what they are entitled to. Contracts between content and hardware companies like the CSS license, however, do not themselves step on the toes of anyone's copyright privileges, at least not directly, so it is difficult to imagine how the preemption doctrine could be brought to bear. Instead, these licenses obligate the manufacturer to produce a technological and economic environment together that just as powerfully regulates users' activities, and keeps out competitors who might want to cater to those activities.

Protecting CSS

So how is the DMCA prohibition of circumvention tools, the rule that makes posting DeCSS illegal, a way to fortify the CSS license? At the time the *Universal v. Reimerdes* suit was brought, there were no authorized DVD player applications for the Linux operating system. This meant Linux users could not play DVDs on their computers, discs they had purchased and therefore presumably had authorization to use. Here is a personal use restricted (purposefully or not) by the business strategies of the film industry, and ensured by the CSS access control. The defendants claimed that DeCSS was part of a development effort to design a DVD player for the Linux operating system, and that a legitimate tool was being squelched by the stipulations of the DMCA.

Admittedly, the claim that DeCSS was part of a Linux project probably belongs in the grey area between accurate and convenient. But what is important here is not the validity of the defense, but the principles by which it was rejected. In the preliminary injunction, Judge Lewis Kaplan dismissed the Linux defense when he stated that, "although defendants contended at oral argument that DeCSS was not designed primarily to circumvent CSS, that argument is exceptionally unpersuasive."[54] This is not what they argued, of course. DeCSS was precisely to circumvent CSS, but for a legitimate purpose. Nevertheless, the court rejected the argument by saying that the question was not about use at all. In Judge Kaplan's eyes, even if DeCSS was for playing DVDs on Linux machines, doing so still entailed circumvention of CSS without authorization, violating the DMCA.

Notice how fair use gets hamstrung between access controls and hardware restrictions; there is simply no place for its consideration. The question ignored is not whether DeCSS developers circumvented to infringe, but whether they circumvented to infringe fairly. It was the law that stopped them from circumventing; it was the lack of authorized Linux players that kept them from making use of their DVDs. The tools do not even get their day in court as potentially contributing to copyright infringement the way the VCR and Napster did, where they might enjoy the protection afforded by the *Sony* doctrine.

The legal system seems singularly uninterested in dealing with the way fair use is now trapped between a technological rock and a legal hard place. Legislators and jurists cannot even see the problem. Consider how responsibility is subtly abrogated inside of this statement from Judge Kaplan's injunction: "In consequence, even though the fair use doctrine permits limited copying of copyrighted works in appropriate circumstances, the CSS encryption of DVD movies, coupled with the characteristics of licensed DVD players, limits such uses absent circumvention of CSS."[55] What is described as "the characteristics of licensed DVD players" is treated as a natural phenomenon, as if DVD players sprout from the ground without Record buttons. In fact, such characteristics are explicitly mandated in the CSS license at the whim of the movie studios. By hiding the system of control inside the technology, not in the CSS encryption but in the hardware itself, the content providers avoid judicial scrutiny, all in the glorious name of preventing piracy and ensuring the continued strength of the American economy.

It is clear, then, why it was so important to the movie studios that the courts protect the security of the CSS algorithm. The threat was not that copyrights would be infringed, but that DeCSS would undermine the power of the CSS license to bind this coalition of content, hardware, and software manufacturers. The designers of DeCSS were not so much pirates as they were upstart manufacturers, of a sort. Their efforts to design a tool outside of the terms of the licensing agreement they didn't want to sign made them a threat to the studios, to the forced collusion with manufacturers that the CSS license ensures, and to the profit streams that collusion aims to generate.[56]

Instead of getting hung up on the fact that DeCSS was designed by a teenage hacker who, by all evidence, wanted people to pirate movies, imagine this in terms of two competing consumer electronics companies. The first, an established vendor, designs a DVD player for the market that adheres to the CSS license, that plays movies but cannot copy them. A second consumer electronics company wants to compete with the first by marketing a device that plays DVDs and allows users to copy them—a DVD player with a Record button. The second company has two choices: it could sign the CSS license and then violate its terms, but this would put the company in breach of contract and make it vulnerable to legal challenge. Or, it could not sign the CSS license, but then it would not have the necessary decryption keys. Now imagine that this company employs some clever computer science graduates, and one of them figures out how to get around the CSS encryption. In a world without the DMCA, it could then go ahead and design a device that will play the film by circumventing CSS, and allow users to do what they please (be it fair or infringing). With the DMCA, the studios can sue these manufacturers, not for copyright violation, but for designing and distributing a circumvention tool, in much the same way as they did here. Manufacturers are left with no choice: signing the CSS license and agreeing to its terms is the only way to avoid legal jeopardy. The DMCA then ends up distinguishing between legitimate and illegitimate manufacturers, making the choice to sign the CSS license no choice at all.

Sleight of Hand

In the *Universal v. Reimerdes* decision, the courts decided to forego the messy work of adjudicating copyright, despite the congressional mandate that makes this their responsibility. The DMCA gave them leave to do this by shifting copyright from a constitutional guideline arbitrating the balance between proper and improper use, to a sanction strengthening technological controls designed and implemented by copyright owners. DRM encryption, and the license that lies beneath it, were given the legal teeth that the studios had requested. Hollywood could lock up its films and demand that hardware manufacturers and software designers enforce its preferred uses; Congress would ensure that the system remained secure by prosecuting hackers, discouraging circumventors, and shutting down the channels by which decryption tools might circulate; the courts rejected the suggestion that this policy solution might have injurious effects on the constitutional balance copyright was designed to preserve.

It is these two dimensions that distinguish the DRM system imposed on DVDs from the failed SDMI effort of the music industry. The encryption itself offered the kind of binding force that the voluntary SDMI effort did not have: Manufacturers of DVD players are hard-pressed to refuse this arrangement, because to do so would mean their devices will not play Hollywood movies, hardly a viable economic decision when the overwhelming majority of films watched by American consumers are studio produced. There was no negotiation to walk away from, in that the studios could simply begin encrypting and wait for manufacturers to accept their terms. And shifting the point of control from the adjudication of use to the enforcement of access control could only work with a law like the DMCA in place. Users who tried to elude the technical barrier could face real legal consequences and, more important, upstart manufacturers couldn't do their own reverse engineering and then undercut the authorized manufacturers by designing a DVD player without the required restrictions.

The sleight of hand here is that the call for the protection of copyright, the heightened fears of piracy, and the careful characterization of the Internet as a fundamentally unsafe space for cultural expression, have all helped usher in a legally sanctioned, technologically enforced collusion of corporate content providers and hardware and software manufacturers. Together they can dictate not only the range of possible uses of cultural expression, but also how, when, and to what extent we will be charged for them.

As Lessig has noted, the law plays a crucial role in building such regimes: not just as part of the arrangement or its moral justification, but as the very authority that holds it together.[57] It is in a unique position to give regimes of alignment their sticking power, and it is where the characterization of technology as an effective intervention has the most resonance and consequence. Lawmakers seem to increasingly prefer this indirect intervention, rather than taking the more traditional role of imposing explicit restrictions through law. This, more than anything else, will be how the Internet is subsumed into systems of control, particularly systems of control that assure the workings of commerce and make all other concerns secondary. As Lessig explains,

Even if it is hard to regulate behavior given the Internet as it is, it is not hard for the government to take steps to alter, or supplement, the architecture of the Net. And it is those steps in turn that could make behavior on the Net more regulable. This is a regulatory two-step: the Net cannot be regulated now, but if the government regulates the architecture of the Net, it could be regulated in the future. And when government regulation of the architecture of the Net is tied to the changes that commerce is already introducing, I argue, the government will need to do very little to make behavior on the Net highly regulable. This strategy of regulation is nothing new. From the beginning of the modern state, government has been regulating to make its regulations work better.[58]

What is lost are the venues in which the public interest side of copyright might effectively counterbalance the demands of copyright owners, who can only envision the value of culture through a lens of their own commercial survival and success. There is nothing to remind us that whatever rules we set about information will powerfully regulate cultural expression, social participation, and the production of knowledge. Perhaps not only the act of expression, but also the act of circulation, can be a valuable element of social participation and learning, but this is shrouded by a system entrusted only to sell, deliver, and collect.

Most of all, as Litman has pointed out, it is Congress who has abrogated their responsibility to raise the question of the public interest. Perhaps this should not come as a surprise. Congressional apathy is endemic to the history of copyright legislation in general.[59] The question of the rights and values regarding cultural expression, once argued in the legal arena, has now been handed to technologists and private corporations to decide for themselves and hardwire in. What was a question of the rights of citizens becomes a question of the preferences of consumers, as characterized by producers. Lawmakers, who might still have an opportunity to demand that this shift include a debate about users' rights, seem debilitated by the technological sheen the debate has taken on. Consider how the following comment, from the House of Representatives discussion of the DMCA before its implementation, first acknowledges the risks of the pay-per-view society, then reveals a sense of futility about turning the inevitable tide of technological progress:

The growth and development of the Internet has already had a significant positive impact on the access of American students, researchers, consumers, and the public at large to informational resources that help them in their efforts to learn, acquire new skills, broaden their perspectives, entertain themselves, and become more active and informed citizens. A plethora of information, most of it embodied in materials subject to copyright protection, is available to individuals, often for free, that just a few years ago could have been located and acquired only through the expenditure of considerable time, resources, and money . . . Still, the Committee [on Commerce] is concerned that marketplace realities may someday dictate a different outcome, resulting in less access, rather than more, to copyrighted materials that are important to education, scholarship, and other socially vital endeavors. This result could flow from a confluence of factors, including the elimination of print or other hard-copy versions, the permanent encryption of all electronic copies, and the adoption of business models that depend on restricting distribution and availability, rather than upon maximizing it.[60]

The language is telling: "marketplace realities" might cause the benefits of the Internet for wide dissemination of information and debate to diminish, because of "the elimination of" alternatives and "the adoption of business models that depend on restricting distribution." Treating these business models as marketplace realities erases Congress's responsibility to regulate the market, something it has been less and less willing to do in recent years. Even in light of a foreseeable and potentially tragic shift, Congress sees itself as only able to adjust to these changes rather than orchestrate preferred alternatives.

The industries involved have been adamant in encouraging this hands-off approach to regulation. A 2003 joint statement from the record, computer, and software industries expressed worry that future congressional intervention might actually demand that copy and access controls include public interest caveats, and asserted that

how companies satisfy consumer expectations is a business decision that should be driven by the dynamics of the marketplace, and should not be legislated or regulated . . . The role of government, if needed at all, should be limited to enforcing compliance with voluntarily developed functional specifications reflecting consensus among affected interests. If government pursues the imposition of technical mandates, technology and record companies may act to ensure such rules neither prejudice nor ignore their interests.[61]

It is the DMCA that is facilitating the adoption of these very business models, handing over authority to technologies and licenses designed by content owners rather than laws designed by government. Congress is creating this world and giving it the authority of law, even as they claim they are merely watching it happen. In their sullen myopia, Congress even believes that the Internet brings us information that "just a few years ago could have been located and acquired only through the expenditure of considerable time, resources, and money," forgetting that much of this information was and is available in public libraries—a quiet reminder of a moment when the government was more than willing to design public institutions to permit the availability of free information, regardless of the commercial interests of publishers.

The legislature and the courts have consistently argued that strengthening copyright is the best and only way to pursue the public interest in cultural expression. The exceptions balanced in fair use, long squeezed, are at risk of being displaced in the paradigmatic shift from use to access, from infringement to circumvention, from policing to preemption, from law to license. It has become nearly unthinkable that the public interest should be served in any way other than ensuring that authors are also owners. The question of whether any of this is justified under the constitutional authority of the copyright doctrine has nearly disappeared within the skirmishes over code and circumvention. And in statutes like the DMCA, this logic is used not just to tip the copyright scales toward corporate owners, but to construct and stabilize particular arrangements of cultural distribution that work hand in hand with these interests, and often against the public welfare.

With this law and license system in place, the encryption of DVDs and the trusted system it imposes have the force of law to control users who circumvent it. More than that, the DMCA was as much about regulating manufacturers as it was users, by providing the backing not for the trusted system itself, but for the licensing arrangement it needed to even exist. All of this was facilitated by CSS as a means to lock up films so that both manufacturers and users would have to embrace the entire protection apparatus; the movie studios were fortunate to have been able to impose this encryption from the start, and with little oversight from government. When, however, they looked to extend this regulation to the new medium of digital television, they found that the public requirements about "free television" and "universal service" would make it untenable to encrypt their material at the source. Their solution was to turn this government oversight into an advantage, seeking a government mandate to impose the alignments required for a trusted system onto manufacturers, perhaps even more comprehensively and with greater authority.

Although the technical constraint is the first and most visible line of defense in the current copy protection on DVDs, it can only function with the support of a set of institutional and ideological alliances: the alliance between content and technology industries to produce the hardware and software that will do the regulating, and the alliance between industry and government to give the technology legal authority and criminal consequence. These institutions have typically enjoyed only tense and temporary alignments, symbiotic relationships but with different worldviews. In pursuit of the DRM strategy, they are by necessity coming more perfectly into alignment. This alignment is sometimes achieved forcibly, sometimes induced along shared commercial interests; always it is warmed by the embrace of a persuasive world view: the tale of Internet piracy and its consequences that the content industries have championed.

What is most difficult to achieve here is the kind of comprehensiveness that the vision of the trusted system requires—a control mechanism affecting all users, obligating all manufacturers, required whether it's in one's best self-interest or not. This is something no commercial entity, no matter how dominant in their own market, and no coalition of corporations, can accomplish. Only the state has the kind of reach and force necessary. In the DMCA, Congress lent both the consequence and the legitimacy of law to the technical measures for protecting digital content: Circumvent encryption or design a tool that does so, and face the consequences. But it did not go the additional step of requiring that such protection measures be imposed.

Content owners have been ambivalent about whether to seek such a mandate. Clearly the hope was that voluntary industry agreement (in SDMI) and industry licenses made persuasive by encryption (CSS) would be sufficient to bind together the various elements necessary for these regimes of alignment to work. But even in the case of DVD copy protection, violation of the system was quick to occur and impossible to undo, consequences were difficult to impose, and restitution was hard to achieve. Other proponents of the DRM strategy have argued that private arrangements will never be sufficient. Economic competitors are unlikely to agree on an encryption standard, when going it alone offers such financial potential, and accepting standards risks locking in an existing oligopoly. Plus, to the extent that the trusted system aspires to manage not only the DVD player but also every device that may connect to the Internet, there may simply be too many players to ever achieve consensus. Only the state has the authority to compel every manufacturer of every digital device to honor a set of rules; only the state has the power to bring economic antagonists to the bargaining table.

Turning to the state as the binding authority for a DRM system is, by all accounts, a double-edged sword. Engineering technical infrastructures is part of the responsibility of the state. But every highway system or electrical grid the state builds is always also an ideologically loaded manifestation of its power. Mukerji reminds us that "state power does not emerge simply from a balancing of interest groups or a definition of the legal bases for administering an area of the world, but from strategic uses of material advantages—engineering for power that includes weapons development but requires more than that. Western states have grown in significance since the early modern period as roads have been constructed, bridges built, telegraphs stretched, railroads laid, schools opened, libraries expanded, and dams erected."[1] Technical infrastructures are built not just to serve citizens or facilitate their economic transactions. They help publicly perform the state's authority, they organize the activities of its constituents in ways amenable to the state's aspirations, they symbolically model and thereby reinforce the state's societal ideals. The Great Wall of China is both a barrier to invaders and a symbol of the nation to itself and to the world; the U.S. railroads were both a means to travel west and a marker of America's commitment to exploration, a rendering of "manifest destiny" in wood, steel, and stone.

So to call upon the state to build technology or enforce the terms of its implementation, while it does bring with it the force and legitimacy of government power, also necessarily invests that engineering project with the political and ideological priorities of the state. State-authorized technology, whether built by the state, paid for through government funding, or built privately but then granted the state's imprimatur, must "speak" the state in both its design and its consequence.

And if it seems like it would be difficult to draw a range of competing corporations into alignment around a common project like DRM, the state may be the most unruly participant of them all: Bureaucratically complex, at least nominally beholden to its citizens and also to those who most persuasively have its ear, constrained by required procedures and schedules, and committed to multiple and often contradictory goals. Most important, however a state agency chooses to act, its actions must be articulated and justified in terms of public principles, regardless of how self-serving or beholden to special interests it may actually be. Though a particular governmental body may want to support a particular strategy, it may be simply unable to fit it discursively into the terms that it is required to serve.

There have been a number of attempts in recent years to develop legislation not just to give the DRM strategy legal teeth, as the DMCA did, but to directly impose obligations upon manufacturers of digital communication technologies—all manufacturers—to abide by some system of encryption-based copy protection. The first, and arguably most successful, was the 1992 Audio Home Recording Act (AHRA). Concerned that the emerging music format known as Digital Audio Tape (DAT) would facilitate digital-quality music piracy, the record industry called for legislation to compel DAT manufacturers to include a "serial copy management system." This system would allow the user to make one initial copy of a sound recording, but would mark that copy with a watermark indicating that it could not be copied again. DAT players are required to both impose this watermarking procedure and honor the watermark by refusing to copy a copy. The law passed without much fanfare; many have argued that it contributed to the lackluster performance of DAT as a consumer format. DAT continues to be used in recording studios, with its copy protection system in place.

The AHRA was deliberately written only for the DAT format, as it seemed to pose a unique threat. Since the explosion of recordable digital media like blank CDs, the shift in consumer habits toward using the computer as the primary storage and playback device for music, and the arrival of the Internet and the ease with which it allows digital copies of copyrighted content to circulate, subsequent legislative proposals have had to go well beyond regulating this or that technology, to designing rules that will regulate all digital media technologies, present or future. The Consumer Broadband and Digital Television Promotion Act (CBDTPA), known also as the "Hollings Bill" for the Senator who first championed it, was the most visible attempt to impose copy protection obligations on manufacturers of all digital media technologies. The bill was first circulated in August 2001 as the Security Systems and Standards and Certification Act (SSSCA). The bill's emphasis on computer security carefully cloaked what was an audacious effort to impose a DRM trusted system on all devices that came into contact with digital media content. Updated as the CBDTPA, the bill would have prohibited the manufacture, sale, import, or provision of any "interactive digital media device" that didn't incorporate certain security technologies. The consumer electronics and content industries would have one year to develop these security technologies, or else the FCC would step in and take over. The bill was allowed to die in committee after outcry from both the public and information technology manufacturers, who pointed out that the definition of "digital media device" was so broad that it could apply to nearly everything. Innovation in the technology sector could be hamstrung by forced adherence to a single encryption standard.

A similar effort to mandate DRM copy protection appeared in negotiations hosted by the FCC about cable systems and consumer hardware. The FCC hoped to establish "plug-and-play" rules to ensure that third party manufacturers could compete in the market for cable receivers, or "set-top boxes," so that consumers would not be compelled to use the hardware provided by their cable companies, and manufacturers would be able to start incorporating cable descrambling directly into digital televisions themselves. This meant requiring that cable providers separate the process of limiting access to authorized subscribers from the rest of the hardware services—channel navigation, interactive features, etc.—so that consumers could opt for a third-party device to handle those tasks. In the course of the negotiations, content interests led by the MPAA called for the FCC to require that set-top manufacturers use anticopying encryption. The MPAA hoped to include a system allowing marked content to trigger the "downrezzing" of digital or high-definition signals to a lesser analog quality if the device in question had the kind of output connections that allow copies to be made, and a function dubbed "selectable output control" in which coded instructions in the signal itself could trigger the device to shut off particular analog and digital outputs altogether.

The FCC rejected both of these encoding strategies in the case of broadcast television signals, but has thus far allowed for the possibility of "downrezzing" for pay-per-view, on-demand services, and premium channels like HBO, which recently took advantage of this to incorporate copy protection mechanisms into its signal.[2] Beyond restricting the use of these specific techniques, the FCC set caps on the extent to which copying can be prohibited: The basic tier of broadcast television must remain unscrambled and available for duplication; pay television, nonpremium subscription channels, and other "basic" cable options must allow one copy but can restrict additional copies; on demand and pay-per-view services can prohibit all copying, but must allow viewers the ability to pause the signal. Implicit in these caps is the understanding that Hollywood and cable providers will settle on a DRM system that can impose these restrictions, although technically the FCC order does not require them to do so.

More recent legislation seeks to impose similar obligations on the manufacturers of analog recording devices, in response to industry worries about the "analog hole." No matter how successfully DRM protects digital content, at some point it must be transformed into an analog signal (to reach the speaker, the screen, or the printed page). At that moment, it is vulnerable to being rerecorded without its protective encryption. This has often been used by critics of DRM to point out the futility of copy protection schemes, but has since become part of the puzzle DRM advocates hope to solve. To design copy protection that can survive the transition from digital to analog and back requires some system of rights management that does not depend on encryption, but rather on watermarks encoded in the data itself that cannot be stripped by intrepid hackers—the SDMI plan. But it would also depend on somehow compelling manufacturers of analog devices to incorporate systems for detecting and obeying these watermarks, and reencrypting any digital copies the user makes.

Drafted by the MPAA and introduced to the House in 2005, the Digital Transition Content Security Act (DTCSA) would require manufacturers of devices capable of converting analog to digital to look for and preserve watermarks that signal whether the content is permitted to be copied or not. The proposed legislation specifies the encryption system to be used, a combination of the "Content Generation Management System—Analog" (CGMS-A) developed by the Consumer Electronics Association, which inserts coded data in the same information channel that already carries closed captioning and V-chip data in broadcast signals, and the newer Video Encoded Invisible Light Technology (VEIL), a watermark inserted directly into the image so that the analog device can check what rights have been specified—so that if the CGMS-A data is removed, restrictions will still be imposed.

Finally, the major U.S. movie studios joined U.S. broadcasters in a call for the state to impose a system of technical protection as part of the transition to digital television broadcasting. Because of a number of peculiarities of this situation, the technical approach had to differ from that already adopted for DVDs. To impose technical copy protection onto U.S. television required enlisting the FCC as arbiter and enforcer of the trusted system the movie industry and its manufacturer partners had in mind. It was the FCC's jurisdiction over all TV manufacturers, not just those convinced to participate, that would give this DRM system its most expansive grip on the new medium. And it was the FCC's legitimacy as an independent agent, not beholden to strict economic imperatives, that would give this plan additional legitimacy.

But, again, enlisting the state in this kind of regime of alignment poses new challenges that corporations alone do not face; as this case makes clear, including the state also introduced new forces that kept such an alignment from taking shape. This is not to suggest that such a coalition could never develop, but rather to reveal the kind of political mobilization necessary, and to explore some of the fault lines that undercut it.

The Transition to Digital Television

Even as cable television has shifted over to an entirely digital service, and satellite television and digital recording devices like TiVo and DVRs have proliferated, traditional broadcast television has retained the analog format it embraced decades ago. However, during the 1990s Congress and the FCC together began orchestrating a digital transition for U.S. over-the-air broadcasting. In response to Japanese innovations in high-definition televisions (HDTV) in the 1980s, Congress held hearings in 1987 to consider how to spur similar innovations in the United States, both in display and in transmission. In 1990 the FCC officially called for the development of a new advanced television (ATV) standard for a digital broadcast signal. After several years of collaboration with industry partners, a suite of standards was made official in 1997.[3] That same year, the FCC granted existing commercial broadcasters free access to a portion of the broadcast spectrum dedicated to this transition to digital.

According to its proponents, digital television broadcasting promises an improvement of the current television experience, and eventually its transformation. Digital broadcasts are visually clearer and crisper, offer CD-quality sound, present images in the 16×9 aspect ratio of movie screens, and suffer less of the interference and ghosting common to analog signals. But the transition to digital offers more than just improvements in quality. Broadcasters will have a choice of broadcasting a DTV or HDTV signal. An HDTV signal occupies the same amount of frequency range (6MHz) as analog, but offers dramatically greater picture resolution. A DTV signal offers slightly lesser image quality, though still better than analog, but uses much less of the allotted frequency spectrum, meaning a broadcaster could offer several channels of DTV in the same frequency, called "multicasting." Some of those channels could offer data services rather than traditional television signals, or provide the means for some degree of interactivity with the consumer, such as on-demand services.[4]

There was some public controversy at the time about this "spectrum giveaway." Critics and activists were outraged that the frequencies dedicated to digital broadcasting were handed over, free of charge, to the entrenched, commercial broadcasters. Many believed that the frequencies should have been auctioned off to the highest bidder, so that resources nominally belonging to the public would at least have fetched a high price (estimates of the value of this portion of the spectrum were around $70 billion[5]) and provided revenue for public broadcasting or other social services. Some saw it as a sign that Congress, and especially the FCC, were fully in the back pocket of the powerful broadcasters, a charge that has dogged the FCC since its inception.[6] With the high-profile entertainment industry mergers in the 1990s, this concern has deepened; broadcasters are increasingly just small holdings of a very small and very powerful klatch of corporate entities that already exerts unprecedented influence over the federal government.

The digital spectrum did not, in fact, come without a price. Congress recognized that converting to digital broadcasting would incur significant costs for established broadcasters: new equipment and transmitters, changes in production and storage, potential consumer aggravation. These might not immediately produce sufficient returns in the form of additional viewers or increased advertising revenue, which meant broadcasters might be reluctant to invest in the transition. In order to spur this transition, the FCC argued it needed to offer broadcasters an incentive. Further, after the transition to digital is complete, the broadcasters are required to "return" their analog spectrum. This spectrum would then be of economic and political value for Congress; they could auction much of it off for commercial uses like wireless networking and essential social services like police communications, and set some aside for public interest purposes. This exchange is scheduled to happen no later than December 31, 2006,[7] although substantial exceptions allow for some drift in that deadline, the foremost question being whether the television audience has embraced digital television sets to a sufficient degree. Still—and this is crucial to understanding the disputes that followed—Congress made the assumption that this transition deadline would be met, and incorporated into future budgets the economic windfall the returned analog spectrum would produce, somewhere in the range of thirty to seventy billion dollars.[8]

The controversy regarding the allocation of this digital spectrum to existing commercial broadcasters drew most of the limited public attention that existed for this issue. Beyond it, the concerns raised were the perennial ones familiar to the history of broadcasting regulation: the cost of the transition for broadcasters and for viewers, and the public interest obligations that should accompany it. However, another concern was quietly being raised by the movie industry, one less familiar to the FCC. At the time, content producers were grappling with the explosion of file-trading over the Internet via peer-to-peer networks. While the music industry was being hardest hit, movies were beginning to appear online, and the major U.S. studios worried that the problem would only grow as consumer-grade bandwidth improved.

In the transition to digital television the studios saw, once again, both risk and opportunity. The move to digital broadcasting, they argued, would render it even easier for unscrupulous consumers to trade their films online, undercutting their economic value. At the same time, if technical and legal measures could be adopted as part of the digital transition, the studios could protect their content more thoroughly than ever before. If those were put into place early, before anyone even knew the full potential of digital television, they could avoid the more difficult task faced by the music industry—convincing users to accept less than they had already enjoyed. Just as with the Internet, the studios proclaimed that the new technology would fail if broadcasters and studios were reluctant to offer their content in the new format, and that stronger copyright protections were the only assurance they would accept.[9] Copyright and the fear of piracy, therefore, were put on the table for discussion—a discussion with a limited timeframe, one that Congress felt a certain financial as well as political imperative to meet.

But digital television posed a curious problem for the proponents of a technical scheme for copy protection. Congress and the FCC had indicated that they would not accept any arrangement in which terrestrial television broadcasts were encrypted at the source (as opposed to satellite). "Under current FCC regulations, most digital terrestrial television broadcasts are delivered in unencrypted form ('in the clear'). Thus, unlike prerecorded encrypted digital media such as DVD, or premium digital cable and satellite video transmissions delivered via conditional access, there may not be any licensing predicate to establish conditions for the secure handling of such content."[10] The justification for this tended to vary from moment to moment. Sometimes it was based on a theoretical commitment to the idea of broadcasting as a "free" and public service. At other times it was based on the more practical concern that switching to an encrypted broadcast signal would render all existing digital television sets obsolete and force all of those early adopters to replace their sets, which Congress and the FCC were loathe to ask of people.

Regardless of the reason, this meant that the trusted system model of copy protection, in which content is encrypted by its owner and authorized decryption devices protect that content by only permitting users to use, copy, or distribute it in particular ways, would not work here. The challenge then faced by the content industry was twofold. The technical challenge was how to design a system of technical control measures where the content is delivered "in the clear" and unencrypted. The institutional challenge was, as with DRM encryption, how to construct some binding obligation by which *all* devices would follow the rules. The movie studios and their allies attempted as before to answer the first challenge themselves, but opted to reach beyond industry coalitions for the second. This transformed the institutional challenge into a political question of: how to get a government mandate regulating all digital television technology, and how to convince that government body that such a mandate was necessary.

The way in which this plan was accomplished reveals the sociopolitical mechanisms necessary to produce a seemingly technical fix. What were necessary were industry and government venues within which a coherent plan could be authorized and implemented—an institutional alignment in which an often contentious group could achieve, or at least appear to achieve, some consensus. Whether this partnership between corporations and government could actually produce a system of copy protection for digital television, and regardless of what implications their solution might have for users, the commercial and political alignments required to even contemplate and build such a system have consequences. The future of digital culture, and copyright's role in it, face a deeper problem than just the imposition of technological constraints. In pursuit of these constraints, both the stakes and the stakeholders have changed.

The Broadcast Flag and All It Entails

Let me say first that, as I write, the "broadcast flag" copy protection system is on hold. After the FCC agreed to the plan proposed by the movie studios and major technology manufacturers and mandated it for all digital televisions and receivers, the District of Columbia Court of Appeals ruled that doing so was an overreach of the agency's authority. The issue is by no means over. The court clearly offered the possibility that Congress could grant the FCC the authority to impose the broadcast flag if they wanted to. So beyond this being a useful case for the consideration of technological regulation and the political alignments it requires, it is a plan that might still come to fruition, and it is still very much an ongoing controversy in the battle over digital copyright.

What the broadcast flag "is" is in many ways the heart of the controversy, of course, so it's important to be circumspect when describing it. The very nature of the technology (writ large) is contingent, contentious, and still under negotiation. That said, the basic premise is this: Digital broadcasts would be accompanied by a mark that indicated whether the owner of that content would permit it to be redistributed or not. Any digital tuner that transformed this signal into a displayable form would be required to check for and honor this flag. If the content was flagged, the tuner would allow it to be recorded only in specific formats—formats that would preserve the broadcast flag if that copy were passed to another device. Moreover, the tuner would only allow the flagged content to be distributed to other devices or across a network after encrypting it using one of a limited set of authorized encryption technologies. Encryption would assure that this content, while it could be played without limit, could only be distributed under specific circumstances, and not indiscriminately across the Internet.[11]

The broadcast flag began as a "redistribution control descriptor," a purely technical standard proposed by Fox Broadcasting (part of News Corporation) in May 2001. Fox brought the idea—at this point just the technical elements, not the accompanying rules or the legal and institutional arrangements it would require—to both the Advanced Television Systems Committee (ATSC), an independent organization that manages the technical standards of broadcast television, and the Digital Transmission Licensing Administrator (DTLA), the DRM licensing arm of the "5C" coalition of consumer electronics corporations: Sony, Matsushita/Panasonic, Intel, Toshiba, and Hitachi. Making the flag a technical standard was a small victory, as the flag does little by itself. It was the proposal made to the DTLA that started the process of building the institutional mechanisms to surround and support the broadcast flag. The Fox proposal was updated by the 5C companies and, in November 2001, presented to the Copy Protection Technical Working Group (CPTWG), the same group responsible for devising the CSS encryption system used to protect DVDs.

In the push for digital television, the studios once again saw both the chance to extend these technical protection strategies to broadcasting, and the danger that, if they did not, their investments would be undercut by increasing Internet piracy of their movies and television shows.[12] This imperative was articulated in the 5C presentation: "Currently, there is no enforceable technical means to prevent unauthorized redistribution of unencrypted digital terrestrial broadcasts,"[13] although, of course, there had been no such means for analog broadcasts either. What looks like redressing a deficit from one vantage point can be seen as pursuing new restrictions from another.

The Broadcast Protection Discussion Group (BPDG), formed under the authority of the CPTWG in late 2001, included representatives from each of the major studios and each of the 5C companies. It also included representatives from other consumer electronics corporations (including Philips, Pioneer, Sharp, Zenith), information technology and software companies (including Microsoft, IBM, the Computer and Communications Industry Association [CCIA]), companies specializing in existing forms of copy protection (including Macrovision, Secure Media, Digimarc), and consumer and public advocate groups (including the Electronic Frontier Foundation [EFF], Digitalconsumer, Public Knowledge). The composition of this group indicates a recognition that to impose such a system would require widespread agreement across several industries, or at least the appearance of it. As the CPTWG put it, "Because the solution will have to be implemented in products manufactured by companies in multiple industries, it would be most effective to develop the solution in a forum with dedicated participation from members of the affected industries."[14] But, as much as the plan required the commitment of these industries to be implemented, it also needed their stamp of approval to convince the FCC that the plan was indeed the product of cross-industry consensus.

In sixteen face-to-face and teleconference meetings, the BPDG discussed how digital television devices that received a flagged signal should treat that content—that is, what kind of restrictions were possible and necessary to impose a functional trusted system.[15] The arrangements described in the BPDG's "Final Report" differed significantly from previous DRM arrangements. As per congressional requirements, the digital broadcast would not be encrypted at the source. The digital TV signal would only have the flag, a mark indicating whether or not it required protection. Restriction would instead begin at the point of "demodulation," wherever the broadcast signal was transformed from code into image and sound. The BPDG proposed that any device capable of demodulating an over-the-air digital signal be required to check for the broadcast flag, and then, if the content was flagged, to limit how this content could be displayed, copied, or transferred to another device. Output would only be in authorized encryption formats—digital rights management (DRM) systems that prevented "indiscriminate redistribution" outside of the home or secure personal network. These "compliance" rules would need to be accompanied by "robustness" rules: Not only must the demodulation device follow a set of guidelines for what it could and could not do, it must materially frustrate attempts by users to undo or circumvent those limitations.[16]

Manufacturing Consensus

Under the aegis of a cross-industry coalition, a plan generated by one movie studio and expanded by its technology partners was given legitimacy as a widely accepted, cross-industry solution. While the FCC's justification for mandating the broadcast flag was clearly founded on the congressional mandate to facilitate the transition to digital television,[17] the details of that plan came almost entirely from the BPDG's final report. The FCC depended on this plan not only for convenience, but also because (internal caveats notwithstanding) the document seemed to represent industry consensus.

This consensus, whether apparent or real, was by no means an easy achievement. The fact that this was a coalition effort meant that, as the plan moved through the process, participants had the opportunity to take issue with its purpose and approach. A leakproof DRM system would require the participation of *all* the relevant hardware manufacturers, yet even some of those present were less than thrilled about a plan that would require these mechanisms to be built into all television devices. They may also have been less than thrilled about the market dominance that could quickly be achieved by the 5C companies were this plan to take effect, since that group was proposing the broadcast flag and simultaneously nominating their own encryption systems as components for its enforcement.

In large part, the development of the broadcast flag was a smooth process because the premise of the flag and how it would work was already agreed upon at the start, or agreed upon by enough of the major players that critics could be pushed aside. The BPDG's official charter already noted the need for some kind of "signal" marking copyrighted works and for the "effective technologies and legal enforcement mechanisms"[18] that would allow this signal to function effectively as a control mechanism. So, from the start, the basis for what would become the broadcast flag was already the frame within which the BPDG was even organized, imported directly from the Fox/5C presentation. Consensus was, if not a foregone conclusion, than at least partly achieved just by virtue of the formulation of the group. Further, the powerful rhetoric of Internet piracy and the narrative offered by the movie industry about its impact on digital television offered a compelling context for the effort, helping to cast the alignment of content industries, technology manufacturers, and government regulators as noble, necessary, and obvious. Finally, as many of these technology manufacturers were increasingly also DRM providers, their economic interests had changed in ways that encouraged closer alignment with the content industries; their fear of Internet piracy, once a nuisance, was now a profitable business opportunity.

However, while there was substantial consensus on the issue, a number of disputes did arise along the way. One participant described the process as "rife with acrimony, arbitrariness and confusion,"[19] charging that powerful members of the group were able to choreograph consensus by marginalizing those more critical of the plans being put forth. Some concerns persisted throughout the debates, while others erupted at particular moments and along particular fault lines. Some could not be entirely reconciled and appeared in the final report of the BPDG, shaping in important ways the discussions with the FCC that followed. Together these concerns are indicative of the kinds of problems that arise when technology is used as a regulatory mechanism, and contentious institutions are asked to align regarding the design and enforcement of these technical regulations.

Though the discussion taken on by the BPDG was already framed in terms of *how* a technical control mechanism would be imposed, activist groups like the EFF were in some instances able to momentarily revive the question of *why*, challenging the project along two lines. First, should broadcasting, intended as a free and public resource, even be subject to strict no-copy rules? This was not merely an ideological critique, but also a practical one. The EFF suggested that making the technology do less might not be wise just as Congress was hoping to convince more users to adopt the technology. Second, was it appropriate in light of the risk that standards could stifle innovation? A standard affecting nearly all consumer electronics and computing technologies, whether established by government or industry, would run counter to the open platform approach thus far embraced by the computer and networking industries.

Considering the initial mandate of the BPDG and the institutional affiliations of most of the attendees of these meetings, these concerns may have been raised mostly for symbolic value. It's unlikely that the consortium would have halted its discussion on the basis that its underlying purpose was untenable or misguided. The challenge may have been more of a gesture intended to force this initial justification to remain on the table for possible scrutiny, or to establish the EFF's reservations early so that more "reasonable" critiques might be more clearly heard later. As the BPDG discussions produced hardened proposals and were passed along to the FCC, the EFF relinquished this critique in order to maintain their standing to participate in and comment on subsequent decisions. Notably, none of the representatives from technology companies shared the EFF's concerns, at least publicly.

A more central and recurring concern was the range of activities that the broadcast flag and its regulatory framework would prohibit. Many of the consumer electronics representatives in the BPDG were concerned that the initial mandate "to prevent unauthorized redistribution of unencrypted digital over-the-air broadcast content on a worldwide basis (including unauthorized redistribution over the Internet)"[20] had morphed in its scope. All participants seemed to agree that redistribution within the home and secure personal networks should be allowed, and that posting programs on the Internet should not. In between was a grey area very much in dispute. The content industries wanted to prevent "unauthorized redistribution outside the home or personal digital network environment,"[21] whereas the technologists preferred a more narrow definition of what was prohibited, so as to prevent only "indiscriminate redistribution of such content over the Internet or through similar means."[22] In particular, the MPAA and the consumer electronics manufacturers parted ways on the question of whether secure e-mail transmission of a recorded program might be acceptable. The clearest and perhaps only major crack in the otherwise united front of the MPAA and the 5C companies revolved around this issue. In a comment sent to the FCC, the DTLA asserted that it "disagrees with the MPAA suggestion that the focus of unauthorized redistribution should be on the unauthorized redistribution beyond a 'local environment' consisting of a set of devices within a tightly defined geographic area around a Covered Product."[23]

The dispute came down to a couple of words: Should the prohibition be on redistribution "including" or "only" over the Internet? Should it prevent "unauthorized" or "indiscriminate" redistribution? At times it was a metaphorical difference more than anything else: The MPAA's interests were generally articulated in terms of spatial boundaries, restricting the movement of content to a "local environment," while the technologists framed their concerns in terms of permission and purpose, distinguishing between secure and insecure connections, and authorized and "indiscriminate" distribution. Still, the dispute gets to the heart of what little disagreement does remain between the content industries and technology manufacturers. While the consumer electronics companies, 5C in particular, could see the economic advantage of an alliance with the movie industry and the chance to be first to market, other manufacturers saw the economic value of getting beyond older visions of the home theater; perhaps it could be a central device that stored and organized all of a user's media, then sent it wirelessly not only to any device in the house but to remote devices and to other authorized users. The desire to offer their consumers wider choice in how they relocate their content led some electronics manufacturers to resist the tighter constraints sought by the MPAA.

Regardless of its scope, the broadcast flag proposal would have little effect if, though the DTV tuner couldn't copy flagged programming, a user could simply pass the content to another device that could. Somehow, *all* devices that dealt with digital television content would have to be compelled to honor the broadcast flag and help prevent redistribution. This threatened to expand the scope of regulation well beyond television sets, and to eclipse the alignment between the MPAA and 5C, by pushing the issue onto manufacturers of computers, handheld devices, software, and communication networks. Would any device (and potentially even those not yet invented) that could connect via a network to a digital television tuner have to honor the same rules? What if the DTV tuner was a computer with a DTV card, meaning it could conceivably be connected to any kind of device computers are now, or will be, connected to? What would compel all of those manufacturers to design their devices to accommodate this system of control?

The solution reached by the group was to return to encryption. If a regulated digital television receiver passed flagged programming to another device, it must first encrypt it using an authorized encryption system—returning the broadcast flag question to the familiar logic of the trusted system. The regulation of "downstream devices" would then be enacted not through legislative mandate, but through the particular licensing arrangements struck between technology manufacturers using that encryption. A second device, to be compatible with files encrypted in a particular encryption format, must honor the license for that form of encryption. The license would require the device to obey the same broadcast flag rules the first device did, just as the CSS license requires DVD players to honor the rules associated with CSS. This, of course, could lead to a number of complications, in that the various licensing arrangements could produce not one but a dizzying array of regulation schemes, could end up fostering incompatible formats, and might be used to also impose regulations that might go well beyond the limited "indiscriminate redistribution" prohibition.[24]

This led to the most substantial dispute: Which encryption schemes should be authorized, by whom, and according to what criteria? The focal point of this dispute was "Table A," the proposed list of authorized encryption and output technologies that would accompany the broadcast flag mandate. Some participants wanted certain widely used DRM mechanisms automatically added to Table A as part of the proposal to the FCC. It's no surprise that the 5C companies were eager to see their own DRM schemes preapproved in this way. Others wanted the criterion for inclusion to be industry agreement, although how this agreement would be determined was itself disputed—would it require a quorum of willing industry reps, or would the market decide? Others called for an independent body to decide which DRM systems would receive authorization according to some more neutral criteria such as what functions should and should not be allowed.

Interestingly, the BPDG passed on deciding this issue, calling for a parallel discussion group to be formed. It is the one significant issue in which the group's final report does not offer a single conclusion. Perhaps, as with SDMI, the economic and ideological worldviews of the various participants were too disparate to allow for a compromise, although in this case the disagreement did not unravel the entire effort. The final report put forth two competing plans culled from the discussions: one, favored by the MPAA and 5C companies, in which DRM systems could be approved by three major studios, or ten electronics companies and two studios, or by some measure of market acceptance;[25] the other, sponsored by Philips Electronics, suggesting independent adjudication according to more functional criteria.[26]

Of this entire effort to build the kind of coalition necessary to then call upon the FCC to act, the schism between Philips and its competitors may be the most revealing. Not a member of the 5C coalition, Philips clearly had much to lose if its competitors were to get a jump on the market for digital television tuners. The 5C encryption systems are designed only to be compliant with each other; if they were handed an early lead on DTV devices, that incestuous design feature would further exclude Philips products from competition. Early in the discussions, Philips proposed an alternative scheme to the Fox/5C model, called the "Open Copy Protection System." It also proposed an alternative model for authorizing DRM systems for inclusion in Table A.[27] In April 2002, while the BPDG negotiations were underway, their North American CEO Lawrence Blanford felt compelled to address the House Energy and Commerce Subcommittee on Telecommunications and the Internet to complain about the inner workings of the consortium. Expressing a lack of confidence that consensus would be achieved, he told Congress, "Private industry should be given a chance to reach a consensus, but the process should be cleansed by the sunlight of government. Further discussion should be held in an open forum, with the involvement of those who are entrusted with the development of public policy."[28]

The EFF was more vocal than Philips about its concerns throughout the effort to gather industry consensus, claiming afterward that the appearance of consensus was itself manufactured: "There appears to be some support for some or all of our positions among other members of the Discussion Group. We perceive that no consensus exists on these issues. We believe that the draft report is not only incorrect in failing to report the lack of consensus, but that it is part of a deliberate attempt to force a particular outcome on the so-called consensus process."[29] Philips, along with the Computer and Communications Industry Association, signed on to the EFF's critique of the BPDG final report, which criticized not only the application of technical constraints to digital television and the manner in which they would regulate, but also the process by which the BPDG handled the production of its report.[30]

This friction was downplayed by those who wanted the BPDG report to seem as consensual as possible. The MPAA remarked, "There were a few dissenting views regarding some compliance and robustness recommendations, but of some 70 organizations that participated in the BPDG, only some 14 submitted dissenting comments on one or more issues. Of these 14 dissenters, six were self-styled 'consumer' groups that appear to be opposed in principle to any restraints whatsoever on the reproduction and redistribution of content."[31] This comment not only reveals the way groups like the EFF get marginalized, it helps accomplish it. The disputes raised by Philips, however, and the frustration it expressed over the way the BPDG made its recommendations, suggests that the capacity to achieve a real consensus around this issue was far from complete.

Beyond making proposals for a viable technology and the legal mechanisms it would require, and bringing industry players into agreement, the

BPDG was designed to manufacture and put onstage the necessary industry consensus to bolster the idea that stronger copyright protection is in everyone's interest. To choreograph the installation of this kind of technical measure on this scale, and to eventually convince the FCC to back it, meant obviating the criticism that the proposal was mere economic self-interest. To a large extent, the final report of the BPDG accomplished this. While the report acknowledged some points of internal dispute, it presented itself as a finished product, including a draft of a broadcast flag mandate that elided those disputes in favor of the MPAA and 5C companies' perspective. On the other hand, the inability to achieve consensus on the final issue of how a DRM system would be granted Table A authorization, introduced a gap in this demonstration of consensus that would prove crucial as the broadcast flag moved from proposal to mandatory federal regulation in the hands of the FCC.

Calling Upon the State

To make it possible for these rules to be imposed, not just on those manufacturers who were already willing to accept them but on every manufacturer of digital television tuners, this plan would require the mandate of law. The failure of SDMI suggested that achieving voluntary agreement from such a varied set of interested parties was an unlikely accomplishment. The reasonably successful DVD encryption system depended on the consensus of a smaller group of producers and manufacturers, with closely aligned interests, to develop a system that could subsequently compel all others to agree to it through a kind of technological extortion. For the broadcast flag plan to work, however, the studios would need every television manufacturer (whether party to these discussions or not) to agree, and would reshape a cultural form that had traditionally been expected to serve a wider public interest than pop music or Hollywood films. To do this, the plan would need governmental authority to have persuasive power over all parties. In addition, this state imprimatur would lend the plan legitimacy in the eyes of the public—a public that was skeptical of the "spectrum giveaway" that had initiated the transition to digital television, enamored with peer-to-peer file trading, and relatively unfazed by the fears of piracy expressed by the content industries.

The FCC responded to the BPDG proposal in August 2002 with a "notice of proposed rulemaking" in which it raised a number of questions regarding the plan as it stood, and remarked that "despite the consensus reached on the technical standard to be implemented, final agreement was not reached on a set of compliance and robustness requirements to be associated with use of the ATSC flag, enforcement mechanisms, or criteria for approving the use of specific protection technologies in consumer electronics devices."[32] In November 2003, after receiving additional commentary from many of the BPDG participants as well as critics outside of it, the FCC ordered that broadcast flag regulations be imposed on all digital television devices. Its plan was almost entirely copied from the MPAA and 5C version of the BPDG final report. The FCC did, however, issue a "further notice of proposed rulemaking" in which it extended some of the questions about its proper application, particularly about the way the "downstream" DRM encryption technologies would be authorized.

By not having resolved this question itself, the BPDG had given the FCC an opportunity to interject itself into the process. The FCC dismissed the MPAA proposal of industry oversight, recognizing that it could leave digital television with "one industry segment exercising a significant degree of control over decisions regarding the approval and use of content protection and recording technologies in DTV-related equipment."[33] FCC co-chairman Michael Copps put his concern more bluntly: "Granting a small set of companies the power to control all digital video content through a government-mandated technology in order to promote digital television is neither necessary nor wise. A broadcast flag mandate that lacked adequate protections and limits would be reprehensible public policy."[34]

Instead, the FCC decided it would be in charge of arbitrating over Table A, judging on functional criteria—an idea that approximates Philips's proposal. Whether or not this would have been an interim or a permanent solution, the decision raised some concerns. First, the FCC has little experience arbitrating over and guiding technological design, particularly involving computational algorithms. As an organization, it has traditionally been charged with monitoring broadcast content and overseeing the granting of licenses. Although this has at times included the material technology of radio and television, the recent convergence of broadcasting and computing and the addition of technical copy protection to the issue would pull the FCC well beyond its traditional expertise. Some suggested that the FCC would end up turning back to the technology manufacturers for guidance in such cases, which would hand back to the major technology manufacturers the power to set the terms upon which such decisions were made—again "granting a small set of companies the power to control all digital video content through a government-mandated technology."

It is possible to argue here that the FCC was taking an independent stance, rejecting the MPAA and 5C's most egregious attempt to insert themselves into a lucrative gatekeeper role, and taking on the burden of adjudicating DRM systems themselves. The recurring charge that the FCC is captured by the industry, and structurally incapable of challenging the industry on substantial issues, cannot fully account for this move. On the other hand, it is also possible to downplay this as a small dispute inside of a broader embrace of the MPAA's and 5C's underlying purposes and perspectives. The Fox proposal, which begat the 5C presentation, which begat the BPDG final report, more or less begat the FCC order. Regardless of whether the industry gets to define the DRM systems of its choice or must appeal to the FCC as arbitrator, it did convince the FCC that technical copy protection is an obvious and necessary component of digital television, and successfully articulated digital piracy as a threat grave enough to warrant a complex and unprecedented regulatory constraint on television manufacturers and on the viewers.

A second concern was whether the FCC even had jurisdiction over such issues. The agency would not only be regulating consumer electronics technology, but also regulating for the purposes of copyright protection. While it is not surprising that those who supported the broadcast flag mandate claimed the FCC did have jurisdiction and critics tended to say it did not, the character of their explanations pointed to the way in which the question itself is changing. The FCC had played no direct part in any previous copyright regulation.

In 2001 the chief of the FCC's Mass Media Bureau said that "copy protection technology and licensing is almost entirely outside the Commission's control."[35] When the agency later published its first notice of proposed rulemaking on the broadcast flag issue, one of the questions it posed for comment was whether the FCC has such jurisdiction; the agency was unsure itself. However, the congressional mandate to the FCC was to promote the transition to digital television. To the extent that the movie industry had successfully persuaded everyone involved that the transition would not happen without new forms of copyright protection, the question of copyright seemed to increasingly fall into the FCC's court. By 2003, the FCC was stating confidently that they had the authority to regulate consumer electronics technology instrumentalities. Critics pointed out that their only previous involvement in regulating technology—the requirement that TVs include UHF reception in 1962, closed captioning in

1990, and the V-chip in 1996—all followed explicit and narrow mandates from Congress to do so. But the FCC argued that the statutory language granting them authority over the "instrumentalities, facilities, apparatus and services"[36] incidental to broadcasting is relatively clear, and justified their involvement.

It is crucial that we note the complexity of what is going on here. We could say that the FCC, in a few short years and in response to concerns expressed by a select few corporations, expanded what it took to be its regulatory jurisdiction, over both copyright enforcement and a broad range of technologies it had never dealt with before. But the FCC, Congress, and all those interested in digital medial have been grappling with the "convergence"—both real and imagined—of communication technologies and industries. Whatever actual rearrangement of digital media this convergence represents, it means both that regulatory institutions like the FCC must reconsider their role in such matters, and that commercial institutions like the MPAA may take advantage of the moment to introduce new imperatives. The convergence of media motivates the questions now faced by the FCC, it provides an opportunity for interested parties to change the terms of those questions, and it provides justification for the FCC to change the way it responds to those questions. So it may not be wildly unreasonable for the FCC, in this new and murky context, to claim it needs to regulate not just broadcast content but the televisions that receive it, and not just televisions but TiVos, DVD players, home theater systems, and computer software, and not just ownership rules or freedom of speech protections but copyright enforcement. What remains a question is whether that claim is justified, whether it is being handled effectively, and whether it is honoring the spirit of the law and serving the best interests of the public. This complex shift and its strategic exploitation are certainly not unique to this case.

The particular dynamics of this "regime of alignment" approach may have also made the expansion of jurisdiction easier to swallow. The FCC could impose the broadcast flag rules onto digital television tuners, a technology that is reasonably within its jurisdiction, because the downstream devices would be regulated not by the FCC mandate but by the private licensing arrangements that accompany the DRM systems. Of course, the selection and implicit authorization of those DRM systems would be overseen by the FCC, but the FCC would not be requiring such systems to be used. And because the system of control is accomplished only through the combination of the flag itself, the DTV hardware recognizing it, the subsequent imposition of encryption, the licenses that govern other devices that access the encryption, and the rules therefore built into that hardware, no one element appears by itself to have dramatic consequences; therefore no single agency seems to be making a particularly dramatic intervention. The way in which copyright regulation increasingly depends here not on a single rule, but on the careful arrangement of technical, legal, and economic elements, makes it more difficult not only for critics to challenge it, but even for those imposing the rules to see the full scope of what they're doing.

This elision is facilitated by the efforts of the proponents of the broadcast flag plan, and of all trusted systems, to portray these technological constraints as not constraining. In the official order mandating the broadcast flag, the FCC argued that "in light of our decision to adopt a redistribution control scheme and to avoid any confusion, we wish to reemphasize that our action herein in no way limits or prevents consumers from making copies of digital broadcast television content."[37] They even note, in a footnote, that the "name of this proceeding has been changed from Digital Broadcast Copy Protection to Digital Broadcast Content Protection."[38] To believe this, the FCC must willfully ignore the obvious implications of its decision. The broadcast flag mandate does not itself limit consumers from making copies, but it quite clearly puts into place the system of control the MPAA and 5C companies sought, which was designed to do just that.

An Unruly Ally

The broadcast flag rule came to an abrupt halt in May 2005, when the court decided the FCC did not have the jurisdiction to impose such a rule. Although it is not articulated in these terms, the ruling reads like a symposium on the trusted system strategy. The court undercuts some but not all of the fundamental principles of the trusted system, although it's not clear that they saw themselves as doing so. The ruling also raises some uncertainty about whether content owners will ever be able to enlist the federal government in helping to impose a trusted system. And it reveals the way in which, in a heterogeneous effort to construct a technical control system and the political consensus necessary to install it, the state not only brings the authority to impose the system comprehensively, but can also introduce additional demands that must be satisfied and that can derail the effort if they are not.

In the order imposing the broadcast flag, the FCC had claimed that its mandate, Title I of the Communications Act of 1934, granted it jurisdiction over "all interstate and foreign communication by wire or radio,"[39] including "all instrumentalities, facilities, apparatus, and services (among other things, the receipt, forwarding, and delivery of communications) incidental to such transmission."[40] To the extent that the television receiver is an instrument incidental to the transmission of DTV, it felt its jurisdiction extended to its design. Further, it felt it could impose rules when "the regulations are reasonably ancillary to the Commission's effective performance of its statutorily mandated responsibilities,"[41] which it believed included aiding the transition to digital television. Echoing the technical turn in copyright, the FCC presumed that a concern about the use of digital content was also an issue of regulating access to the content, and of the design of the technology involved. The petitioners were a collection of library, consumer, and digital technology advocate groups led by the American Library Association (ALA). They challenged the FCC's decision on three grounds: (1) that the agency's ancillary jurisdiction did not extend to what DTV receivers did with content after they had received it, (2) that the broadcast flag rule violated the spirit of copyright law, for which the FCC had no statutory jurisdiction, and (3) that the rule itself was capricious and arbitrary and did not derive from or satisfy any proven need.

Focusing on the first of these challenges, the court decided that, while the FCC may have the right to regulate the design of television receivers, it can only regulate those aspects that have to do with the reception of a broadcast signal: "The insurmountable hurdle facing the FCC in this case is that the agency's general jurisdictional grant does not encompass the regulation of consumer electronics products that can be used for receipt of wire or radio communication when those devices are not engaged in the process of radio or wire transmission. Because the *Flag Order* does not require demodulator products to give effect to the broadcast flag until *after* the DTV broadcast has been completed, the regulations adopted in the *Flag Order* do not fall within the scope of the Commission's general jurisdictional grant."[42] To put it another way, the FCC does not have the authority to regulate the color of TV sets or the range of appropriate volume settings. These aspects of the technology are not closely related to the reception of the broadcast itself, which is the heart of the FCC's mandate. In declaring that encrypting received signals and protecting them against redistribution are separate from the reception of the signal itself, the court implicitly refuses the trusted system logic that posits these as crucially interrelated, and the Valenti logic that without the one there will not be the other. The reception of a signal and the subsequent technical protection of that content are distinct functions, in the eyes of the court.

Not all of the ideological dimensions of the trusted system were addressed by this decision. The charge that the FCC should not have jurisdiction over copyright concerns, perhaps the most germane to our inquiry, sadly was not considered. The Court of Appeals followed the U.S. legal tradition of judging on as little as is necessary; once the court had decided that the FCC did not have jurisdiction over functions of DTV receivers beyond reception itself, it needed go no further with the complaint. This repeats how we regularly overlook the deeper implications of the regime of alignment being pursued here. Just as the court in *Universal v. Reimerdes* focused only on the fact that circumvention had occurred and thus the DMCA had been violated, but was unwilling to see how fair use got hamstrung between technical protection and the use regulations that followed, the court in this case would not go beyond the specifics under consideration to determine whether the FCC even had the right to make rules in the name of copyright.

The court also focused its attention on the way the FCC rule would regulate functions of DTV receivers that went beyond reception, but did not acknowledge that the broadcast flag rule would be the key to a regulatory system that would extend to "downstream devices." Surely, if the FCC does not have jurisdiction over incidental aspects of TV sets, it does not have jurisdiction over computer hard drives, video iPods, and Sony Playstations. Again, the diffuse arrangement of the trusted system helps obscure the character and scope of the regulation being installed. Had the court decision gone the other way and supported the FCC's claim of jurisdiction over all aspects of DTV receivers, would it have noticed that the FCC rule would also regulate all information devices by proxy?

Perhaps most revealing was the argument made by the MPAA that the entire case should be dismissed on a technicality. Before the court could rule on the question of FCC jurisdiction, they needed to address the procedural question of whether the petitioners had legal standing to challenge the rule in this court. To do so, the petitioners had to prove that a broadcast flag rule might reasonably harm one of them in some substantive way. To make this point, the ALA included an affidavit describing a North Carolina State University librarian who assisted professors by providing short television clips for downloading by students. The suggestion was that this legal and valuable service would be inhibited by a broadcast flag rule.

The MPAA, speaking in support of the FCC, argued that the affidavit did not prove that the harm described actually stemmed from the broadcast flag rule. In its logic, once the broadcast flag rule were imposed, manufacturers would design encryption systems that allowed for secure online redistribution while still protecting against indiscriminate redistribution over the Internet. If they failed to do this, the MPAA argued, it would be the absence of technologies that would inhibit the librarian, not the rule itself. Therefore, the librarian example was not germane to a dispute about the rule per se. This is the same mindset as was reflected in the BPDG's explanation for why the broadcast flag would not squelch innovation or hamper fair use: New uses that did not compromise the security of the digital content would naturally develop in the market and be approved. If they did not, it was not the rule's fault. The court, however, rejected this argument, calling it "specious."

As I have argued, it is in fact the combination of the rule itself, the license between content and hardware providers, and the technology it produces that constrains the activity of the user. This librarian would be inhibited from her educational and fair use of TV broadcasts by the lack of technology, as mandated by the broadcast flag rule and constrained by the approval process for authorized encryption technologies. No one element fully imposes the regulation. The MPAA attempted to take advantage of that fact. In a context where the rule is being held up to scrutiny, the MPAA claims it's the lack of technology that imposed the restriction. The rule itself, it says, is neutral. One might imagine a second scenario, in which a manufacturer proposes an innovative encryption scheme for authorization, and the studio representatives call upon the authority of the rule to reject it. The responsibility lies everywhere, and therefore nowhere, when the system is taken to task. The proponents of the trusted system can describe all these pieces as powerfully linked when pitching it to their industrial partners, then disassociate it back to its individual components in order to abrogate responsibility for its most egregious consequences. That the court rejected this argument suggests that this diffusion of responsibility across the heterogeneous elements of the system is not as persuasive as the industry had hoped.

The attempt to draw on the authority of the FCC to compel an alignment of manufacturers, content providers, and technologies of digital television failed. While the judgment reached by the court seems in principle to reject the use/access logic of the trusted system, the language of its decision suggests that this was not explicitly their purpose. What did happen here was a clash of paradigms. A new regulatory strategy, the trusted system and all it requires, found itself posed against some much older notions of how and why regulation should be imposed, assumptions built into the now sedimented rules of agency jurisdiction. First, a DRM system in which content was encrypted at the source was unacceptable, not only because of the practical costs of upgrading the technology and alienating early adopters, but also because Congress has a historical commitment to the "public interest" when regulating television, a commitment counter to this premise of locked content. Then, despite the trusted system vision in which access to content and its misuse are fundamentally connected, and regulating one can regulate the other, the FCC's authority was deemed to be over broadcasting and nothing more. The agency has statutory authority over any aspect of the transmission and reception of a signal communication, but not over the protection of that content in any operation that follows. The MPAA had successfully argued in other contexts that the promiscuity of online distribution had changed the game: Consumption and distribution are now nearly one and the same activity, and it has become necessary to regulate distribution at the point of consumption. Yet they were unable to convince the courts of this here. Despite sharing some of the goals of the content industries, the government is in many ways an unruly ally in that it brings with it historically sedimented paradigms (like public interest) that must be honored, and bureaucratic rules (such as jurisdiction) that cannot be circumvented.

Still, the *ALA v. FCC* decision did leave one very large door open, such that an FCC-imposed trusted system for digital television is still a real possibility. According to the mandate of the FCC, Congress can at any time pass legislation extending the agency's authority or jurisdiction in any way it sees fit, particularly when warranted by new technologies or communication practices. This is how the FCC did have the authority to require television manufacturers to build in closed captioning and the V-chip. Thus attention has turned back to Congress, who had granted the FCC authority to oversee the transition to digital broadcasting in the first place. The MPAA has already begun to petition Congress to revive the broadcast flag plan in the same or in some slightly altered form, either as a law requiring it, or as a mandate granting the FCC the authority it needs. Discussions about inserting the broadcast flag into an bill concerning the digital television transition occurred in the Senate Commerce Committee in early 2006.[43] The broadcast flag is by no means a dead issue, or a quaint historical case study.

The Consequences of Alignment

The recurring concerns about DRM—that fair use will be squelched by its technical constraints and that innovation will be stifled by the restrictive, industry-wide standards it requires—most certainly apply to the broadcast flag. As Susan Crawford argues,

The technological approach the MPAA is suggesting in the broadcast flag/analog hole proposals will instantiate a particular vision of copyright law in mandatory code that will eventually be globally pervasive. But law is supposed to be a social conversation about collective values. Using code in this way to mandate one view of copyright law may create path dependencies that will be very difficult to change, cut off all social conversation about the course of the law, and allow one regime to set rules for another without a social agreement that such rules are necessary. This description states the issue far too mildly. The MPAA is attempting to create an alternate, technical walled garden that will seek to control the channel for worldwide expressions—without a social consensus that such control is appropriate.[44]

Alongside this concern I would like to consider another, addressing the political shifts upon which these strategies are founded. The greatest risk to fair use and innovation is not the broadcast flag and its complementary regulations. It is the tight interlocking of industries and government regulators that makes these regulations even possible. Whether or not the broadcast flag regulation itself would have the consequences Crawford describes (arguably, cable and satellite providers will continue to earn a greater share of television audiences, and the question of broadcasting itself will be less of an issue for consumers), the bigger question is what this rhetorical and political confluence will mean for copyright and technology more generally.

The broadcast flag is just one element of the growing push toward technically imposed copyright protections that depend on encrypted content, technologies that abide by a set of rules applied to that content, and laws making it illegal to tamper with or produce alternatives to those technologies. The broadcast flag is a curious case only because traditional notions of broadcasting and the "public interest," and the particular functions and procedures of the agency designed to oversee it, interrupted its imposition. The failure to impose this system reveals the cracks in the system, cracks that may go unnoticed as it is more successfully implemented in other domains.

The MPAA and 5C companies were not only attempting to build a trusted system for digital television, they were also building a coalition of industry partners so that regulatory strategies that depend on the interlocking of hardware and software could be pursued by similarly interlocking industries. This larger project is of greater concern, and its success depends on the persuasive demonstration of a confluence of interests between content owners, technology manufacturers, and government regulators.

What interests the public may have, either in fair use, technological innovation, choice of providers, or diversity of content, are rarely voiced within such debates. Consumer and citizen advocacy groups like the Electronic Frontier Foundation and Public Knowledge have been somewhat successful in insinuating themselves into the decision-making process, by claiming to represent the "public interest." Yet it is still easy for industry representatives to marginalize their contributions. Government regulators do have some, at least indirect, dependence on public confidence, which can ebb and flow with the sense that the public interest is being served. But in the current political climate, they more often see their role as smoothing market mechanisms rather than intervening in them.

Beyond the presence and limited impact of advocacy groups, and the increasingly core moments when lawmakers and regulators are willing to oppose industry goals, the public interest is primarily served only at the points of disagreement between the major industry players. Consumer electronics manufacturers want to give consumers more choice and functionality than the movie studios would like; computer and IT manufacturers tend to see their customers as users more than consumers and generally assume that open platform design is preferable to specialized tools. These fissures become disagreements about the imposition of copyright: As the Center for Democracy and Technology argued, "The consumer electronics (CE) companies have a symbiotic relationship with the content industry. But while CE companies want to support the content industry's efforts at protecting content, they also wish to protect their users' ability to make wide use of the content they acquire. This tension has led to some divergence of opinion among CE companies about how best to approach the digital copyright issue . . . Although the companies do not wish to jeopardize their relations with the content industry by appearing to sell products that exacerbate the digital piracy problem, they want to provide consumers with innovative new devices."[45]

This tension is important, particularly for copyright. As noted in the previous chapter, copyright laws are generally drafted not by Congress, but by stakeholders convened by Congress, who typically include content producers, technology manufacturers, and occasionally artists' organizations and public advocacy groups such as library associations. There is typically no significant public voice present (including Congress itself, which plays no active role in the process). Unsurprisingly, the laws created by stakeholders who all benefit from copyright are almost always increasingly strong copyright arrangements that continue to benefit those in attendance.[46]

Litman notes, however, that because consumer electronics manufacturers have competing interests—a fundamental symbiosis with content providers, as well as a desire to offer consumers the capacity to copy and redistribute—they are sometimes the voice of reason when film and music industry representatives call for tighter copyright controls.[47] For example, it was the consumer electronics companies that, during the discussions that produced the Audio Home Recording Act, pushed for the rule to allow one copy but prevent serial copying; the RIAA wanted to prohibit copying altogether.[48] The victory may have been a minor one, because the DAT format it applied to did not take off as a consumer-grade format, but it is indicative of how the politics of copyright have differed between these industries in the past. And this predates the involvement of information technology manufacturers, who have less investment in the interests of film and music producers, and who have benefited from a legal environment in which innovation occurred in a relatively open context.

However, these worldviews are clearly changing. Information technology manufacturers are increasingly seeing high-value film and music content as crucial to the economic value of their products. Many of them are spearheading the production of their own DRM encryption products, which means they are dramatically more invested in the success of these systems than they ever were. Consumer electronics manufacturers are increasingly making Faustian bargains with content producers, recognizing that with encryption, those who don't comply face a possibility that even producing legitimate DVD players and digital television receivers may be technically and legally impossible. Technological convergence and increasingly deregulated corporate mergers mean it is often the same corporation that is producing media content, electronics, computers, and networks, and that therefore has even more invested in finding solutions that fit them all. Finally, as DRM and trusted systems are repeatedly described as the only solution to the threat of Internet piracy, and this story of a devastating problem and an appealing solution is taken increasingly as gospel, these three industries are increasingly falling into lockstep, resulting in a convergence necessary to produce the technical and legal elements of a trusted system, closing those once-productive gaps where, almost by accident, the public was represented.

The aspirations of the content industries are clear: Shift the regulation of copyright to the technology, and bring into alignment the manufacturers, the legislators, the courts, and the cultural expectations that together regulate the duplication of digital content and its use. While no system has yet been fully effective, the tactic appeals to content providers, both as protection against piracy and as an opportunity to regulate and monetize a vast new array of uses and functions. While most of the concerns for this strategy have to do with how uses are regulated in ways that diverge from the traditional balance of copyright law, there is another set of questions that need to be asked: How does this copy protection strategy affect the design of the technology? How does the restriction of some uses through technical design set the terms for users and their relationship with their tools? The regime of alignment behind the trusted system not only requires docile manufacturers; it also needs the technology itself to be a partner in the effort—by making some uses impossible, and by being impenetrable to those who might examine its inner workings so as to evade those limits. The licenses behind these trusted systems require that the technologies be designed to be "robust" against user investigation—in both the software code and the hardware itself, the hood must be welded shut. This radical shift, from a cultural logic of technology in which we are invited to understand the device by peering inside, to one in which we're shut out and can only use it as directed, will have consequences for the use and innovation of technology, just as technical copyright rules will have consequences for the use and innovation of culture.

Certainly, the appeal of DRM and technical copy protection is clear, at least for the major stakeholders in the market for cultural goods. The trusted system, at least in its ideal form, promises the consumer a rich media experience with a seemingly endless array of choices; at the same time it promises the copyright owner precise regulations on those uses that are most financially damaging, as well as those that can be more effectively remade as pay-per-view services. Digital media devices will offer such a rich array of functions, they hope, that the limitations will soon disappear and be forgotten. But there are lots of ways to build a speed bump. The choices that are still to be made about how such technolegal constraints will actually be designed and imposed will make a dramatic difference for the character of that technology and the experience of its use.

The recurring tensions between those who produce and distribute culture and those who consume it and find it meaningful have been shifted to technical terrain. Fans continue to argue about whether a band that signs with a major record label is "selling out," whether prices of CDs or DVDs or digital downloads are too high, and whether movie stars are entertaining cultural icons or vacuous, corporate puppets. Collage artists and hip-hop samplers and literary parodists continue to do legal battle with the owners of the content they appropriate. But the embrace of technical copy protection has opened up a new front in this war that revolves around digital tools: what can be done using legitimate electronics and software, how limitations may be circumvented, and to what extent users opt for black market devices that permit uses that producers hope to abolish.

The efforts to design and impose trusted systems based on digital encryption, to mobilize economic and political actors, and to give the project a sense of cultural legitimacy have had to confront a competing and powerful counterparadigm: the widespread embrace of peer-to-peer file-trading, especially by the young, and a general lack of concern over legal and moral assertions that such activities are wrong. This worldview has merged with longstanding debates about the cultural value of music and critiques of the economic practices of corporate producers, and has found a neat fit with the political and technical priorities of hacker culture and the economic tactics and ideological motives of those who design and support peer-to-peer networks.

Users have challenged DRM systems in a number of ways—most powerfully, perhaps, through the continued use of peer-to-peer networks. The fact that millions of users still download and make available music and movies through such networks despite technical and legal efforts to prevent it poses a real, if politically oblique, challenge to DRM advocates.[1] In addition, software designers continue to produce the kind of circumvention tools that the DMCA prohibits, treating each subsequent DRM system as an engineering challenge to be toppled. These efforts are sometimes articulated as oppositional tactics and celebrated as political victories, while others see them simply as neat ways of getting something for nothing or as clever technical gamesmanship.[2]

Public debate about DRM strategies has also persisted since their introduction, not just in the halls of academia or in policy circles, but in mainstream journalism and in tech-savvy online discussion spaces like Slashdot and Engadget. Some have championed alternatives to copyright law itself, such as the "copyleft" model of GPL-protected software and the Creative Commons licensing schemes, hoping to win over artists and users to a more open regime. And an implicit critique is made by users every time they defy limits and create artistic works that duplicate and rework commercial culture in the ways DRM systems would like to inhibit: music mashups, video collages, gaming hacks.

Users find themselves having to accept or renegotiate the rules of culture as they have been materialized in their tools and, more obliquely, embedded in the political and legal arrangements beneath them. And they do so in a number of ways: explicitly challenging the technology in public venues, interpreting the technology in their own preferred terms, creatively using the technology in ways unanticipated by its designers, and redesigning the technology itself to have different cultural and political implications. In some ways, the very agency that users have and expect to have with the culture they consume and the tools they use is the greatest challenge to a system of technical copy protection that not only aspires to prevent copyright infringement, but also takes as its ideal the frequent, monitored, metered, and, most important, passive consumption of cultural goods.

In the face of the political, technical, and cultural criticisms of DRM, as well as the political and financial costs of building such systems, some content owners have wondered whether these protection systems need only provide "curb-high protection" to dissuade casual users, rather than aspiring to a leakproof system.[3] The desire to pursue perfect regulation, regardless of expense and difficulty, is a seductive one. The culture industries fret that a single leak renders the entire apparatus irrelevant. Once one copy of the film or song reaches the "darknet"[4] of peer-to-peer trading networks, it can replicate endlessly. In this light, curb-high regulation is tantamount to no regulation at all. More important, these systems want to govern not just copying but also purchase and use; while copy control might be able to tolerate the occasional leak, a system that manages the purchase of media cannot.

So while some have lowered the walls in order to entice users—most notably Apple, which uses DRM encryption in its iTunes Music store but imposes relatively lenient rules about copying—most DRM advocates have attempted to further fortify the leakproof systems they hope to achieve, not only by building rules into devices and backing them with laws against their circumvention, not only by lining up partner industries and regulatory agencies to produce and authorize the necessary components, but also by demanding that the devices be designed such that they cannot be tampered with, hacked, or unbuilt. If the DVD player or the DTV application can somehow render its inner workings invisible so that it is impervious to the efforts of hackers, the copyright rules will be perfectly enforced and never circumvented. Programmers often chuckle at this aspiration as hopelessly naïve. But whether or not it's even possible, the implications of trying—for copyright, for innovation, and most of all for users' experience with their technology and culture—are significant.

Thus far in my analysis and in the work of most others on this subject, concerns about the implications of technical copy protection have centered on what users can or can't do with their technology and with the content it grants them access to. If users are being technically barred from doing things the law would otherwise allow, then there is a political problem, a shift in the balance between content owners and the public that copyright was supposed to manage. But DRM is not just about walling off some uses to encourage others. These walls may stop some of us from copying and distributing protected content; maybe they will stop most of us. But prohibition does not solve the problem of how to stop those who are willing and able to break the rules. Content owners hope, therefore, to build walls that can't be climbed, which means making the workings of the technology inscrutable to those who might circumvent it. Doing so requires changing these technologies in fundamental ways, and in the process changing the relationship between technology and its users in equally fundamental ways. Increasingly what is at stake here is the user's ability not only to act with a tool, but to act on that tool; the user's agency, their own perception that they have the capacity and the right to operate and manipulate their own technology, must be actively frustrated.

To frustrate people's actions is less politically problematic than to convince them that they have no such agency to be frustrated. To consider this problem, we need to discard the belief that as individuals we are entirely free to act as we please on an inert world waiting for our intervention. Our capacities develop within, are defined by, and contest the structural dimensions of the society around us. If we borrow from Anthony Giddens's theory of "structuration" and Wanda Orlikowski's extension of that theory to technology, we can recognize that the capacity for a user to act in the world is bound by both institutional and semiotic structures, and these structures are themselves the result of human action.[5] Our assent to these structures is implicit in our choice to act, and we legitimate these structures in doing so. At the same time, structures can be transformed through reflective action.

But even within this understanding of human agency bound by societal structures of our own making, we must recognize not just how action is limited or encouraged, but also how the very possibility of acting is staged, made visible or invisible, gently encouraged or quietly rebuked. The possibility of my writing an editorial for my local newspaper may be limited by the rules of editorial page content, the economics of the publishing process, the politics of my local community. These are structures that I can accept, challenge, or refuse. How (or whether) I write my editorial will depend on these structural conditions, and the act of writing the editorial within those conditions implicitly reaffirms them. But beyond these structural constraints, my choice to write the editorial or not may also be shaped by the extent to which, in my cultural experience, I have been invited to see myself as a writer and a contributor to the public discussion, or just as a reader and a consumer of what I am told. My actions are constrained not only by the social world around me, but also by my sense of myself as having the ability and right to engage with it.

Part of the DRM strategy is to match the technical limitations on use with a political and economic framework that supports and authorizes those limits; part is to positively articulate cultural reasons for why it is the approach needed to solve the pressing problem. But another part is to subtly encourage users to adopt a different perspective on technology and culture itself, one in which they embrace the docile use of tools and the passive consumption of content. This need not be a deliberate, mustache-twiddling, nefarious plot—it is something much more subtle. Those who design and deploy DRM systems tend to think of culture as something to be sold and consumed; fair use, remaking, tinkering, and critique are outside of the paradigm within which they understand what they do. This paradigm is powerfully reinforced by the economic imperative they face in their businesses, where commercial success is everything. It should come as no surprise, then, that the way in which content owners understand the use of culture informs their interpretation of copyright law and the rights it grants them, motivates the particular kind of protection strategies they pursue, and subtly colors their intervention when those strategies require concomitant changes in the dynamics of technology and its use. Seeing culture as a commodity (as DRM does) fits neatly with, and thereby subtly encourages, a passive consumer; building technology to regulate culture in commodity terms similarly wants and reinforces passivity in the users of that technology. The trusted system ends up urging us to be both.

Robustness

In most forms of technical copy protection, the rules imposed on the manufacturers of the technology come in two parts. The first requires that manufacturers build their devices such that they regulate the users' interaction with the protected work: the devices will allow or prohibit copying, they will restrict whether the user can transmit a file to another device, etc. The files themselves are encrypted, meaning access can only be gained under authorized conditions. The enforcement of those rules requires that the devices themselves be the perfect chaperones, only allowing users to behave appropriately. Manufacturers, then, are abiding by a set of rules that dictate how to design their devices to be those perfect chaperones. In the FCC's broadcast flag mandate, these were called "compliance" rules: check for the flag watermark, encrypt the file, regulate copying, prevent "indiscriminate redistribution" over the Internet. The DVD-CCA license accompanying CSS encryption and signed by DVD manufacturers articulates a similar set of rules: how DVD players and software applications must be designed so that users are prevented from duplicating or distributing protected films. These compliance rules are what makes a device a trust-worthy element in the trusted system.

While these compliance rules are the heart of the trusted system and the flashpoint for most of the digital copyright debates, they are nevertheless only part of the rules necessary for this elaborate control system to work. Every time the culture industries deploy a particular encryption system, they run the risk that a single hacker may disable that system and spread the word over the Internet as to how it's done—or worse, design an application that hacks for them. This can be a colossal setback. By the time an encryption system has reached the consumer market, it has already been extensively researched and tested, imposed on millions of files, built into millions of devices. The industries involved have come to rely on it, and the possibility of having to upgrade or replace that system is a daunting and costly one. This is the scenario that Hollywood faced when a group of teenagers in Norway figured out the secret to their CSS encryption, designed DeCSS, and spread it far and wide over the Internet, rendering the encryption system used to protect their movies on DVD vulnerable to circumvention.

DRM advocates in the content industries need to win—or better yet, avoid—this digital arms race. Toward this end, they have supported laws like the Digital Millennium Copyright Act (DMCA), prohibiting not only the circumvention of an encryption system but also the provision of infor-mation or tools that help others do so. The suit brought in *Universal v. Reimerdes* was an attempt to stem the tide of DeCSS by punishing those who posted it online, and in the process to demonstrate the risks to hackers of undertaking similar attempts to crack similar encryption systems. Still, even with a legal victory in that case the damage could not be undone, and DeCSS (and its clones) could not be effectively erased from the web. So while the suit may have had symbolic value, and may have deterred casual users from posting DeCSS, making the application somewhat harder to find, it did not solve the problem. If the appeal of DRM as a mechanism for copyright is that it promises to preempt infringement instead of responding to it after the fact, the content industries would like a similarly preemptive way to prevent circumvention as well.

To prevent hackers from discovering how a technical copy protection system works, manufacturers are contractually obligated to follow a second set of rules—"robustness" rules—to go along with the compliance rules. Like DRM itself, robustness takes a technological barrier, this time the hard casing of the device and the interface of the software, and braces it with an unwieldy cooperation between content producers and technology manufacturers. These rules require that manufacturers make their technologies harder to circumvent, more resistant to hacking and tampering, and more unwilling to give up the secrets of how they work to those who, with that knowledge, could reverse engineer the tool and build its constraint-free twin. The robustness rules require manufacturers to enlist in this digital arms race, to help defeat hackers by making unbreakable encryption and impervious devices. Perhaps more important, they make the manufacturers liable for the cost when they fail.

Who and Why to Frustrate

As discussed earlier, the DRM encryption that protects DVDs is implemented through a license. This contract, which must be assented to by any manufacturer of a DVD player or application in order to get the decryption key necessary to play a DVD, is primarily a series of compliance rules: specifications according to which DVD players must be manufactured so that encrypted DVDs stay encrypted and copying is forbidden. But alongside these compliance rules is a set of restrictions made to frustrate hackers by design. Whether it be software or hardware, the manufacturer must be "reasonably certain" that the player is "clearly designed in a manner that would effectively frustrate each of the following: (1) attempts to defeat the copy protection functions . . . ; (2) attempts to discover decrypted confidential DVD Keys embodied therein; (3) attempts to discover Highly Confidential Information in the form of CSS Security Algorithms."[6] The license goes on to specify how this might be achieved: by encrypting the encryption process and the decryption keys themselves; by "closely coupling" the elements of the device that handle authentication and decryption with elements that perform other functions, such as playback; and by building in mechanisms that self-check the integrity of the system, and fail if the system has been compromised.

Clearly, these mandates make very specific demands on technological design, demands driven not by functional efficiency, cost, or engineering aesthetic, and certainly not by the goal of user-friendliness. This has consequences not only for the design of DVD players, but for their repair. The license acknowledges this, and in fact demands it: "Licensee shall not disclose to end users any diagnostic information relating to such implementations and shall protect the confidentiality of integrated circuit specifications relating to CSS."[7]

To make DVD players and applications resistant to the intrusions of hackers, manufacturers must render the workings of the CSS encryption so obscure within a deliberately complex technology that those who want to circumvent will find themselves unable to discover how. Encryption will protect the data; the technology will honor the encryption; compliance rules will direct the design of the technology; the design of the technology will frustrate invaders; robustness rules will ensure the frustrating design. And while compliance rules, at least in principle, have a check on their reach in copyright law and fair use, there is no such legal counterbalance to robustness requirements.

The fact that the CSS encryption was successfully circumvented may not be evidence of the futility of this approach, it may actually justify it. The genesis of DeCSS and the *Universal v. Reimerdes* case came not from the violation of compliance rules, but from the failure of one manufacturer to follow the robustness rules. As noted earlier, Jon Johansen, DeCSS's designer, discovered the key to CSS encryption when he found that RealNetworks had failed to encrypt their key in their DVD software.[8] DeCSS, then, was not a lock pick but a ring full of copied keys, developed from one accidentally left on the back porch.

The FCC's broadcast flag mandate made an oblique reference to a similar set of robustness requirements, leaving their implementation vague: "The content protection requirements set forth in the Demodulator Compliance Requirements shall be implemented in a reasonable method so that they cannot be defeated or circumvented merely by an ordinary user using generally-available tools or equipment."[9] The tone of this statement belies the prickly controversy that preceded it. Several of the points of contention in the interindustry debates hosted by BPDG, and in the comments that followed during the FCC discussion period, concerned the character of these requirements.

The central issue was how robust DTV devices would need to be to meet this part of their obligation: that is, who or what they must be designed to frustrate. Does a digital television tuner that protects flagged broadcasts have to be able to withstand the efforts of a skilled hacker to crack the system, or just an average user attempting to sneak past the technical restrictions? The MPAA and 5C companies argued for the stricter standard, defined in terms of frustrating, as critics put it, "even the most knowledgeable professional technicians,"[10] or in terms of the tools that might be used, that is, professional grade software as well as the household screwdriver. The MPAA went so far as to suggest tactics by which this stricter standard could be achieved, borrowed from those outlined in the DVD-CCA license: for instance, entangling different functions within the device so that the decryption process is less easily identified and studied. The IT companies and consumer advocate groups generally argued for the less stringent standard, requiring manufacturers to frustrate only ordinary users from getting around the technical barriers.

This dispute parallels the tension in defining the underlying purpose of the broadcast flag, and of all DRM protection systems, about whether to offer "leakproof" or "curb-high" protection, whether to prevent determined attacks or merely casual infringement. The FCC rejected the stricter standard, making the broadcast flag more curb than container. They even justified their decision by turning a statement made by the MPAA against them, noting that the

MPAA itself describes the flag as a limited mechanism to inhibit theft of content: "A person who hacks their device will simply achieve the disabling of that single device, and no other impact. While hacks of individual devices will result in the theft of some content, it is wrong to presume that every consumer is a thief, and it is equally mistaken to assert that [because] some burglars know how to pick locks, it is not worthwhile to lock the door. The Broadcast Flag will keep widespread unauthorized redistribution under control because most consumers will not hack their devices." We therefore conclude that an expert level of robustness is incongruous with the scope of protection offered by an ATSC flag system and that an "ordinary user" level is more appropriate in these circumstances.[11]

This incongruous statement by the MPAA (incongruous in that so many of their other efforts do imply that all users are at least potential thieves) became the basis for the FCC to adopt the gentler "ordinary user using generally-available tools or equipment"[12] standard. At the same time, they made sure to emphasize that this standard was only a minimum, one that "represents a floor that manufacturers are free to exceed."[13]

The device specifications that were the result of Phase I of the SDMI efforts also included a set of robustness requirements, although in that case what was meant by "robustness" was a combination of protecting the content and making it difficult for users to discover how it was protected. Many of these suggestions focused on designing the technology to fail if a self-check of the system's integrity indicated that it had been tampered with. But the specifications also included the obligation of "in every case of implementation of software, using techniques of obfuscation to disguise and hamper attempts to discover the approaches used,"[14] and proposed a number of these techniques. The SDMI rules also addressed the problem of how robust to be, by defining three categories of tools that someone might use—"widely available," "specialized," and "professional"—and expecting that the device be designed so that it "cannot be defeated" using the first two and "only with difficulty be defeated" using the third.[15]

The SDMI obligations also recognized the likelihood that such technical barriers would eventually be circumvented, no matter how robust their implementation; as such, the robustness requirements even prepared for their own failure:

> If an Implementation when designed and shipped complies with the requirements set forth above, but at any time thereafter circumstances arise which—had they been existing at the time of design—would have caused such Implementation to fail to comply with the Specification . . . then upon having reasonable notice of such New Circumstances, the developer of such Implementation . . . shall promptly redesign affected product(s) or make available upgrades to its affected product(s), and, as soon as reasonably practicable, consistent with ordinary product cycles and taking into account the level of threat to Content under the New Circumstances, shall incorporate such redesign or replacement into its affected product(s), cease manufacturing such affected product(s) and cease selling such affected product(s).[16]

Clearly, robustness is not just about thwarting investigation, but about loading the cost of doing so squarely on the shoulders of manufacturers.

The Open Source Critique

The question of who and what these robustness requirements are meant to inhibit is an important one, most obviously for manufacturers. Whether the standard of robustness is the ordinary user with generally available tools or the expert user with professional resources sets the terms for how hard manufacturers must work to design an "effectively frustrating" artifact, and how liable they may be if they fail. It is also important for ordinary users. While they would presumably be prevented from investigating the inner workings of their devices by either standard, the professional standard might also mean that the only available repair services come directly from the manufacturer or from authorized third parties, who could artificially inflate the costs of repairs.

But perhaps the users most affected by this dispute, and by robustness rules in general, are those overlooked by this familiar dichotomy of ordinary users and professional experts. Users who are skilled but not professional, who are capable of developing uncommon tools and able to make them easily accessible online, are forgotten by this convenient categorization. In this context they are most often dubbed "hackers," but we should be careful to resist the narrowness of this pejorative term. In nearly all fields of technology in which the raw materials are publicly available, there exists a class of amateur experts somewhere between the poles of consumer and professional, who are regularly marginalized by the way we narrate the history of technological innovation.

Such amateurs are certainly not a product of the Internet; the antecedents to the modern hacker include kit car builders, ham radio enthusiasts, and garage computer hobbyists.[17] But on the Internet they are perhaps more visible, can more easily form communities of interest and share their expertise, and, in the case of digital media and software, can even share the work itself. Amy Bruckman argues that the Internet helps complicate the seemingly clean categories between amateurs and professionals in the art world, making possible a venue and a distribution network for "semi-published artists" and blurring the implied, bright-line distinction between two now untenable extremes.[18] The same may be said for a number of creative practices, where the Internet offers easy and wide distribution and a foundation for social interaction and community. Those interested in and skilled in a particular practice can become, not professionals in the traditional sense, marked by the trappings of career, institutions, and widely agreed-upon standards of performance, but a community of expert practitioners, ranked by reputation as determined by their peers.

One example of this kind of expert community, and the one that represents the clearest problem with DRM robustness rules, is the open source software design community. In the discussions during and following the BPDG meetings, and later in response to the FCC's rulemaking proposals, critics like the Electronic Frontier Foundation argued that requiring trusted devices to be robust could hamper innovation. They noted that the robustness requirements, if imposed, would systematically close out the possibility of designing a DTV device using an open source approach, which, they maintained, would squelch innovation and slow the DTV transition itself.

"Open source" is in fact a catch-all term for a number of approaches to the design of computer software. Most commercial software applications are designed by a single corporation in code that is withheld from both users and competitors as a trade secret and valuable corporate property. By contrast, open source advocates suggest that software is better designed in loosely organized collaborative projects, where the code is freely made public to any and all interested contributors. Code that is worked over by many interested and disparate designers will be more responsive to the needs of multiple user groups, will suffer from fewer bugs, and will benefit from unexpected innovations. This movement has experienced a number of successes, depending on the definition of success being applied: The Linux operating system was the result of an extended open source collaboration, and Apache is now the most widely used web server tool. Many argue that such open source efforts produce better and more innovative software than do traditional commercial design arrangements, and some argue that the nonhierarchical and nonproprietary approach is more politically progressive than that of the vertically scaled software industry.[19] At the very least, it is a compelling and provocative experiment in how to choreograph technological innovation along very different economic and political lines, what Benkler has more broadly described as "commons-based peer production."[20]

While the participants in these open source software projects often disagree about the details, one of the foundational principles is that the underlying computer code must be public and available to anyone. Once code is locked away, early design directions are ratified, subsequent innovations are squelched, and overlooked bugs persist. Open source enthusiasts rail against commercial software providers for their "closed code" approach, and lambaste anyone who dares to turn an open code application into a closed code commodity, regularly designing their product licenses to prohibit it.[21] Generally, the open source community is also reluctant to draw a tight boundary around those who are participating in the design process and those who are not. Anyone who expresses interest may contribute, and the aggregate achievement is better for it. The boundary of what is "inside" and "outside" of the technology, the design process, and the community is rendered blurry, if nonexistent.[22]

The approach espoused by the open source software movement is crucially at odds with the "robustness" component of the DRM strategy. In trusted systems the technology acts as part of the barrier to use, which means it must be designed so as to frustrate investigation by others; open source design assumes investigation by users is part of the design process. By extension, those specifically authorized to know about the workings of a DRM tool must be clearly demarcated from those who are not, to prevent the secrets of the system from leaking; open source design dictates that no such boundary should exist.

Imposed not for its current design value or with an eye toward possible future innovation, the principle of robustness threatens to have systematic consequences for the sites and dynamics of technological change, at a moment when those dynamics, at least for information technologies, may be shifting in more progressive directions. The risk of this approach goes well beyond the concern that innovation in digital television will be hampered, or that future possibilities for the distribution and use of digital media will go unexplored. It tips the scales in the debate about technological design itself, marginalizing a new[23] approach to technology that complicates the simple dichotomy between passive consumers and professional designers.

The manner in which digital communication technologies will be innovated can hardly be anticipated. As a society we are continually challenged by the need to protect innovation we cannot predict but nevertheless want to cultivate. The past teaches us that innovation is often constrained by the same kind of concentrated oligopoly that currently dominates the technology industries—the kind being solidified through these very DRM control strategies. Crawford argues that innovation withers when variety and chance are severely restricted, yet this tends to be in the financial interests of industry giants. Drawing on ecological metaphors she suggests that the innovation environment should be neither a "monoculture" in which all adaptation is scripted and controlled, nor complete chaos, in which change cannot emerge.[24]

We are in the midst of a debate, centered in but not exclusive to the software industry, about this very question. Alternative models for organizing design are challenging the limitations of closed, hierarchical, "monocultural" corporate design methods. Perhaps, open source advocates suggest, we can design better technologies if the process by which they are designed is collaborative, open, distributed, and driven by enthusiasm, rather than hierarchical, closed, centralized, and powered by profit.

It is no surprise, then, that critics of the centralized approach hold up open source design as an emblem for why the DRM robustness requirements are a danger to our technological future. As the EFF pointed out, "although one can imagine open source software developers creating a 'compliant' demodulator or downstream application, requiring that such a demodulator or application be 'robust' against user modification is the problem . . . To the extent the open source development model embraces the freedom to modify, however, this necessarily means that open source software cannot be made 'tamper-resistant' in the fashion contemplated by the broadcast flag mandate."[25] For a digital television tuner or application to comply with the broadcast flag, it would have to be closed to any inquisitive user and robust enough to withstand purposeful intervention; tamper resistance is antithetical to the open source design philosophy, where design *is* tampering, where innovation demands investigation. The robustness standard, then, would have functionally prohibited open source designers from ever participating in the market for digital television software. Any tool designed according to open source standards would be a violation of the robustness regulations, and perhaps of the DMCA.

Designing against User Agency

The EFF's criticism of the broadcast flag was strategic, framing the tension between robustness rules and the open source design movement as a problem for innovation. This was an astute rhetorical tactic for offering comments to the FCC, in that it accepted the agency's market-centric approach to regulation and spoke to the underlying purposes of the entire effort: Closing off the possibility of an open source digital television application would preclude innovations that might bring better and cheaper tools to the market; such innovations would encourage the transition Congress was so eager to foster. However, what is at issue, I believe, is a broader question of user agency: The open source software design community encourages and depends on it; a trusted system is antithetical to and forbids it.

Most revealing was a moment in which the EFF responded to a criticism from the MPAA:

The MPAA Comments respond by pointing out that many open source software applications offer security features, citing firewall software as an example. This discussion betrays a fundamental confusion regarding the difference between security—securing a PC *for* its owner—and "tamper resistance"—securing a PC *against* its owner. Open source software has been very successful at the former goal (in fact, products based on open source software have proven to be more secure than closed source software). The latter goal—enforcing restrictions *against* the wishes of a computer's owner—is much harder in an open source environment, where the owner can modify the software.[26]

What the robustness rules require is security against the owner of the technology, which can only now be contemplated because of the techniques of encryption and the embrace of technolegal control strategies like DRM. To the extent that the trusted system needs its technologies to hide their inner workings from their own users and be fortified against committed inquiry, it is fundamentally at odds not only with the open source model of design, but also with broader cultural presumptions about the commonplace principles of tool use.

Technological design can anticipate users and build in roles for them. Certainly a great deal of discussion about who is using a technology, and why, goes into the design process—though it is a discussion often built more on presumptions about use and the aspirations of the designers than on interactions with actual users. But "along with negotiations over who the user might be, comes a set of design (and other) activities which attempt to define and delimit the user's possible actions."[27] Woolgar suggests that designers "configure" the user through the artifact, designing the tool so that particular uses are prominent, difficult, or unavailable, and further characterizing the nature of these uses in supplementary materials like manuals and ads.[28] These roles can be quite compelling, subject positions that most users will tend to inhabit.[29]

But beyond anticipating the user, and in the process favoring some uses over others (which arguably happens in all technical design), the robustness principle asks designers to go one step further: to also design against the very possibility of user agency. It makes quite a difference if you weld a car's hood shut—not only for what users can and cannot do, but for how users will understand themselves as users, around whether having agency with that technology is possible, or even conceivable. This has significant impact on our ideas about technology and its role in society, and on the direction of culture and information that technolegal versions of copyright hope to choreograph.

My sense of agency with my own tools is constituted by and within a set of competing cultural forces. For example, I am encouraged to examine, manipulate, and even innovate my car by a number of mechanisms: books and courses on car maintenance, friends who share their love of tinkering, local competitions and subcultures that celebrate individual innovations. Furthermore, the commercial gain of saving on car repair, and the back-and-forth of innovations and innovators between amateur design communities and the auto industry, are financial encouragements to tinker as well. The law of property implies that what is mine is available to me as something to investigate, change, break, or redesign. These are all subtle reminders that I can not only operate my car but also maintain, repair, customize, adjust, destroy, or redesign it; I can conceive of it both as a tool I use and an object upon which I can act.[30]

Beyond these legal, commercial, and social forces, I can also be encouraged by the design of the car itself: the latch that opens the hood, the kickstand that props it up, the orientation of the engine components toward my line of sight. Each of these is an oblique encouragement of user agency built into the technology itself: not just the right to use, but the creative agency to trick out, to tinker, to dismantle, to reinvent. I may never take advantage of these opportunities to do anything innovative with my car, but I am regularly reminded that I might. And even if I don't do so with my car, I might with my computer, or my VCR, or my broken toaster.

Historians of technology have begun to note the importance of this give-and-take between users and their technologies, both for the social character of technologies and for their subsequent innovation:

People are not merely malleable subjects who submit to the dictates of a technology; in their consumption, they are not the passive dupes suggested by crude theorists of ideology, but active, creative and expressive—albeit socially situated—subjects. People may reject technologies, redefine their functional purpose, customize or even invest idiosyncratic symbolic meanings in them. Indeed they may redefine a technology in a way that defies its original, designed, and intended purpose . . . However, the appropriation of a technology cannot be entirely separated from its design and development: technologies are designed for particular purposes.[31]

This emphasis on the role of users is an attempt to counter the tendency, both in academic thought and in Western culture at large, to think of technologies as independent forces that act upon the social world with predictable and universal consequences. The possibility that users can reimagine or innovate a technology in ways unexpected by the designer suggests that these technologies do not follow some independent trajectory, either inherent in the thing itself or as intended by designers.

User interventions are not so rare or idiosyncratic as one might imagine. Ron Kline and Trevor Pinch describe rural farmers in the early days of the automobile who removed the wheels of their Model Ts and connected their farm equipment to the driveshaft, transforming their cars into stationary power sources. Such innovations quickly spread beyond individual farmers. Magazines reported on some of the innovations, third-party manufacturers developed devices that facilitated the connection between auto and tool, and some auto manufacturers even incorporated the uses into their advertising.[32] The agency of users, in negotiation with the technology itself (what's possible) and the designers and manufacturers (what's intended), puts twists and turns in the paths of innovation these technologies follow.

Perhaps most important, these user appropriations and innovations can be implicit challenges by those marginal to the centers of power and technological production.[33] Farmers transform their Model Ts into stationary power generators, hackers crack commercial filtering software to reveal the list of sites being blocked, researchers turn toy robot dogs into roving "sniffers" that can identify hazardous chemicals in residential areas.[34] If technologies are then marked by the specific power relations within which they were designed, and more generally by the systems of power in which those sites are embedded, their very shape tends to propose ways of engaging with the world that quietly ratify those power relations. The act of appropriating a technology, making it one's own through use and sometimes through its unauthorized redesign, extracts that technology from these power dynamics and can even turn it back against them. Discovering the copy protection algorithms in a DVD player and turning them into an illicit duplication tool may be childish rule breaking, but it does repurpose a tool dedicated to consumption of culture to allow its user to become a distributor. As such it is an implicit, materialized challenge to the systems of power that produced digital locks in the first place, and the judgment that it is illegal or wrong is always also a judgment about the challenge it poses and the system it challenges.

But what if such user innovations are rendered impossible by the technology itself, that is, if the hood is welded shut? Or if prying it open is illegal? What if this strategy increasingly becomes the norm, and a generation of users grows up never knowing there is a hood there at all? If the tools available for the consumption and circulation of music, movies, e-books, and digital information[35] are designed to robustly withstand user intervention, our sense of technological agency will diminish. The more that the technology itself is designed to be closed to the user, and the more its functions are obscured within its design, the less likely unauthorized users are to work out its encryption secrets and crack the code upon which the technical constraints are based. Technologies already submerge their workings for a number of reasons: protecting the innovative design or code from the eyes of economic competitors, giving users an uncluttered and aesthetically appealing interface that does not require them to understand how things work, subtly preventing users from making adjustments that pose safety risks or would make authorized repair of the device more difficult. Now, the "black box"[36] of technology is itself being further black boxed.

The idea being imagined here is a relatively new one. With traditional machines, it is only possible to prevent users from accessing the internal workings of the device by regulating their access to it. I cannot open the hood of the commuter train or the jet airplane I am on because the panels are locked, because the crew is authorized to stop me, because doing so is illegal. This depends on the fact that the technology is controlled by an entity with the authority to limit my access to it. Such restrictions are lent a legitimacy both by the tenets of property (I can't tamper with what isn't mine) and safety (I shouldn't tamper when doing so might cause physical harm). When the technology is legally and materially in my possession, it has until now been nearly impossible to prevent me from opening it up and seeing how it works; I can just lift the casing of my VCR to see where the tape meets the head.

How manufacturers and their content industry partners hope to prevent user alterations is also new. In Kline and Pinch's story of the rural automobile, some car manufacturers were disturbed by the farmers' unexpected innovation. Their reaction, however, was merely to contractually require their dealers not to perform conversions for their customers, not to actually try to stop farmers from doing it themselves.[37] When AT&T wanted to discourage the use of telephone peripherals such as the Hush-a-Phone mouthpiece, the company appealed to the FCC and to the courts to make the peripheral device illegal—and failed.[38] What these industry giants did *not* do was redesign their devices to make user innovation less possible, presumably because they couldn't. No device could be closed that could not also be opened. Ownership implied the right to access, and the authority to grant others access. However, with digital technology and particularly with the techniques of encryption, the software I buy today can work *for* me without ever being open *to* me. This offers a qualitatively new degree of control to the designer and, by extension, to the designers' economic allies.

A Right of Inquiry into Technology and Culture

The robustness rules built into trusted systems are intended to frustrate user agency materially and legally, and therefore conceptually. The risk here is that our ontological relationship to technology will shift. It has already shifted dramatically over the past two centuries, from one where we were often the makers of the tools we used, to one where our tools are largely mass-produced elsewhere, but we nevertheless have access to their inner workings.[39] With the manufacturers' desire for a technology that can prevent access to itself, this relationship shifts again, to one in which users are discouraged, materially and legally, from investigating their own tools and from using them in ways other than those for which they were intended and authorized. The design of these technologies encourages some uses and forbids others, and it also suggests a passivity toward the technology itself by forbidding more active interventions. Passivity may be acceptable to culture providers who profit from "couch potato" consumption, but it certainly is not the ideal version of technological agency we might want to encourage as a society.

This shift only makes sense within a worldview in which everything users do besides consume is framed as a problem. First, it assumes that all users, given the opportunity, will work around any rules built into a technology. All users are nearly pirates, and all pirates nearly hackers. Second, it requires a battle mentality, in which every device must be fortified against the inevitable attack. If the trusted system is sufficiently robust, every device will work perfectly according to the compliance rules, allowing some uses and disallowing others, and barring any intervention, whether mechanical or digital. In this way, the digital Wild West can become a neatly appointed shopping mall. What is left for users is to act as passive consumers, using the technology appropriately.

Perhaps unsurprisingly, this strategy of designing against user agency demonstrates a striking parallel to the politics of the content industries in regard to copyright and culture. Cutting up films into a digital montage, generally protected by fair use, is a manifestation of cultural agency. Opening up a DVD player or digital application and reworking the tool to make it better suited for some unanticipated use is technical agency. Both are structurally disabled by DRM systems, where technical barriers squelch cultural and technical innovation in their effort to inhibit infringement. The fear of tampering (whether with the content or with the tool) seems to justify measures that, because they cannot discern between circumvention and creative tinkering, simply prohibit both.

In the end, the impact on our experience with culture and with technology may be the same. Content owners, in seeking stricter and more preemptive copyright rules, are working to turn users of culture into mere consumers, to discourage consumers from being (fair) users. To do so through a technological DRM regime, and to robustly protect it against tampering, requires designing for the same passivity with the technology, to create consumers of technology rather than users. In this effort to bring manufacturers and materials and rules into lockstep, what is endemic to the trusted system is an underlying distrust of users, both of culture and of technology. It is a politics of culture and technology that is very much at odds with our common sense and our democratic notions of what individuals should be able to do with both, but a neat fit to the principles of commercial, mass-produced culture.

One comment from the EFF is particularly telling. Before they shifted early in the debates about the broadcast flag, they argued that fair use would be squelched by the measures being proposed. It is a warning regularly posed as a critique of DRM, but the language they chose to use in this moment is important: "Manufacturers and the public, including hobbyists and individual technologists, have a basic right of inquiry, to access any unencrypted signal and to process it as they wish. No technological restrictions on the ability to process, record, transmit, play, or otherwise handle signals should be created, promulgated, or perpetuated."[40] Though their comments to the FCC shifted to focus on the effect of robustness rules on open source innovation, this "basic right of inquiry," be it cultural or technical, is arguably the same. The trusted system envisioned by the content industry, and pursued in regulatory strategies like that of the broadcast flag, works to close down both, and in similar ways.

This regulatory strategy is likely to continue. Copyright protection continues to be consistently and energetically pursued by the MPAA, RIAA, and publishing industry, and has gained ground with legislators and regulators. Consumer electronics and information technology manufacturers are increasingly embracing and lending support to this approach rather than resisting it. The impact is not limited to open source digital television tuners. Increasingly, for a coherent and comprehensive trusted system to work, these robustness requirements must apply to all technologies that deal in any way with digital content. These may be applied through law, as with the proposed broadcast flag or the Hollings Bill, or through DRM licensing agreements that impose many of the same requirements, as with the downstream devices involved in digital television and with DVD players. As more and more "technologies of culture" are required to be robust, and user agency is both designed away and outlawed by statutes like the DMCA, user agency itself is likely to evaporate.

Users Sometimes Matter

Technologies are in many ways defined by the practices and perceptions of their users; as Nelly Oudshoorn and Trevor Pinch put it, "Users matter."[41] And perhaps we can distinguish four ways in which they matter.[42] First, users help to define a technology in the moment of use, treating it as something and not something else, thereby together giving life to the technology as a cultural artifact. This meaning-making process may be perfectly aligned with the intentions of designers, or it may involve a "reinterpretation"[43] of the artifact according to different semantic associations, but in the end it can only work with what's offered. Some DRM systems fail because they simply never get bought, or never find a place in people's social activities.

Second, users can, explicitly or obliquely, speak about a technology and its appropriate uses. They do this through consumer reports, while beta testing with manufacturers, in complaints to regulators, and as occasional public outcries. The mockery that followed the CD protection scheme that could be circumvented with a magic marker[44] radically altered the social meaning of the DRM technologies; they became not a neutral and legal requirement but a laughable and inept effort to tilt at windmills. This characterization did as much to undermine DRM's effectiveness as the magic marker did. Those posting DeCSS often did so as part of a political critique of DRM, of technical control, and of the music and movie industries and their business practices.[45]

Third, users sometimes adapt the technology for novel uses unanticipated by its designers; this adaptation by users can, if it becomes widespread or noted in public venues, substantially change the social meaning of the technology.[46] The outrage expressed after it was revealed that Sony's CD protection scheme rendered users' computers vulnerable to rootkit viruses reminds us that Sony's protection scheme could be adapted to more nefarious uses than was intended.

Fourth, users sometimes remake the technology, if they have the skills, opportunity, and desire to do so: As Gieryn reminds us, "Once unleashed by designers and builders, artifacts become available for later reconfiguration as they are returned to the hands of human agents for more or less creative redefinition, reevaluation and even re- (or de-) construction. Reconfiguration may be discursive or material. In the first instance, the black box is left unopened, but it is shrouded in novel interpretations and assessments . . . In other instances, a black box is pried opened and the artifact is materially remade—or destroyed, possibly abandoned to the junk heap."[47] Ron Eglash suggests that this reinvention is the most important kind of user appropriation, because while reinterpretation changes only the technology's meaning, and adaptation changes only its meaning and its use, reinvention alters its meaning, its use, and its structure. In doing so it can create new functions, and reimagine the "contours of social power"[48] embedded in the device and the "structures of participation"[49] that accompany it. And if these redesigners decide to distribute their reworked technology, it can become a useful tool for others, and have a different social impact than its predecessor.

In all four ways, users have a say in the material and discursive construction of the technology and its place in society. What DRM reveals, however, is that designers may actually have some sway over how much users can matter, at least in the first and fourth senses. As Hugh Mackay and Gareth Gillespie observe, "Some technologies are more open than others, more amenable to being used for a range of purposes."[50] If designers choose, or are compelled by government fiat or commercial license, they can design against user agency itself—by welding shut the hood, encrypting the data, making the artifact robust against user inquiry. The roles designers build into their devices will then be systematically passive ones, guiding not only particular uses but also the underlying sense of agency that accompanies that use.

Not only does this have implications in the debates about DRM, copyright law, and the regulation of digital culture; it also has implications for theories of the social shaping of technology that optimistically hold up user innovation as a counterbalance to designer intentions.[51] If the ability of users to innovate is contingent on whether designers build for it or against it, particular attention must be paid to those commercial and legislative efforts that design against user agency. Since this technolegal strategy curtails the user agency demonstrated only through material reworking, but not through public critique and political mobilization, these other forms of agency may be of greater significance, if the very idea of user agency is to remain in our cultural vocabulary.

We have benefited as a culture from the balance struck in copyright, between the rights of owners of culture and the ability of a public who can fruitfully build off of that work. This balance is arguably being tipped by the efforts of a powerful set of content owners to use encryption to lock up cultural work and push the use of culture toward more thoroughly commodified and structurally passive forms of consumption. What is revealed in the debates about DRM robustness rules is that we have also benefited from a balance between different modes of technological innovation—closed, hierarchical, corporate design, and the messier innovations of a curious public of users. This balance is similarly at risk of being tipped by DRM. Open forms of innovation could be shut down as part of preventing copyright piracy. If there is a democratic imperative to balance copyright in order to encourage production over consumption, and to ensure the public's right to remix in the face of a near-monopoly power of culture owners, then there is a similar imperative in the politics of technology. Here, we must encourage agency over passivity, assert the public's "freedom to tinker"[52] over the near-monopoly power of technology manufacturers, who are being drawn into tighter and tighter collusion with culture owners. It is this second power of users, the power to speak back to designers through purchase, complaint, and outcry, that must be used to challenge the possibility that agency in culture and technology will be encrypted against the very users on whom they depend.

Encryption, then, is not only the technical foundation of the trusted system, but a means by which copyright owners gain political leverage, both against established manufacturers and against users who might fancy themselves manufacturers of a sort. The license it backs obligates the makers of machines to frustrate users' efforts. Encryption, a technique for ensuring secrecy and therefore fundamentally a means to include and exclude by design, allows for the technical protection of copyright—and is being used for far more than copy control. In the end, it not only serves as a powerful element in the sociotechnical restriction of copyright, but also imposes and enforces very particular market dynamics on the movement and use of culture. While we do have a forum for debating the legal consequences of changing copyright law, we are less able to recognize that market strategies can also regulate speech and constrain use. These consequences are also important to copyright and to its cultural and political goals.

Throughout this book, I have argued that it is crucial for us to think of DRM as much more than a technological phenomenon. More than technology is required to make it work, and it may be that those political, economic, and institutional shifts and alignments will be of greater consequence than DRM itself for cultural expression in a digital age. This is part and parcel of current thinking about technology in its social context— what we think of as technical is never exclusively so, though it gains much of its power from seeming to be so. The trusted system is no different, benefiting from the way technological interventions both appear neutral and obscure the real social and political work that put them in place and gave them force.

But while encryption may only be the leading edge of the sociopolitical regulation scheme imagined for the future of digital copyright, it is significant for the way it gives shape to the activity that can occur within it. The paradigmatic relationship between participants that encryption has required in its traditional application—secret military communication— is being forced upon public, commercial, and cultural exchanges that never before worked on such terms. By considering encryption in its historical context and asking why it is now being used in cultural distribution in the way it is, we can examine the consequences of this strategy not only for copyright, but for something larger: the further commodification of culture. Under the persuasive rubric of anti-piracy, what is being built here is not copy protection, but content protection. The distinction is a crucial one. Copyright has always been both a legal and an economic arrangement, and as such we have regularly had to grapple with the way that both legal and economic structures shape the rights we associate with it. Now, content owners are once again attempting to shift and expand the commercial choreography of culture, in ways that will again impact the rights we associate with culture—and they are again using copyright to do it, this time through its technical implementation.

In the end, DRM is not a means to regulate duplication and distribution; it is a way to guide and track purchase, access, and use in ways that monetize what users do, and only then to constrain redistribution and reuse through commercial and technical boundaries. This helps to explain why—despite abundant evidence that a perfect DRM system simply cannot be affordably built, that patrolling that system is costly and publicly damaging, that achieving interindustry agreement or federal mandates is arduous and perhaps futile—content companies keep pursuing it. When content is locked and devices promise to love, honor, and obey their built-in rules, every use of a cultural work can be tagged with a price, and every right can come with a bill. Just as digital technology has expanded copyright law from something only businesses cared to litigate into something affecting every one of us, the logic of copyright is expanding from the Record button to every point of interaction with culture. Not only is content commodified, but our rights to interact with it are as well.

Encryption For, and Against

Humans have been practicing the art of cryptography for thousands of years. As long as people have competed for political or economic resources, conveying information to allies without revealing it to competitors has been a powerful way to gain the upper hand in such contests. Information is power, but it is also vulnerable to interception, which always makes that power precarious. For this reason, we have pursued innovations not only in communication, but also in making that communication selectively legible only to trusted recipients. Primarily, these practices of information secrecy have been pursued by and for military and government interests, that is, those charged with strategically competing with enemies. Generals in the field need to receive commands from leaders back home without revealing the plans to the other side; spies need to get sensitive information out of hostile territory without revealing that they are doing so.

The techniques of cryptography demonstrate these particular priorities.[1] Cryptography presumes that the primary goal is keeping a message secret between two speakers, in the face of hostile agents who are determinedly seeking to discover this message and may have the capacity to interrupt its movement. A checkpoint on a road may stop the messenger; the message then must be either hidden, unrecognizable as a message, or indecipherable. The earliest techniques were mere masquerade: the clever hiding of messages on the body, inside objects, or anywhere they might go undiscovered. Messengers are only suspicious to the enemy if it is clear they are messengers. But this system of secrecy, called stenography, is only as good as its hiding place. A discovered message is a compromised one. A better technique, at the heart of traditional cryptography, is to transmit the message in a coded language, so that the hostile interceptor cannot understand it even if it is discovered, but the recipient armed with the appropriate knowledge can undo the code and read the message within.

The means of obscuring information using code are myriad, and it is beyond the scope of this book to relate them. Driven by the imperative need for secure information in political conflicts, modern governments have called upon linguists and mathematicians to come up with ever more complex systems of encryption; driven also by the need for any clue as to the enemy's whereabouts or intentions, the same governments have called upon the same linguists and mathematicians to pursue techniques for breaking encoded information. This has led to a cryptographic arms race, spurred by centuries of military and political conflicts, that has helped fuel an intellectual and technological commitment to encryption, particularly over the last century.

Each new communication technology presents new challenges for the transmission of secret information. So long as information traveled along with a human messenger, that information was only vulnerable at the moment of his capture. Telephone allows for the transmission of information nearly instantaneously, but wires are vulnerable to uninvited listeners anywhere along their path. With the advent of radio, military instructions could be transmitted powerfully and instantly far and wide, but anyone with a receiver tuned to the correct frequency could hear those instructions as well. As the delivery of information becomes less and less protectable through the sheer physical control of the messenger, encryption increasingly becomes the only means by which information can be shielded from prying eyes. Hiding the message itself or rendering it unrecognizable as a message are less and less feasible techniques; only encryption of the message can suffice. To put it another way, "the safest option is to assume that all transmissions can be intercepted."[2]

Communication networks also expanded the need for cryptography beyond its military origins. When personal or commercial messages must be put into the hands of a telegraph operator or a postman or delivered through a network run by a telephone company, even messages that aren't state secrets may be vulnerable.[3] The presence of that disinterested third party can be exploited. Business rivals might pay to overhear your economic plans and undercut them; distributors of your message may not guard it as carefully as you would; vital personal information could be gathered and exploited. For the same reasons that we seal our envelopes before mailing them, an increasingly wide range of civilian users are turning to encryption to protect their messages to trusted partners as they travel the public byways of communication networks.

The unquestioned rule, until a few decades ago, was that encryption depends on having previously and carefully shared a decryption key, so that both participants in the exchange know how to encode and decode messages. This way the message itself can travel along vulnerable networks, and even a hostile interceptor who receives it presumably cannot decipher it, yet the recipient can. The gold standard of this technique is the "one-time pad"; sender and receiver have in their possession a copy of the same pad, each page of which offers a system for replacing the letters of the message with other letters. The message is sent encoded, including the number of the page used to encode it, which tells the recipient which page to use to decode it. Without a copy of that one-time pad, the hostile interceptor is left with gibberish and no way to decipher it; even if he does crack the code today, a different code will be used tomorrow.

The value of this system also reveals its limitation: There must first be a way to ensure that both participants start with matching pads. This means that at some point the pad has to be delivered, and presumably not along the same avenues by which the messages will be sent, as they are obviously vulnerable. The pad itself must be vigorously protected. A compromised encryption system of this sort cannot easily be salvaged. And if the enemy were able to obtain the key without its users knowing it, they might continue their secret communication, oblivious that its security had been compromised.

Even if the key is kept safe, encryption is not perfect. Breaking codes without the benefit of knowing how they were encoded, called cryptanalysis, depends on finding and exploiting flaws in the encryption. Simple codes can be broken because underlying patterns common to language are often visible. This is why simple letter substitutions are the stuff of puzzle magazines and not of military secrecy: By knowing what words, letters, or letter combinations are common to a language, the hostile interceptor can make educated guesses, building up insight not only into the coded message but also into the cipher itself. The more messages intercepted, the easier this pattern recognition becomes. Therefore, stronger and stronger encryption was developed to produce coded messages that did not give away telltale patterns. This meant complex substitutions, multiple encryptions, and the introduction of onetime variations that would be known only to the sender and the recipient.

It should come as no surprise, then, that cryptographers and cryptanalysts alike turned to machines to manage the complexity of these substitutions. The computer more than any other machine fit this need particularly well, so much so that much of the innovation in computing technology has been driven by the needs of military cryptography. It became clear that massive mathematical algorithms could be used to make systematic changes to a message, changes that could only be undone by knowing the algorithms. Series of changes could be built into a piece of machinery, like the Enigma used by Allied forces in WWII, so that alterations too complex for an individual to comprehend could be undone by a matching device at the other end. This did not solve the problem, of course, of having to first deliver the machine itself and the instructions by which it would be run in a given instance, which made the Enigma a particularly valuable trophy for the enemy.

At the same time, mechanical and digital computing power is useful not only in encrypting messages, but also in breaking encryption. If the key to breaking a code is pattern recognition, computers can be programmed to recognize and tease out subtle patterns that a human operator might not have the time or capacity to recognize; as an alternative, computers can much more rapidly run "brute force attacks" on a code, that is, simply trying all available combinations until a recognizable message is revealed. Stronger and stronger computational encryption became the only way to maintain information secrecy in a context in which the enemy also had computers working to break the code.

With the rise of the PC, the computing power to handle cryptography not only grew, but also moved beyond the hands of military, government, and business interests and onto the desktops of individual users. What was once possible only with massive and expensive mainframes could be handled by a relatively inexpensive consumer device, shifting the power both to use and to break encryption. And with computer networks, just as with previous communication networks, even more people found encryption valuable for more information tasks. In particular, online e-commerce has called for a new level of encryption to be put in the hands of retailers and consumers, who exchange credit card and personal information across the Internet, hoping it will not be vulnerable to identity thieves, business competitors, even the government.

This call for consumer-grade encryption benefited from a discovery made only a decade or two before that overturned some of the deepest assumptions about how cryptography works. Now widely used, "public key cryptography" depends on the fact that some mathematical equations are relatively easy to perform but extremely difficult to reverse.[4] From this discovery, cryptographers realized that encryption could involve two keys, with only those in possession of both able to decrypt. Users could publish their "public" key for anyone to see; any sender could encrypt a message to them using this public key, but only that user could decipher the message using the matching "private" key, which wouldn't be published. Even if the hostile interceptor knows the public key, without the private one the message is still indecipherable. It's as if I can leave an open lock box in the middle of the town square with my name on it; you can put something inside for me and lock it, without needing a key to do so; even if our enemy knows that the box is there, that there is something in it, and that it is for me, without the key only I have he cannot open it. This "asymmetrical" form of cryptography obviates the problem of having to agree upon and deliver matching keys and keep them secret throughout an entire transaction. Each user need only protect their own private key, and anyone can initiate contact with them using the published key, without having planned to do so beforehand. This technique is the basis to current e-commerce transactions; your browser automatically encrypts your personal information using the public key of the retailer, so only that retailer can open it.

With this innovation, and the proliferation of computing power beyond select institutions to all users, encryption has taken on a qualitatively new role in communication practices. Consumer-grade cryptography is readily available and built into most networking software as a way to protect all manner of information traveling public communication networks. Still, the underlying goal remains the same: to ensure that two trusted individuals may speak with reliable secrecy without a hostile interceptor discovering the content of that conversation. Encryption makes a clear distinction between who is inside the communication and who is outside of it, and attempts to honor and protect that distinction despite the interceptor's best efforts. It assumes a fundamental trust between participants and takes an implicitly hostile, or at least skeptical, posture toward everyone else. The roles already imagined in communication—producer/consumer, sender/receiver, artist/audience—are hardened into a battle paradigm where communicators are under relentless attack. This provokes an obvious set of questions: Who has the authority to access the information? Was this arranged beforehand? What private goal are these trusted partners together pursuing? Who can break the code, and what happens when they do?

Secret Machines

DRM content protection techniques take advantage of all of these encryption innovations, but put them toward a dramatically new purpose. In all the uses outlined in the preceding section, the sender and recipient are using encryption to together keep their communication safe from prying eyes. The encryption builds a barrier around the information for the duration of its journey through hostile territory, and those unauthorized to read it are unable to do so because they lack the necessary key. Once the message is delivered, the encryption mechanism becomes a decryption mechanism, and the information is freed from its shackles by the recipient. This ability to cloak one's communicative exchange is a powerful tool, sometimes to exert power and sometimes to evade it. In fact, the developers and promoters of public-key cryptography imagined it to be a tool of liberation. Putting "crypto" in the hands of many, they hoped, would put the power of privacy in the hands of all; what once was the exclusive ability of governments and militaries to keep their information and their actions secret from others could now be shared by anyone.

But up to this point, encryption was a wall around information that kept out the unauthorized, and nothing more. With DRM encryption, not only is the encryption designed to exclude, it is also designed to regulate what the recipient does with the information. This curious shift is only made possible with the reimagining of the tools involved. The decoder ring, the Enigma, and decryption software were tools that users could employ to free information from its protective shield; fitted with the right key, a computer could decipher a message and make it available to a reader. With DRM, the recipient technology is designed both to decrypt *and* to regulate the user's encounter with the information. Decryption of the message becomes decryption-with-conditions. It is the perfect match with copyright: how to regulate what people do with your work the moment you send it to them.

Another way to think about it is that the receiver of DRM-encrypted information is not actually the consumer but the consumer's device. The sender (a film studio) encrypts their message so that prying eyes cannot see. The recipient, your DVD player, has already been given the proper key to decrypt that message after it successfully travels the public byways—the production, distribution, and retail systems. The "trust" in the trusted system is between the content provider and the devices. In this framework, *we* are the hostile interceptors. We are the ones who want to see the content while it is being delivered from sender to receiver, and we are unable to do so because of the encryption. Once it is safely in the hands of the device, we are then limited by its functions as chaperone, not by the encryption itself.

This also reveals the fundamental weakness of the DRM strategy. While it is the technology's job to chaperone its users, it must also have the means to decrypt. The secret code that ensures the content's safe journey between producer and device is built into the tool and handed to any and all users, no matter how nefarious their intent. If the conundrum of copyright is how to control the use of a work after it is given to those who will use it, the DRM solution has a parallel conundrum: how to keep content secret from someone while also handing them the tools for revealing that secret. In this sense, encryption does not and cannot solve the problem. As Cory Doctorow put it, "At the end of the day, all DRM systems share a common vulnerability: they provide their attackers with ciphertext, the cipher and the key. At this point, the secret isn't a secret anymore."[5]

This is why the real story, the real power behind DRM, is not the rise and embrace of encryption itself, but the institutional negotiations to get technology manufacturers to build their devices to chaperone in the same way, the legitimation to get consumers to agree to this arrangement, the political machinations to get the government to authorize these rules for building the technology according to specs, and the legal wrangling to make it criminal to circumvent. The DMCA tries to make homegrown cryptanalysis illegal; robustness rules demand that manufacturers bury that decryption mechanism deep inside the workings of the technology; and efforts to legitimate these DRM-protected distribution arrangements hope to convince users that the code is there for their own benefit and should not be undone. Most important, DRM encryption requires and reinforces a particular idea about technologies and their users. The device is the content owner's "man inside," a technology that in principle belongs more to them than to us.

It should come as no surprise that the contest over digital copyright has become a military-style battle between industry and consumers, between encryption technologists and hackers, as the very strategy of control is fundamentally and historically a military one. The tactics of DRM are precisely the same tactics used against military enemies, and therefore are couched in the language of threat, attack, distrust, secrecy, vulnerability, and the risk of cataclysm. This is not the best paradigm for understanding and encouraging either the delicate flows of information and culture or a rich ecology for technical and cultural innovation, but it is a persuasive way of framing the battle as the protection of copyright versus the onslaught of piracy. And unlike the law, which is designed to arbitrate over conflicts according to shared values, this militaristic framework lends itself to forceful intervention, hard-fought battle lines, and the even more troubling logic of the preemptive strike.

Preemption

Anderton said: "You've probably grasped the basic legalistic drawback to precrime methodology. We're taking in individuals who have broken no law."

"But surely they will," Witwer affirmed with conviction.

"Happily they *don't*—because we get to them first, before they can commit an act of violence. So the commission of the crime itself is absolute metaphysics. We claim they're culpable. They, on the other hand, eternally claim they're innocent. And, in a sense, they *are* innocent."

The lift let them out, and they again paced down a yellow corridor. "In our society we have no major crimes," Anderton went on, "but we do have a detention camp full of would-be criminals."[6]

In "Minority Report," Philip K. Dick invites us to ponder the implications of a criminal system that could prevent crime rather than merely punish it. In his tale, psychics capable of seeing a crime before it is committed are enlisted in the service of law enforcement and given powerful stimulants to enhance their visions; a team of "precrime" law enforcers interpret the visions seen by the psychics to discover the location of the crime about to be committed, and rush to the scene to stop the perpetrator before he or she can act. The precriminal is arrested and detained for having been about to violate the law, thus preventing the crime; at the start of the story, the city has been murder-free since the program was initiated. The narrative is an extended chase sequence, the director of the program trying to elude his officers and his fate. The premise of the story asks us to grapple with the ethical question of whether, if we had the means, it would be morally acceptable to intervene before a crime occurred, holding someone responsible for something they had not yet done. And as in any good science fiction, Dick suggests that such a system would not only likely be flawed, it would also be prone to abuse.

While we have no such mechanism for predicting criminal behavior in the specific, we do have ways of predicting criminal behavior in the abstract. And we have grappled with the ethical and legal ramifications of acting on such information. As a society, we have considered, and experimented with, the sterilization of convicted sex offenders (while it follows a crime, it is considered to be less a form of punishment and more a way to make unlikely or impossible a repeat offense), we have engaged in and debated the ethics of racial profiling, and we continue to try to prevent terrorism by imposing restrictions on immigration from those populations from which terrorists seem to emerge. In recent years we have adopted a military foreign policy, sometimes known as the "Bush doctrine" for President George W. Bush's invasion of Iraq beginning in 2003, of engaging in preemptive military strikes when they seem justified by a pending threat. The relative merit of those justifications in hindsight reveals, as well as Dick's fiction could, the risks of a preemptive approach.

The imposition of technological barriers is the most common form of preempting criminal or other unwanted actions. Trigger locks prevent the trigger from being pulled unless the weapon is in the hands of its authorized user; automatic seatbelts close for the driver without participation, or prevent the driver from starting the car until the belt is in place; courts have required recidivist drunk drivers to modify their cars to include a breathalyzer that prevents ignition until the driver has demonstrated sobriety. The V-chip blocks television programs with questionable content before that content can be seen or assessed, while filtering software does much the same for websites. Some new cars used to be sold fitted with a "governor" that would prevent the driver from exceeding moderate speeds, in order to habituate the engine to regular use. And, most mundanely, we install locks in our front doors, build fences around our property, lock away valuables in safes, and build walls around important buildings to keep out unwanted visitors before they can enter or make off with our precious things.

The regulation of copyright through DRM also attempts to impose a preemptive measure, shifting the point at which regulation is imposed from after a violation to before. Whereas copyright law leaves the discretion to act in the hands of the users, allowing them to determine whether to risk activity that might result in legal penalties, DRM forecloses such discretion, allowing only those actions deemed appropriate in advance by the information producer. This is part of DRM's appeal. Technical protections promise to automatically prevent copyright violations from ever occurring; for content owners, this is certainly preferable to a law that can only be applied after illicit copies have already been made and distributed, the economic damage never to be undone. The fact that these measures apply to all users equally offers a comforting sense of justice, more so than a law that applies only to those who get caught, and only when the copyright holder sees it as economically viable to bring suit.

However, there are three significant problems with a restriction that pre-empts behavior rather than applying consequences after the behavior has occurred. The first, discussed already, is that the kind of exceptions and special cases the law is able to accommodate may be rendered unavailable. While we have a law prohibiting murder, and there is relatively little hes-itation on either deontological or utilitarian grounds as to the merit of such a law, we also have a series of caveats built into the law that we value as a society. Killing someone in self-defense is still murder, but it is murder that, in the eyes of the law and after deliberation in a courtroom, can under particular circumstances be excused. Such an exception would cease to exist were the act of murder somehow preemptible in all cases.

Though we aspire to a legal regime that precisely and clearly regulates behavior in both morally and socially justifiable ways, we recognize that the real world is always more complex than a statute can ever anticipate. In these messy cases we rely on judges and juries to apply the abstractions of law, and in the process to both honor those laws and recognize those moments in which exceptions should be allowed. Such discretion requires that the law be applied after the fact, even though this means that crimes will be committed before they can be adjudicated. If the behavior has yet to occur, it cannot be judged, or can only be judged categorically and without consideration for individual circumstances.

This concern has been the focus of the strongest critiques of DRM. Copy-right as a legal doctrine attempts to strike a balance among the interests of authors, owners, and the public they serve. In pursuit of this balance, the otherwise exclusive rights granted to the owner of a copyrighted work are delimited by a set of important exceptions. Some of these exceptions, such as fair use, are akin to self-defense in that they are legally sanctioned exceptions to the rule, rather than affirmative rights of their own. While the rights of the copyright owner may have been violated, a judge may take into consideration the context and consequences of that viola-tion to determine whether the use fits a prescribed set of criteria protect-ing certain unauthorized but socially valuable uses. Critics of DRM have noted that technologically enforced rules prohibiting duplication and dis-tribution of copyrighted works render unavailable almost all such exemp-tions.[7] By preempting copying, DRM intervenes before use is made, meaning no unauthorized use can ever be accommodated, permissible or otherwise.

Second, preemption endangers the hallowed practice of protesting a law by breaking it. Just as we recognize that our laws are abstract and require constant adjudication, we also recognize that they are imperfect and require regular reconsideration. While we have ways of making such changes, through legislation by our political representatives, we know this system often suffers from calcified unresponsiveness, bureaucratic inertia, and the powerful bias of moneyed interests. Often it is those citizens unfairly restricted by a rule who must rise up to challenge it; sometimes, the most viable means to do so is to break the rule as an act of political defiance, as civil rights protesters in the United States and South Africa historically did by willfully ignoring segregationist or apartheid laws. They did not presume that they would get to avoid the consequences the law set out for their actions; they decided that the statement made by defying the law, and the possibility of change that might follow, made it worth accepting those consequences.

Hackers who have challenged DRM restrictions have sometimes adopted a similar rationale, dubbing their circumventing activities a form of "electronic civil disobedience."[8] The comparison to human rights agitation is not meant to overdramatize digital copyright law and its discontents, nor to suggest that everyone who provides decryption tools intends political critique. It is merely meant to point out that the mechanism used by protesters in both cases—defying the law to call attention to its immoral principles or unjust consequences—is an important tactic for an imperfect democratic system. Preemption, however, makes such critiques impossible—unless hackers can get around them. Such circumventions will continue to be made, for fun, for profit, and as a political statement. But in the dream of DRM providers, such circumvention will eventually be preempted itself, through more powerful encryption and more robustly designed technologies.

Third, preemption raises an even more fundamental issue, about the very justification of law itself and the right to impose restrictions on others. DRM, especially in its state-sponsored form, can be seen as a denial of the responsibility, and so of the autonomy, otherwise accorded to information users. Because DRM preempts the discretion of information users, denying them control over how information products are to be used, it treats them as morally immature or incompetent—blocked from, and by implication incapable of, making a moral decision to obey the law. Like the V-chip and filtering software, DRM places information producers in the role of parent, treating users as children, locking away the cookie jar because users are incapable of independently determining responsible use of the treat inside.

Of course, the individual user may seek the owner's consent in order to use content. But putting the user at the whim of the content owner only underscores the implicit infantilization at work here.

Rules are only effective if they are seen as legitimate by the majority of the people to whom they apply; rules we all find pointless or repugnant are not likely to be rules we as a society will follow. A traditional system of law—in which particular behaviors are prohibited, and perpetrators proven to have violated the prohibition are duly punished—assures its own legitimacy on at least two grounds. First, the code of appropriate behavior articulated by a legal system roughly matches an underlying and widely shared morality. While the particular prohibitions may not always be the most exact, fair, or perfectly described, and the system by which they are enforced may be plagued by the frailties of human and institutional capacity, those subject to it will nevertheless accept it if it feels like a sufficiently close match to their own personal and communal sense of right and wrong. Second, in a democratic society, we expect that these laws have been written and enacted according to the general wishes of the public upon which they are to be imposed, at least by way of their elected officials. The process that produces them, although again an imperfect system in practice, lends the laws legitimacy in the eyes of those subject to them.

Still, there may be another way in which the laws to which we are subject earn their legitimacy, beyond their moral congruence and democratic origins. In fact, there must be. In a nation this large and complex, individual citizens often feel quite distant from the government that designed and imposed they laws they must obey. The chain of people and decisions linking them to their representatives can feel long and flimsy; the democratic process can appear flawed and unjust. And individual citizens do not always feel a perfect congruence between their own moral beliefs and the laws they nevertheless obey. Some laws feel inane and pointless and irrelevant to their daily lives—and some of them are. Yet we generally obey the law, even those laws we feel do not match our values, or that we suspect were not designed according to the ideals of democratic governance.

Every time someone chooses to obey a law, they offer that law, and the entire system of law, a tiny bit of legitimacy, both in their own mind and for those around them. Law itself is marked as something worth honoring, something we all consent to in every moment. And this depends on having the choice to obey or not. The fact that a law can be broken, that I could pocket that candy bar if I wanted to, means that in every moment I am choosing not to. Every time I make this choice, I am certifying that the law is worth obeying, not just because the possible punishment is worth avoiding but because it is simply right. It is my autonomy that grants the law legitimacy. And I am surrounded by others doing the same, a constant reminder of the collective acceptance of these norms and the society they represent. It may only be at the moment of violation—when the kid next to us grabs a candy bar and takes off, when the driver in front of us runs the red light—that we even notice how rare it is to break the law, how many millions of choices are made not to do so.

This may be easy to overlook because most laws are enforced after they are broken, such that the autonomy of citizens to obey them is always assured. A preemptive restraint such as DRM, however, precludes this sense of agency. The average citizen cannot break the law, and in fact may not even know exactly what this law prohibits or why. In place of a rule that must be contemplated and accepted in every instance, DRM regulates by obviating that choice altogether. The legitimacy of its authority over people, then, cannot be built on the active consent of its subjects. Instead, by intervening before behavior and preempting possible uses whether authorized or not, DRM instrumentalizes users as mechanisms designed to collectively pay the artist's salary, nothing more. Of course, critics of peer-to-peer trading may say that without this preemption, millions of people continue to defy the law of copyright. But this should raise the question of whether, in the face of widespread violation, the rule is being legitimately applied in a culturally valuable way; it appears not to carry the moral imperative that would warrant the stringent impositions and harsh punishments the content industries have sought.

For all of these reasons, it seems vital that preemptive measures be held to a significantly higher standard than prohibitive measures in their enactment. They affect everyone without discriminating between criminals and lawful users, and they risk closing off legitimate activities along with illegitimate ones. They render civil disobedience impossible, or reserve it for only those with particular technical skills. Most of all, it is impossible to know what innovations would have developed had these preemptive rules not been in place, or to know the value of activities that have been prevented. Granted, to the extent that we allow people to lock up their homes and possessions, we do embrace state-authorized preemptive restrictions. The value of such restrictions legitimately outweighs whatever meager benefit there might be in allowing strangers access to our things. However, locking up copyrighted material and preempting use is much more controversial, because of the tenuous balance of interests that intellectual property law is supposed to preserve. Most of all, the preemptive approach to imposing rules undercuts the agency and autonomy of people who are subject to those rules, further encouraging a cultural mindset that undermines people's sense of participation and responsibility and replaces it with a patronizing "do what you're told with what you're sold."

Perhaps a more appropriate standard would look something like the First Amendment doctrine of "prior restraint."[9] The First Amendment requires that the speech of individuals be protected from any and all restriction, be it imposed by the state or effected by another individual, but the rule is not without exceptions. Laws may restrict the time, place, or manner in which speech occurs (e.g., not in the middle of a busy intersection), and some speech does not enjoy First Amendment protection (such as child pornography, or speech that will "incite" violence against another person or the government). However, the courts give more leeway to laws that impose consequences after the speech has occurred; they are much less tolerant of laws that preempt speech. "Gag" laws (or judicial injunctions, for that matter) that impose "prior restraint"—that is, restraint before the speech can be committed or published—must pass a much more rigorous test to prove there is a national interest in squelching that speech, and great harm if it is allowed to proceed.

The premise is that the danger of censoring speech is nearly always greater than the harm of allowing some speech that turns out to be obscene, incendiary, slanderous, or treasonous. Just as we hold that it is better to allow ten guilty to go free than to jail one innocent, it is also better to allow illegal speech to be spoken and impose consequences afterwards than to risk that legal speech be silenced. The punitive consequences that can follow unlawful speech are chilling enough, but preemption means the speech will never see the light of day, will never be heard or criticized, and could be lost forever. DRM and technological barriers are a form of prior restraint, one that assumes that the activity of the citizen is not valuable enough to warrant its day in court.

Regional Coding

Questions about fair use in a digital context reveal the problem of technological preemption most visibly, and may be the most politically viable way to counter the claim that DRM is the solution to the "problem" of digital culture. But in focusing exclusively on copyright, this line of inquiry can overlook the way the technolegal scheme enforced through DRM and trusted computing extends well beyond the activities regulated by that law.

We need to ask not only about how technical copy protection and the regime of alignment it requires intervene in user practices once regulated by law, but also about how and where they shape our relationship with information and culture more broadly. What have the rhetoric of digital copyright and the threat of piracy been used to justify, and how have they expanded the domain of copyright itself? To put it another way, the pre-emption made possible by DRM is not only a mechanism for stopping infringement before it happens, but a way to command users to be docile, not just in terms of appropriate and inappropriate use, but in relation to all engagements with the content—especially its purchase.

With the CSS encryption built into DVDs, and the DMCA as a legal guardian not only against users who circumvent but also against the makers of tools that facilitate circumvention, encryption becomes the means to compel manufacturers to build limits into their tools, limits that subsequently regulate users. The new law, premised as always on the threat of a pandemic of copyright violation, serves as a restriction as much on what devices can be manufactured as on what uses may be made of the copyrighted work. If a studio wants to lock up their movie, manufacturers must follow their rules or risk the charge of contributing to piracy. The agreement produces a cartel of legitimate manufacturers that abide by the rules, and criminalizes anyone who dares to work outside of this agreement. But the DMCA supports technical barriers that prevent access, not copying; this means that any reason the content provider might have to want to restrict access would now have legal and contractual backing. Encrypting digital data becomes a means of both preventing users from making unauthorized uses of the work and harnessing manufacturers into building tools the film industry wants—not only to more effectively prevent copying, but to institute any and all control measures that industry desires.

The bulk of the DVD-CCA license signed by every DVD player manufacturer is geared toward copyright protection. For the most part, it ensures that the DVD player in question will not output the film in a digital format other than those approved by the film industry. But there is an additional component to this license, one that does not protect copyright or regulate unauthorized distribution: regional coding. DVDs and DVD players include deliberate regional incompatibility in order to segment international markets. When the DVD was first being designed, the film industry mapped the global market into six distinct regions, roughly by continent.[10] Every DVD player must check for a single bit of information on each disc that indicates its region of origin, and compare it to its own. If the codes do not match, the device must refuse to play the disc. A disc purchased in the United States will not play on a European device, and vice versa.[11] A region-free device is a violation of the DVD-CCA license, though it does exist.[12] Regional coding depends on the encryption and technological barriers of DRM, and allows the studios and their distributors to choreograph the sales and consumption of their films, releasing DVDs in markets around the world at different moments and at different prices. It does this by inventing a technical incompatibility, and through the license, requiring manufacturers to enforce it.

Technical incompatibilities in media technologies between regions of the world are not new. Specific infrastructures for electricity and transportation often reflect early choices that imposed strong path dependencies on future developments. Sometimes we only discover the obstacle when we attempt to interconnect these infrastructures across national borders.[13] Military purposes often justified strategic incompatibilities in widely used technologies, such as national differences in the gauge of train tracks or the caliber of rifles. Incompatible standards have also been used to insulate domestic markets, raising the costs of entry to foreign competitors.[14] Television signals have long had competing standards,[15] established back when television was only delivered via an airborne signal, and the national broadcast systems were relatively distinct. Television manufacturers built different kinds of televisions for different markets; when the VCR was introduced, this incompatibility meant that devices and tapes built for one standard could not be exported for sale in another. Consumers might not be likely to try to resell their VCRs on an international scale, but VHS tapes were cheap enough to distribute that the "arbitrage," buying in one market to ship and resell to another, might be viable. However, the technical incompatibility, though it was not intended as a way of regulating trade, did have that effect of preventing this kind of international arbitrage.

In the information age, major efforts have been made to overcome such fragmentation of standards, in the name of both free trade and the benefit of network effects. Formal and informal international standards-setting processes, now essential features of global information networks, are maintaining the fragile compacts of compatibility that have given us a small set of interoperable standards to govern major communications infrastructures: the Internet, a few input/output (I/O) designs, air traffic control.[16]

With the DVD, however, the film industry has turned this kind of inadvertent incompatibility into a deliberate and strategic tool. The studios purposefully designed in regional coding as a mechanism for distinguishing and separating international markets. The incompatibility is as simple as a "1" on a disc and a "2" on a DVD player. There is no bureaucratic or technical legacy underlying the region code, only a market logic that encourages inefficiencies at one level (interregional trade) to achieve greater market power at another (price discrimination by region). The cartel power of the major film studios allows them to shift the costs of this bargain to hardware manufacturers (who must license the technology) and to consumers, who find their consumption habits tied to regional infrastructures.

The purpose of this technological measure has little to do with copyright. Besides frustrating travelers, it is designed primarily to allow studios to release DVDs in markets around the world at different moments and at different prices.[17] The film industry has historically discriminated among various markets—by time, medium, and location—to sell its product at a price optimally suited to each. Studios typically cascade the release dates of their films in various media. In the United States this means a progression through first-run theaters, second-run theaters, pay-per-view, hotel rental and in-flight screenings, video sales and rental, premium cable, basic cable, and network broadcast. Each version is usually cheaper for the consumer than the previous one, and often of lesser perceived quality (aesthetic or experiential). International market segmentation follows similar strategies, from staggered international release schedules[18] to price discrimination in the international marketing of DVDs, primarily as a way to steer prices closer to the relative purchasing power of customers outside the United States and Europe.

Such price discrimination would be undercut if consumers could purchase DVDs from any place in the world. Importers could load up on a cheap release in the United States and undercut the Asian market for the same film if it was being released at a higher price or at a later date. Consumers could buy DVDs online from sellers in different countries if the shipping costs were less than the savings. And, in the case of a DVD being released in one market before the film even hits theaters in another, international DVD sales could undercut the box office for the theatrical release.

Regional coding works to eliminate some of this arbitrage, to ensure that the studios get to set region-specific prices themselves. The ability to block arbitrage also assures opportunities for secondary, exclusive distribution deals between studios and local partner companies. Partner companies' products will not have to compete with discs imported from other regions. In practice, studios need not even release a film in all regions if they think its market prospects are poor. Under these circumstances, a film may be completely unavailable in a region. Although this is rarely the case with major Hollywood releases, it is routinely the case with foreign releases, which have no distribution networks in the U.S. market.

DVDs are the most prominent example of this kind of regional coding, although they are not alone. Sony has a regional coding scheme in its Playstation games and game consoles; Hewlett-Packard has a similar mechanism matching ink cartridges to printers by region. This technique is likely to expand: "Even though it costs manufacturers more to make region-specific gear, the combination of obvious currency variations plus cheap international transport means 'regionality' is a growing trend."[19]

It is important to note that, again, the technology can't accomplish this restriction alone. Not only must the technology distinguish regional players and discs, which requires a licensing arrangement that affects all manufacturers, but a cultural justification for the barrier—something more powerful than economic self-interest—must also be in place. If the only reason the airlines require that the buyer of a ticket also be the passenger was to help them engage in price discrimination, consumers would not tolerate it. However, the airlines have a powerful rationale for this practice: homeland security. While this practice does allow them to engage in a very intricate form of price discrimination, it is justified as a security measure, a bulwark against terrorism. There is no more powerful justification today than that. Similarly, the film studios have conveniently leaned on the fear of piracy as their justification for these measures. And they've done so in a particularly subtle way. The fears of piracy offered a powerful rationale for the DMCA; they are also a powerful justification for CSS encryption and the licensing arrangement that supports it. The license does indeed enact technological measures that limit duplication and redistribution of protected movies, which are copyright restrictions by another name. But the license also demands that manufacturers honor regional coding, even though it is entirely a means of price discrimination and market control. To market a device that ignores the regional codes would violate the license, a license "necessary" in the name of copyright protection. To circumvent the "access control" of regional coding would violate the DMCA, which is necessary to prevent piracy.

Here the regime of alignment—technological access control by means of encryption, legal prohibition of circumventing such a barrier, and contractual license compelling manufacturers to abide by a set of restrictions designed to regulate use—is in the employ not of copyright protection, but of a surgical intervention into the consumer practices of purchasing and viewing films. The scope and dynamics of marketing a film were once regulated by the physical and practical limits of material distribution; now these "natural" constraints have been replaced by artificial and intentional ones, built into the devices themselves. Yet there has been little debate about whether the film industry has the right to regulate where and how its goods are consumed according to location in this way, or whether such differentiation has any cultural implications. Copyright and the fear of piracy offer a powerful rhetorical justification for a system that, in truth, regulates activities outside of the scope of copyright and distant from the aims of that law.

There has been only one glimmer of recognition in the courts about the way copyright rhetoric has been used to justify such regional coding mechanisms—not in the United States, but in Australia. Sony Computer Entertainment has brought a number of lawsuits in the United States, the United Kingdom, and Australia, against providers of "mod chips"—mechanical devices designed to be affixed to PlayStation game consoles that allow them to play unauthorized games. These include bootleg games, but also games from other regions. After winning injunctions in the United States and the United Kingdom, the first Australian court to hear the case found for the defendants.[20] The court argued that the measures built into the PlayStation to honor regional coding and reject bootleg games are not "technological protection measures" because they are "not designed to prevent or inhibit post-access infringement of copyright, but simply deterred such infringement."[21] On appeal, the Full Federal Court overturned the lower court ruling. Still, in that moment, the question of regional coding, and of pairing content encryption and hardware restriction for strictly marketing purposes, slipped briefly out from behind the shadow of the copyright wars.

However, it may be that such moments will be less likely to appear in court; the U.K. has proposed a directive that would include in their copyright law a clearer prohibition on "illegal technical devices."[22] And the CSS encryption even allows movie studios to handle this issue themselves. Some DVD players have been designed to be "region-free," and sites on the Internet have explained how users can modify their own devices to ignore region coding. In response, Warner Brothers upgraded their CSS DVDs with "Region Code Enhancement"; if a region-free or modified player is detected, the film will not play, displaying instead a message warning the viewer that the device is unauthorized. As it turns out, these new RCE discs will be incompatible with some old DVD players; apparently, this is a drawback the studios and manufacturers are willing to accept.[23]

Rules for You

The "celestial jukebox"[24] that the culture industry has promised, now enhanced with the distribution power of the Internet, aspires to instant delivery, interactivity, massive choice, clever organization and recommendation systems, and intuitive interfaces. These have long been the promise of the Internet itself, where the narrowcasting of cable television can become individualized programming, where interactivity allows content to be adjusted to suit the personalized tastes of the individual user. But as we have seen, digital technology also allows for more specific, individualized means of monitoring and controlling the access to and use of digital content. A trusted system can distinguish between authorized and unauthorized users, but can also distinguish between different *types* of users, who can be granted different levels of access and use depending on how much they pay, their technical profile, or a host of other attributes.

It is, of course, possible that, once the film industry fully commits to digital delivery instead of DVD, they might do away with regional coding, allowing their Internet storefront to serve a single, integrated, global market. But the more likely scenario is that, with Internet broadband connectivity, the technique behind regional coding might develop into an even more intricate cascade of purchase and use options, not unlike the cascade of releases we experience today, but exploded in number and in detail. With an encryption system in place, founded on the fear of piracy but designed also to ensure access on the studios' terms, this release schedule could be ported entirely to digital downloads, and expanded to include whether the film could be copied, whether it could be played for a certain time period, whether it could be lent out to others, and so forth.

With the shift to digital distribution, technically enforced regionalized pricing can be deployed even more effectively. Apple's iTunes Store, for example, has established different pricing structures for different countries; their DRM protects against consumer arbitrage, and their servers ensure that anyone trying to log onto, say, the U.S. iTunes website from a U.K. computer will be automatically redirected to the British site. This discrimination can be further enforced by accepting credit cards only from the same country in which the content is being purchased. This ability to offer multiple interfaces to the same products, and to redirect users to the "appropriate" one, makes possible price discrimination on a much more complex scale, and is designed deliberately to do so.

But the technology already available could be used to extend this price discrimination an additional step, from regional coding to what we might call "individual coding." The clumsiness of the brick-and-mortar distribution of DVDs makes it difficult to distinguish between markets in a way much more fine-grained than by continent and format; the cascading release can only distinguish in the broadest strokes. But with online delivery, paired with databases that record consumer purchases and preferences, pricing schemes and release dates could be tailored to each individual consumer.[25] This is already commonplace in the music subscription services such as Napster 2, where downloaded music is rendered inert if the subscription is terminated.[26] Similar interventions have been suggested to regulate use in different ways: Cable providers are considering time limits on their popular programs, so that shows recorded onto DVRs will only last for a few weeks. Their "death" could be timed with the release of that season on DVD.[27]

This is the promise of the trusted system—to allow "versioning"[28] of the content or service for different users or groups of users, depending on how much they are willing to pay and for what. Charges might be adjusted not only by region, but by previous purchases, by Internet service provider, or with membership in studio-specific "frequent buyer clubs." This kind of price discrimination can be cloaked as "bundling," where a package of goods and services are priced together—buy your iPod now and your iTunes downloads are half off, subscribe to HBO and AOL Music for one low price. These techniques could go even further. Charges could also vary with the consumer's consent to have their personal information sold to other marketers, or to watch advertisements (which would be encrypted such that they could not be skipped, as they are on many current DVDs). DRM providers are already offering ways to make the personal information required by DRM into a commercial asset of its own. As one provider promised,

With Active Internet's DRM, retailers and record labels can set up Internet music stores to distribute digital media files. Content providers can also remain confident that their digital media files will stay protected, no matter how widely they are distributed. The license acquisition process allows companies to gather targeted customer information. For example, many music distribution Web sites now request the consumer's e-mail address in exchange for audio file licenses. Music distribution companies can then use this e-mail address to keep the consumer up-to-date on concert schedules and new compact disc (CD) releases, or to market related merchandise. Alternatively, unsigned bands can upload and market their music directly to fans using DRM technology, while record labels can generate interest in new bands by offering free downloads of their new music.[29]

Recent innovations in DRM systems suggest that these possibilities will only expand, and that this expansion is what is fueling their innovation. Where DRM systems once assigned private keys to classes of devices (e.g., all DVD players of a specific brand or model), now they can assign keys to each individual device.[30] Once your DVD player has a unique decryption key, more precise regulations can be imposed on your unique usage, rather than on all users with the same kind of device or all devices on the same continent. And while micropayment schemes that could allow fractions of a cent to be automatically debited from a bank account with every download (or viewing or lending period or copy or skipped ad) have yet to prove technically or financially viable, practitioners continue to dream of their one day being commonplace.[31]

"Always on" network connectivity is also increasingly common for both computers and cultural appliances, further expanding what's possible with DRM. Despite the demise of DIVX video disc technology (in part because the device required its own dedicated and constant connection to a phone line in order to accept instructions from the vendor), more and more cultural appliances are being built with connectivity as a required function. HD-DVD technology that uses the AACS encryption system will likely require online connectivity as a way to revoke licenses for compromised DRM.[32] Regular software upgrades help to convince users to allow their application to interface with the manufacturer's server, or even accept an automated contact to occur invisibly underneath the software's regular functions. As an example, Windows Media Player connects with Microsoft's server every time a DVD is played, in order to get the title and chapter information.[33] This is not required, but is presented as a "feature," helping to justify regular contact and data transfer to Microsoft, who can then use this and other information about the user to more specifically regulate and charge that user and to better market to others. As Microsoft's literature notes, "Because licenses and digital media files are stored separately, licensing terms can be changed on the licensing server without the need to redistribute or repackage the digital media file."[34] Critics have noted a similar dynamic with Apple's iTunes, where changes in their DRM restrictions, automatically imposed by the upgraded version of the iTunes application, affect music the user had downloaded before the change went into effect.[35] Whether it is required by the format or presented as a feature, regular online contact with the copyright owner or their vendor will ensure that more specific and current information can be used to price discriminate for each user—even information that was not explicitly provided by the user.

Because personal information is fundamental to the workings of the trusted system, it is likely that it will increasingly be exploited, to determine pricing as well as to regulate use. DRM encryption, when combined with license-bound devices that honor it, regularly serves two distinct but interconnected purposes.[36] First, the trusted system can regulate access, typically through user verification. The software assesses whether you are the authorized user, and only decrypts the data after authorization is assured. This requires that the software know something about you (your digital signature, your ability to correctly enter the serial number or password, your having the correct kind of device, etc.). And second, as we have seen, the trusted system regulates use, rendering certain functions unavailable, either entirely or to certain users under restricted conditions. The culture industries are attempting to put DRM to both purposes, and it is their combination that is troubling. Because DRM systems can and must know their user, that information becomes available in subsequent regulation of use.

Once the movie studios and record labels have established, purportedly in the service of the protection of copyright, that they must install legally backed, technological barriers regulating access, and include functions that can distinguish use and price by region, device, user, or use, a number of possible steps might follow. The consequences they pose are not themselves copyright issues, so it is difficult to pinpoint the individual rights that are at stake. However, what are clearly affected are the ways we consume culture and the ways culture is commodified.

By necessity, price discrimination requires impinging on privacy; the seller must know something about the buyer in order to assess what price category they belong in. DRM, then, both depends on and exacerbates the privacy problems already endemic to digital technology.[37] Region-specific DVD players force users to "tell" the seller what region they're from, in that they must buy discs matched to their player. This is hardly a substantial breach of privacy. Once the digital distribution of culture is commonplace, however, the array of potentially available information about each user could be used as the gatekeeping mechanism for access to and use of digital content. For example, consider what would happen if you were directed to "please sign in to activate your downloaded film." If this were the only way to enjoy the latest summer blockbuster, it might not sound like too distasteful a compromise. Joseph Turow notes that as traditional media providers have migrated into digital environments and faced both the fragmentation of the mass audience and the rise of "ad-skipping" technologies, they have increasingly embraced a combination of direct marketing and customer relationship management techniques. These techniques depend not only on massive information databases and programs to parse and recognize patterns, but also on the discovery that "consumers will agree to give up important demographic, psychographic, and lifestyle information about themselves when marketers and media reward them or treat them as special through material that appears tailored for them."[38]

Content providers could then do any number of things with that information. They could target advertisements according to the user's other downloads. They could adjust how much each user should pay for the work, and for any future downloads, based on purchase history or demographic desirability. Turow worries that the content not just of ads but of entertainment as well could be customized for each user in a desperate attempt to encourage brand loyalty.[39] They could streamline the viewing experience for those who have made amenable purchases: For instance, viewers of Warner Bros. films might be allowed to skip ads if they were also subscribers to Time Warner ISP broadband or the AOL portal, while others would have to wade through movie trailers and merchandise offers; this "walled garden" technique is increasingly being explored by content providers as a counter to the sheer magnitude of choices available to their consumers.[40] (A similar technique has often been proposed by cable Internet providers, to speed your connection to their partner websites and slow connections to others.[41])

Such systems could also facilitate the "self-help" measures that content owners have pursued in response to piracy. Seeding peer-to-peer networks with bogus files has become commonplace; the music industry lobbied for but failed to get legislation that would allow them to automatically disable users' computers if illegal mp3 files were found.[42] With a fully installed trusted system such measures could take the war against peer-to-peer much further, using the purchase of goods as both the carrot and the stick to keep users honest. Studios could automatically issue cease and desist letters for copyright violations if they found evidence of unauthorized copies of their works on a user's computer, or they could automatically remove those files.

This individualized, technically imposed price discrimination would also be well suited to turning fair use into "fared use,"[43] giving users the opportunity to pay more to enjoy the kinds of transformative reuses once given safe harbor by the law. Even the Congressional Budget Office has worried that "DRM would enable copyright owners to charge a price for their creative works that varied according to the particular use(s) made of them.

Literally, consumers would pay a price that depended on the amount of 'rights' that they were able to exercise over a copyrighted work in digital form."[44] What once was a protected right could become a further dimension of the commodification of culture: one price to watch, an additional price to edit.

Such a system could further regulate redistribution, not simply by prohibiting it technically, but by enlisting users as local distributors in the service of the content owner. As a representative of Intertrust, a commercial provider of DRM, described it: "You can do things like superdistribution, for example, where you can e-mail the song and say, 'If you get 10 of your best friends to buy it, I'll give you free tickets to the Britney Spears concert next month.' So you get on AOL and you e-mail the thing to 50 of your best friends and so on. And with Intertrust you can go down as many levels as you want, so they can e-mail it to 50 of their best friends, turning the consumer into a distributor of sorts. We think offers like that are going to be very compelling."[45] Here, a right of the owner (licensing distribution) is combined with techniques of price discrimination to become a means to convince users not just to buy but to sell.

Most troubling is that all of this could be automated. Your device could decide whether you are authorized to purchase or use a digital file in a certain way, without indicating it is doing so or revealing what criteria it is using. A downloaded film could be encrypted with a "smart contract" click-through agreement that authorizes the system to automatically see what other films the user has on his or her computer, or to examine the web browser cache to see what sites have recently been visited. The trusted software could report back to the content owner what files users have on their computers, how often they have accessed them, where they were purchased, and all in a context in which, as Mosco sees it, "the laws that protect against the misuse of such information are popguns against an elephant."[46]

Currently, both economic and technological conditions are more amenable to the practice of price discrimination than ever before. It is increasingly seen as an economically efficient and culturally legitimate way of doing business, at least in abstract terms, although consumers often have lingering hesitations about its fairness. The ability to effectively price discriminate is qualitatively expanded with computational technology. Massive data collection and new techniques of consumer profiling allow vendors to collect and store a great deal of information about consumers; e-commerce sites increasingly encourage consumers to volunteer personal information, as a means to develop an ongoing "service" relationship from a series of discrete transactions; online commerce can only be handled through credit cards or online payments, leaving further data trails connecting purchaser to purchase; cookies allow a simple way for sites to record and retain individual information by storing it on the user's computer.

In the past, individualized price discrimination has been frowned upon by consumers, though not consistently. In 1887, the Interstate Commerce Act ended the longstanding tradition of individual price discrimination for train tickets, and was widely praised by frustrated passengers, yet today we accept the same arrangements for air travel. While people may grumble about the perceived inequities of the airline pricing system, we have generally embraced it as "the way it is," and take pleasure in saving a few dollars when we're on the right side of its myriad distinctions. And there are real benefits to the arrangement. For example, "versioning" was the technique that most successfully allowed independent news outlets to stay online: read *Salon* online for free if you watch an ad a day, or pay for a subscription and get "premium" access; pay extra to get *Wired News* headlines on your Blackberry PDA or your cell phone.

But should culture work like airline tickets? Like air travel, the economics of cultural goods are particularly suited to price discrimination: Cultural goods have high and fixed initial costs but smaller marginal costs. Once you commit to producing this good, it is economically beneficial to secure as many customers as possible, at whatever price they're willing to pay. Both benefit from the "network effects" of having wider service to more customers. But unlike air travel, cultural goods have both a social and an economic significance; copyright law says as much. People as members of society need to have culture; information is both a resource for democracy and a commodity in the market. As C. Edwin Baker notes, price discrimination in information markets raises an issue of fairness. "When and why should some consumers have to pay more than others for the same good, thereby reducing or eliminating their potential 'consumer surplus,' in order to achieve distribution to others who willingly pay the marginal cost but would not pay the higher price necessary to cover infrastructure or first-copy costs?"[47]

In making communication policy we have struggled with the fairness of information pricing, setting rates on everything from mail delivery to telephony to musical adaptations, allowing some to pay less for the same service, but always in the name of pursuing some other equity: universal service, greater inclusion of rural communities, educational value, freedom of expression. In fact, copyright ensures the economic viability of cultural goods only because the framers of the Constitution believed doing so would support the social value of those goods. And copyright law imposes limits, precisely for those cases in which the cultural product's life as a commodity interferes with its life as a public resource: Exclusion through monopoly power and overpricing to stir demand are restrained by fair use and duration limits.

Price discrimination through DRM does not advance these equity concerns; it in fact undercuts them. Content owners can charge more for the same work to those who are able to pay, in greater need, or interested in making new uses of it. Of course, it is possible that the kinds of individualized price discrimination I have imagined here will prove too costly.[48] But when we evaluate the societal merits of DRM, we must look beyond its expense to consider also these secondary costs: the social costs of hierarchical pricing schemes, increasingly restricted use, the prosecution of circumvention cases, user frustration, and constrained innovation.

"Content Protection" and a Pay-per-Use Society

To the extent that current DRM-based restrictions have already taken political cover under the umbrella of copyright rhetoric, a move toward individualized price discrimination could also fall under its shelter. Encryption will continue to be protected under laws like the DMCA, regardless of what rules that encryption enforces. As we saw in the FCC's recasting of the broadcast flag issue, "copy protection" increasingly becomes "content protection," and the imperative that fueled the first lends its authority to the second. The rhetorical back-and-forth in Microsoft's description of their Windows Media DRM exemplifies this:

Windows Media digital rights management (DRM) is a flexible platform that makes it possible to protect and securely deliver a la carte and subscription content for playback on a computer, portable device, or network device. This benefits everyone who wants to create, deliver, or play digital media content by offering the content protection necessary to ensure that content owners make high-quality content available, and the portability to ensure that consumers can enjoy their content wherever they may be, on the device of their choice.

The rapid development of online distribution and consumption of digital media has received great notoriety. There are a variety of technical, legal, and business-related issues impacting this market.

The net result is that for a wide variety of digital audio and video content to be available, it has to be protected—but this protection needs to be as transparent as possible so it doesn't impact the consumer experience. Windows Media DRM is platform technology that makes it possible for:

- Content owners to protect their digital media content by packaging files with robust encryption algorithms
- Content owners and content service providers to experiment with new business models through the flexibility of the Windows Media DRM platform
- Consumers to find, acquire, and play content virtually anywhere[49]

The "notoriety" of online distribution and its "legal issues" are subtle reminders of the piracy argument regularly trumpeted by the content industries, even Valenti's specific claim that DRM offers "the content protection necessary to ensure that content owners make high-quality content available." Yet this rationale serves as the foundation for a DRM system that lets content owners "experiment with new business models," all of which is further framed in terms of best helping "consumers to find, acquire, and play content virtually anywhere." The term "content protection" does a lot of work here. First and foremost, it suggests an implicit understanding that what is being protected against is probably piracy, and in any case is certainly bad and worth preventing. But what content is actually being protected from by systems such as these is sometimes copyright infringement, sometimes arbitrage, sometimes consumers switching away from a particular service, sometimes fair use practices, and sometimes personal, noncommercial uses.

While it poses challenges for copyright in a new medium, DRM is also an intervention in a very old struggle: the relentless commodification of culture by its powerful commercial providers. Marketing strategies not only shape the production and distribution of culture in ways suited more to the corporations' economic self-interest than to democratic society; they also shape our experience of culture in similar ways. The manner in which cultural goods are served up as commodities choreographs how users are likely to engage with them, and how they envision their subject position vis-à-vis culture: as consumers who merely receive content, or as participants with a sense of their agency in the selection from and contribution to a store of cultural knowledge. Though, as Benkler notes, "information . . . is both the input and the output of its own production process,"[50] this can easily be forgotten, or obscured by the relentless rhetoric of consumer culture.

The concern, broadly, is that we are moving inexorably toward a "pay-per-use" society, in which every instance in which we interact with culture will be commodified. This concern has been voiced by a wide array of constituencies. House Representative Rick Boucher, one of the few outspoken critics of the DMCA within Congress, used the term to criticize the Library of Congress decision not to build a fair use exception into the DMCA:

"Given the importance of fair use to society as a whole, my hope is that Congress will re-calibrate the DMCA to balance more evenly the interests of copyright owners and information consumers. With today's failure of the Library of Congress to protect the public's fair use rights, Congress in its next session should act to prevent the creation of a 'pay per use' society, in which what is available today on the library shelf for free is available in the future only upon payment of a fee for each use."[51] Robin Gross, executive director of IP Justice, used similar language to critique statements coming from the United Nations' sponsored World Summit on the Information Society: "WSIS organizers held a summit under the auspices of the UN to endorse a particular agenda for the information society, but made little serious attempt to promote human rights or reduce poverty through information technologies, seeing them instead as a means to extract wealth from people and more control over the daily lives of individuals."[52]

Such worries typically hinge on whether cultural material will continue to be available in free venues, such as libraries, alongside their commercial counterparts. The public library has played a fundamental role in democratic thinking since its genesis, but the library system in the United States has enjoyed less and less ideological and real support in recent years. Mosco frets that this is part and parcel with the push toward the privatization and deregulation of communication and information systems, "part of a wider attack on the public information institutions in North America" that includes the erosion of public broadcasting, universal telephone service, even the postal service.[53] A parallel concern, represented by the arguments of Boyle, is that copyrighted materials currently in the public domain are being "enclosed" as private and controlled works, both through the regular extension of copyright terms and through the imposition of DRM onto otherwise publicly available cultural works.[54]

However, DRM substantially extends these concerns, raising the further issues of whether all culture will be commodified, and in what way. The kind of "individual coding" price discrimination made possible by DRM raises an initial set of worries: the possibility that different consumers will be charged different prices for different uses based on different criteria. But if a trusted computing environment were also linked into a system of digital online micropayment systems, as many have proposed, not only would uses be commodified in different ways, but the very experience of how viewers pay and use would change. Payment would infiltrate use rather than largely preceding it; the experience of culture could inexorably become one of insistent "impulse buying" where consumers decide in the moment whether to pony up for another listen to a hit song, or another viewing of the newest blockbuster film, or another glimpse of an important scientific report.

The move toward payment being weaved into the experience of culture rather than preceding it is not a conspiracy; it is also hard to condemn, because it makes a certain kind of sense. It is difficult to hold the culture industries responsible for what appears to be a move to ensure that customers are satisfied, that we pay for what we're supposed to, and that their legal rights remain protected. But again, what is overlooked here, and regularly ignored by commercial media producers, is that culture cannot be just another commodity, because our relationship to it must be more than that of a consumer. How we encounter cultural goods shapes how we think of culture itself. If cultural goods are insistently sold and delivered, mere trinkets meant only to be collected, viewed, and discarded, then viewers are encouraged to be consumers and nothing more. If cultural goods are seen as a churning storm of ideas that we engage, reject, change, and pass along, then viewers are encouraged to also be artists, educators, critics, activists. If cultural goods are widely and easily available to all, then viewers feel like part of a community—perhaps just an audience, at first, but potentially something greater. If viewers are atomized by the insistent marketing efforts of the culture industry, they experience culture as lone individuals disconnected from any larger community of taste or fandom or politics or interpretation.

Furthermore, when the symbols and meanings that surround us are of our own making, we have a kind of agency in the cultural democracy in which we participate; in a mass-mediated society, in which the raw materials for understanding ourselves and our place in the world are largely provided to us by a small set of dominant, interconnected, and commercial vendors of culture, we are forced to make these our own and negotiate with their meanings.[55] If this process of semiotic appropriation is further undercut by the commercial tactics of those vendors, we are left only to drown in a sea of meanings that are not our own. These arrangements are built into the technology of DRM, and by extension into the digital culture it regulates. As Jackson argues, "The ultimate outcome of technological control and other attempts to re-privatize copyright . . . is a dramatic reduction in the utility of communication networks like the Internet. This trend is transforming the Internet from a two-way medium of active cultural participation among citizens into a one-way medium for content distribution to passive consumers."[56]

Any law of commerce, copyright included, lays out a set of criteria according to which the transfer of goods may and may not occur; inside those terms, whatever they may be, capitalism assures that commerce will flourish. Vendors find the most viable way to profit while remaining on the right side of the legal lines. When the lines shift, commercial activity pours into the space that opens up. For this reason, the consideration of a law's consequences must go beyond whether the legal principle is just; it must reasonably anticipate the commercial arrangements that are likely to grow up around it. If the practices of commerce that develop in the shadow of a new copyright law run counter to the public mandate it was designed to serve, then that law is problematic, even if its abstract principles are not. This interconnection of legal rule and commercial practice must be part of the policy question, although all too often we focus our concern on the law in the abstract and assume that "markets will be markets."

We have seen just this kind of problem, again and again, in the history of copyright, and for some of these problems we have responded by changing the law. Under the broad protections of copyright, content owners might find it to their best financial or ideological advantage to price their content out of the reach of those who might use it critically, or to deny permission to use it altogether. This is not a failing of the law itself; it is an economic strategy that actually obeys the law, yet does not serve its ends. So we add a caveat that says that such economic tactics can be ignored under certain "fair" circumstances. We have similar exceptions in the doctrine of free speech. Although the First Amendment merely says "no law" shall infringe on a citizen's right to speak, we recognize that the business practices of distributors and broadcasters, of technology manufacturers, and even of audiences can also end up squelching speech in ways detrimental to the original purpose.[57] So we develop further rules, be they broadcast licensing or ownership limits, that make certain demands on broadcasters, whether they find those rules economically satisfying or not.

Business practices are forever outpacing the law's consideration of them, and it is time once again to ask whether this is the case with copyright. DRM is, primarily if not wholly, a way to regulate the sale of cultural expression, and it does so in ways that profoundly reshape what users can do with culture once they have it. Traditional rights such as those expressed in the fair use doctrine are constrained by this technoeconomic arrangement; if for no other reason, legislators should cast a skeptical eye toward these arrangements. But more important, we have an opportunity to examine not only what is lost, but also what could now be gained. The Internet and digital computing, though not a "revolution" as first imagined, do offer the possibility of powerful innovations for cultural expression—new tools for recombination and for collaboration, new opportunities for access to cultural works, new social and institutional arrangements for production and distribution. They seem to also make possible, even encourage, a new mindset for thinking about cultural participation, where people can be users as much as consumers.

Thus it is vital that when we apply the law of copyright—which at its core reifies the roles of producer and consumer, and only addresses users in its caveats and exceptions—to digital culture, we notice how the law tends to reimpose these roles onto digital cultural practice. Moreover, we must notice that DRM strategies, which are becoming the accepted method of enforcing digital copyright, further extend the dynamics of commodification into the practices of use, sharing, redistribution, commentary, and subsequent creative expression. Their imposition, especially under the protective rubric of copyright, undercuts the priorities that drove copyright law in the first place, and throws into question the Internet's capacity to help us innovate not only new tools and genres, but the very dynamics of communication on cultural, social, political, and structural levels.

A Question of How Becomes a Question of Why

DRM applications and devices, the material artifacts themselves, merely allow producers to circulate their work publicly, in a hidden form available only to those who have the key; it is the regime of alignment of which they are part that allows the attachment of rules to digital works, and the automatic regulation of use according to those rules. There is nothing inevitable about how such material affordances must be designed or used, and public debate could conceivably change how they should and will work. But with the legal and institutional arrangements developing around these technological innovations, we are witnessing a significant restructuring of the very dynamics of culture as it moves to a digital, networked environment. DRM technologies are not only a means of regulating users but also a means of reorganizing the market for culture. As regional coding and the claims of DRM providers indicate, this regime can extend its influence well beyond copyright to every facet of the production, distribution, and consumption of culture. Whatever room there might currently be to discuss the mechanics and purposes of DRM infrastructures is quickly disappearing.

The debate about DRM needs to be extended beyond the question of pop music and peer-to-peer; it applies to all forms of digital information. It needs to be extended beyond the question of copyright, because DRM is a mechanism that exists as much to regulate commerce as to limit infringement. It needs to be extended past questions of content, because DRM is increasingly encroaching on how technologies are designed and innovated, and by whom. And it must be extended beyond questions of law, because the regulation being pursued is as much technological, commercial, institutional, social, and ethical as it is legal.

The debate about DRM is, in the end, a debate about the shape of digital culture. Will digital culture be bound into a system of "public secrecy," where encryption technologies and the licenses they enforce close out users from the workings of their own technologies and position them as docile consumers of content in a pay-per-view society? Or will we embrace the "remix culture" flourishing not just since the emergence of the Web but ever since modernist collage, audio mix tapes, and hip-hop sampling became viable artistic ways to respond to, make sense of, and participate in an all-consuming popular culture? Will we continue to think about information in terms of who created it and what rights they have to regulate its movement through society, or in terms of who has access to it and how it becomes a means to cultural participation and further innovation of ideas?

In some ways, I take solace from the recent interest the public is showing in these questions—not only the broad, if sometimes selfish, embrace of peer-to-peer file-trading, but also the energy growing in the Free Culture movement[58] and around Creative Commons,[59] in the various communities of open source software design, in the musical genres of mashups and remixes, in the wide and thoughtful participation in Wikipedia and collaborative blogs.[60] These efforts are grassroots, and are often naïve about the power of structural alignments, institutional inertia, and legal authority. But the heterogeneous engineering involved in putting together a cohesive and comprehensive "regime of alignment" to govern the movement of culture requires not only technical mechanisms, legal boundaries, institutional alliances, and cultural norms—it also, at least in the last instance, requires public consent. And this is by no means easy to earn. Consent can never be taken by force, and all the legal and technical arrangements in the world will fail in the face of broad disregard.

In addition, the expansion of the DRM strategy and the aggressive legal stance taken by content owners are increasingly putting them in opposition not just to college hackers and fledgling peer-to-peer companies, but to commercial behemoths like Verizon, Apple, and Google. Whether, like Apple, they are seeking a "third way" between the extremes of the copyright wars, or, like Verizon, their business is the smooth delivery of information rather than its restriction—or, like Google, they aspire to both—these "new media" corporations increasingly have the economic motivation and the political heft to challenge the music and film industries when their preferred control strategies start to impinge on the movement of information more broadly. While the optimist in me hopes the grassroots cultural and technical creativity of users will in the aggregate open up new practices and shift the debate away from a locked-down vision of commercial culture, the realist in me fears the debate will be won by those who have access to the halls of power and money to burn. The music and film industries in the U.S. have had the upper hand in the copyright debate from the beginning, in large part because they get to present their characterization of the issue to Congress, to the courts, to the press. Their political and financial influence means that they more often get to set the terms, framing culture as a commodity that must be protected and chaperoned, and marginalizing the public resistance as simply the lure of free content, and a disregard for the law and for those it is designed to protect. But when the party on the other end of their lawsuit is Google,[61] that kind of economic and political power is no longer their exclusive weapon.

On the other hand, what we are consenting to or rejecting is itself drawn from a menu of alternatives already selected and shaped by interested parties, and there is no way to overestimate the power of what can be made to appear normal. DRM content protection has gained much more ground in the world of film than in music, primarily because the film industry waited until they could introduce a new format, the DVD, that was encrypted from day one. Recent attempts to add technical protection to CDs struck consumers who were used to unprotected music as an egregious restriction; similar technical protection on DVDs did not strike people used to VHS tapes as any problem at all. What we should or should not be able to do is in some ways framed by what we expect to be able to do, and these expectations are themselves being constructed in these debates. It may be easiest to institute DRM, and the regime of alignment it requires, when it is sold to the public not as a restrictive intervention for the public's own good, but in the more persuasive terms of technological progress and consumer satisfaction.

Notes

1 The Technological Fix

1. Alvin Weinberg, "Can Technology Replace Social Engineering?," in Albert Teich, ed., *Technology and the Future* (Boston: Bedford/St. Martin's, 2000), 32.

2. Carolyn Marvin, *When Old Technologies Were New: Thinking about Electric Communication in the Late Nineteenth Century* (New York: Oxford University Press, 1988), 235.

3. Rob Kling, "Hopes and Horrors: Technological Utopianism and Anti-Utopianism in Narratives of Computerization," in Rob Kling, ed., *Computerization and Controversy: Value Conflicts and Social Choices* (San Diego: Academic Press, 1996), 53.

4. See Susan Douglas, *Inventing American Broadcasting: 1899–1922* (Baltimore: Johns Hopkins University Press, 1987); Claude Fischer, *America Calling: a Social History of the Telephone to 1940* (Berkeley: University of California Press, 1992); Marvin, *When Old Technologies Were New*; Adrian Johns, *The Nature of the Book: Print and Knowledge in the Making* (Chicago: University of Chicago Press, 1988).

5. James Carey and John J. Quirk, "The Mythos of the Electronic Revolution," in James Carey, *Communication as Culture: Essays on Media and Society* (New York: Routledge, 1992), 114. Though their essay, written in 1970, discusses futurists like Marshall McLuhan and Alvin Toffler and their accelerated claims about cybernetics, the lesson also applies to the discussions surrounding the emergence of the Internet.

6. Paul Duguid, "Material Matters: The Past and Futurology of the Book," in Geoffrey Nunberg, ed., *The Future of the Book* (Berkeley: University of California Press, 1996), 65. To put this in a different light, these two principles are similar to Leo Marx's description of American attitudes toward technological progress: the "Enlightenment belief in progress," which supposed that new technology would draw us closer to the social values we aspire to, and the "technocratic concept of progress," which seemed less concerned with social values, believing instead that scientific and technological innovation is in and of itself a kind of progress. We might link Duguid's idea of liberation to the Enlightenment view, and supersession

to the technocratic view; however, Marx claims that these two views are contradictory, while Duguid sees them as coterminous, though paradoxical. I prefer Duguid's description, not because I think Marx is wrong, but because I see these views, if historically sequential in their genesis, as cohabitant in contemporary discourse on digital technology. Leo Marx, *The Machine in the Garden: Technology and the Pastoral Ideal in America* (New York: Oxford University Press, 1964).

7. This, of course, is not true: First, in the literal sense, in that radio did not kill the newspaper, nor will the Internet kill television. It is also not true in a metaphorical sense, in that the interrelation between new and old media is always much more complex. As Jay David Bolter and Richard Grusin argued, an emergent medium tends to "remediate" existing forms—simultaneously claiming to supercede the old in its ability to deliver unmediated experience, yet also drawing on and sustaining the aspirations and conventions of old media. Jay David Bolter and Richard Grusin, *Remediation: Understanding New Media* (Cambridge, MA: MIT Press, 1999). Existing technologies are already encrusted with a recognizable grammar for conveying meaning and asserting legitimacy; it is no surprise that as cultural traditions they provide "reservoirs of metaphors" for the new form to borrow from. Lev Manovich, "Cinema as a Cultural Interface" (1998), http://www.manovich.net/TEXT/cinema-cultural.html. And new media must distinguish themselves as superior without being incomprehensible to users familiar with older forms; to negotiate this balance, new media play off of the conventions of the old, resuscitating old forms even as they claim to extinguish them. An example of this is the metaphors that are typically built into the interfaces of computer software. For an example, see my discussion of Macromedia's Director and Dreamweaver and the implications of their interface metaphors for digital authorship. Tarleton Gillespie, "The Stories Digital Tools Tell," in John Caldwell and Anna Everett, eds., *New Media: Theses on Convergence, Media, and Digital Reproduction* (London: Routledge, 2003), 107–126.

8. Bolter and Grusin suggest that this mindset may be specific to the United States: "That digital media can reform and even save society reminds us of the promise that has been made for technologies throughout much of the twentieth century: It is a peculiarly, if not exclusively, American promise. American culture seems to believe in technology in a way that European culture, for example, does not . . . In America, however, collective (and perhaps even personal) salvation has been thought to come through technology rather than through political or even religious action." Bolter and Grusin, *Remediation*, 61.

9. Duguid, "Material Matters," 76.

10. Carey, *Communication as Culture*, 123.

11. Marvin notes that the technological experts were themselves driven by the same fantasies of social progress. "With the more general application of electricity throughout society, electricians believed, the world could change only to their advantage. For them, electricity was the transformative agent of social possibility.

Through their power over it, it would be a creator of social miracles." Marvin, *When Old Technologies Were New*, 63.

12. John Caldwell, "Introduction: Theorizing the Digital Landrush," in John Caldwell, ed., *Electronic Media and Technoculture* (New Brunswick, NJ: Rutgers University Press, 2000), 1–31; Eric Klinenberg and Claudio Benzecry, "Introduction: Cultural Production in a Digital Age," *The Annals of the American Academy of Political and Social Science* 597.1 (January 2005): 13–16.

13. Henry Jenkins and David Thorburn, "Introduction: The Digital Revolution, the Informed Citizen, and the Culture of Democracy," in Henry Jenkins and David Thorburn, eds., *Democracy and New Media* (Cambridge, MA: MIT Press, 2003): 10.

14. "The Wired Scared Shitlist," *Wired* 3.01 (January 1995): 110.

15. Simson Garfinkel, *Database Nation: The Death of Privacy in the 21st Century* (Sebastopol, CA: O'Reilly & Associates, 2001); Michael Froomkin, "The Death of Privacy?" *Stanford Law Review* 52 (2000): 1461–1543.

16. There is a complex array of questions being raised concerning digital copyright; I do not intend to touch on many of them directly. For a useful primer on the many concerns, I suggest National Research Council, *The Digital Dilemma: Intellectual Property in the Information Age* (Washington, DC: National Academy Press, 2000).

17. Lawrence Lessig, *Free Culture: How Big Media Uses Technology and the Law to Lock Down Culture and Control Creativity* (New York: Penguin Books, 2004); Siva Vaidhyanathan, *The Anarchist in the Library: How the Clash between Freedom and Control Is Hacking the Real World and Crashing the System* (New York: Basic Books, 2004). See also Siva Vaidhyanathan, "Afterword: Critical Information Studies: A Bibliographic Manifesto," *Cultural Studies* 20.2–3 (2006): 292–315.

18. *A&M Records, Inc., et al. v. Napster, Inc.*, 239 F.3d 1004 (9th Cir. 2001).

19. Julie Cohen, "Copyright and the Jurisprudence of Self-Help," *Berkeley Technology Law Journal* 13 (1998): 1089–1143.

20. Including Ann Bartow, "Electrifying Copyright Norms and Making Cyberspace More Like a Book," *Villanova Law Review* 48 (2003): 101–206; Stefan Bechtold, "From Copyright to Information Law—Implications of Digital Rights Management," in Tomas Sander, ed., *Security and Privacy in Digital Rights Management. Vol. 2320: Lecture Notes in Computer Science* (Berlin: Springer, 2002), 213–232; Stefan Bechtold, "The Present and Future of Digital Rights Management: Musings on Emerging Legal Problems," in Becker Eberhard, Willms Buhse, Dirk Günnewig, and Neils Rump, eds., *Digital Rights Management—Technological, Economic, Legal and Political Aspects* (Berlin: Springer, 2003), 597–654; Tom Bell, "Fair Use vs. Fared Use: The Impact of Automated Rights Management on Copyright's Fair Use Doctrine," *North Carolina Law Review* 76 (1998): 557–619; Stuart Biegel, *Beyond Our Control? Confronting the Limits of Our Legal System in the Age of Cyberspace* (Cambridge, MA: MIT Press, 2001);

Dan Burk, "Anti-Circumvention Misuse," *UCLA Law Review* 50 (2003): 1095–1140; Julie Cohen, "Some Reflections on Copyright Management Systems and Laws Designed to Protect Them," *Berkeley Technology Law Journal* 12 (1997): 161–190; Julie Cohen, "Lochner in Cyberspace: The New Economic Orthodoxy of 'Rights Management,'" *Michigan Law Review* 97.2 (1998): 462, 480–515; Julie Cohen, "Pervasively Distributed Copyright Enforcement," *Georgetown Law Journal* 95.1 (2006): 1–48; Niva Elkin-Koren, "It's All About Control: Rethinking Copyright in the New Information Landscape," in Niva Elkin-Koren and Neil Netanel, eds., *The Commodification of Information* (Hague: Kluwer Law International, 2002), 79–106; Edward Felten, "A Skeptical View of DRM and Fair Use," *Communications of the ACM* 46.4 (2003): 57–59; William Fisher, *Promises to Keep: Technology, Law, and the Future of Entertainment* (Stanford, CA: Stanford University Press, 2004); Tarleton Gillespie, "Copyright and Commerce: The DMCA, Trusted Systems, and the Stabilization of Distribution," *The Information Society* 24.4 (2004): 239–254; John Gilmore, "What's Wrong with Copy Protection" (February 16, 2001), http://www.toad.com/gnu/whatswrong.html; Jane Ginsburg, "Copyright and Control over New Technologies of Dissemination," *Columbia Law Review* 101 (2001): 1613–1647; Jane Ginsburg, "From Having Copies to Experiencing Works: The Development of an Access Right in U.S. Copyright Law," *Journal of the Copyright Society of the USA* 50 (2003): 113–132; Mike Godwin, "What Every Citizen Should Know about DRM, a.k.a. 'Digital Rights Management,'" Public Knowledge, Washington, DC (2004), http://www.public-knowledge.org/pdf/citizens_guide_to_drm.pdf; Matt Jackson, "Using Technology to Circumvent the Law: The DMCA's Push to Privatize Copyright," *Hastings Communications and Entertainment Law Journal* 23 (2001): 607–646; Matt Jackson, "From Private to Public: Reexamining the Technological Basis for Copyright," *Journal of Communication* 52.2 (2002): 416–433; Lawrence Lessig, *Code, and Other Laws of Cyberspace* (New York: Basic Books, 1999); Lawrence Lessig, *The Future of Ideas: The Fate of the Commons in a Connected World* (New York: Random House, 2001); Lawrence Lessig, *Free Culture: How Big Media Uses Technology and the Law to Lock Down Culture and Control Creativity* (New York: Penguin Books, 2004); Joel Reidenberg, "Lex Informatica: The Formulation of Information Policy Rules through Technology," *Texas Law Review* 76.3 (1998): 553–584; Pamela Samuelson, "DRM {and, or, vs.} the Law," *Communications of the ACM* 46.4 (2003): 41–45; Rajiv Shah and Jay Kesan, "Manipulating the Governance Characteristics of Code," *Info* 5.4 (2003); Siva Vaidhyanathan, *Copyrights and Copywrongs: The Rise of Intellectual Property and How It Threatens Creativity* (New York: New York University Press, 2001); Fred von Lohmann, "Fair Use and Digital Rights Management: Preliminary Thoughts on the (Irreconcilable?) Tension between Them," paper presented at Computers, Freedom, and Privacy (April 16, 2002), http://www.eff.org/IP/DRM/fair_use_and_drm.html.

21. The term "cultural policy" has been increasingly used as an explicitly analytical term in the study of media and culture to examine the array of formal, institutional, and tacit rules that shape the production of culture. Two texts offer a useful start:

Toby Miller and George Yudice, *Cultural Policy* (London: Sage Publications, 2002); Justin Lewis and Toby Miller, eds. *Critical Cultural Policy Studies: A Reader* (Oxford: Blackwell, 2003). This is a promising line of inquiry, combining insights into the political economy of media and information with an attention to the dynamics of culture derived from the best of cultural studies. Surprisingly, the issue of copyright is often absent from this literature, despite being one of the central rules that organize cultural production and distribution, overseeing the transformation of culture into a commodity—something this literature is otherwise deeply concerned about. Three exceptions are Siva Vaidhyanathan, "Remote Control: The Rise of Electronic Cultural Policy," *The Annals of the American Academy of Political and Social Science* 597.1 (January 2005): 122–133; Shalini Venturelli, "From the Information Economy to the Creative Economy: Moving Culture to the Center of International Public Policy," discussion paper, Cultural Comment, Center for Arts and Culture, Washington, DC, 2001; Ren Bucholz, "File Sharing, Information Policy, and Democratic Public Spheres," discussion paper, Necessary Knowledge for a Democratic Public Sphere, Social Science Research Council, 2005.

22. Marvin, *When Old Technologies Were New*, 233.

23. Thomas Streeter, *Selling the Air: A Critique of the Policy of Commercial Broadcasting in the United States* (Chicago: University of Chicago Press, 1996), 326.

24. Scholars of the Internet are only now getting over the "dazzling light" of the new medium and asking these kinds of questions. A useful example is the February 2004 special issue of the journal *New Media & Society*. See Stephen Graham, "Beyond the 'Dazzling Light': From Dreams of Transcendence to the 'Remediation' of Urban Life—A Research Manifesto," *New Media & Society* 6.1 (February 2004): 16–25; Leah Lievrouw, "What's Changed about New Media? Introduction to the Fifth Anniversary of *New Media & Society*," *New Media & Society* 6.1 (February 2004): 9–15.

25. These fields, though they have long shared an interest in many of the same phenomena, have until recently had very little dialogue between them. In part because of the deliberate efforts by a community of young scholars to bridge these fields, and in part because computing and the Internet have provided such a compelling (and fundable) object of study for all three fields, they have begun to intersect and share their insights. I hope this book will be one of the bricks in this bridge; for a very useful consideration of the fields and their potential overlaps, see Pablo Boczkowski and Leah Lievrouw, "Bridging STS and Communication Studies: Scholarship on Media and Information Technologies," in Edward Hackett et al., eds., *New Handbook of Science and Technology Studies* (Cambridge, MA: MIT Press, forthcoming). For a different literature review that focuses on building on the kind of analysis being tackled by copyright scholars and extending it to the critical study of information in its sociopolitical context, see Siva Vaidhyanathan, "Afterword: Critical Information Studies: A Bibliographic Manifesto," *Cultural Studies* 20.2–3 (2006): 292–315.

2   The Copyright Balance and the Weight of DRM

1. Jessica Litman, *Digital Copyright: Protecting Intellectual Property on the Internet* (Amherst, NY: Prometheus Books, 2001), 19.

2. Peter Jaszi, "Toward a Theory of Copyright: The Metamorphoses of 'Authorship,'" *Duke Law Journal* 2 (1991): 464.

3. U.S. Constitution, art. I, § 8, cl. 8. I will describe some of the fundamental elements of this law in a moment, but it is important to note that current copyright law is a deeply complicated affair whose myriad details cannot be explained here because of space constraints. For those who want a primer on copyright law as it stands, consult the U.S. Copyright Office's "Copyright Basics" (http://www.copyright.gov/circs/circ1.html). The current statutes are available at the "Legal Information Institute" of Cornell University's Law School (http://www.law.cornell.edu/topics/copyright.html). I will also not be dealing with copyright law outside the United States; though much of U.S. doctrine was built on the model of European laws, and many of the mechanisms are similar, especially after recent global treaties, the historical tradition and legal particulars of copyright elsewhere is significantly different than the U.S. model.

4. William Fisher, "Theories of Intellectual Property," in Stephen Munzer, ed., *New Essays in the Legal and Political Theory of Property* (Cambridge: Cambridge University Press, 2001), 168–200.

5. Ginsburg notes that there is some confusion as to whether the author's rights were considered by the framers of the Constitution to be subservient to the public benefit copyright was designed to offer, or of equal weight, or simply congruent in a way in which distinction between the two was simply unnecessary. Jane Ginsburg, "A Tale of Two Copyrights: Literary Property in Revolutionary France and America," *Tulane Law Review* 64 (1990): 991–1031.

6. Matt Jackson, "Using Technology to Circumvent the Law: The DMCA's Push to Privatize Copyright," *Hastings Communications and Entertainment Law Journal* 23 (2001): 613.

7. Ronald Bettig, "Critical Perspectives on the History and Philosophy of Copyright," *Critical Studies in Mass Communication* 9.2 (1992): 146.

8. Yochai Benkler, "Freedom in the Commons: Towards a Political Economy of Information," *Duke Law Journal* 52 (2003): 1245–1276.

9. William Fisher, "The Growth of Intellectual Property: A History of the Ownership of Ideas in the United States," in *Eigentum im Internationalen Vergleich* (Göttingen: Vandenhoeck & Ruprecht, 1999): 265–291, http://cyber.law.harvard.edu/people/tfisher/iphistory.pdf.

10. Although Melville Nimmer, whose multivolume text is treated by scholars and jurists as the key reference for copyright law, does a phrase-by-phrase reading of the constitutional language, he does not speculate as to what the word "progress" means in this context. In discussing how "to promote the progress of science and useful arts," he suggests that the courts have chosen to accept this *term* in the most vague terms—encouraging all creativity, with the least governmental intervention regarding what kind of creativity, is in the best public interest. Melville Nimmer, *Nimmer on Copyright: A Treatise on the Law of Literary, Musical, and Artistic Property, and the Protection of Ideas* (1963; reprint, New York: M. Bender, 1983). For a consideration of what "progress" has meant in Western culture, see Robert Nisbet, *History of the Idea of Progress* (New Brunswick, NJ: Transaction Publishers, 1994).

11. This logic is almost the opposite of the "sweat of the brow" interpretation: Precisely because someone put effort into producing creative work, it should be made more available so that others do not waste their time duplicating that effort.

12. John Stuart Mill, "On the Liberty of Thought and Discussion," in John Stuart Mill, *On Liberty* (London: Longman, Roberts & Green, 1869).

13. Karl Popper, *Conjectures and Refutations: The Growth of Scientific Knowledge* (London: Routledge, 1963).

14. I do not intend to cite these as self-evident truths; they are homilies more than established facts. Critics in the sociology of science and technology have challenged the premise of the scientific principle, and asked whether scientists ever really follow its dictates; see Michael Mulkay and Nigel Gilbert, "Replication and Mere Replication," *Philosophy of the Social Sciences* 16.1 (1986): 21–37; and more generally, Harry Collins and Trevor Pinch, *The Golem: What You Should Know about Science*, 2nd ed. (Cambridge: Cambridge University Press, 1998). Economic theorists since Smith have questioned whether "perfect information" is possible, and whether it would coax the market to some fair balance even if it existed. My point is that these platitudes are widely held to be true in principle, and each calls for the circulation of information and culture to be more open rather than less.

15. See Yochai Benkler, "Intellectual Property and the Organization of Information Production," *International Review of Law and Economics* 22 (2002): 81–107; Yochai Benkler, *The Wealth of Networks: How Social Production Transforms Markets and Freedom* (New Haven: Yale University Press, 2006); William Landes and Richard Posner, "An Economic Analysis of Copyright Law," *Journal of Legal Studies* 18.2 (1995): 325–363; Hal Varian, Joseph Farrell, and Carl Shapiro, *The Economics of Information Technology: An Introduction* (Cambridge: Cambridge University Press, 2004).

16. In fact, as Adrian Johns notes, the line between legitimate publisher and pirate is not a clean, obvious, or universal one; in the history of printing, publishers quite often moved between the two categories, gaining legitimacy after building a business on pirated works, or being challenged as pirates not for violations of

unauthorized printing but for breaching the rules of propriety that governed publishers and stationers, or as a challenge to claims made within the work in question. Adrian Johns, *The Nature of the Book: Print and Knowledge in the Making* (Chicago: University of Chicago Press, 1998), 167. To this day, these categories are more intertwined than they seem, and much of the work of debating an issue like copyright is articulating where the line between them should be drawn and why.

17. There are, of course, black market sneakers as well as other material goods whose manufacture may resemble piracy. But this has more to do with (1) using cheaper materials to recreate the appearance of the sturdier good, and (2) using the trademark of a respected good so as to lure customers to the knock-off—which is not piracy of the sneaker, but unauthorized use of the trademarked brand, and thus the piracy of intellectual property.

18. Julie Cohen, "Lochner in Cyberspace: The New Economic Orthodoxy of 'Rights Management,'" *Michigan Law Review* 97.2 (1998): 560.

19. The Copyright Act of 1790 set the copyright term at fourteen years, with a renewal period of fourteen years. In 1831, the term grew to twenty-eight and fourteen; with the Copyright Act of 1909, it grew again to twenty-eight and twenty-eight. The Copyright Act of 1976, arguing that the duration of copyright needed to match increasing lifespans, lengthier market potential of new technologies, and increasing copyright terms in other nations, changed the term to the life of the author plus fifty years. The Sonny Bono Copyright Term Extension Act brought it to its current length, life of the author plus seventy years. See Edward Walterscheid, "Defining the Patent and Copyright Term: Term Limits and the Intellectual Property Clause," *Journal of Intellectual Property Law* 7 (2000): 315–394; Ruth Okedji, "Givers, Takers, and Other Kinds of Users: A Fair Use Doctrine for Cyberspace," *Florida Law Review* 53 (2001): 107–182.

20. See Jessica Litman, "The Public Domain," *Emory Law Journal* 39 (1990): 965–1023.

21. This concern developed specifically around the press, which enjoys its own special kind of legal protection; imagine if a corporation were to write a puff piece about a controversial new product, and then could shut down criticism by bringing an infringement suit against anyone who wrote an article about that same subject.

22. See Nimmer, *Nimmer on Copyright*, 1.10[B].

23. James Boyle, *Shamans, Software, and Spleens: Law and the Construction of the Information Society* (Cambridge, MA.: Harvard University Press, 1996), 57–58.

24. These four factors were drawn primarily from Justice Story's decision in the *Folsom v. Marsh* case, where he established three of the four (he did not address the "nature of the copyrighted work"). *Folsom v. Marsh*, 9 9F Cas. 342 (C.C.D. Mass.

1841). The language changed slightly from Story's rendering to the suggested legislation to the statute; Patry makes a useful comparison between the different versions in an attempt to show subtle changes in priority and the semantic compromises made to assuage different interests. See William Patry, *The Fair Use Privilege in Copyright Law*, 2nd ed. (Washington, DC: Bureau of National Affairs, 1995).

25. Patry, *The Fair Use Privilege in Copyright Law*, 364; see also Nimmer, *Nimmer on Copyright*, 13.05[A].

26. Patry, *The Fair Use Privilege in Copyright Law*, 413.

27. 17 U.S.C. §§ 108.

28. Dan Burk and Julie Cohen, "Fair Use Infrastructure for Rights Management Systems," *Harvard Journal of Law and Technology* 15.1 (2001): 43, http://jolt.law. harvard.edu/articles/pdf/15HarvJLTech041.pdf.

29. Burk and Cohen, "Fair Use Infrastructure for Rights Management Systems," 44.

30. Fred von Lohmann, "Fair Use and Digital Rights Management: Preliminary Thoughts on the (Irreconcilable?) Tension between Them," paper presented at Computers, Freedom, and Privacy (April 16, 2002): 3, http://www.eff.org/IP/DRM/fair_use_and_drm.html.

31. Jessica Litman, "War Stories," *Cardozo Arts & Entertainment Law Journal* 20 (2002): 337–365. For the curiously parallel battles over printed sheet music at the turn of the twentieth century, see Adrian Johns, "Pop Music Pirate Hunters," *Daedalus* 131 (2002): 67–77; Lisa Gitelman, "Media, Materiality, and the Measure of the Digital, or, the Case of Sheet Music and the Problem of Piano Rolls," in Lauren Rabinovitz and Abraham Geil, eds., *Memory Bytes: History, Technology, and Digital Culture* (Durham, NC: Duke University Press, 2004), 237–262.

32. Thomas Streeter, *Selling the Air: A Critique of the Policy of Commercial Broadcasting in the United States* (Chicago: University of Chicago Press, 1996).

33. David Harvey, *The Condition of Postmodernity: An Enquiry into the Origins of Cultural Change* (Oxford: Blackwell, 1989).

34. Esther Dyson, "Intellectual Property in the Net," Electronic Frontier Foundation (1995), http://www.eff.org/Misc/Publications/Esther_Dyson/ip_on_the_net.article; Esther Dyson, "Intellectual Value," *Wired* 3.07 (July 1995): 136–141, 182–184.

35. See, for example, John Perry Barlow, "Selling Wine without Bottles: The Economy of Mind on the Global Net," in Peter Ludlow, ed., *High Noon on the Electronic Frontier: Conceptual Issues in Cyberspace* (Cambridge, MA: MIT Press, 1996): 9–35.

36. Janet Abbate, *Inventing the Internet* (Cambridge, MA: MIT Press, 1999), 36.

37. See Paul Edwards, *The Closed World: Computers and the Politics of Discourse in Cold War America* (Cambridge, MA: MIT Press, 1996), 115–125.

38. Again, to relate the history of the Internet is beyond the scope of my work; I will only be pointing at a few developments that are implicated in the more theoretical issues I am discussing. For a history of the Internet, see Abbate, *Inventing the Internet*; Edwards, *The Closed World*; Katie Hafner and Matthew Lyon; *Where Wizards Stay Up Late: The Origins of the Internet* (New York: Simon & Schuster, 1996); Howard Rheingold, *The Virtual Community: Homesteading on the Electronic Frontier* (Reading, MA: Addison-Wesley, 1993).

39. Abbate, *Inventing the Internet*, 85.

40. Hafner and Lyon, *Where Wizards Stay Up Late*, 189.

41. Abbate, *Inventing the Internet*, 96–111.

42. See Fred Turner, *From Counterculture to Cyberculture: Stewart Brand, the Whole Earth Network, and the Rise of Digital Utopianism* (Chicago: University of Chicago Press, 2006).

43. John Gilmore, qtd. in Rheingold, *The Virtual Community*, 7.

44. Stewart Brand, *The Media Lab: Inventing the Future at MIT* (New York: Viking, 1987), 202. Pinning down the first appearance of this aphorism has apparently been quite difficult; Clarke tracked it to Brand's presentation at the first Hackers Conference in 1984; see Roger Clarke, "'Information Wants to Be Free...'" (2000), http://www.anu.edu.au/people/Roger.Clarke/II/IWtbF.html.

45. Paul Duguid, "Material Matters: The Past and Futurology of the Book," in Geoffrey Nunberg, ed., *The Future of the Book* (Berkeley: University of California Press, 1996), 74.

46. Rheingold, *The Virtual Community*, 276.

47. Rheingold, *The Virtual Community*, 57–59.

48. Barlow, "Selling Wine without Bottles," 10.

49. Dyson, "Intellectual Value."

50. See Kevin Kelly, *Out of Control: The Rise of Neo-Biological Civilization* (Reading, MA: Addison-Wesley, 1994), 4–28.

51. Barlow, "Selling Wine without Bottles," 17–18.

52. For a powerful argument regarding the international aspirations of Clinton's policies, see Herbert Schiller, "The Global Information Highway: Project for an Ungovernable World," in Iain A. Boal and James Brook, eds., *Resisting the Virtual Life: The Culture and Politics of Information* (San Francisco: City Lights, 1995), 17–34.

Schiller argues that the NII and the accompanying "Global Information Infrastructure" (GII) proposed to the world were clearly about extending American global power through control of information. But he also notes that this plan was nearsighted; the policies being proposed hoped to extend the strength of American private interests, but it was precisely private interests that, in the information economy, were overshadowing the power of nations altogether.

53. National Information Infrastructure, "Agenda for Action: Executive Summary" (1993).

54. Pamela Samuelson, "The Copyright Grab" *Wired* 4.01 (January 1996), http://www.wired.com/wired/archive/4.01/white.paper_pr.html.

55. U.S. Department of Commerce, Information Infrastructure Task Force, "Intellectual Property and the National Information Infrastructure: The Report of the Working Group on Intellectual Property Rights," Washington, DC, 1995, 11 [hereafter referred to as NII White Paper].

56. NII White Paper, 12.

57. See also Jane Ginsburg, "Copyright and Control over New Technologies of Dissemination," *Columbia Law Review* 101 (2001): 1613–1647; Jane Ginsburg, "From Having Copies to Experiencing Works: The Development of an Access Right in U.S. Copyright Law," *Journal of the Copyright Society of the USA* 50 (2003): 113–132. For an argument that anticipates this concern well before the rise of the web, see Ann Branscomb, "Law and Culture in the Information Society," *The Information Society* 4.4 (1986): 279–311.

58. Samuelson, "The Copyright Grab."

59. Gandy, Oscar. "The Real Digital Divide: Citizens versus Consumers," in Leah Lievrouw and Sonia Livingstone, eds., *The Handbook of New Media* (London: Sage, 2002), 448–460.

60. NII White Paper, 16.

61. Four public hearings were held by the Information Infrastructure Task Force (IITF) Working Group on Intellectual Property Rights: September 14, 1994, in Chicago, September 16, 1996, in Los Angeles, and September 22 and 23, 1994, in Washington, DC. The EFF has posted copies of the transcripts online at http://www.eff.org/Infrastructure/Govt_docs/ipwg091494_hearing.transcript, http://www.eff.org/Infrastructure/Govt_docs/ipwg091694_hearing.transcript, http://www.eff.org/Infrastructure/Govt_docs/ipwg092294_hearing.transcript, and http://www.eff.org/Infrastructure/Govt_docs/ipwg092394_hearing.transcript.

62. National Research Council: Committee on Intellectual Property Rights in the Emerging Information Infrastructure, *The Digital Dilemma: Intellectual Property in the Information Age* (Washington, DC: National Academy Press, 2000), 76–95.

63. For a more journalistic account of the trajectory of online music (i.e., less scholarly but more entertaining), see John Alderman, *Sonic Boom: Napster, MP3, and the New Pioneers of Music* (Cambridge, MA: Perseus, 2001); Bruce Haring, *Beyond the Charts: MP3 and the Digital Music Revolution* (Los Angeles: JM Northern Media LLC, 2000).

64. "Codec," short for "compression-decompression," is an algorithm for reducing the amount of data required to transmit a body of data. Data can be digitized in an uncompressed form; in text, each character receives an 8-bit binary code, in images, each pixel is given a hexadecimal color value that is then encoded in binary. For text, this poses no problem in terms of transmission, because text files are not of an unwieldy size. But the encoding of other forms of media, whether images, music, or video, can quickly add up to massive file sizes, which then become arduous to transmit over low-bandwidth Internet connections. A codec will mathematically alter the digital code such that it takes less storage space to encode the same information—or its close approximation. Some codecs are "lossless," meaning the algorithm does not lose any information in the process of compression (for example, "gif" files are compressed by noticing sequences of pixels of the same color; rather than recording them as "blue blue blue blue" they are encoded as "4 blue," which requires less code). But most are "lossy," meaning that some information is discarded in the process. The goal then is to discard enough information to shrink the file without discarding so much that the quality of the file is unduly compromised. The "jpg" image format does this by finding similarities in the image and choosing a single color to encode very similar areas. For music files, it depends on removing sounds that the human ear does not register. Some music formats, like Real Audio, compromise the quality of the sound significantly in order to make very small files; the mp3 format is popular in part because the compression incurs relatively little loss quality; though some audiophiles disagree, mp3 is regularly touted as "near-CD quality."

65. Levels 1 and 2 were related compression standards exclusive to high-end devices.

66. Charles Mann, "The Heavenly Jukebox," *Atlantic Monthly* (September 2000): 39–59.

67. Mann, "The Heavenly Jukebox."

68. Jonathan Sterne, "The MP3 as Cultural Artifact," *New Media & Society* 8.5 (2006): 825–842).

69. Mike Tanner, "MP3 Music Pirates Avoid Legal Action," *Wired News* (May 23, 1997).

70. Steven Brull, "Net Nightmare for the Music Biz," *Business Week* (March 2, 1998): 89–90.

71. Richard Barbrook, "The High-Tech Gift Economy," in Josephine Bosma, ed., *Readme! Filtered by Nettime: ASCII Culture and the Revenge of Knowledge* (Brooklyn: Autonomedia, 1999), 133–139.

72. Steve Jones, "Music That Moves: Popular Music, Distribution and Network Technologies," *Cultural Studies* 16.2 (2002): 219–224; Siva Vaidhyanathan, *The Anarchist in the Library: How the Clash between Freedom and Control Is Hacking the Real World and Crashing the System* (New York: Basic Books, 2004), 15–24, 41–64.

73. "Warez" is a term for illegal copies of soft*ware*; the "z" was a common designator of hacker activity.

74. The No Electronic Theft Act, or NET Act, was passed in 1997 in an attempt to counter the increasing circulation of unauthorized copies of software circulating online. It closed the loophole in existing copyright law where infringement in which there was no commercial gain could not be prosecuted as a criminal offense, only for civil damages. The Act made it possible for noncommercial infringement to be considered a criminal violation by redefining "commercial advantage or private financial gain" to include the exchange of copies without money changing hands. It depends on, and I would argue has helped to legitimize, the argument that a traded copy is a lost sale, an argument that gained a lot of ground during the lawsuits against Napster and other peer-to-peer networks. See Stuart Biegel, *Beyond Our Control?: Confronting the Limits of Our Legal System in the Age of Cyberspace* (Cambridge, MA: MIT Press, 2001), 141–148.

75. Amy Harmon, "Potent Software Escalates Music Industry's Jitters," *New York Times* (March 7, 2000): A1, C6; Spencer Ante, "Shawn Fanning's Struggle," *Business Week* (May 1, 2000): 197; Steven Levy, "The Noisy War over Napster," *Newsweek* (June 5, 2000): 46–53; Amy Kover, "Who's Afraid of This Kid?" *Fortune* (June 26, 2000): 129; Karl Greenfeld, "Meet the Napster," *Time* (October 2, 2000): 59–68.

76. Nelson Minar and Marc Hedlund, "A Network of Peers: Peer-to-Peer Models through the History of the Internet," in Andy Oram, ed., *Peer-to-Peer: Harnessing the Power of Disruptive Technologies* (Sebastopol, CA: O'Reilly & Associates, 2001): 3–20.

77. *A&M v. Napster*, "Expert Report of Professor Lawrence Lessig to Federal Rule of Civil Procedure 26(a)(2)(B)" (June 2000): 17.

78. This should not come as a surprise, considering the military/academic origins of the network. While the U.S. military had reasons to want their information and personnel to be distributed, instantly available, and geographically scattered, they certainly did not want just any individual to become an information provider on this network. They needed to retain some sense of authority about who speaks, what they say, and how we know to listen. The global aspirations of the American military make it that much more crucial that information be certified and reliable. In the academic community, a need for reliable information in research and the special importance of reputation similarly demanded that information be provided only by certain sources under certain conditions. So, while this distributed network does flatten that system of authority, it does not remove it.

79. As I suggested, it is important to remember that although peer-to-peer applications renovated the architecture of the Internet, their contribution is not "new" in

any dramatic way. One of the first protocols designed for the Internet was FTP, or "file transfer protocol"; it allowed files to be requested and delivered before the emergence of a web interface. This in itself worked within the client-server system of the web; but others took advantage of it, creating programs like IRC (Internet Relay Channel) and Hotline that allowed individuals to serve files themselves. Before the Internet, many models of distributed communication proliferated under the radar of more mainstream systems: the bootleg trading of concert recordings or amateur pornography, for instance; the publication and distribution of 'zines; and chain letters and Ponzi schemes that took advantage of the "distributed" nature of the postal service to communicate without a central point of distribution. The Gingrich Republicans became famous for using a network of fax machines to get their daily talking points out to their constituents; they were not the first to use the telephone system and its related technologies for organized publication within or by a community. Describing what he called the "Victorian Internet," Standage describes a system of pneumatic tubes set up between telegraph offices to ease the bottleneck in busy cities. Tom Standage, *The Victorian Internet: The Remarkable Story of the Telegraph and the Nineteenth Century's On-Line Pioneers* (New York: Walker and Company, 1998). To extend the history further, we might argue that all communication followed this model in the days before print and broadcast technologies arrived. News, stories, and songs traveled where bards did, possibly multiplying at the moment of performance or retelling when another chose to take them up and share them again. In fact, the ascension of centralized, authorized, mass-distributed cultural expression is, in relative terms, a very recent phenomenon.

80. Interestingly, peer-to-peer technologies must, in the process, make further demands on the user's privacy. The first concern, of course, is that a clever hacker could see and even download everything on your computer, not only your music. This has not proven to be a major problem so far. But participation on a peer-to-peer network requires logging in and urges that you make your designated files as available as others do—your MP3 collection is public, meaning your preferences are visible. Of course some have noted that, even as Napster was being heralded as an emblem of sharing, not everyone was that generous; the Napster application allowed users to prevent people from downloading their files while still being able to download themselves, which some users called "leeching." But, at least in principle, though many did not use Napster to serve files, it was designed to do so. This concern for the privacy of the users reveals more, in the end, about those concerned than about the application. We generally worry about consumers losing their privacy because consumers do not expect to provide anything. When we remember that peer-to-peer, at least in principle, allows anyone to be a provider of information, this "invasion" of privacy is no more substantial than that of any author or distributor—publishers do not have the same privacy concerns, because making themselves publicly available is, by definition, the accepted price of participation in a public system of cultural distribution, which is their goal.

81. *A&M v. Napster*, "Complaint for Contributory and Vicarious Copyright Infringement, Violations of California Civil Code Section 980(a)(2), and Unfair Competition" (December 7, 1999): 1.

82. They would later extend this argument by claiming a "space-shifting" practice analogous to Sony's time-shifting—that users who owned music would download it at another location, say at the office, to avoid carting CDs back and forth.

83. Benkler does an excellent job of pointing out precedents for when the law does embrace the "sharing" of goods rather than their sale, and how this might apply to the distribution of information. Yochai Benkler, "Sharing Nicely; On Shareable Goods and the Emergence of Sharing as a Modality of Economic Production," *Yale Law Journal* 114.22004): 273–358.

84. *Metro-Goldwyn Mayer Studios, Inc. v. Grokster, Ltd.*, 123 2764 (S. Ct. 2005).

85. Sudip Bhattacharjee, Ram Gopal, Kaveepan Lertwachara, James Mardsen, and Rahul Telang, "The Effect of P2P File Sharing on Music Markets: A Survival Analysis of Albums on Ranking Charts," working paper #05-26, Networks, Electronic Commerce, and Telecommunications Institute, October 2005; Robert Danay, "Copyright vs. Free Expression: The Case of Peer-to-Peer File-Sharing of Music in the United Kingdom," *International Journal of Communications Law & Policy* 10 (2005); Seung-Hyun Hong, "The Effect of Napster on Recorded Music Sales: Evidence from the Consumer Expenditure Survey," discussion paper #03-18, Stanford Institute for Economic Policy Research, Stanford, CA, January 30, 2004; Stan Liebowitz, "Policing Pirates in the Networked Age," Policy Analysis, #438. Cato Institute (May 15, 2002); Norbert Michel, "Internet File Sharing: The Evidence So Far and What It Means for the Future," #1790, Policy Research & Analysis, The Heritage Foundation (August 23, 2004); Felix Oberholzer-Gee and Koleman Strumpf, "The Effect of File Sharing on Record Sales: An Empirical Analysis" (March 2004), available at http://www.unc.edu/~cigar/papers/FileSharing_March2004.pdf; Martin Peitz and Patrick Waelbroeck, "The Effect of Internet Piracy on CD Sales: Cross-Section Evidence," #1122, CESifo Working Paper Series (January 2004); Tatsuo Tanaka, "Does File Sharing Reduce Music CD Sales? A Case of Japan," Working Paper #05-08, Institute of Innovation Research, Hitotsubashi University (December 13, 2004).

86. Chuck Philips, "Time Warner Tunes in New Delivery Channel (Interview with Richard Parsons)," *Los Angeles Times* (July 25, 2000): C1+.

87. I will discuss the workings of DRM only in broad strokes, and then focus on a few specific examples. For a useful primer on the workings of DRM, see John Erickson, "Fair Use, DRM, and Trusted Computing," *Communications of the ACM* 46.4 (2003): 34–39; Mike Godwin, "What Every Citizen Should Know about DRM, a.k.a. 'Digital Rights Management,'" Public Knowledge, Washington, DC (2004), http://www.public.knowledge.org/pdf/citizens_guide_to_drm.pdf; Jeff Howe, "The Shadow Internet," *Wired* 13.01 (January 2005); National Research Council:

Committee on Intellectual Property Rights in the Emerging Information Infrastructure, *The Digital Dilemma: Intellectual Property in the Information Age* (Washington, DC: National Academy Press, 2000), 152–198.

88. Erickson, "Fair Use, DRM, and Trusted Computing," 35–36.

89. Godwin, "What Every Citizen Should Know about DRM, a.k.a. 'Digital Rights Management.'"

90. An article from the National Cable & Telecommunications Association (NCTA), reprinted in Cable Labs' newsletter, suggests that this term was first coined by the Copy Protection Technical Working Group (CPTWG), a coalition of content and technology corporations brought together to discuss the technical possibilities of copy protection. This is surprising, since the work of this group on DVD protection and, more recently, for digital television, aspires to much more protection than this term suggests. See "The Copy Protection Issue and its Impact on Cable," *SPECS Technology* (June 1998), http://www.cablelabs.com/news/newsletter/SPECS/spectechjune/. See also National Research Council: Committee on Intellectual Property Rights in the Emerging Information Infrastructure, *The Digital Dilemma: Intellectual Property in the Information Age* (Washington, DC: National Academy Press, 2000), 218.

91. The description of such "trusted systems" is drawn primarily from Mark Stefik, who has described them in the context of legal debates and inside the world of digital publishing. But similar plans crop up in press and industry reports, and some elements are beginning to appear in announcements about the two digital music subscription services, Pressplay and MusicNet, since established by the major record companies, and the more recent and somewhat less restrictive system established by Apple. Mark Stefik, "Letting Loose the Light: Igniting Commerce in Electronic Publication," in Mark Stefik, ed., *Internet Dreams: Archetypes, Myths, and Metaphors* (Cambridge, MA: MIT Press, 1996): 219–254; Mark Stefik, "Shifting the Possible: How Trusted Systems and Digital Property Rights Challenge Us to Rethink Digital Publishing," *Berkeley Technology Law Journal* 12.1 (1997): 137–159.

92. Erickson, "Fair Use, DRM, and Trusted Computing," 35.

93. Stefik, "Shifting the Possible," 140.

94. Roger Parloff, "Copy This! Can 'Military' Technology Beat Digital Piracy?" *Inside.com* (March 12, 2001).

95. Bruno Latour, *Science in Action: How to Follow Scientists and Engineers through Society* (Cambridge, MA: Harvard University Press, 1987), 130–131.

96. Lawrence Lessig, *Code, and Other Laws of Cyberspace* (New York: Basic Books, 1999), 130.

97. Erickson, "Fair Use, DRM, and Trusted Computing," 37.

98. Stefik, "Shifting the Possible."

99. Deirdre Mulligan, John Han, and Aaron Bernstein, "How DRM-Based Content Delivery Systems Disrupt Expectations of 'Personal Use,'" *3rd ACM Workshop on Digital Rights Management* (Washington DC: ACM Press, 2003), 77–89.

100. Stefik, "Letting Loose the Light," 241.

101. Stefik, "Letting Loose the Light," 241.

102. Stefik, "Letting Loose the Light," 235.

103. Stefik, "Letting Loose the Light," 120–123.

104. Vincent Mosco, "Introduction: Information in the Pay-per Society," in Vincent Mosco and Janet Wasko, eds., *The Political Economy of Information.* (Madison: University of Wisconsin Press, 1988), 8.

105. William Fisher, *Promises to Keep: Technology, Law, and the Future of Entertainment* (Stanford: Stanford University Press, 2004), 237.

106. Tom Bell, "Escape from Copyright: Market Success vs. Statutory Failure in the Protection of Expressive Works," *University of Cincinnati Law Review* 69 (2001): 741–805; Kenneth Dam, "Self-Help in the Digital Jungle," *Journal of Legal Studies* 28.2 (1999): 393–412.

107. Litman, *Digital Copyright,* 22–34.

108. Lessig, *Code, and Other Laws of Cyberspace,* 131.

109. Joel Reidenberg, "Lex Informatica: The Formulation of Information Policy Rules through Technology," *Texas Law Review* 76.3 (1998): 582–583.

110. This market dominance was threatened by a high-profile antitrust suit brought by the U.S. Department of Justice as well as a coalition of state authorities; while the most visible violation was that Microsoft built their web browser into their operating system, many more of the less public concerns were about the kinds of standards Microsoft built into Windows and how they systematically worked against Microsoft's competitors like Sun, RealNetworks, and Netscape. Lessig served as court expert for the case. The district court found against Microsoft and threatened to break up the company, but the appeals court backed away from that ruling, urging gentler measures. In 2001, Microsoft reached an agreement with the DOJ, signing a Consent Decree and offering to donate computers and software to schools, in exchange for almost all of the punitive measures being dropped. Lawrence Lessig, "It's Still a Safe World for Microsoft," *New York Times* (November 9, 2001): A27.

111. Ted Bridis, "Tech Giants out to Ambush MP3," *ZDNet* (2001).

112. Lessig, *Code, and Other Laws of Cyberspace,* 135.

113. Dan Burk, "Muddy Rules for Cyberspace," *Cardozo Law Review* 21 (1999): 121–179.

114. Cohen, "Lochner in Cyberspace," 558.

115. Edward Felten, "A Skeptical View of DRM and Fair Use," *Communications of the ACM* 46.4 (2003): 58.

116. Erickson, "Fair Use, DRM, and Trusted Computing," 37.

117. Lev Manovich, "Filters, Plug-ins, Menus: From Creation to Selection," *Le Numérique Intégral/The Digital Whole* (Imagina '98, Bry-sur-Marne, France: l'Institut National de l'Audiovisuel, 1998).

118. Lessig, *Code, and Other Laws of Cyberspace*, 139–140.

119. Tom Bell, "Fair Use Vs. Fared Use: The Impact of Automated Rights Management on Copyright's Fair Use Doctrine," *North Carolina Law Review* 76 (1998): 619.

120. Stefik, "Letting Loose the Light," 243.

121. Pamela Samuelson, "DRM {and, or, vs.} the Law," *Communications of the ACM* 46.4 (2003): 44.

122. Even if fair use were mandated and successfully coded for, to do so raises other concerns, such as the privacy, anonymity, and spontaneity typically guaranteed by fair use. Burk and Cohen fret that even the fair-use-friendly DRM system they propose, which might be more flexible about what counts as fair use and fair about who gets to enjoy its privileges, would still depend on every user providing their identity to some authority, making their action visible to copyright holders and permanent in the records of the licensing authority. The fact that fair use currently not only allows for unauthorized use, but also allows authors and critics to do so spontaneously and anonymously, may itself enrich public culture in ways that fair use, and the copyright doctrine itself, intend. Burk and Cohen, "Fair Use Infrastructure for Rights Management Systems," 59–61.

123. *Campbell v. Acuff-Rose Music, Inc.*, 510 U.S. 569 (U.S. S. Ct. 1994).

3 The Speed Bump

1. Lawrence Lessig, *Code, and Other Laws of Cyberspace* (New York: Basic Books, 1999), 64.

2. Daniel Bell, "The Social Framework of the Information Society," in Michael Dertouzos and Joel Moses, eds., *The Computer Age: A Twenty-Year Vie* (Cambridge, MA: MIT Press, 1979), 163–211; Manuel Castells, *The Rise of the Network Society*, 2nd ed. (Oxford: Blackwell Publishers, 2000); Elizabeth Eisenstein, *The Printing Revolution in Early Modern Europe* (Cambridge: Cambridge University Press, 1983); Jack Goody, *The Domestication of the Savage Mind* (Cambridge: Cambridge University Press, 1977); Harold Innis, *Empire and Communications* (Oxford: Clarendon Press, 1950); Harold Innis, *The Bias of Communication* (Toronto: University of Toronto

Press, 1951); Walter Ong, *Orality and Literacy: The Technologizing of the Word* (London: Methuen, 1982); Denise Schmandt-Besserat, *How Writing Came About* (Austin: University of Texas Press, 1996).

3. A useful challenge to this perspective is Adrian Johns's history of print, in which he argues that it is not the fact of print that had consequence for Western culture, but the sociopolitical efforts made during the proliferation of print to make print be what it is now taken to be: reliable, trustworthy, permanent, consistent. These were not truths about print technology, but the result of the efforts of political and economic institutions who together produced the "print culture" surrounding it. Adrian Johns, *The Nature of the Book: Print and Knowledge in the Making* (Chicago: University of Chicago Press, 1998). There is also a useful debate between Johns and Eisenstein that extends this line of inquiry: Elizabeth Eisenstein, "An Unacknowledged Revolution Revisited," *American Historical Review* 107.1 (2002): 87–105; Adrian Johns, "How to Acknowledge a Revolution," *American Historical Review* 107.1 (2002): 106–125; Elizabeth Eisenstein, "Reply," *American Historical Review* 107.1 (2002): 126.

4. Bettig, "Critical Perspectives on the History and Philosophy of Copyright," 132.

5. Donald MacKenzie and Judy Wajcman, eds., *The Social Shaping of Technology*, 2nd ed. (Buckingham: Open University Press, 1999), 19; Steve Woolgar, "The Turn to Technology in Social Studies of Science," *Science, Technology, & Human Values* 16.1 (1991): 30.

6. Mackenzie and Wajcman, *The Social Shaping of Technology*, 4.

7. For a particularly interesting point/counterpoint on whether technologies can be said to have material capabilities independent of the claims and assertions made about them, that among many topics addresses the role of guns in American society, see Steve Woolgar, "The Turn to Technology in Social Studies of Science," *Science, Technology, & Human Values* 16.1 (1991): 20–50; Rob Kling, "Computerization and Social Transformations," *Science, Technology, & Human Values* 16.3 (1991): 342–367; Steve Woolgar and Keith Grint, "Computers and the Transformation of Social Analysis," *Science, Technology, & Human Values* 16.3 (1991): 368–378; Rob Kling, "Reply to Woolgar and Grint: A Preview," *Science, Technology, & Human Values* 16.3 (1991): 379–381; Rob Kling, "Audiences, Narratives, and Human Values in Social Studies of Technology," *Science, Technology, & Human Values* 17.3 (1992): 349–365; Keith Grint and Steve Woolgar, "Computers, Guns, and Roses: What's Social about Being Shot?," *Science, Technology, & Human Values* 17.3 (1992): 366–380; Rob Kling, "When Gunfire Shatters Bone: Reducing Socio-Technical Systems to Social Relationships," *Science, Technology, & Human Values* 17.3 (1992): 381–385. "Without a gun, it is hard to tear so much flesh and splinter so much bone so rapidly and readily and with such focus while standing 10 feet away from an intended victim. Today, they also have special capabilities in expediting murders, capabilities that should not be lost in endlessly iterative reinterpretations." Kling, "Audiences, Narratives, and Human Values in Social Studies of Technology," 362. "The gun lobby would have us believe that guns

are innocent tools in the hands of killers; their opponents (and we assume Kling to be one of them) will try to persuade us that it is the ease of access to weapons that facilitates such actions. . . . But both perspectives are undermined by stressing that problems arise only when *killers unite with guns*. Gunless killers do not shoot people anymore than killerless guns; it is a particular alliance of humans and nonhumans that can lead to devastating results." Grint and Woolgar, "Computers, Guns, and Roses: What's Social about Being Shot?" 373.

8. Leah Lievrouw, "Determination and Contingency in New Media Development: Diffusion of Innovations and Social Shaping of Technology Perspectives," in Leah Lievrouw and Sonia Livingstone, eds., *The Handbook of New Media: Social Shaping and Consequences of ICTs* (London: Sage, 2002), 192.

9. The theoretical tools I draw upon in this chapter emerge largely from the field of science and technology studies. Though the work coming from this young discipline has generally not focused on information and communication technologies, it has most directly struggled with the question of how technologies shape society. The field of communication and media studies has not done as substantial a job thinking about the materiality of communication, as it has so exclusively focused on the persuasive power of the message, its psychological and social effects, and, more recently, the sociocultural relations that develop around the production and consumption of texts. The little attention that has, until recently, been paid to technology has too often been held in the sway of McLuhan's provocative but flawed work proclaiming that "the medium is the message." Marshall McLuhan, *Understanding Media: the Extensions of Man* (New York: McGraw-Hill, 1964); Paul Levinson, *The Soft Edge: A Natural History and Future of the Information Revolution* (London: Routledge, 1997); Joshua Meyrowitz, *No Sense of Place: The Impact of Electronic Media on Social Behavior* (New York: Oxford University Press, 1985).

An opposing line of inquiry that looks at the history of communication technology has offered a quieter counterpoint to the brash claims of McLuhan: see John Caldwell, ed., *Electronic Media and Technoculture* (New Brunswick, NJ: Rutgers University Press, 2000); James Carey, *Communication as Culture: Essays on Media and Society* (New York: Routledge, 1992); Daniel Czitrom, *Media and the American Mind: From Morse to McLuhan* (Chapel Hill: University of North Carolina Press, 1982); Susan Douglas, *Inventing American Broadcasting, 1899–1922*, Johns Hopkins Studies in the History of Technology (Baltimore, MD: Johns Hopkins University Press, 1987); Claude Fischer, *America Calling: A Social History of the Telephone to 1940* (Berkeley: University of California Press, 1992); Lisa Gitelman, *Always Already New: Media, History and the Data of Culture* (Cambridge, MA: MIT Press, 2006); Lisa Gitelman and Geoffrey Pingree, eds., *New Media, 1740–1915* (Cambridge, MA: MIT Press, 2003); Lisa Gitelman, *Scripts, Grooves, and Writing Machines: Representing Technology in the Edison Era* (Stanford: Stanford University Press, 1999); Clifford Lynch, "The Battle to Define the Future of the Book in the Digital World," *First Monday* 6.6 (2001); Lary

May, *Screening Out the Past: The Birth of Mass Culture and the Motion Picture Industry* (New York: Oxford University Press, 1980); David Morton, *Off the Record: The Technology and Culture of Sound Recording in America* (New Brunswick: Rutgers University Press, 2000); Chandra Mukerji and Michael Schudson, eds., *Rethinking Popular Culture: Contemporary Perspectives in Cultural Studies* (Berkeley: University of California Press, 1991); David Nye, *American Technological Sublime* (Cambridge, MA: MIT Press, 1994); Paul Starr, *The Creation of the Media: Political Origins of Modern Communications* (New York: Basic Books, 2004); Jonathan Sterne, *The Audible Past: Cultural Origins of Sound Reproduction* (Durham, NC: Duke University Press, 2003); Thomas Streeter, *Selling the Air: A Critique of the Policy of Commercial Broadcasting in the United States* (Chicago: University of Chicago Press, 1996); David Thorburn and Henry Jenkins, eds., *Rethinking Media Change: The Aesthetics of Transition* (Cambridge, MA: MIT Press, 2003).

Increasingly, useful work has developed as the fields of communication, science and technology studies, and computer and information science have begun to collaborate around the study of computers and networked communication. Of particular relevance here is the work of Rob Kling and the "social informatics" line of inquiry he pioneered, although his focus was generally on the process of computerization, rather than on the negotiation that followed once computers were in place. Rob Kling, ed., *Computerization and Controversy: Value Conflicts and Social Choices*, 2nd ed. (San Diego: Academic Press, 1996). See also John Seely Brown and Paul Duguid, *The Social Life of Information* (Boston: Harvard Business School Press, 2000); Joseph Walther, Geri Gay, and Jeffrey Hancock, "How Do Communication and Technology Researchers Study the Internet?" *Journal of Communication* 55.3 (September 2005): 632–657.

Finally, a body of work has recently been developing around the values embedded in technological design, with information and communication technologies (especially the Internet) as a preferred site for consideration: Geoffrey Bowker and Susan Leigh Star, "How to Infrastructure," in Leah Lievrouw and Sonia Livingstone, eds., *The Handbook of New Media: Social Shaping and Consequences of ICTs* (London: Sage, 2002), 151–1162; Mary Flanagan, Daniel Howe, and Helen Nissenbaum, "Embodying Values in Technology: Theory and Practice," unpublished manuscript (August 31, 2005), http://www.nyu.edu/projects/nissenbaum/papers/Nissenbaum-VID.4-25.pdf; Batya Friedman and Helen Nissenbaum, "Bias in Computer Systems," *ACM Transactions on Information Systems* 14.3 (1996): 330–347; Tarleton Gillespie, "The Stories Digital Tools Tell," in John Caldwell and Anna Everett, eds., *New Media: Theses on Convergence, Media, and Digital Reproduction* (London: Routledge, 2003): 107–126; Lucas Introna and Helen Nissenbaum, "Defining the Web: The Politics of Search Engines," *IEEE Computer* 33.1 (2000); Leah Lievrouw and Sonia Livingstone, eds., *The Handbook of New Media: Social Shaping and Consequences of ICTs* (London: Sage, 2002); Robin Mansell and Roger Silverstone, eds., *Communication by Design: The Politics of Information and Communication Technologies* (Oxford: Oxford University Press, 1996); Helen Nissenbaum, "How Computer Systems Embody Values," *IEEE*

Computer 34.3 (2001): 120, 118–119; Christian Sandvig, "Shaping Infrastructure and Innovation on the Internet: The End-to-End Network that Isn't," in David Guston and Daniel Sarewitz, eds., *Shaping Science and Technology Policy: The Next Generation of Research* (Madison, WI: University of Wisconsin Press, 2006).

10. I am borrowing the speed bump example from, among others, Latour. Bruno Latour, "Which Politics for Which Artifacts?" *Domus* (2004), http://www.ensmp.fr/%7Elatour/presse/presse_art/GB-06%20DOMUS%2006-04.html.

11. Latour, "Which Politics for Which Artifacts?"

12. Langdon Winner, "Do Artifacts Have Politics?" *Daedalus* 109.1 (1980): 123.

13. Steven Johnson, *Interface Culture: How New Technology Transforms the Way We Create and Communicate* (San Francisco: HarperEdge, 1997): 44.

14. Michel Foucault, *Discipline and Punish: The Birth of the Prison*, 1st American ed. (New York: Pantheon, 1977), 195–228.

15. Latour, "Which Politics for Which Artifacts?"

16. Their inability to satisfactorily prove that and thereby debunk Winner's argument leads them to note the importance and fluidity of academic parables. Steve Woolgar and Geoff Cooper, "Do Artefacts Have Ambivalences? Moses' Bridges, Winner's Bridges, and Other Urban Legends of STS," *Social Studies of Science* 29.3 (1999): 433–449.

17. Dan Lockton maintains a useful site and blog that collects a number of modern examples in the analog and digital environments, pointing particularly to whether their goals are for social engineering or commercial gain. See Dan Lockton, "Architectures of Control in Design," http://architectures.danlockton.co.uk/.

18. Friedman and Nissenbaum, "Bias in Computer Systems," 331.

19. Introna and Nissenbaum, "Shaping the Web."

20. Richard Dyer, "Making 'White' People White," in Donald MacKenzie and Judy Wajcman, eds., *The Social Shaping of Technology*, 2nd ed. (Buckingham: Open University Press, 1999), 134–140.

21. Rachel Weber, "Manufacturing Gender in Commercial and Military Cockpit Design," *Science, Technology, & Human Values* 22.2 (1997): 237–239.

22. Thanks to Trevor Pinch for this observation.

23. Winner, "Do Artifacts Have Politics?," 130.

24. See Tarleton Gillespie, "Engineering a Principle: 'End-to-End' in the Design of the Internet," *Social Studies of Science* 36.3 (2006): 427–457; W. Russell Neuman, Lee McKnight, and Richard Jay Solomon, *The Gordian Knot: Political Gridlock on the*

Information Highway (Cambridge, MA: MIT Press, 1997), 45–84; Sandvig, "Shaping Infrastructure and Innovation on the Internet."

25. Kling, "Computerization and Social Transformations," 355–360.

26. Gillespie, "Engineering a Principle." See also Jody Berland, "Cultural Technologies and the 'Evolution' of Technological Cultures," in Andrew Herman and Thomas Swiss, eds., *The World Wide Web and Contemporary Cultural Theory* (New York: Routledge, 2000), 235–258; Woolgar, "The Turn to Technology in Social Studies of Science"; Sally Wyatt, "Talking about the Future: Metaphors of the Internet," in Nik Brown, Brian Rappert, and Andrew Webster, eds., *Contested Futures: A Sociology of Prospective Techno-Science* (Aldershot: Ashgate Press, 2000), 109–126.

27. Bruno Latour (a.k.a. Jim Johnson), "Mixing Humans and Nonhumans Together: The Sociology of a Door-Closer," *Social Problems* 35 (1988): 298–310.

28. Latour, "Mixing Humans and Nonhumans Together," 298–310.

29. Latour, "Mixing Humans and Nonhumans Together," 302.

30. Latour, "Mixing Humans and Nonhumans Together," 276.

31. Latour, "Technology Is Society Made Durable," in John Law, ed., *A Sociology of Monsters: Essays on Power, Technology and Domination* (London: Routledge, 1991), 103–131.

32. Winner, "Do Artifacts Have Politics?," 124.

33. Thomas Gieryn, "What Buildings Do," *Theory and Society* 31 (2002): 35.

34. Latour, "Which Politics for Which Artifacts?"

35. Ellen van Oost, "Materialized Gender: How Shavers Configure the Users' Femininity and Masculinity," in Nelly Oudshoorn and Trevor Pinch, eds., *How Users Matter: The Co-Construction of Users and Technology* (Cambridge, MA: MIT Press, 2003), 193–208.

36. Johnson, *Interface Culture*; Brenda Laurel, *The Art of Human-Computer Interface Design* (Reading, MA: Addison-Wesley, 1990); Lev Manovich, *The Language of New Media* (Cambridge, MA: MIT Press, 2001).

37. Gillespie, "The Stories Digital Tools Tell."

38. Roger Silverstone, *Television and Everyday Life* (London, New York: Routledge, 1994), 82–83.

39. Madeleine Akrich, "The De-scription of Technical Objects," in Wiebe Bijker and John Law, eds., *Shaping Technology/Building Society: Studies in Sociotechnical Change* (Cambridge, MA: MIT Press, 1992), 208.

40. Steve Woolgar, "Technologies as Cultural Artefacts" in William Dutton, ed., *Information and Communication Technologies—Visions and Realities* (Oxford: Oxford University Press, 1996), 87–102.

41. Madeleine Akrich, "User Representations: Practices, Methods, and Sociology," in Arie Rip, Thomas Misa, and John Schot, eds., *Managing Technology in Society: The Approach of Constructive Technology Assessment* (London: Pinter Publishers, 1995), 167–184.

42. Steve Woolgar, "Configuring the User: The Case of Usability Trials," in John Law, ed., *A Sociology of Monsters: Essays on Power, Technology, and Domination* (London: Routledge, 1991), 58–100.

43. Hugh Mackay, Chris Carne, Paul Beynon-Davies, and Dough Tudhope, "Reconfiguring the User: Using Rapid Application Development," *Social Studies of Science* 30.5 (2000): 737–757.

44. Bruno Latour, "Where Are the Missing Masses? The Sociology of a Few Mundane Artifacts," in Wiebe Bijker and John Law, eds., *Shaping Technology/Building Society: Studies in Sociotechnical Change* (Cambridge, MA: MIT Press, 1994), 225–258.

45. John Law, "Technology and Heterogeneous Engineering: The Case of the Portuguese Expansion," in Wiebe Bijker, Thomas Hughes, and Trevor Pinch, eds., *The Social Construction of Technical Systems: New Directions in the Sociology and History of Technology*, (Cambridge, MA: MIT Press, 1987), 111.

46. Silverstone, *Television and Everyday Life*, 80.

47. Trevor Pinch and Wiebe Bijker, "The Social Construction of Facts and Artefacts: Or How the Sociology of Science and the Sociology of Technology Might Benefit Each Other," *Social Studies of Science* 14.3 (1984): 399–441; see also Wiebe Bijker, Thomas Hughes, and Trevor Pinch, eds., *The Social Construction of Technological Systems: New Directions in the Sociology and History of Technology* (Cambridge, MA: MIT Press, 1987); Wiebe Bijker, "Do Not Despair: There Is Life after Constructivism," *Science, Technology, & Human Values* 18.1 (1993): 113–138; Wiebe Bijker, *Of Bicycles, Bakelites, and Bulbs: Toward a Theory of Sociotechnical Change* (Cambridge, MA: MIT Press, 1995).

48. This kind of user manipulation of the tool itself is certainly not specific to digital technologies, although "hacking" and amateur coding are prized as valuable activities inside of the world of software. Kline and Pinch relate stories about early automobile users in the rural United States, who ingeniously converted their cars into stationary power sources for farm and domestic tasks—an intervention not always appreciated by the auto manufacturers. Ronald Kline and Trevor Pinch, "Users as Agents of Technological Change: The Social Construction of the Automobile in the Rural United States," *Technology and Culture* 37.4 (1996): 763–795. This will be discussed further in chapter 8.

49. Roger Silverstone and Leslie Haddon, "Design and Domestication of Information and Communication Technologies: Technical Change and Everyday Life," in Robin Mansell and Roger Silverstone, eds., *Communication by Design: The Politics of Information and Communication Technologies* (Oxford: Oxford University Press, 1996), 44–74.

50. Woolgar, "Technologies as Cultural Artefacts"; Nelly Oudshoorn and Trevor Pinch, eds., *How Users Matter: The Co-Construction of Users and Technologies* (Cambridge, MA: MIT Press, 2003), 99.

51. Bijker, *Of Bicycles, Bakelites, and Bulbs.*

52. Streeter, *Selling the Air*, 7.

53. Grint and Woolgar, "Computers, Guns, and Roses," 371.

54. Paul Edwards, *The Closed World: Computers and the Politics of Discourse in Cold War America* (Cambridge, MA: MIT Press, 1996), 147–174.

55. William Gaver, "Technology Affordances," *Proceedings of the SIGCHI Conference on Human Factors in Computing Systems: Reaching through Technology* (New Orleans: ACM Press, 1991), 79–84; James Gibson, "The Theory of Affordances," in Robert Shaw and John Bransford, eds., *Perceiving, Acting, and Knowing: Toward an Ecological Psychology* (Hillsdale, NJ: Lawrence Erlbaum Associates, 1977), 62–82; Donald Norman, *The Psychology of Everyday Things* (New York: Basic Books, 1988).

56. Hugh Mackay and Gareth Gillespie, "Extending the Social Shaping of Technology Approach: Ideology and Appropriation," *Social Studies of Science* 22.4 (1992): 685–716; Langdon Winner, "Upon Opening the Black Box and Finding It Empty: Social Constructivism and the Philosophy of Technology," *Science, Technology, & Human Values* 18.3 (1993): 362–378. See also Stewart Russell, "The Social Construction of Artefacts: A Response to Pinch and Bijker," *Social Studies of Science* 16.2 (1986): 331–346; Trevor Pinch and Wiebe Bijker, "Science, Relativism and the New Sociology of Technology: Reply to Russell," *Social Studies of Science* 16.2 (1986): 347–360; Sergio Sismondo, "Some Social Constructions," *Social Studies of Science* 23.3 (1993): 515–553; Hans Klein and Daniel Kleinman, "The Social Construction of Technology: Structural Considerations," *Science, Technology, & Human Values* 27.1 (2002): 28–52.

57. I am using this term in a way suggested by a loose coalition of scholars from communication, cultural psychology, cognitive science, and anthropology, who have attempted to analyze cognitive development in terms of systems of activity: "Cultural mediation implies a special importance of the social world in human development since only other human beings can create the special conditions needed for that development to occur." Michael Cole and Yrjö Engeström, "A Cultural-Historical Approach to Distributed Cognition," in Gavriel Salomon, ed., *Distributed Cognitions: Psychological and Educational Considerations* (Cambridge:

Cambridge University Press, 1993), 9. Drawing on the Russian cultural-historical school of psychology—Lev Vygotsky, Alexonder Luria, Evald Ilyenkov—the cultural anthropology of Clifford Geertz and Gregory Bateson, and the sociology of George Herbert Mead, these scholars have made inroads into finding a theoretical language to explore the links between social activity and material artifacts without falling into simple and determinist dichotomies. There are some very useful connections between this field and the technology scholars I discuss in this chapter, although bringing them together is beyond the task at hand. One likely obstacle is that the theories of mediation, because they emerged from a psychological domain, tend to see mediation in terms of individuals manipulating their *own* environment, not in terms of how we use tools to intervene in the environments of others. The closest these scholars have gotten to my use of the term may be their thoughts about pedagogy, where the use of classroom artifacts purposefully intervenes in the child's environment. See Gregory Bateson, *Steps to an Ecology of Mind* (Chicago: University of Chicago Press, 2000); Cole and Engeström, "A Cultural-Historical Approach to Distributed Cognition"; Michael Cole, *Cultural Psychology: A Once and Future Discipline* (Cambridge, MA: Belknap Press of Harvard University Press, 1996); Clifford Geertz, *The Interpretation of Cultures: Selected Essays* (New York: Basic Books, 1973), 55–86; Edwin Hutchins, *Cognition in the Wild* (Cambridge, MA: MIT Press, 1995); Jean Lave, *Cognition in Practice: Mind, Mathematics, and Culture in Everyday Life* (Cambridge: Cambridge University Press, 1988); Lucy Suchman, *Plans and Situated Actions: The Problem of Human-Machine Communication* (Cambridge: Cambridge University Press, 1987); Lev Vygotsky and Michael Cole, *Mind in Society: The Development of Higher Psychological Processes* (Cambridge, MA: Harvard University Press, 1978). For an application of these ideas to the design of computing technologies, see Geri Gay and Helene Hembrooke, *Activity-Centered Design: An Ecological Approach to Designing Smart Tools and Usable Systems* (Cambridge, MA: MIT Press, 2004).

58. Both Michael Mulkay and Thomas Gieryn, discussing scientists, noted the way in which they strategically position themselves and their profession so as to maintain the best balance of independence and support from other institutions such as government. This effort to preserve their "functional autonomy" often requires defining what they do as neutral (therefore needing no regulation or oversight) and beneficial (therefore deserving funding and praise), and maintaining that the benefit comes best when it is unobstructed. Michael Mulkay, "Norms and Ideology," *Social Science Information* 15 (1976): 637–656. Gieryn extends Mulkay's observation by noting how scientists have to present themselves differently to different audiences to achieve this goal. This same kind of "boundary work" is done by engineers, and it very often requires downplaying the political or cultural significance of what is being engineered. Thomas Gieryn, "Boundary-Work and the Demarcation of Science from Non-Science: Strains and Interests in Professional Ideologies of Scientists," *American Sociological Review* 48 (1983): 781–795; Thomas Gieryn, *Cultural Boundaries of Science: Credibility on the Line* (Chicago: University of Chicago Press, 1999).

59. Gieryn, "What Buildings Do," 42.

60. Brian Pfaffenberger, "Technological Dramas," *Science, Technology, & Human Values* 17.3 (1992): 283.

61. Woolgar, "Technologies as Cultural Artefacts," 89.

62. Pfaffenberger, "Technological Dramas," 282–283.

63. Latour, "Which Politics for Which Artifacts?"

64. I'm thinking here about the work done in media and cultural studies in the 1980s and 1990s, especially around television audiences. Ien Ang, *Desperately Seeking the Audience* (London: Routledge, 1991); Ien Ang, *Living Room Wars: Rethinking Media Audiences for a Postmodern World* (London: Routledge, 1996). Charlotte Brunsdon, Julie D'Acci, and Lynn Spigel, eds., *Feminist Television Criticism* (Oxford: Clarendon Press, 1997); John Caldwell, *Televisuality: Style, Crisis, and Authority in American Television* (New Brunswick: Rutgers University Press, 1995); John Corner, *Critical Ideas in Television Studies* (Oxford, Oxford University Press, 1999); John Fiske, *Television Culture* (London: Methuen, 1987); Todd Gitlin, *Watching Television: A Pantheon Guide to Popular Culture*, 1st ed. (New York: Pantheon Books, 1986); Stuart Hall, "Encoding/Decoding," in Stuart Hall, ed., *Culture, Media, Language* (London: Hutchinson Educational Ltd., 1980): 128–138; Justin Lewis, *The Ideological Octopus: An Exploration of Television and Its Audience.* (New York: Routledge, 1991); George Lipsitz, *Time Passages: Collective Memory and American Popular Culture* (Minneapolis: University of Minnesota Press, 1990); David Morley, *Family Television: Cultural Power and Domestic Leisure* (London: Comedia Publishing Group, 1986); David Morley, *Television, Audiences, and Cultural Studies* (London: Routledge, 1992); David Morley and Charlotte Brunsdon, *The 'Nationwide' Television Studies* (London: Routledge, 1999); Roger Silverstone and Eric Hirsch, *Consuming Technologies: Media and Information in Domestic Spaces* (London, New York: Routledge, 1992); Lynn Spigel, *Make Room for TV: Television and the Family Ideal in Postwar America* (Chicago: University of Chicago Press, 1992); Lynn Spigel and Denise Mann, eds., *Private Screenings: Television and the Female Consumer* (Minneapolis: University of Minnesota Press, 1992); Lynn Spigel and Jan Olsson, *Television after TV: Essays on a Medium in Transition* (Durham, NC: Duke University Press, 2004).

65. See Grint and Woolgar, "Computers, Guns, and Roses," 372.

66. Gieryn, "What Buildings Do," 65.

67. James Carey, *Communication as Culture: Essays on Media and Society* (New York: Routledge, 1992), 13–36.

68. Carey, *Communication as Culture*, 18.

69. Silverstone, *Television and Everyday Life*, 80.

70. Foucault, *Discipline and Punish*, 195–228.

71. Lessig, *Code, and Other Laws of Cyberspace*, 53.

72. Lessig, *Code, and Other Laws of Cyberspace*, 100–110; Steve Weber, *The Success of Open Source* (Cambridge, MA: Harvard University Press, 2004).

73. Gieryn, "What Buildings Do," 43.

74. Joel Reidenberg, "Lex Informatica: The Formulation of Information Policy Rules through Technology," *Texas Law Review* 76.3 (1998): 568.

75. Lessig, *Code, and Other Laws of Cyberspace*, 96.

76. Bijker, *Of Bicycles, Bakelites, and Bulbs*, 274.

77. However, we do contemplate these possibilities from time to time. The home-owner on a quiet street with a speed bump directly in front of his home may wish it gone every time he pulls out of his driveway; every prisoner has dreamed of smashing a wall or digging a tunnel to freedom; many a driver who has found herself locked in when she arrived too late to the parking garage has envisioned slamming her car through those flimsy gates. We fantasize about such destruction all the time in our action movies and TV dramas—our heroes always saddled with a sufficiently urgent and noble reason—yet we rarely act on these impulses ourselves.

78. Bernward Joerges, "Do Politics Have Artefacts?" *Social Studies of Science* 29.3 (1999): 424.

79. Chandra Mukerji, "Intelligent Uses of Engineering and the Legitimacy of State Power," *Technology and Culture* 44.4 (2003): 655–658.

80. Thomas Hughes, "The Evolution of Large Technological Systems," in Wiebe Bijker, Thomas Hughes, and Trevor Pinch, eds., *The Social Construction of Technical Systems: New Directions in the Sociology and History of Technology* (Cambridge, MA: MIT Press, 1987), 51–82. See also W. Bernard Carlson, "Artifacts and Frames of Meaning: Thomas A. Edison, His Managers, and the Cultural Construction of Motion Pictures," in Wiebe Bijker and John Law, eds., *Shaping Technology/Building Society: Studies in Sociotechnical Change* (Cambridge, MA: MIT Press), 175–200.

81. Thomas Hughes, "The Seamless Web: Technology, Science, Etcetera, Etcetera," *Social Studies of Science* 16.2 (1986): 281–292.

82. Law, "Technology and Heterogeneous Engineering," 115.

83. Law, "Technology and Heterogeneous Engineering," 117.

84. Law, "Technology and Heterogeneous Engineering," 114.

85. Mark Stefik, "Letting Loose the Light: Igniting Commerce in Electronic Publication," in Mark Stefik, ed., *Internet Dreams: Archetypes, Myths, and Metaphors* (Cambridge, MA: MIT Press, 1996), 240.

86. Dean Marks and Bruce Turnbull, "Technical Protection Measures: The Intersection of Technology, Law and Commercial Licenses," paper presented at Workshop on Implementation Issues of the WIPO Copyright Treaty (WCT) and the WIPO Performances and Phonograms Treaty (WPPT), Geneva, Switzerland (1999), 1.

87. Mark Rose, *Authors and Owners: The Invention of Copyright* (Cambridge, MA: Harvard University Press, 1993), 9–30.

88. Joerges, "Do Politics Have Artifacts?," 414.

4 A Heroic Tale of Devilish Piracy and Glorious Progress, by Jack Valenti

1. Joseph Schumpeter, *Capitalism, Socialism, and Democracy*, 3rd ed. (New York: Harper & Row, 1950). For this idea applied to the peer-to-peer controversy, see Raymond Ku, "The Creative Destruction of Copyright: Napster and the New Economics of Digital Technology," *University of Chicago Law Review* 69.1 (2002): 263–324.

2. See Sanjay Jain and Yanfeng Zheng, "The Incumbent's Advantage? Charting the Institutional Response of Incumbent Firms to the Threat Posed by Emerging Technologies," unpublished manuscript (2004).

3. Pamela Samuelson, "The Copyright Grab," *Wired* 4.1 (January 1996): 134–138, 188, 190–191.

4. Brian Pfaffenberger, "Technological Dramas," *Science, Technology, & Human Values* 17.3 (1992): 294.

5. Debora Halbert, *Intellectual Property in the Information Age: The Politics of Expanding Ownership Rights* (Westport, CT: Quorum, 1999), 101.

6. See, for example, John Perry Barlow, "The Next Economy of Ideas," *Wired* 8.10 (October 2000); Marco Montemagno, "P2P Manifesto" (January 15, 2005), http://rothko.hmdnsgroup.com/~montemag/p2pmanifesto_en.pdf.

7. Jessica Litman, "Revising Copyright Law for the Information Age," *Oregon Law Review* 75 (1996): 19–46; Pamela Samuelson, "Questioning the Need for New International Rules on Author's Rights in Cyberspace," *First Monday* 1.4 (1996).

8. Chuck Philips, "Time Warner Tunes In New Delivery Channel (Interview with Richard Parsons)," *Los Angeles Times* (July 25, 2000): C1.

9. John Logie, "A Copyright Cold War? The Polarized Rhetoric of the Peer-to-Peer Debates," *First Monday* 8.7 (2003).

10. Motion Picture Association of America, "Jack Valenti Announces Resignation after 38 Years as Head of MPAA/MPA," press release, Washington, DC (July 1, 2004).

11. Janet Abbate, *Inventing the Internet* (Cambridge, MA: MIT Press, 1999), 191–199.

12. Jack Valenti, "Protecting America's Most Prized Export in the Digital World," paper presented at Summer Internet World '98, Chicago, IL (July 16, 1998).

13. Jack Valenti, "Home Recording of Copyright Works," U.S. House of Representatives, Committee on the Judiciary, Subcommittee on Courts, Civil Liberties, and the Administration of Justice (April 12, 13, 14, June 24, August 11, September 22, 23, 1982).

14. In order to analyze Valenti's efforts in this regard, I have conducted a close reading of twenty-three speeches given to public audiences or government commissions, twenty-three MPAA press statements that included quotes from Valenti, two interviews given to journalists and academics, and one deposition given by Valenti in the process of a legal suit pressed by the major Hollywood studios. These documents begin in 1996 (well before the appearance of Napster and the earliest file-trading networks, and before the formal introduction of the DVD, but already in the midst of the booming popularity of the Internet) and extend to the July 1, 2004, announcement of his retirement. Most are available on the MPAA's web site; a few were drawn from the archives of the EFF.

15. The title to what later became his stump speech in 2002–2003. Jack Valenti, "A Clear Present and Future Danger: The Potential Undoing of America's Greatest Export Trade Prize. An Accounting of Movie Thievery in the Analog and Digital Format, in the U.S. and around the World," U.S. Senate, Committee on Foreign Relations (February 12, 2002).

16. Jack Valenti, "International Intellectual Property Piracy: Stealing America's Secrets," U.S. Senate, Committee on Foreign Relations (June 9, 2004).

17. Jack Valenti, "Protecting America's Grandest Trade Prize," U.S. Senate, Foreign Relations Committee on WIPO Copyright Treaties Implementation Act and the Online Copyright Liability Limitation Act (September 10, 1998).

18. Jack Valenti, "Let Us Build Together a Global Alliance Whose Mandate It Is to Protect Creative Works in the Digital World: A Call for Germany, the European Union and the United States to Forge Strong Barriers to Digital Piracy," paper presented at DVD Entertainment Trade Forum, Munich (October 22, 2002).

19. Jack Valenti, "WIPO One Year Later: Assessing Consumer Access to Digital Entertainment on the Internet and Other Media," U.S. House of Representatives, Committee on Commerce, Subcommittee on Telecommunications, Trade, and Consumer Protection (October 28, 1999).

20. Jack Valenti, "'Quo Vadis?'" paper presented to Consumer Electronic Manufacturers Association, Orlando, FL (May 23, 1996).

21. Jack Valenti, "Protecting America's Grandest Trade Prize," U.S. Senate, Foreign Relations Committee: on WIPO Copyright Treaties Implementation Act and the Online Copyright Liability Limitation Act (September 10, 1998).

22. See, for example, Jack Valenti, ". . . With a Wild Surmise, Silent, upon a Peak in Darien . . .' The Audiovisual Revolution in the Americas," paper presented at Intellectual Property Conference of the Americas, Los Angeles, CA (July 15, 1996). For more on the frontier metaphor, see Frederick Turner, "Cyberspace as the New Frontier? Mapping the Shifting Boundaries of the Network Society," discussion group post, Red Rock News Eater Service (June 6, 1999), http://commons.somewhere.com/rre/1999/RRE.Cyberspace.as.the.Ne.html?Search=cyberspace.

23. Jack Valenti, "Copyright and Creativity—The Jewel in America's Trade Crown: A Call to Congress to Protect and Preserve the Fastest Growing Economic Asset of the United States," paper presented at International Trademark Association, Santa Monica, CA (January 22, 2001).

24. Jack Valenti, "If You Can't Protect What You Own—You Don't Own Anything," U.S. House of Representatives, Subcommittee on Courts & Intellectual Property: On WIPO Copyright Treaties Implementation Act and the Online Copyright Liability Limitation Act (September 16, 1997).

25. Jack Valenti, "'Oh, To Have the Visionary Gifts of Ninon de Lenclos!' A Recital of Why Visual Entertainment, and in Particular the American Movie, Remains Immune to the Economic Blahs," paper presented to Merrill Lynch Business Conference, Pasadena, CA, (September 25, 2002).

26. *A&M Records, Inc., et al. v. Napster, Inc.*, 239 F.3d 1004 (9th Cir. 2001).

27. Jessica Litman, "Sharing and Stealing," *Hastings Communication and Entertainment Law Journal* 27 (2004): 18–20. Litman notes not only that the presumption that posting music online is direct infringement clumsily overlooks some standard distinctions in traditional copyright law, but that Congress is making further efforts to clarify that merely having an unauthorized copy of a digital work on your computer in a way that is conceivably available to the public (e.g., in a "shared music" folder of a peer-to-peer application) is tantamount to unlawful distribution—raising the problematic possibility that a hyperlink to a copyrighted work could be considered unlawful distribution as well. See also Michael Carroll, "A Primer on U.S. Intellectual Property Rights Applicable to Music Information Retrieval Systems," *Illinois Journal of Law, Technology, & Policy* 2003.2 (2003): 313–328.

28. Valenti, "WIPO One Year Later" (October 28, 1999).

29. See Jessica Litman, "The Demonization of Piracy," paper presented at Challenging the Assumptions; Tenth Conference on Computers, Freedom & Privacy, Toronto, Canada (2000).

30. Halbert has a particularly useful discussion of how the term "piracy" was used to export American notions of copyright to nations that did not share it, and was constructed as a legitimate trade issue. The techniques she describes are quite similar to those seen here (and were, in fact, tactics deployed by the very same people, Valenti included): building a narrative around good, hard-working people and lazy

and greedy pirates, making it a moral issue more than a legal one, using this moral narrative as justification for political intervention. Debora Halbert, *Intellectual Property in the Information Age: The Politics of Expanding Ownership Rights* (Westport, CT: Quorum, 1999), 81–94.

31. Litman, "The Demonization of Piracy," 8.

32. Recording Industry Association of America, "Issues: Anti-Piracy" (2003), http://www.riaa.com/issues/piracy/default.asp.

33. Valenti, "A Clear Present and Future Danger" (February 12, 2002).

34. Jack Valenti, "'There is No Force under Heaven Which Can Tear a Nation's Allegiance from its Culture.' Some Testimony about the Endurance of a Country's National Culture as Well as Some Remarks and Cautionary Observations about the Audiovisual Future," paper presented at Global Media Dialogue, Denmark (October 10, 1996).

35. Peter Jaszi, "Toward a Theory of Copyright: The Metamorphoses of 'Authorship,'" *Duke Law Journal* 2 (1991): 481. Jaszi argues that, to the extent that copyright has been expressed as a set of rights given to authors, the romantic notion of the author—"that the essence of true 'authorship' resides in a privileged connection between the inspired individual and the world of natural phenomena" (p. 494)—has been readily available as a cultural trope, to be deployed when strategically useful by those who want to defend their economic self-interest in somewhat more noble terms.

36. Halbert, *Intellectual Property in the Information Age*, 89.

37. Motion Picture Association of America, "Protecting Movie Magic in the Digital Age," press release, Washington, DC (June 15, 2004). This strategy was also employed in the MPAA's 2003 public education campaign that briefly appeared on television and in the trailers before major movies, in which anonymous gaffers, make-up artists, and stuntmen spoke of the impact of file-trading to their livelihood. See Motion Picture Association of America, "Film/TV Industry Launches Public Service Announcements as Part of Nationwide Awareness Campaign on the Impact of Digital Piracy," press release, Los Angeles, CA (July 22, 2003).

38. Valenti, "'Oh, To Have the Visionary Gifts of Ninon de Lenclos!'"

39. Jack Valenti, "Thoughts on the Digital Future of Movies, the Threat of Piracy, the Hope of Redemption," U.S. Senate, Committee on Governmental Affairs, Permanent Subcommittee on Investigations: On "Privacy & Piracy: The Paradox of Illegal File Sharing on Peer-to-Peer Networks and the Impact of Technology on the Entertainment Industry" (September 30, 2003).

40. Valenti, "'. . . With a Wild Surmise, Silent, upon a Peak of Dorien.'"

41. Valenti, "WIPO One Year Later" (October 28, 1999).

42. Motion Picture Association of America, "Motion Picture Association Vows Support of WIPO Treaty and Implementation Bill" (July 29, 1997).

43. Valenti, "Copyright and Creativity—The Jewel in America's Trade Crown."

44. Oliver Boyd-Barrett, "Media Imperialism: Towards an International Framework for an Analysis of Media Systems," in James Curran, Michael Gurevitch, and Janet Woollacott, eds., *Mass Communication and Society* (London: Edward Arnold, 1977), 116–135; Armand Mattleart, *Mapping World Communication: War, Progress, Culture* (Minneapolis: University of Minnesota Press, 1994); Herbert Schiller, *Mass Communications and American Empire* (New York: A. M. Kelley, 1969); John Tomlinson, *Cultural Imperialism: A Critical Introduction* (Baltimore: Johns Hopkins University Press, 1991).

45. Valenti, "If You Can't Protect What You Own—You Don't Own Anything" (September 16, 1997).

46. Jack Valenti, "The Perils of Movie Piracy and Its Dark Effects on Consumers, the Million People Who Work in the Movie Industry, and the Nation's Economy: Some Facts, Worries and a Look at the Uncharted Future," U.S. Senate, Commerce Committee (September 17, 2003).

47. Corey Robin, *Fear: The History of a Political Idea* (Oxford: Oxford University Press, 2004), 16.

48. Robin, *Fear*, 16.

49. Political, but especially cultural, discourse marked by moral panics: Chas Crichter, *Moral Panics and the Media* (Philadelphia: Open University Press, 2003); Chas Crichter, *Critical Readings: Moral Panics and the Media* (Maidenhead: Open University Press, 2005); Arnold Hunt, "'Moral Panic' and Moral Language in the Media," *The British Journal of Sociology* 48.4 (1997): 629–648; Angela McRobbie and Sarah Thornton, "Rethinking Moral Panic for Multi-Mediated Social Worlds," *British Journal of Sociology* 46.4 (1995): 559–574; Steven Starker, *Evil Influences: Crusades against the Mass Media* (New Brunswick: Transaction Publishers, 1989).

50. Hunt, "'Moral Panic' and Moral Language in the Media," 631.

51. Malcolm Spector and John Kitsuse, *Constructing Social Problems* (Menlo Park, CA: Benjamin Cummings, 1977), 72. Quoted in Crichter, *Moral Panics and the Media*, 20.

52. McRobbie and Thornton, "Rethinking Moral Panic for Multi-Mediated Social Worlds," 562.

53. Jack Valenti, "'Man Is the Only Animal Who Both Laughs and Weeps, Because Man Is the Only Animal Who Understands the Difference between the Way Things Are and the Way They Ought to Be': Some Comments on the Moral Imperative," paper presented at Duke University (February 24, 2003).

54. Valenti, "'. . . With a Wild Surmise, Silent, upon a Peak in Darien . . . .'"

55. Valenti, "'These Is No Force under Heaven Which Can Tear a Nations Allegiance from Its Culture.'"

56. Motion Picture Association of America, "Valenti, Copyright Assembly Call on Congress to Protect and Support Copyright in Internet Age," press release, Washington, DC (February 16, 2000).

57. Jack Valenti, "There's No Free Hollywood," editorial, *New York Times* (June 21, 2000).

58. Valenti, "Copyright and Creativity—The Jewel in America's Trade Crown."

59. Valenti, "Copyright and Creativity—The Jewel in America's Trade Crown."

60. Valenti, "Copyright and Creativity—The Jewel in America's Trade Crown."

61. Jack Valenti, "If You Can't Protect What You Own, You Don't Own Anything! A Brief Report Concerning the Dark Underside of Internet Piracy as Well as the Possibility of a Cleansing Redemption to Benefit the American Consumer," U.S. Senate, Committee on Commerce, Science, and Transportation (February 28, 2002).

62. Motion Picture Association of America, "Copyright Community Forms United 'Copyright Assembly,'" press release, Washington, DC (February 14, 2000).

63. Valenti, "If You Can't Protect What You Own, You Don't Own Anything!" (February 28, 2002).

64. Motion Picture Association of America, "Valenti, Copyright Assembly Call on Congress to Protect and Support Copyright in Internet Age."

65. Valenti, "Protecting America's Most Prized Export in the Digital World."

66. Valenti, "'. . . With a Wild Surmise, Silent, upon a Peak in Darien . . .'"

67. Valenti, "A Clear Present and Future Danger" (February 12, 2002).

68. Valenti, "'Quo Vadis?'"

69. Valenti, "'Quo Vadis?'"

70. Valenti, "WIPO One Year Later" (October 28, 1999).

71. Valenti, "The Perils of Movie Piracy and Its Dark Effects on Consumers, the Million People Who Work in the Movie Industry, and the Nation's Economy" (September 17, 2003).

72. Valenti, "Protecting America's Grandest Trade Prize" (September 10, 1998).

73. Jack Valenti, "Emerson's Doctrine: The Very Good, the Not-So-Good, the Brooding Menace, and the Wonder and the Beauty of 'Human Behavior,'" paper presented at ShoWest, Las Vegas, NV (March 4, 2003).

74. Valenti, "Thoughts on the Digital Future of Movies, the Threat of Piracy, the Hope of Redemption" (September 30, 2003).

75. Valenti, "Thoughts on the Digital Future of Movies, the Threat of Piracy, the Hope of Redemption" (September 30, 2003).

76. Valenti, "The Perils of Movie Piracy and Its Dark Effects on Consumers, the Million People Who Work in the Movie Industry, and the Nation's Economy" (September 17, 2003).

77. Valenti, "Thoughts on the Digital Future of Movies, the Threat of Piracy, the Hope of Redemption" (September 30, 2003).

78. Motion Picture Association of America, "Protecting Movie Magic in the Digital Age."

79. Jack Valenti, "International Copyright Piracy: Links to Organized Crime and Terrorism," U.S. House of Representatives, Committee on the Judiciary, Subcommittee on Courts, the Internet, and Intellectual Property (March 13, 2003).

80. Valenti, "International Intellectual Property Piracy" (June 9, 2004). The internal quote in Valenti's statement belongs to Ron Noble, the secretary general of Interpol, speaking at the first Global Congress on Combating Counterfeiting in Brussels in May 2004.

81. Valenti, "A Clear Present and Future Danger" (February 12, 2002).

82. Valenti, "Thoughts on the Digital Future of Movies, the Threat of Piracy, the Hope of Redemption" (September 30, 2003).

83. Valenti, "Thoughts on the Digital Future of Movies, the Threat of Piracy, the Hope of Redemption" (September 30, 2003).

84. Robin, *Fear*, 3.

85. A term made popular in Goldstein's 1995 treatise on copyright. Paul Goldstein, *Copyright's Highway: From Gutenberg to the Celestial Jukebox*, 1st ed. (New York: Hill and Wang, 1994). Importantly, the term is referenced in the NII White Paper, U.S. Department of Commerce, Information Infrastructure Task Force, "Intellectual Property and the National Information Infrastructure: The Report of the Working Group on Intellectual Property Rights," Washington, DC, 1995. This concept harkens back to the classical desire to collect all information in a single location, not unlike the Library of Alexandria; the inability to anticipate the decentralized collection of cultural works represented by the Internet may suggest why the music

and film industries have had such conceptual objections to peer-to-peer networks, beyond their economic concerns. Charles Mann calls it the "heavenly jukebox," and suggests that the pursuit of the one dream may interfere with the other: "In the short run the struggle is for control of the heavenly jukebox . . . at stake in the long run is the global agora: the universal library-movie theater-television-concert hall-museum on the Internet." Charles Mann, "The Heavenly Jukebox," *Atlantic Monthly* 3 (September 2000): 39–59.

86. Yochai Benkler, "From Consumers to Users: Shifting the Deeper Structures of Regulation Toward Sustainable Commons and User Access," *Federal Communications Law Journal* 52 (2000): 561–579.

87. Valenti, "A Clear Present and Future Danger" (February 12, 2002).

88. Valenti, " 'Quo Vadis?' " (May 23, 1996).

89. Motion Picture Association of America, "Ratification of WIPO Treaties Caps Historical Congress for MPAA," press release, Washington, DC (October 21, 1998).

90. Valenti, "The Perils of Movie Piracy and Its Dark Effects on Consumers, the Million People Who Work in the Movie Industry, and the Nation's Economy" (September 17, 2003).

91. Motion Picture Association of America, "Ratification of WIPO Treaties Caps Historical Congress for MPAA."

92. Motion Picture Association of America, "Statement by Jack Valenti, on RIAA Announcement of Intention to Take Legal Action Against Individuals Illegally Offering Music Online," press release, Washington, DC (June 25, 2003).

93. Valenti, "A Clear Present and Future Danger" (February 12, 2002). See also Helen Nissenbaum, "Hackers and the Contested Ontology of Cyberspace," *New Media and Society* 6.2 (2004): 195–217.

94. Valenti, "If You Can't Protect What You Own—You Don't Own Anything," (September 16, 1997).

95. Valenti, "Thoughts on the Digital Future of Movies, the Threat of Piracy, the Hope of Redemption" (September 30, 2003).

96. Valenti, " 'Oh, To Have the Visionary Gifts of Ninon de Lenclos!' "

97. Valenti, "Protecting America's Most Prized Export in the Digital World."

98. Valenti, "WIPO One Year Later" (October 28, 1999).

99. Motion Picture Association of America, "Protecting Movie Magic in the Digital Age."

100. Valenti, "WIPO One Year Later" (October 28, 1999).

101. Valenti, "WIPO One Year Later" (October 28, 1999).

102. For a useful analysis of these campaigns, see Kelly Gates, "Will Work for Copyrights: The Cultural Policy of Anti-Piracy Campaigns," *Social Semiotics* 16.1 (2006): 57–73.

103. Valenti, "A Clear Present and Future Danger" (February 12, 2002).

104. Cave, Damien. "Studio Technician." *Salon* (February 14, 2000), http://www.salon.com/tech/view/2000/02/14/valenti.

105. Valenti, "'Quo Vadis?'"

106. Turner, "Cyberspace as the New Frontier?"

107. Crichter, *Moral Panics and the Media*, 23.

108. Howard Berman, "Introduction of the Peer to Peer Piracy Prevention Act," U.S. House of Representatives (July 25, 2002), http://www.house.gov/apps/list/speech/ca28_berman/piracy_prevention_act.html.

109. Nissenbaum, "Hackers and the Ontology of Cyberspace," 1.

110. Debora Halbert, "Discourses of Danger and the Computer Hacker," *The Information Society* 13.4 (1997): 361–374.

111. Debora Halbert, "Weaving Webs of Ownership: Intellectual Property in an Information Age," diss., Hawaii Research Center for Future Studies, University of Hawaii at Manoa (1996), http://www.futures.hawaii.edu/dissertation/TOC2.html.

112. Fred Vogelstein, "Is It Sharing or Stealing?" *U.S. News and World Report* (June 12, 2000): 38–40.

113. *A&M v. Napster*, "Notice of Joint Motion and Joint Motion for Plaintiffs for Preliminary Injunction; Memorandum of Points and Authorities" (July 26 2000), 3.

114. Todd Gitlin, *The Whole World Is Watching: Mass Media in the Making and Unmaking of the New Left* (Berkeley: University of California Press, 1980): 1–20.

115. Nissenbaum, "Hackers and the Ontology of Cyberspace," 16.

5 Why SDMI Failed

1. Michael Katz and Carl Shapiro, "Network Externalities, Competition, and Compatibility," *The American Economic Review* 75.3 (1985): 424–440. See also Carl Shapiro and Hal Varian, *Information Rules: A Strategic Guide to the Network Economy* (Cambridge, MA: Harvard Business School Press, 1999); Hal Varian, Joseph Farrell, and Carl Shapiro, *The Economics of Information Technology: An Introduction* (Cambridge: Cambridge University Press, 2004).

2. Richard Posner, "Antitrust in the New Economy," Chicago: University of Chicago Law & Economics, Olin Working Paper, #106 (November 2000): 4.

3. Richard Hawkins, "The Rise of Consortia in the Information and Communication Technology Industries: Emerging Implications for Policy," *Telecommunications Policy* 23.2 (1999): 159–173; Martin Weiss and Carl Cargill, "Consortia in the Standards Development Process," *Journal of the American Society for Information Science* 43.8 (1992): 559–565.

4. Paul David and Mark Shurmer, "Formal Standards-Setting for Global Telecommunications and Information Services." *Telecommunications Policy* 20.10 (1996): 789–815.

5. Mark Lemley, "Intellectual Property Rights and Standard-Setting Organizations," *California Law Review* 90 (2002): 1889–1990; Varian, Farrell, and Shapiro, *The Economics of Information Technology*.

6. Thomas Hemphill and Nicholas Vonortas, "U.S. Antitrust Policy, Interface Compatibility Standards, and Information Technology," *Knowledge, Technology, & Policy* 18.2 (2005): 126–147; Shapiro and Varian, *Information Rules*, 305–306.

7. Federal Trade Commission and U.S. Department of Justice, "Antitrust Guidelines for Collaboration among Competitors" (2000), http://www.ftc.gov/os/2000/04/ftcdojguidelines.pdf.

For a useful consideration of whether the SDMI was a violation of antitrust laws, see Nichelle Levy, "Method to Their Madness: The Secure Digital Music Initiative, a Law and Economics Perspective," *Virginia Journal of Law and Technology* 5.3 (2000): paragraphs 52–54.

8. Dan Burk, "Law as a Network Standard." *Yale Journal of Law and Technology* (Fall 2005).

9. Hawkins, "The Rise of Consortia in the Information and Communication Technology Industries," 166.

10. Hawkins, "The Rise of Consortia in the Information and Communication Technology Industries," 161.

11. Hawkins, "The Rise of Consortia in the Information and Communication Technology Industries," 174–175.

12. David and Shurmer, "Formal Standards-Setting for Global Telecommunications and Information Services," 803.

13. Robert Merges, "From Medieval Guilds to Open Source Software: Informal Norms, Appropriability Institutions, and Innovation," paper presented at Conference on the Legal History of Intellectual Property, Madison, WI (2004).

14. Mark Rose, *Authors and Owners: The Invention of Copyright* (Cambridge, MA: Harvard University Press, 1993).

15. Michel Foucault, "What Is an Author?" in Josue Harari, ed., *Textual Strategies: Perspectives in Post-Structural Criticism* (Ithaca, NY: Cornell University Press, 1979), 141–160; Adrian Johns, *The Nature of the Book: Print and Knowledge in the Making* (Chicago: University of Chicago Press, 1998).

16. Recording Industry Association of America, "Worldwide Recording Industry Announces Precedent-Setting Initiative to Address New Digital Music Opportunities," New York (December 15, 1998).

17. The Audio Home Recording Act (1992) was designed in response to digital audio tape (DAT) recording, a technology now used almost exclusively in professional recording studios but that at one point Sony was pushing as the new consumer format for music. Worried that perfect digital copies would undercut legitimate markets, the RIAA lobbied Congress for a law regulating DAT and digital music devices. The AHRA states that any "digital audio recording device" or "digital audio recording medium" would be required by law to recognize, preserve, and abide by any copyright protection that accompanied a digital audio track. The law anticipated what was dubbed the "Serial Copy Management System," a then fictional set of standards for managing copyright through information attached to a digital file. This system would allow one copy of a digital track to be made, but would mark it as a copy, so that it could not be further duplicated. Stuart Biegel, *Beyond Our Control?: Confronting the Limits of Our Legal System in the Age of Cyberspace* (Cambridge, MA: MIT Press, 2001), 301–302.

18. John Alderman, "Rio Debut Back on Track," *Wired News* (October 27, 1998). Diamond successfully argued that its device was not a "recording device" but only a "playback device," and as such did not need to incorporate SCMS or any other mechanisms for honoring copy protection. This helps explain why current mp3 players do not allow the user to move music from the device to the computer, only in the other direction. Importantly, they noted that it was the computer that did the copying, not the Rio, leaving the question of copying at the doorstep of the IT industry. See *Recording Industry Association of America v. Diamond Multimedia Systems, Inc.*, 180 F.3d 1072 (9th Cir. 1999)—"Diamond Multimedia Systems' Points and Authorities in Opposition to Temporary Restraining Order," October 16, 1998.

19. See Amy Slaton and Janet Abbate, "The Hidden Lives of Standards: Technical Prescriptions and the Transformation of Work in America," in Michael Allen and Gabrielle Hecht, eds., *Technologies of Power: Essays in Honor of Thomas Parke Hughes and Agatha Chipley Hughes* (Cambridge, MA: MIT Press, 2001): 95–144.

20. Cary Sherman, "Presentation to the SDMI Organizing Plenary," Secure Digital Music Initiative, Los Angeles, CA (February 26, 1999).

21. Christopher Jones, "Music Biz Builds a Time Bomb," *Wired News* (May 14, 1999).

22. Secure Digital Music Initiative, "SDMI Announces Standard for New Portable Devices: On-Time Specification Will Enable Creation of New Ways to Deliver Digital Music," Los Angeles, CA (June 28, 1999).

23. Stephanie Miles, "Infighting Threatens to Kill Net Music Antipathy Standard," *CNet* (September 23, 1999).

24. Christopher Jones, "SDMI: Shape Up or Ship Out." *Wired News* (April 28, 2000).

25. Jones, "SDMI: Shape Up or Ship Out."

26. Jones, "SDMI: Shape Up or Ship Out."

27. Secure Digital Music Initiative, "An Open Letter to the Digital Community," Los Angeles, CA (September 6, 2000).

28. Electronic Frontier Foundation, "EFF Calls for Boycott of 'Hack SDMI Challenge,'" Washington, DC (September 18, 2000).

29. Electronic Frontier Foundation, "EFF Renews Its Call to Boycott the 'Hack SDMI' Challenge," (September 29, 2000).

30. Janelle Brown, "Is the SDMI Boycott Backfiring?" *Salon* (October 3, 2000).

31. Scott Craver, Min Wu, Bede Liu, Adam Stubblefield, Ben Swartlander, Dan Wallach, Drew Dean, and Edward Felten, "Reading between the Lines: Lessons from the SDMI Challenge," paper presented at 10th USENIX Security Symposium, Washington, DC (August 13–17, 2001).

32. The suit was dismissed in November 2001 and not appealed after the SDMI and RIAA made public assurances that they would not sue Felten and his students.

33. Secure Digital Music Initiative, "SDMI Reviews Screening Technology Needs," Amsterdam, Netherlands (May 18, 2001).

34. Coral Consortium, "Entertainment, Technology and Consumer Electronics Leaders Unite for DRM Interoperability," Sunnyvale, CA (October 4, 2004).

35. Ryan Naraine, "Sony, Philips Snap Up Intertrust," *Internet News* (November 13, 2002).

36. John Borland, "FAQ: Sony 'Rootkit' CDs," *CNet* (November 11, 2005); J. Alex Halderman and Edward Felten, "Lessons from the Sony CD DRM Episode" (February 14, 2006), available at http://itpolicy.Princeton.edu/pub/sonydrm-ext.pdf.; Bruce Schneier, "Real Story of the Rogue Rootkit," *Wired News* (November 17, 2005).

37. Michael Strangelove, *The Empire of Mind: Digital Piracy and the Anti-Capitalist Movement* (Toronto: University of Toronto Press, 2005).

38. Weiss and Cargill, "Consortia in the Standards Development Process."

39. Brown, "Is the SDMI Boycott Backfiring?"

40. Brown, "Is the SDMI Boycott Backfiring?"

41. John Borland, "SDMI Antipiracy Effort Loses Leader," *CNet* (January 24, 2001).

42. Charles Mann, "The Heavenly Jukebox," *Atlantic Monthly* 3 (September 2000): 39–59.

43. Edward Felten, www.freedom-to-tinker.com, December 3, 2002.

44. The possibility of designing a DRM system that includes a watermark that would survive the transition to analog and back has been extended in the various proposals for "Analog Hole" laws, which would require that analog devices look for and honor a watermark when translating a digital signal to analog. See "Hollywood Wants to Plug the 'Analog Hole,'" Electronic Frontier Foundation, Consensus at Lawyerpoint (May 23, 2002), http://bpdg.blogs.eff.org/archives/000113.html.

45. Craver et al., "Reading between the Lines," 4.

46. Many thanks to Oren Bracha for this observation.

47. Michel Callon, "Some Elements of a Sociology of Translation: Domestication of Scallops and the Fishermen of St. Brieuc Bay," in John Law, ed., *Power, Action and Belief: A New Sociology of Knowledge?* (London: Routledge, 1986), 196–229; Bruno Latour, *Aramis, or, the Love of Technology* (Cambridge, MA: Harvard University Press, 1996).

48. John Borland, "Hardwiring Copyrights: Antipiracy Efforts Spark Battle over Computer Hardware," *CNet* (March 23, 2001).

6 Protecting DVDs: Locks, Licenses, and Laws

1. Jessica Litman, *Digital Copyright: Protecting Intellectual Property on the Internet* (Amherst, NY: Prometheus Books, 2001): 122–150.

2. *Sony Corp. of America v. Universal City Studios, Inc.*, 464 U.S. 417 (U.S. S. Ct. 1984).

3. This agreement was only reached after a heated competition between two competing digital disc formats; in the interest of avoiding the kind of battle waged over the VHS and Betamax VCR formats, representatives of the computer industry were invited in to mediate. For more detail, see Consumer Electronics Association, *Digital America* (2005).

4. See Consumer Electronics Association, *Digital America*, chap. 12, for more.

5. DVD Demystified, "DVD Frequently Asked Questions (and Answers)," http://www.dvddemystified.com/dvdfaq.html (last updated May 19, 2006).

6. Consumer Electronics Association, *Digital America*, chapter 12.

7. As Labriola notes, the fact that many of these have been cracked is not considered a failure by the movie industry: "Most are intended primarily to limit 'casual copying,' in which a consumer cavalierly runs off a quick duplication for a friend. This goal is threatened only when a crack is simple enough and so well-distributed that it gains mass-market appeal. Because so few people are willing to seek out exotic ripper software or learn to navigate Internet Relay Chat, any circumvention that doesn't offer Napster-class ubiquity and ease of use isn't a showstopper for content providers. One justification for packing so many levels of copy protection into DVDs was to make circumvention tools too complicated, specialized, and intimidating for mainstream consumers." Don Labriola, "Digital Content Protection, Part II: How Anti-Piracy Technologies are Transforming Digital Media," *Extreme Tech* (August 25, 2003).

8. Jane Ginsburg, "From Having Copies to Experiencing Works: The Development of an Access Right in U.S. Copyright Law," *Journal of the Copyright Society of the USA* 50 (2003): 113–132.

9. Obviously, the music industry does embrace this access-control strategy for live concerts. But, to date, the bulk of their revenue comes from CD sales.

10. Using video cameras in movie theaters to record films is prohibited by a number of state laws; in September 2004, the House of Representatives passed the Piracy Deterrence and Education Act, part of which would make this a federal offense with a potential first-offense penalty of three years in prison. See HR 4077[108], "Piracy Deterrence and Education Act of 2004."

11. Bruno Latour (a.k.a. Jim Johnson), "Mixing Humans and Nonhumans Together: The Sociology of a Door-Closer," *Social Problems* 35 (1988): 298–310.

12. A number of creative versions of the tiny application are collected at David Touretzky's "Gallery of CSS Descramblers," http://www.cs.cmu.edu/~dst/DeCSS/Gallery/.

13. For details, see Andy Patrizio, "DVD Piracy: It Can Be Done," *Wired News* (November 1, 1999); Andy Patrizio, "Why the DVD Hack Was a Cinch," *Wired News* (November 2, 1999); Lynn Burke, "Teen Hacker's Home Raided," *Wired News* (January 25, 2000); Jeff Howe, "DVD Hackers Take a Hit in NY," *Wired News* (January 21, 2000).

14. Johansen was indicted in January 2002 and faced up to two years in prison. But in January 2003, he was acquitted of all charges. See Associated Press, "DVD-Cracking Teen Acquitted," *Wired News* (January 7, 2003).

15. *Universal City Studios, Inc. v. Reimerdes*, 111 F. Supp. 2d 294 (S.D.N.Y. 2000). The decision was appealed by the defendants, and affirmed on appeal; *Universal City Studios, Inc. et al. v. Eric Corley*, 273 F.2d 429 (2d Cir. 2001).

16. The DVD-CCA also sued seventy-two websites in a California court for providing the application; the charge was trade secret violation. The people operating the sites distributing the application knew or should know that the tool was built around stolen property, namely the decryption key lifted from XingDVD. These lawsuits stalled in anticipation of a resolution in the New York case. But in 2004, the lawsuits were dropped after the California Supreme Court ruled that posting DeCSS could not be trade secret violation because the DVD-CCA had not proved its case that CSS was a trade secret.

17. The NII Working Group on Intellectual Property was not the first U.S. government effort to assess the interplay of copyright and the distribution of information over the Internet. The now defunct Office of Technology Assessment issued two reports, in 1985 and 1994, on the subject; Halbert reports that the suggestions made in the 1985 report were much more measured and subtle than what would later appear from the NII, and were much more in line with the early Netizen claims. The OTA acknowledged that the Internet was a dynamic medium, but focused not on the risk of piracy but on the potential for new forms of authorship. The reports speculated that copyright might not even be up to the job of accommodating all of these changes, and warned against too bold an intervention at such an early stage. In particular, they wondered whether the incentive logic of copyright would even function on the Net. As Halbert notes,

New circumstances meant technology was creating opportunities that previously had not existed. These opportunities were economic, political, and cultural in nature and were responsible for more information and better access to cultural goods. Despite the opportunities provided by these new technologies, conflict was emerging as an increased emphasis on profit and ownership began to clash with the increased ability to exchange information. These opportunities, and the potential for clashing interests, led the OTA group to claim that economic incentives may not have the desired effect, or might not create the environment for creative activity, because they could pit one interests against another. Given the traditional assumption that copyright is supposed to inspire creative work by providing an economic benefit, the OTA acknowledgement that economic incentives may actually hinder creative work is quite radical.

Debora Halbert, *Intellectual Property in the Information Age: The Politics of Expanding Ownership Rights* (Westport, CT: Quorum, 1999): 28. But although the group seemed willing to acknowledge several competing perspectives about the Internet, authorship, and commerce, and even to interrogate the fundamental commercialization of cultural expression built into copyright law, they refused to proactively protect these possibilities. They proposed nothing so intrusive as anticircumvention rules; instead, they urged Congress to hold back and allow the Internet to develop before imposing copyright. Halbut, *Intellectural Property in the Information Age*, 29, 32–33. In not demanding that new possibilities be actively nurtured and shielded from the crushing force of commercial imperatives, even these more measured contributions helped pave the way for laws that would use the Internet as justification to radically alter the balance of interests embedded in copyright.

18. Litman *Digital Copyright*, 97 n.1.

19. Information Infrastructure Task Force, "Intellectual Property and the National Information Infrastructure: The Report of the Working Group on Intellectual Property Rights," Washington, DC, September 1995 [hereafter referred to as NII White Paper].

20. Litman, *Digital Copyright*, 22–34.

21. NII White Paper.

22. A number of legal scholars have examined the NII White Paper and its implications for copyright; see Dan Burk, "Anti-Circumvention Misuse," *UCLA Law Review* 50 (2003): 1095–1140; Julie Cohen, "A Right to Read Anonymously: A Closer Look at 'Copyright Management' in Cyberspace," *Connecticut Law Review* 28 (1996): 981–1039; Jane Ginsburg, "Copyright and Control over New Technologies of Dissemination," *Columbia Law Review* 101 (2001): 1613–1647; Jon Katz, "Napster Aftermath: Fan vs. Corporate Rights," *Slashdot* (July 28, 2000), http://slashdot.org/features/00/07/27/154247.shtml; Jessica Litman, "Revising Copyright Law for the Information Age," *Oregon Law Review* 75 (1996): 19–46; Litman, *Digital Copyright*, 166–191; Neil Netanel, "From the Dead Sea Scrolls to the Digital Millennium; Recent Developments in Copyright Law," *Texas Intellectual Property Journal* 9 (2000): 19–63; David Nimmer, "A Riff on Fair Use in the Digital Millennium Copyright Act," *University of Pennsylvania Law Review* 148 (2000): 673–742; Pamela Samuelson, "Legally Speaking: The NII Intellectual Property Report," *Communications of the ACM* 37.12 (1994): 21–27; Pamela Samuelson, "The U.S. Digital Agenda at the World Intellectual Property Organization," *Virginia Journal of International Law* 37 (1997): 369–439; Pamela Samuelson, "Intellectual Property and the Digital Economy: Why the Anti-Circumvention Regulations Need to Be Revised," *Berkeley Technology Law Journal* 14 (1999): 519–566; Diane Zimmerman, "Adrift in the Digital Millennium Copyright Act: The Sequel," *Dayton Law Review* 26.2 (2001): 279–292.

23. NII White Paper.

24. Motion Picture Association of America, "Copyright Protection Technical Working Group Announces DVD Encryption Achievement" (October 29, 1996).

25. The anticircumvention legislation was sponsored in the Senate by Senator Hatch, Chairman of the Senate Judiciary Committee, as S. 1284, and in the House of Representatives by Congressman Moorhead, as HR 2441. S 105–190, "The Digital Millennium Copyright Act," U.S. Senate (May 11, 1998): 5.

26. Denise Caruso, "A Tough Stance on Cyberspace Copyrights," *New York Times* (January 19, 1998); Litman, *Digital Copyright*, 123–124.

27. WIPO Copyright Treaty, cited in S 105–190: 5.

28. Litman, *Digital Copyright*, 131.

29. HR 105–551, "WIPO Copyright Treaties Implementation and Online Copyright Infringement Liability Limitation," U.S. House of Representatives, 105th Congress, 2nd session (May 22, 1998).

30. In this sense, the DMCA has some kinship with existing statutes regarding "contributory" and "vicarious" infringement, the statutes used to prosecute Napster. These statutes allow someone to be held partially responsible for copyright infringement if they materially helped it happen or benefited from it financially. Like these "secondary liabilities," the DMCA hopes to prevent infringement not by prosecuting the individual infringer, but by stopping those who might facilitate such efforts. This is a common but controversial strategy in cyberlaw. With online, asynchronous, and sometimes anonymous communication, the reality is that it can be difficult to pursue and prosecute individual violators. Putting responsibility on those who have facilitated the violation enlists those people and institutions in the enforcement of the law. Yet this practical solution raises important philosophical and ethical questions as to how far responsibility can be fairly extended, and practical questions as to what consequences there might be when technology makers, service providers, and website operators find it in their best interests to be patrolling their users for illegal activity.

31. Nimmer, "A Riff on Fair Use in the Digital Millennium Copyright Act," 683.

32. Nimmer, "A Riff on Fair Use in the Digital Millennium Copyright Act," 683.

33. In a display of sheer tautological bravado, the House Committee on Commerce tried to reassure themselves by adjusting their bill so that it would be a free-standing law rather than an amendment to Title 17 Copyright Act; without changing any of the bill's language, which clearly worked to regulate copyrighted work and its use, they felt that writing it as a separate law would preserve copyright law as "technology neutral." This separation was not continued as the DMCA made it into law. See HR 105-551: 25.

34. Digital Millennium Copyright Act ("DMCA"), Pub. L. No. 105-304, 112 Stat. 2860 (1998) (codified at 17 U.S.C. 512 and in various sections of Chapter 12 of Title 17 of the U.S.C.).

35. 47 U.S.C. SS 553, "Unauthorized Reception of Cable Service"; See also Anne Branscomb, *Who Owns Information?: From Privacy to Public Access* (New York: Basic Books, 1994), 106–118; David Waterman, "The Political Economy of Audio-Visual Copyright Enforcement," unpublished manuscript (June 2005), http://www.indiana.edu/~telecom/faculty/waterman/piracy_05.pdf.

36. Ginsburg, "From Having Copies to Experiencing Works."

37. For the idea of "paracopyright," see Burk, "Anti-Circumvention Misuse"; Margaret Chon, "Paracopyright and the Digital Divide: Anti-Circumvention Provisions and Control Over Digital Information," paper presented at Copyright's Balance

in an Internet World, University of Dayton School of Law Symposium (2000); National Research Council, Committee on Intellectual Property Rights in the Emerging Information Infrastructure, *The Digital Dilemma: Intellectual Property in the Information Age* (Washington, DC: National Academy Press, 2000); Peter Jaszi, "Intellectual Property Legislative Update: Copyright, Paracopyright, and Pseudo-Copyright," paper presented at Annual Meeting—The Future Network: Transforming Learning and Scholarship, Association of Research Libraries, Eugene, OR (May 13–15, 1998).

38. The DMCA includes an explicit stipulation intended to ensure that its legal domain would not impinge on fair use protections: "Nothing in this section shall affect rights, remedies, limitations, or defenses to copyright infringement, including fair use, under this title." Digital Millennium Copyright Act, 1201(c)(1).

39. Nimmer, "A Riff on Fair Use in the Digital Millennium Copyright Act."

40. Digital Millennium Copyright Act, 1201(c)(1).

41. Ginsburg, "From Having Copies to Experiencing Works," 11.

42. *Universal v. Reimerdes*, 111 F. Supp. 2d 346 (S.D.N.Y. 2000): 45.

43. *Universal v. Reimerdes*, "Appeals Court Transcript," May 8, 2001.

44. Digital Millennium Copyright Act, 1201 (k)(1)(A)(i).

45. "CSS Specifications, Version 1.1," http://www.dvdcca.org/css/; accessed January 18, 2003.

46. Additionally, licensed manufacturers must ensure that their devices restrict the playing of regional DVD discs outside of the appropriate locale. The implications of this set of restrictions is addressed in chapter 9.

47. These restrictions, requiring "robustness" in the device, are of particular concern, and will be addressed in chapter 8.

48. David Nimmer, Elliott Brown, and Gary Frischling, "The Metamorphosis of Contract into Expand," *California Law Review* 87 (1999): 24.

49. Mark Lemley, "Beyond Preemption: The Law and Policy of Intellectual Property Licensing," *California Law Review* 87 (1999): 125–126.

50. This is no longer hypothetical. In the case *ProCD Inc. v. Zeidenberg*, 86 F.3d 1447 (7th Cir. 1996), a provider of a CD-ROM database of White Pages phone listings sued a second provider who copied their listings to create a website serving the similar function. Precisely because the Supreme Court had already decided that telephone book listings do not enjoy copyright protection because they are a collection of facts and not original expression (*Feist Enterprises, Inc. v. Rural Telephone Service Co.*, 499 U.S. 340 [1991]), the provider sued on the basis of breach of contract, in that the user's license on its CD-ROM prohibited making the contents of the data-

base available to users other than the purchaser. While the district court rejected the suit on the basis that contractual obligations could not trump copyright rules, the Seventh Circuit Court of Appeals reversed the decision. See Nimmer, Brown, and Frischling, "The Metamorphosis of Contract into Expand"; Lemley, "Beyond Preemption."

51. Section 301 of the Copyright Act.

52. Lawrence Lessig, *Free Culture: How Big Media Uses Technology and the Law to Lock Down Culture and Control Creativity* (New York: Penguin Books, 2004): 148–153.

53. See Julie Cohen, "Lochner in Cyberspace: The New Economic Orthodoxy of 'Rights Management,'" *Michigan Law Review* 97.2 (1998): 462, 480–563.

54. *Universal City Studios, Inc. v. Reimerdes*, 82 F. Supp 2d 21 (S.D.N.Y. 2000): 12.

55. *Universal City Studios, Inc. v. Reimerdes*, 111 F. Supp. 2d 346 (S.D.N.Y. 2000): 73.

56. Dan Burk argues that the cases brought under the DMCA show that the law has overwhelmingly been used by individual businesses to shut out upstart competitors; often the plaintiffs are not even the relevant copyright holders, as in *RealNetworks, Inc. v. Streambox, Inc.* LEXIS 1889 (U.S. Dist. 2000). Burk, "Anti-Circumvention Misuse." See also Siva Vaidhyanathan, "Remote Control: The Rise of Electronic Cultural Policy," *The Annals of the American Academy of Political and Social Science* 597.1 (January 2005): 129.

57. Lawrence Lessig, *Code, and Other Laws of Cyberspace* (New York: Basic Books, 1999), 90–95.

58. Lessig, *Code, and Other Laws of Cyberspace*, 43–44.

59. Litman, *Digital Copyright*, 89–100.

60. HR 105–551, part 2: 35–36.

61. Business Software Alliance, Computer Systems Policy Project, and Recording Industry Association of America, "Technology and Record Company Policy Principles" (January 14, 2003). See also Associated Press, "'Landmark' Accord on Copyrights," *Wired News* (January 14, 2003).

7 Raising the Broadcast Flag

1. Chandra Mukerji, "Intelligent Uses of Engineering and the Legitimacy of State Power," *Technology and Culture* 44.4 (2003): 657.

2. Home Box Office, "FAQ-HBO Application of CGMS—A Copyright Protection," http://www.hbo.com/corpinfo/cgmsafaq.shtml.

3. National Telecommunications and Information Administration, Department of Commerce; Benton Foundation, "Charting the Digital Broadcasting Future: Final

Report of the Advisory Committee on Public Interest Obligations of Digital Television Broadcasters," Washington, DC (December 18, 1998).

4. NTIA, "Charting the Digital Broadcasting Future."

5. Celia Wexler, "Channeling Influence: The Broadcast Lobby and the $70 Billion Free Ride," (Washington, DC: Common Cause, 1997).

6. Robert Horwitz, *The Irony of Regulatory Reform: The Deregulation of American Telecommunications* (New York: Oxford University Press, 1989).

7. Federal Communications Commission, "In the Matter of: Digital Broadcast Content Protection—Report and Order and Further Notice of Proposed Rulemaking," MB Docket 02-230, #03-273 (November 4, 2003); Michael Grebb, "Uncle Sam Wants Your Airwaves," *Wired News* (September 22, 2004).

8. Mike Godwin, "Harry Potter and the Prisoners of the DTV Transition," Public Knowledge, Washington, DC (2003), http://www.public.knowledge.org/news/analysis/harrypotter.

9. For example, see Fritz Attaway and Tod Cohen, "Comments of the Motion Picture Association of America, In the Matter of Carriage of Transmissions of Digital Television Broadcast Stations, CS Docket #98-120, Amendments to Part 76 of the Commission's Rules," Federal Communications Commission (September 17, 1998).

10. Broadcast Protection Discussion Group, "Final Report of the Co-Chairs of the Broadcast Protection Discussion Subgroup to the Copy Protection Technical Working Group" (June 3, 2002): 1 [hereafter referred to as BPDG Final Report].

11. Center for Democracy and Technology, "Implications of the Broadcast Flag: A Public Interest Primer," Washington, DC (December 2003); Center for Democracy and Technology, "The Broadcast Flag: An Introduction," online FAQ (May 23, 2004); Godwin, "Harry Potter and the Prisoners of the DTV Transition"; Motion Picture Association of America, "Broadcast Flag: Frequently Asked Questions," online FAQ (2005).

12. It is worth explaining here why content owners see the redistribution of broadcast content as a detriment, since it may not be intuitively obvious why it matters when a program broadcast for free is subsequently circulated for free. The classic concern is the same one used to justify the *Sony v. Universal* lawsuit against the VCR: If the viewer can tape a movie and keep it, they won't watch it the next time it is broadcast on television, meaning less ad revenue. The concern now is harm to DVD sales, a worry that increasingly extends to the copyright holders of television programs, who are seeing a booming market for television on DVD. Add to this the potential impact on syndication revenue: Why would affiliate stations pay for a show to go into syndication if all of its fans already had the entire series collected on their laptops, or could easily pull them from peer-to-peer networks? Local ad revenue may be particularly harmed by this redistribution. Premium channels like

HBO and Showtime also worry that, if their content is widely available online, fewer people will pay a monthly fee to subscribe. It is this last concern that is, in some ways, the most important, as these content protection technologies increasingly make possible a pay-per-view or subscription model for the delivery of content. This will be discussed further in chapter 9.

13. BPDG Final Report: Tab A, "5C Presentation to CPTWG: Protecting Against Unauthorized Redistribution of Digital Broadcast Content."

14. BPDG Final Report: Tab B, "Proposal and Work Plan for CPTWG 'Broadcast Protection Discussion Group' to Tackle the Technical Aspects of Preventing Unrestricted and Unauthorized Redistribution of Digital Broadcast Content": 2.

15. BPDG Final Report: 4.

16. I will return to these "robustness" rules in the next chapter.

17. FCC Federal Communications Commission, "In the Matter of: Digital Broadcast Copy Protection—Notice of Proposed Rulemaking," MB Docket 02-230, #02-231 (August 8, 2002): 14.

18. BPDG Final Report: Tab B: 1–2.

19. BPDG Final Report: Tab N2; Electronic Frontier Foundation, "Comments on the Final Report of the Broadcast Protection Discussion Group" (May 29, 2002).

20. BPDG Final Report: Tab B: 1.

21. BPDG Final Report: 14.

22. FCC, "In the Matter of: Digital Broadcast Content Protection" (November 4, 2003): 6.

23. Digital Transmission Licensing Administrator, "Reply Comments," to Federal Communication Commission, "In the Matter of: Digital Broadcast Content Protection," MB Docket 02-230 (March 15, 2004): 3.

24. This will be discussed further in the chapter 9.

25. BPDG Final Report: Tab F1 and F2.

26. BPDG Final Report: Tab G.

27. BPDG Final Report, "Open Copy Protection System, Compliance and Robustness Rules" (May 7, 2002); BPDG Final Report, "Term Sheet for OCPS License" (May 7, 2002); BPDG Final Report: Tab G, "Philips Proposal to the BPDG."

28. Philips Consumer Electronics, "Philips Consumer Electronics North America CEO Warns Congress That Plan Will Raise Costs, Complexity, and Confusion for Millions of Consumers in Digital TV Age," press release, Washington, DC (April 25, 2002); posted on EFF blog "Consensus at Lawyerpoint" (April 26, 2002), http://bpdg.blogs.eff.org/archives/000060.html.

29. BPDG Final Report: Tab N1, Electronic Frontier Foundation, "Comments on Existing Draft Requirements" (May 9, 2002).

30. Interestingly, while this press release is still online at the EFF, and it mentions another press release from Philips expressing similar concerns, neither of these press releases is available on Philips's own corporate website, although it does provide an archive of press releases.

31. MPAA, "Broadcast Flag FAQ."

32. FCC, "In the Matter of: Digital Broadcast Copy Protection" (August 9, 2002): 1–2.

33. FCC, "In the Matter of: Digital Broadcast Content Protection" (November 4, 2003): 26.

34. FCC, "In the Matter of: Digital Broadcast Content Protection" (November 4, 2003): 66–68.

35. Roy Stewart, "Digital Television Transition," presented to the Federal Communications Commission (April 19, 2001).

36. FCC, "In the Matter of: Digital Broadcast Content Protection" (November 4, 2003): 14.

37. FCC, "In the Matter of: Digital Broadcast Content Protection" (November 4, 2003): 6.

38. FCC, "In the Matter of: Digital Broadcast Content Protection" (November 4, 2003): 1, fn 1.

39. *American Library Association et al. v. Federal Communications Commission and United States of America*, 406 F.3d 689 (U.S. App. D.C. 2005): 5.

40. *American Library Association et al. v. Federal Communications Commission and United States of America*, 406 F.3d 689 (U.S. App. D.C. 2005): 24.

41. *American Library Association et al. v. Federal Communications Commission and United States of America*, 406 F.3d 689 (U.S. App. D.C. 2005): 4.

42. *American Library Association et al. v. Federal Communications Commission and United States of America*, 406 F.3d 689 (U.S. App. D.C. 2005): 19.

43. American Library Association, "Senate Holds Broadcast Flag Hearing" (March 22, 2006), http://www.ala.org/ala/washoff/WOissues/copyrightb/broadcastflag/broadcastflag.htm.

44. Susan Crawford, "The Biology of the Broadcast Flag," *Hastings Communications and Entertainment Law Journal* 25.2 (2004): 649.

45. Center for Democracy and Technology, "Mapping the Digital Video Copyright Landscape: Stakeholder Interests and the Internet," (2004): 6.

46. Jessica Litman, *Digital Copyright: Protecting Intellectual Property on the Internet* (Amherst, NY: Prometheus Books, 2001): 22–34.

47. Jessica Litman, *Digital Copyright: Protecting Intellectual Property on the Internet* (Amherst, NY: Prometheus Books, 2001): 122–150.

48. Edwin Outwater, "The History of Digital Copyright Management, Or How the Cows Got on the Ice," *Medialine* (May 2000).

8 Effective Frustration

1. This has at times been articulated as a political act, especially in the rhetoric of the Free Culture movement, which casts culture as belonging to its users in important ways, but is more often used in the apolitical terms of getting music and movies for free only in the sense of not paying for it. See http://www.freeculture.org/.

2. Kristin Eschenfelder and Anuj Desai, "Software as Protest: The Unexpected Resiliency of U.S.-Based DeCSS Posting and Linking," *The Information Society* 20.2 (2004): 101–116.

3. National Research Council: Committee on Intellectual Property Rights in the Emerging Information Infrastructure, *The Digital Dilemma: Intellectual Property in the Information Age* (Washington, DC: National Academy Press, 2000), 218.

4. Peter Biddle, Paul England, Marcus Peinado, and Bryan William, "The Darknet and the Future of Content Distribution," paper presented at ACM Workshop on Digital Rights Management, Stanford, CA (2002).

5. Anthony Giddens, *The Constitution of Society: Outline of the Theory of Structuration* (Cambridge, UK: Polity Press, 1984); Wanda Orlikowski, "The Duality of Technology: Rethinking the Concept of Technology in Organizations," *Organization Science* 3.3 (1992): 398–427.

6. CSS license, v. 1.1, section 6.2.5.1.

7. CSS license, v. 1.1, section 6.2.5.3.

8. Andy Patrizio, "Why the DVD Hack Was a Cinch," *Wired News* (November 2, 1999).

9. Federal Communications Commission, "In the Matter of: Digital Broadcast Content Protection—Report and Order and Further Notice of Proposed Rulemaking," MB Docket 02-230, #03-273 (November 4, 2003): 43.

10. Broadcast Protection Discussion Group, "Final Report of the Co-Chairs of the Broadcast Protection Discussion Subgroup to the Copy Protection

Technical Working Group" [hereafter referred to as BPDG Final Report] (June 3, 2002): 14.

11. FCC, "In the Matter of: Digital Broadcast Content Protection" (November 4, 2003): 23.

12. FCC, "In the Matter of: Digital Broadcast Content Protection" (November 4, 2003): 43.

13. FCC, "In the Matter of: Digital Broadcast Content Protection" (November 4, 2003): 23.

14. Secure Digital Music Initiative, "SDMI Portable Device Specification, Part 1: Version 1.0," Los Angeles, CA (July 8, 1999): 31.

15. Secure Digital Music Initiative, "SDMI Portable Device Specification, Part 1: Version 1.0," Los Angeles, CA (July 8, 1999): 33.

16. Secure Digital Music Initiative, "SDMI Portable Device Specification, Part 1: Version 1.0," Los Angeles, CA (July 8, 1999): 33.

17. Josh Greenberg, "Hackers and Tinkerers and Amateurs . . . Oh My!" unpublished manuscript, George Mason University (2004).

18. Amy Bruckman, "Studying the Amateur Artist: A Perspective on Disguising Data Collected in Human Subjects Research on the Internet," *Ethics and Information Technology* 4.3 (2002): 217–231. See also Tom Coates, "(Weblogs and) The Mass Amateurisation of (Nearly) Everything . . . ," *Plasticbag.org* (September 3, 2003); Dan Hunter and Gregory Lastowka, "Amateur-to-Amateur," *William and Mary Law Review* 46 (2004): 951–1030; Clay Shirky, "Weblogs and the Mass Amateurization of Publishing," *Clay Shirky's Writings about the Internet* (October 3, 2002).

19. For more on open source software design, see Yochai Benkler, "Coase's Penguin, or Linux and the nature of the Firm," *Yale Law Journal* 112.3: 369–446; David Berry, "The Contestation of Code: A Preliminary Investigation into the Discourse of the Free/Libre and Open Source Movements," *Critical Discourse Studies* 1.1 (April, 2004): 65–89; Shay David, "Opening the Sources of Accountability," *First Monday* 9.11 (2004); Tarleton Gillespie, "Book Review: Steven Weber, 'The Success of Open Source,'" *Isis* 97.3 (2006): 592–593; David Nichols and Michael Twidale, "The Usability of Open Source Software," *First Monday* 8.1 (2003); Matt Ratto, "The Pressure of Openness: The Hybrid Work of Linux Free/Open Source Software Developers," diss., University of California, San Diego, 2003; Matt Ratto, "Embedded Technical Expression: Code and the Leveraging of Functionality," *The Information Society* 21.3 (2005): 205–213; Eric Raymond, *The Cathedral and the Bazaar: Musings on Linux and Open Source by an Accidental Revolutionary* (Beijing: O'Reilly, 1999); Richard Stallman, "Why Software Should Not Have Owners," in Richard Stallman, ed., *Free Software, Free Society: Selected Essays of Richard M. Stallman* (Cambridge, MA: Free Software Foundation, 2002), 45–50; Linus Torvalds, "What Makes Hackers Tick? a.k.a. Linus'

Law," in Pekka Himanen, ed., *The Hacker Ethic* (New York: Random House, 2001), xiii–xvii; Steve Weber, *The Success of Open Source* (Cambridge, MA: Harvard University Press, 2004).

20. Yochai Benkler, "Freedom in the Commons: Towards a Political Economy of Information," *Duke Law Journal* 52 (2003): 1245–1276; Yochai Benkler, *The Wealth of Networks: How Social Production Transforms Markets and Freedom* (New Haven: Yale University Press, 2006), 59–132.

21. Weber, *The Success of Open Source*, 157–189.

22. Steve Woolgar, "Configuring the User: The Case of Usability Trials," in John Law, ed., *A Sociology of Monsters: Essays on Power, Technology, and Domination* (London: Routledge, 1991), 58–100.

23. "New" is a problematic word here, and probably the wrong one; the open source approach to design can be linked to many past forms of collaborative and communal work, imported as it is to the digital and networked context. It is new only in the sense that it is newly articulated as a challenge to traditional and dominant modes of commercial software design, and its precedents have tended to be marginalized in these contexts. The dichotomy it challenges, however, is a pervasive and a powerful one.

24. Susan Crawford, "The Biology of the Broadcast Flag," *Hastings Communications and Entertainment Law Journal* 25.2 (2004): 603–652.

25. BPDG Final Report: Tab N1; Electronic Frontier Foundation, "Comments on Existing Draft Requirements" (May 9, 2002): 2–3.

26. BPDG Final Report: Tab N1; Electronic Frontier Foundation, "Comments on Existing Draft Requirements" (May 9, 2002): 2–3.

27. Woolgar, "Configuring the User," 61.

28. Woolgar, "Configuring the User," 61.

29. Madeleine Akrich, "The De-scription of Technical Objects," in Wiebe Bijker and John Law, eds., *Shaping Technology/Building Society: Studies in Sociotechnical Change* (Cambridge, MA: MIT Press, 1992), 205–224.

30. Engeström argues that the fundamental ontological relationship between users and their technology has to do with a regular shifting between these two understandings. Yrjö Engeström, "When Is a Tool? Multiple Meanings of Artifacts in Human Activity," in Yrjö Engeström, ed., *Learning, Working and Imagining: Twelve Studies in Activity Theory* (Helsinki: Orienta-Konsultit, 1990: 171–195).

31. Hugh Mackay and Gareth Gillespie, "Extending the Social Shaping of Technology Approach: Ideology and Appropriation," *Social Studies of Science* 22.4 (1992): 698–699.

32. Ronald Kline and Trevor Pinch, "Users as Agents of Technological Change: The Social Construction of the Automobile in the Rural United States," *Technology and Culture* 37.4 (1996): 774–775.

33. Ron Eglash, "Appropriating Technology: An Introduction," in Ron Eglash, Jennifer Crossiant, Giovanna Di Chiro, and Rayvon Fouché, eds., *Appropriating Technology: Vernacular Science and Social Power* (Minneapolis: University of Minnesota Press, 2004): vii–xxi.

34. Natalie Jeremijenko's project can be seen at http://xdesign.ucsd.edu/feralrobots/.

35. This concern may extend to the technologies of production as well, although this currently remains a separate question.

36. Bruno Latour, *Science in Action: How to Follow Scientists and Engineers through Society* (Cambridge, MA: Harvard University Press, 1987).

37. Kline and Pinch, "Users as Agents of Technological Change," 790–791.

38. Robert Horwitz, *The Irony of Regulatory Reform: The Deregulation of American Telecommunications* (New York: Oxford University Press, 1989), 230–231.

39. Merritt Roe Smith and Leo Marx, eds., *Does Technology Drive History?: The Dilemma of Technological Determinism* (Cambridge, MA: MIT Press, 1994).

40. BPDG Final Report: Tab N1.

41. Nelly Oudshoorn and Trevor Pinch, eds., *How Users Matter: The Co-Construction of Users and Technologies* (Cambridge, MA: MIT Press, 2003): 1–27.

42. I'm borrowing from Ron Eglash's three-part criteria for investigating the appropriation of technology and adding a fourth inspired by Woolgar. Eglash, "Appropriating Technology."

43. Eglash, "Appropriating Technology."

44. Reuters, "CD Crack: Magic Marker Indeed," *Wired News* (May 20, 2002).

45. Eschenfelder and Desai, "Software as Protest."

46. Eglash, "Appropriating Technology."

47. Thomas Gieryn, "What Buildings Do," *Theory and Society* 31 (2002): 45.

48. Eglash, "Appropriating Technology."

49. Joe Karaganis and Natalie Jeremijenko, eds., *Structures of Participation in Digital Culture* (Durham, NC: Duke University Press, 2007).

50. Mackay and Gillespie, "Extending the Social Shaping of Technology Approach," 702.

51. The now iconic work of Kline and Pinch mentioned earlier has been criticized for paying insufficient attention to the social structure in which negotiations around technology exist. Hugh Mackay, Chris Carne, Paul Beynon-Davies, and Dough Tudhope, "Reconfiguring the User: Using Rapid Application Development," *Social Studies of Science* 30.5 (2000): 737–757; Nelly Oudshoorn, Els Rommes, and Marcelle Stiensra, "Configuring the User as Everybody: Gender and Design Cultures in Information and Communication Technologies," *Science, Technology, & Human Values* 29.1 (2004): 30–63. Many who have deployed their argument in their own case studies have been even more enamored and less careful with the idea of "users as agents of technological change" than they were, and unaware of the way in which their agency itself can be curtailed through design and law.

52. Edward Felten, http://www.freedom-to-tinker.com/.

9 The Cultural Implications of Encryption

1. This general discussion of the history of cryptography is only intended as a barebones outline in order to suggest one of the political priorities that have shaped encryption. A number of useful books on the subject have helped me lay out this history in broad strokes, and go into much more detail for those who are interested. Charles C. Mann, "A Web-Only Primer on Public-Key Encryption," *Atlantic Monthly* (September 2002); Dana Mackenzie, "The Code War," *Beyond Discovery* (February 12, 2003); Fred Piper and Sean Murphy, *Cryptography: A Very Short Introduction* (Oxford: Oxford University Press, 2002); Bruce Schneier, *Secrets and Lies: Digital Security in a Networked World* (New York: John Wiley, 2000); Simon Singh, *The Code Book: The Evolution of Secrecy from Mary, Queen of Scots, to Quantum Cryptography* (New York: Doubleday, 1999).

2. Piper and Murphy, *Cryptography*, 12.

3. Singh, *The Code Book*, 61.

4. David Phillips, "Cryptography, Secrets, and the Structuring of Trust," in Philip Agre and Marc Rotenberg, eds., *Technology and Privacy: The New Landscape* (Cambridge, MA: MIT Press, 1997), 250–251.

5. Cory Doctorow, "Microsoft Research DRM Talk," paper presented to Microsoft Research Group, Redmond, WA (June 17, 2004), http://www.craphound.com/msftdrm.txt.

6. Philip K. Dick, *The Philip K. Dick Reader* (New York: Pantheon Books, 2001): 324.

7. Dan Burk and Julie Cohen, "Fair Use Infrastructure for Rights Management Systems," *Harvard Journal of Law & Technology* 15.1 (2001): 42–83; Edward Felten, "A Skeptical View of DRM and Fair Use," *Communications of the ACM* 46.4 (2003): 57–59; Pamela Samuelson, "DRM {and, or, vs.} the Law," *Communications of the ACM* 46.4 (2003): 41–45.

8. *Universal City Studios, Inc. v. Reimerdes*, 111 F. Supp. 2d 294. (S.D.N.Y. 2000): 1, 21, 46. See also John Wilen, "DVD Suit Defendant Pushes Legal Envelope," *USA Today* (August 25, 2000); Carl Kaplan, "Does an Anti-Piracy Plan Quash the First Amendment?" *New York Times* (April 27, 2001).

9. Owen Fiss, *Liberalism Divided: Freedom of Speech and the Many Uses of State Power* (Boulder, CO: Westview Press, 1996): 121–138.

10. The regions are (1) the U.S., its territories, and Canada; (2) Europe, Greenland, the Middle East, Japan, Lesotho, Swaziland, and South Africa; (3) South Korea, Taiwan, Hong Kong, and the Association of Southeast Asian Nations (ASEAN): Brunei, Cambodia, Indonesia, Laos, Malaysia, Myanmar, the Philippines, Singapore, Thailand, and Vietnam; (4) Australia, New Zealand, Mexico, Central and South America; (5) Russia and the ex-Soviet Bloc Eastern European nations, the Indian subcontinent, Mongolia, and the remainder of Africa; (6) China. Region 7 is a reserved category for future use, and region 8 is for international territory, primarily for transcontinental flights and cruise ships. DVDs that are encoded for all regions are sometimes called "region 0." See Wikipedia.org, "DVD," http://en.wikipedia.org/wiki/DVD (accessed August 17, 2005).

11. A device may allow the user to "switch" the region setting for their device in order to play a DVD from another region—but they can only do this a set number of times, usually between three and five.

12. It has also been revealed that many devices and application have secret codes that allow users to render their device region-free. Paul Rubens, "Border Controls Crumble in DVD Land," *BBC News* (August 19, 2002).

13. Paul David, "Clio and the Economics of QWERTY," *American Economic Review* 75.2 (1985): 332–337; Thomas Hughes, "The Evolution of Large Technological Systems," in Wiebe Bijker, Thomas Hughes, and Trevor Pinch, eds., *The Social Construction of Technical Systems: New Directions in the Sociology and History of Technology* (Cambridge, MA: MIT Press, 1987), 51–82.

14. Amy Slaton and Janet Abbate, "The Hidden Lives of Standards: Technical Prescriptions and the Transformation of Work in America," in Michael Allen and Gabrielle Hecht, eds., *Technologies of Power: Essays in Honor of Thomas Parke Hughes and Agatha Chipley Hughes* (Cambridge, MA: MIT Press, 2001), 95–144; Gregory Tassey, "The Roles of Standards as Technology Infrastructure," in Richard Hawkins, Robin Mansell, and Jim Skea, eds., *Standards, Innovation and Competitiveness: The Politics and Economics of Standards in Natural and Technical Environments* (Brookfield, VT: Edward Elgar, 1995), 161–171.

15. NTSC, used in most of North, South, and Central America, as well as Japan, South Korea, and the Philippines; PAL, in most of western Europe, Africa, Australia, China, India, and much of the Middle East; and SECAM, in France and eastern

Europe. The difference has to do with the number of lines on the screen, the color specifications, and the refresh rates.

16. Janet Abbate, *Inventing the Internet* (Cambridge, MA: MIT Press, 1999), 147–180; Scott Bradner, "The Internet Engineering Task Force," in Chris Dibona, Sam Ockman, and Mark Stone, eds., *Open Sources: Voices from the Open Source Revolution* (Cambridge, MA: O'Reilly and Associates, 1999), 47–52; William Drake, "The Internet Religious War," *Telecommunications Policy* 17.9 (1993): 643–649; Alexander Galloway, "Global Networks and the Effects on Culture," *The Annals of the American Academy of Political and Social Science* 597.1 (2005): 19–31; Simson Garfinkel, "The Web's Unelected Government," *Technology Review* (November/December 1998): 38–47; Brian Kahin and Janet Abbate, eds., *Standards Policy for Information Infrastructure* (Cambridge, MA: MIT Press, 1995); Jay Kesan and Rajiv Shah, "Fool Us Once Shame On You—Fool Us Twice Shame on Us: What We Can Learn from the Privatizations of the Internet Backbone Network and the Domain Name System," *Washington University Law Quarterly* 79.1 (2001): 89–220.

17. J. D. Lasica, *Darknet: Hollywood's War Against the Digital Generation* (Hoboken, NJ: Wiley, 2005), 23–26.

18. This strategy is fast disappearing as studios try to diminish the window of opportunity for DVD pirates.

19. Charles Arthur, "Revealed: The Tech Consumer as Prawn," *The Register* (February 7, 2005).

20. *Kabushiki Kaisha Sony Computer Entertainment v Stevens*, 2003 FCAFC 157, Federal Court of Australia (2003).

21. Sue Gilchrist and Sarah Strasser, "Full Federal Court Rules that PlayStation 'Mod-Chipping' Infringes Copyright Law," *FindLaw Australia* 53 (2003).

22. Commission of the European Communities, "Directive of the European Parliament and of the Council—On Measures and Procedures to Ensure the Enforcement of Intellectual Property Rights" (January 30, 2003).

23. Richard Smith, "Serious Privacy Problems in Windows Media Player for Windows XP," *ComputerBytesMan.com* (February 20, 2002), http://www.computer bytesman.cm/privacy/wmp8dvd.htm.

24. Paul Goldstein, *Copyright's Highway: From Gutenberg to the Celestial Jukebox* (New York: Hill and Wang, 1994).

25. Nissenbaum makes this point the key to her reconsideration of information privacy issues: The question is less about whether individuals can maintain the privacy of their own personal information, but whether the availability of massive databases and the capacity of interested parties to collect, aggregate, and mine people's public information raises new questions about what people expect can be

done with their public information. Helen Nissenbaum, "Protecting Privacy in an Information Age: The Problem of Privacy in Public," *Law and Philosophy* 17 (1998): 559–596. Helen Nissenbaum, "Privacy as Contextual Integrity," *Washington Law Review* 79.1 (2004): 101–139. The "individual coding" hypothetical I am playing out here is one such application of this concern, where this collected public information can be made into a mechanism by which we are charged differently for the same content—and in politically troubling ways.

26. While digital distribution systems that impose price discriminations, such as the MusicNet and PressPlay music services, have proven less successful than systems like iTunes, which do not discriminate, it is important to remember that the music industry has yet to impose an encryption system like CSS or a rule like regional coding. See Fred von Lohmann, "Measuring the Digital Millennium Copyright Act Against the Darknet: Implications for the Regulation of Technological Protection Measures," *Loyola of Los Angeles Entertainment Law Review* 24 (2004): 635–648.

27. Rick Ellis, "Is 'Transitional Fair Use' The Wave Of The Future?" *AllYourTV.com* (November 28, 2004).

28. Carl Shapiro and Hal Varian, *Information Rules: A Strategic Guide to the Network Economy* (Cambridge, MA: Harvard Business School Press, 1999), 53–82.

29. Active Internet, "DRM Benefits," http://www.activeInternet.com/drm/drm_benefits.asp.

30. AASC, "Introduction and Common Cryptographic Elements v0.90," section 3.1. http://www.aacsla.com/specifications/AACS_Spec-Common_0.90.pdf.

31. For a consideration of the pros and cons and the possible future of micropayments, see Jakob Neilsen, "The Case for Micropayments," blog entry, *Alertbox: Current Issues in Web Usability* (January 25, 1998); Clay Shirky, "The Case against Micropayments," blog entry, *OpenP2P* (December 19, 2000); Clay Shirky, "Fame vs. Fortune: Micropayments and Free Content," blog entry, *Clay Shirky's Writings about the Internet* (September 5, 2003); Scott McCloud, "Misunderstanding Micropayments: BitPass, Shirky and the Good Idea that Refuses to Die," blog entry, *Scott McCloud.com* (September 11, 2003).

32. The Blu-ray format for high-definition DVDs will combine AACS encryption with the ability to regularly check for revoked licenses and compromised content, requiring online connectivity. Bill Rosenblatt, "Blu-Ray Group Announces Content Protection Strategy," *DRM Watch* (August 11, 2005). Windows Media Player connects with Microsoft's server every time a DVD is played, in order to gather title and chapter information. Smith, "Serious Privacy Problems in Windows Media Player for Windows XP."

33. Smith, "Serious Privacy Problems in Windows Media Player for Windows XP."

34. Microsoft, "Features of Windows Media DRM," http://www.microsoft.com/windows/windowsmedia/drm/features.aspx.

35. Andrew Orlowski, "Apple De-Socializes iTunes," *The Register* (March 15, 2005); Jason Schultz, "Meet the New iTunes, Less than the Old iTunes?" *LawGeek* (April 29, 2004).

36. This is related to Lessig's observation that encryption has two purposes: keeping information secret and ensuring identity. Lawrence Lessig, *Code, and Other Laws of Cyberspace* (New York: Basic Books, 1999), 36.

37. Philip Agre and Marc Rotenberg, eds., *Technology and Privacy: The New Landscape* (Cambridge, MA: MIT Press, 1997); Philip Agre, "The Architecture of Identity: Embedding Privacy in Market Institutions," *Information, Communication and Society* 2.1 (1999): 1–25; Julie E. Cohen, "The Law and Technology of Digital Rights Management: DRM and Privacy," *Berkeley Technology Law Journal* 18 (2003): 575–617; Nissenbaum, "Protecting Privacy in an Information Age"; Nissenbaum, "Privacy as Contextual Integrity"; Rohan Samarajiva, "Surveillance by Design: Public Networks and the Control of Consumption," in Robin Mansell and Roger Silverstone, eds., *Communication by Design: The Politics of Information and Communication Technologies* (Oxford: Oxford University Press, 1996): 129–156. Joseph Turow, "Audience Construction and Culture Production: Marketing Surveillance in the Digital Age," *The Annals of the American Academy of Political and Social Science* 597 (2005): 103–121.

38. Turow, "Audience Construction and Culture Production," 115; Samarajiva, "Surveillance by Design," 135–146.

39. Turow, "Audience Construction and Culture Production," 105.

40. Turow, "Audience Construction and Culture Production," 116–117.

41. Benkler raises this point in reference to a 1999 White Paper published by Cisco called "Controlling Your Network—A Must for Cable Operators," http://www.democraticmedia.org/issues/openaccess/cisco.html; Yochai Benkler, "Freedom in the Commons: Toward a Political Economy of Information," *Duke Law Journal* 52 (2003): 1267.

42. HR 5211, "Peer-to-Peer Piracy Prevention Act," introduced July 25, 2002, http://thomas.loc.gov/cgi-bin/bdquery/z?d107:h.r.05211. The bill died in committee.

43. Tom Bell, "Fair Use vs. Fared Use: The Impact of Automated Rights Management on Copyright's Fair Use Doctrine," *North Carolina Law Review* 76 (1998): 557–619.

44. Congressional Budget Office, "Copyright Issues in Digital Media" (August 2004): 23.

45. Talal Shamoon, Executive VP of Intertrust, qtd. in Damien Cave, "Watermarks in Music?" *Salon* (July 31, 2000).

46. Vincent Mosco, "Introduction: Information in the Pay-per Society," in Vincent Mosco and Janet Wasko, eds., *The Political Economy of Information* (Madison: University of Wisconsin Press, 1988), 12.

47. C. Edwin Baker, *Media, Markets, and Democracy* (Cambridge: Cambridge University Press, 2002), 10.

48. Congressional Budget Office, "Copyright Issues in Digital Media," 26.

49. Microsoft, "Benefits of Windows Media DRM," http://www.microsoft.com/windows/windowsmedia/drm/benefits.aspx.

50. Benkler, "Freedom in the Commons," 1253.

51. Rick Boucher, "'Pay-Per-Use' Society One Step Closer," Washington, DC (November 2, 2000).

52. Robin Gross, "World Summit to Create 'Pay-Per-Use' Society: Human Rights Ignored as Big Business Dominates Geneva," IP Justice, Geneva, Switzerland (December 21, 2003), http://www.ipjustice.org/WSIS/IPJ_WSIS_Report.html.

53. Mosco, "Introduction," 12.

54. James Boyle, "The Second Enclosure Movement and the Construction of the Public Domain," *Law and Contemporary Problems* 66.1+2 (2003): 33–74.

55. Rosemary J. Coombe, *The Cultural Life of Intellectual Properties: Authorship, Appropriation, and the Law* (Durham, NC: Duke University Press, 1998); Jane Gaines, *Contested Culture: The Image, the Voice, and the Law* (Chapel Hill, NC: University of North Carolina Press, 1991), 228–240; Dick Hebdige, *Subculture: The Meaning of Style* (London: Methuen, 1979); Dick Hebdige, *Cut 'n' Mix: Culture, Identity, and Caribbean Music* (London; New York: Routledge, 1990); Andrew Herman and John Sloop, "The Politics of Authenticity in Postmodern Rock Culture: The Case of Negativland and The Letter 'U' and the Numeral '2'," *Critical Studies in Mass Communication* 15.1 (March 1998): 1–20; Sam Howard-Spink, "Grey Tuesday, Online Cultural Activism and the Mash-up of Music and Politics," *First Monday* 9.10 (October 2004); Matt Jackson, "Commerce versus Art: The Transformation of Fair Use," *Journal of Broadcasting & Electronic Media* 39.2 (Spring 1995): 190–199; Henry Jenkins, "Quentin Tarantino's Star Wars?: Digital Cinema, Media Convergence, and Participatory Culture," in David Thorburn and Henry Jenkins, eds., *Rethinking Media Change: The Aesthetics of Transition* (Cambridge, MA: MIT Press, 2003): 281–312; Lawrence Lessig, *Free Culture: How Big Media Uses Technology and the Law to Lock Down Culture and Control Creativity* (New York: Penguin Books, 2004); Thomas Schumacher, "'This Is a Sampling Sport': Digital Sampling, Rap Music, and the Law in Cultural Production," *Media, Culture and Society* 17.2 (April 1995): 253–274; Siva Vaidhyanathan, *Copyrights and Copywrongs: The Rise of Intellectual Property and How It Threatens Creativity* (New York: New York University Press, 2001), 132–145; Lauren Yamamoto, "Copyright Protection and Internet Fan Sites: Entertainment Industry Finds Solace

in Traditional Copyright Law," *Loyola of Los Angeles Entertainment Law Review* 20.1 (2000): 95–128.

56. Matt Jackson, "Using Technology to Circumvent the Law: The DMCA's Push to Privatize Copyright," *Hastings Communications and Entertainment Law Journal* 23 (2001): 610.

57. C. Edwin Baker, *Human Liberty and Freedom of Speech* (New York: Oxford University Press, 1989), chap. 9; Robert Horwitz, "The First Amendment Meets Some New Technologies: Broadcasting, Common Carriers, and Free Speech in the 1990s," *Theory and Society* 20.1 (February 1991): 21–72.

58. http://www.freeculture.org/.

59. http://www.creativecommmons.org/.

60. David Berry, "The Contestation of Code: A Preliminary Investigation into the Discourse of the Free/Libre and Open Source Movements," *Critical Discourse Studies* 1.1 (April 2004): 65–89; Tom Coates, "(Weblogs and) the Mass Amateurisation of (Nearly) Everything . . . ," *Plasticbag.org* (September 3, 2003), http://www.plasticbag .org/archives/2003/09/weblogs_and_the_mass_amateurisation_of_nearly_every thing.shtml; Howard-Spink, "Grey Tuesday, Online Cultural Activism and the Mash-up of Music and Politics"; Lasica, *Darknet*, 67–85; Clay Shirky, "Weblogs and the Mass Amateurization of Publishing," *Clay Shirky's Writings about the Internet* (October 3, 2002); Michael Strangelove, *The Empire of Mind: Digital Piracy and the Anti-Capitalist Movement* (Toronto: University of Toronto Press, 2005), 99–133; Siva Vaidhyanathan, "The State of Copyright Activism," *First Monday* 9.4 (2004); Siva Vaidhyanathan, "Afterword: Critical Information Studies: A Bibliographic Manifesto," *Cultural Studies* 20.2–3 (2006): 292–315.

61. For a discussion of the lawsuit brought by the Association of American Publishers against Google for its "Google Library," see Jonathan Band, "The Google Print Library Project: A Copyright Analysis," *Association of Research Libraries, Bimonthly Report* 242 (October 2005): 6–9; Tarleton Gillespie, "Everything to Everyone," *Inside Higher Ed* (January 27, 2006); Lawrence Lessig, "Google's Tough Call," *Wired* 13.11 (November 2005); Wade Roush, "The Infinite Library: Does Google's Plan to Digitize Millions of Print Books Spell the Death of Libraries, or Their Rebirth?" *Technology Review* (May 2005); Siva Vaidhyanathan, "A Risky Gamble with Google," *The Chronicle of Higher Education* 15 (December 2, 2005): B7.

References

A&M Records, Inc., et al. v. Napster, Inc. 239 F.3d 1004. 9th Cir. 2001.

Abbate, Janet. *Inventing the Internet.* Cambridge, MA: MIT Press, 1999.

Agre, Philip, and Marc Rotenberg, eds. *Technology and Privacy: The New Landscape.* Cambridge, MA: MIT Press, 1997.

Akrich, Madeleine. "The De-scription of Technical Objects." In Wiebe Bijker and John Law, eds., *Shaping Technology/Building Society: Studies in Sociotechnical Change*, 205–224. Cambridge, MA: MIT Press, 1992.

Akrich, Madeleine. "User Representations: Practices, Methods, and Sociology." In Arie Rip, Thomas Misa, and Johan Schot, eds., *Managing Technology in Society: The Approach of Constructive Technology Assessment*, 167–184. London: Pinter Publishers, 1995.

Alderman, John. "Rio Debut Back on Track." *Wired News* (October 27, 1998). http://www.wirednews.com/news/print/0,1294,15847,00.html.

Alderman, John. *Sonic Boom: Napster, MP3, and the New Pioneers of Music.* Cambridge, MA: Perseus, 2001.

American Library Association, et al. v. Federal Communications Commission and United States of America. 406 F.3d 689. U.S. App. D.C. 2005.

Ang, Ien. *Desperately Seeking the Audience.* London: Routledge, 1991.

Ang, Ien. *Living Room Wars: Rethinking Media Audiences for a Postmodern World.* London: Routledge, 1996.

Ante, Spencer. "Shawn Fanning's Struggle." *Business Week* (May 1, 2000: 197).

Arthur, Charles. "Revealed: The Tech Consumer as Prawn." *The Register* (February 7, 2005). http://www.theregister.co.uk/2005/02/07/regionalism_analysis/.

Attaway, Fritz, and Tod Cohen. "Comments of the Motion Picture Association of America, In the Matter of Carriage of Transmissions of Digital Television

Broadcast Stations, CS Docket #98-120, Amendments to Part 76 of the Commission's Rules." Federal Communications Commission (September 17, 1998). "Audio Home Recording Act." *17 U.S.C. §§1001–1010* (1992).

Baker, C. Edwin. *Human Liberty and Freedom of Speech.* New York: Oxford University Press, 1989.

Baker, C. Edwin. *Media, Markets, and Democracy.* Cambridge: Cambridge University Press, 2002.

Band, Jonathan. "The Google Print Library Project: A Copyright Analysis." *Association of Research Libraries, Bimonthly Report* 242 (October 2005): 6–9. http://www.arl.org/newsltr/242/google.html.

Barbrook, Richard. "The High-Tech Gift Economy." In Josephine Bosma, ed., *Readme! Filtered by Nettime: ASCII Culture and the Revenge of Knowledge*, 133–139. Brooklyn: Autonomedia, 1999.

Barlow, John Perry. "Selling Wine without Bottles: The Economy of Mind on the Global Net." In Peter Ludlow, ed., *High Noon on the Electronic Frontier: Conceptual Issues in Cyberspace*, 9–35. Cambridge, MA: MIT Press, 1996.

Bartow, Ann. "Electrifying Copyright Norms and Making Cyberspace More Like a Book." *Villanova Law Review* 48 (2003): 101–206.

Bateson, Gregory. *Steps to an Ecology of Mind.* Chicago: University of Chicago Press, 2000.

Bechtold, Stefan. "From Copyright to Information Law—Implications of Digital Rights Management." In Tomas Sander, ed., *Security and Privacy in Digital Rights Management*, 2320. Lecture Notes in Computer Science, 213–232. Berlin: Springer, 2002. http://www.jura.uni-tuebingen.de/bechtold/pub/2002/DRM_Information_Law.pdf.

Bechtold, Stefan. "The Present and Future of Digital Rights Management: Musings on Emerging Legal Problems." In Eberhard Becker, Willms Buhse, Dirk Günnewig, and Neils Rump, eds., *Digital Rights Management—Technological, Economic, Legal and Political Aspects*, 597–654. Berlin: Springer, 2003.

Bell, Daniel. "The Social Framework of the Information Society." In Michael Dertouzos and Joel Moses, eds., *The Computer Age: A Twenty-Year View*, 163–211. Cambridge, MA: MIT Press, 1979.

Bell, Tom. "Fair Use vs. Fared Use: The Impact of Automated Rights Management on Copyright's Fair Use Doctrine." *North Carolina Law Review* 76 (January 1998): 557–619.

Bell, Tom. "Escape from Copyright: Market Success vs. Statutory Failure in the Protection of Expressive Works." *University of Cincinnati Law Review* 69 (2001): 741–805. http://www.tomwbell.com/writings/(C)Esc.html.

Benkler, Yochai. "Coase's Penguin, or Linux and the Nature of the Firm." *Yale Law Journal* 112.3 (2002): 369–446.

Benkler, Yochai. "From Consumers to Users: Shifting the Deeper Structures of Regulation toward Sustainable Commons and User Access." *Federal Communications Law Journal* 52 (May 2000): 561–579. http://www.nyu.edu/pages/lawreview/74/2/benkler.pdf.

Benkler, Yochai. "Intellectual Property and the Organization of Information Production." *International Review of Law and Economics* 22 (2002): 81–107. http://www.law.nyu.edu/benklery/IP&Organization.pdf.

Benkler, Yochai. "Freedom in the Commons: Towards a Political Economy of Information." *Duke Law Journal* 52 (2003): 1245–1276. http://www.law.duke.edu/shell/cite.pl?52+Duke+L.+J.+1245.

Benkler, Yochai. "Sharing Nicely; On Shareable Goods and the Emergence of Sharing as a Modality of Economic Production." *Yale Law Journal* 114.2 (2004): 273–358. http://www.yalelawjournal.org/archive_abstract.asp?id=94.

Benkler, Yochai. *The Wealth of Networks: How Social Production Transforms Markets and Freedom*. New Haven: Yale University Press, 2006.

Berman, Howard. "Introduction of the Peer to Peer Piracy Prevention Act." U.S. House of Representatives (July 25, 2002). http://www.house.gov/apps/list/speech/ca28_berman/piracy_prevention_act.html.

Berry, David. "The Contestation of Code: A Preliminary Investigation into the Discourse of the Free/Libre and Open Source Movements." *Critical Discourse Studies* 1.1 (April 2004): 65–89.

Bettig, Ronald. "Critical Perspectives on the History and Philosophy of Copyright." *Critical Studies in Mass Communication* 9.21992: 131–155.

Bhattacharjee, Sudip, Ram Gopal, Kaveepan Lertwachara, James Mardsen, and Rahul Telang. "The Effect of P2P File Sharing on Music Markets: A Survival Analysis of Albums on Ranking Charts." Working Paper #05–26 Networks, Electronic Commerce, and Telecommunications Institute (October 2005). http://www.netinst.org/Telang2005.pdf.

Biddle, Peter, Paul England, Marcus Peinado, and Bryan William. "The Darknet and the Future of Content Distribution." Paper presented at ACM Workshop on Digital Rights Management, Stanford, CA (2002). http://crypto.stanford.edu/DRM2002/darknet5.doc.

Biegel, Stuart. *Beyond Our Control?: Confronting the Limits of Our Legal System in the Age of Cyberspace*. Cambridge, MA: MIT Press, 2001.

Bijker, Wiebe. "Do Not Despair: There Is Life after Constructivism." *Science, Technology, and Human Values* 18.1 (Winter 1993): 113–138.

Bijker, Wiebe. *Of Bicycles, Bakelites, and Bulbs: Toward a Theory of Sociotechnical Change*. Cambridge, MA: MIT Press, 1995.

Bijker, Wiebe, Thomas Hughes, and Trevor Pinch, eds. *The Social Construction of Technological Systems: New Directions in the Sociology and History of Technology*. Cambridge, Mass.: MIT Press, 1987.

Bijker, Wiebe E., and John Law, eds. *Shaping Technology/Building Society: Studies in Sociotechnical Change*. Cambridge, MA: MIT Press, 1992.

Boczkowski, Pablo, and Leah Lievrouw. "Bridging STS and Communication Studies: Scholarship on Media and Information Technologies." In Edward Hackett, Olga Amsterdamksa, Michael Lynch, and Judy Wajcman, eds., *New Handbook of Science and Technology Studies*. Cambridge, MA: MIT Press, forthcoming.

Bolter, J. David, and Richard Grusin. *Remediation: Understanding New Media*. Cambridge, MA: MIT Press, 1999.

Boorstin, Eric. "Music Sales in the Age of File Sharing." B.A. thesis, Princeton University (2004).

Borland, John. "SDMI Antipiracy Effort Loses Leader." *CNet* (January 24, 2001). http://news.com.com/SDMI+antipiracy+effort+loses+leader/2100-1023_3-251465.html.

Borland, John. "Hardwiring Copyrights: Antipiracy Efforts Spark Battle over Computer Hardware." *CNet* (March 23, 2001). http://news.com.com/Hardwiring+copyrights/2009-1023_3-254549.html.

Borland, John. "FAQ: Sony 'Rootkit' CDs." *CNet* (November 11, 2005). http://news.com.com/FAQ+Sonys+rootkit+CDs/2100-1029_3-5946760.html.

Boucher, Rick. "'Pay-Per-Use' Society One Step Closer." Washington, DC (November 2, 2000). http://www.arl.org/info/frn/copy/boucherpr.html.

Bowker, Geoffrey, and Susan Leigh Star. "How to Infrastructure." In Leah Lievrouw and Sonia Livingstone, eds., *The Handbook of New Media: Social Shaping and Consequences of ICTs*, 151–1162. London: Sage, 2002.

Boyd-Barrett, Oliver. "Media Imperialism: Towards an International Framework for an Analysis of Media Systems." In James Curran, Michael Gurevitch, and Janet Woollacott, eds., *Mass Communication and Society*, 116–135. London: Edward Arnold, 1977.

Boyle, James. *Shamans, Software, and Spleens: Law and the Construction of the Information Society*. Cambridge, MA: Harvard University Press, 1996.

Boyle, James. "The Second Enclosure Movement and the Construction of the Public Domain." *Law and Contemporary Problems* 66.1+2 (Winter/Spring 2003): 33–74. www.law.duke.edu/pd/papers/boyle.pdf.

Bradner, Scott. "The Internet Engineering Task Force." In Chris Dibona, Sam Ockman, and Mark Stone, eds., *Open Sources: Voices from the Open Source Revolution*, 47–52. Cambridge, MA: O'Reilly and Associates, 1999. http://www.oreilly.com/catalog/opensources/book/ietf.html.

Branscomb, Ann. "Law and Culture in the Information Society." *The Information Society* 4.4 (1986): 279–311.

Branscomb, Anne. *Who Owns Information?: From Privacy to Public Access*. New York: Basic Books, 1994.

Bridis, Ted. "Tech Giants out to Ambush MP3." *ZDNet* (April 12, 2001). http://www.zdnet.com/filters/printerfriendly/0,6061,2707267-2,00.html.

Broadcast Protection Discussion Group. "Final Report of the Co-Chairs of the Broadcast Protection Discussion Subgroup to the Copy Protection Technical Working Group" (June 3, 2002). http://www.cptwg.org/html/Bpdg_home_page.htm.

Brown, Janelle. "Is the SDMI Boycott Backfiring?" *Salon* (October 3, 2000). http://www.salon.com/tech/feature/2000/10/03/hacksdmi_fallout/print.html.

Brown, John Seely, and Paul Duguid. *The Social Life of Information*. Boston: Harvard Business School Press, 2000.

Bruckman, Amy. "Studying the Amateur Artist: A Perspective on Disguising Data Collected in Human Subjects Research on the Internet." *Ethics and Information Technology* 4.3 (2002): 217–231. http://www.nyu.edu/projects/nissenbaum/ethics_bru_full.html.

Brull, Steven. "Net Nightmare for the Music Biz." *Business Week* (March 2, 1998): 89–90. http://www.businessweek.com/1998/09/b3567132.htm.

Brunsdon, Charlotte, Julie D'Acci, and Lynn Spigel, eds. *Feminist Television Criticism*. Oxford: Clarendon Press, 1997.

Bucholz, Ren. "File Sharing, Information Policy, and Democratic Public Spheres." Discussion paper, Necessary Knowledge for a Democratic Public Sphere, Social Science Research Council (2005). http://www.ssrc.org/programs/media/publications/bucholz.4.final.doc.

Burk, Dan. "Muddy Rules for Cyberspace." *Cardozo Law Review* 21 (October 1999): 121–179.

Burk, Dan. "Anti-Circumvention Misuse." *UCLA Law Review* 50 (2003): 1095–1140. http://ssrn.com/abstract=320961.

Burk, Dan. "Legal and Technical Standards in Digital Rights Management Technology." Minnesota Legal Studies Research Paper #05-16 (2005). http://ssrn.com/abstract=699384.

Burk, Dan. "Law as a Network Standard." *Yale Journal of Law and Technology* (Fall 2005). http://islandia.law.yale.edu/isp/GlobalFlow/paper/Burk.pdf.

Burk, Dan, and Julie Cohen. "Fair Use Infrastructure for Rights Management Systems." *Harvard Journal of Law & Technology* 15.1 (2001): 42–83. http://jolt.law .harvard.edu/articles/pdf/15HarvJLTech041.pdf.

Burke, Lynn. "Teen Hacker's Home Raided." *Wired News* (January 25, 2000). http://www.wired.com/news/print/0,1294,33889,00.html.

Business Software Alliance, Computer Systems Policy Project, and Recording Industry Association of America. "Technology and Record Company Policy Principles" (January 14, 2003). http://www.riaa.com/News/newsletter/pdf/techprincipalsfinal. pdf.

Caldwell, John. *Televisuality: Style, Crisis, and Authority in American Television*. New Brunswick, NJ: Rutgers University Press, 1995.

Caldwell, John, ed. *Electronic Media and Technoculture*. New Brunswick, NJ: Rutgers University Press, 2000.

Caldwell, John. "Introduction: Theorizing the Digital Landrush." In John Caldwell, ed., *Electronic Media and Technoculture*, 1–31. New Brunswick, NJ: Rutgers University Press, 2000.

Callon, Michel. "Some Elements of a Sociology of Translation: Domestication of Scallops and the Fishermen of St. Brieuc Bay." In John Law, ed., *Power, Action and Belief: A New Sociology of Knowledge?* 196–229. London: Routledge, 1986.

Campbell v. Acuff-Rose Music, Inc. 510 U.S. 569. U.S. S. Ct. 1994.

Carey, James. *Communication as Culture: Essays on Media and Society*. New York: Routledge, 1992.

Carey, James, and John J. Quirk. "The Mythos of the Electronic Revolution." In James Carey, ed., *Communication as Culture: Essays on Media and Society*, 113–141. New York: Routledge, 1992.

Carlson, W. Bernard. "Artifacts and Frames of Meaning: Thomas A. Edison, His Managers, and the Cultural Construction of Motion Pictures." In Wiebe Bijker and John Law, eds., *Shaping Technology/Building Society: Studies in Sociotechnical Change*, 175–200. Cambridge, MA: MIT Press.

Carroll, Michael. "A Primer on U.S. Intellectual Property Rights Applicable to Music Information Retrieval Systems." *Illinois Journal of Law, Technology, & Policy* 2003.2 (Fall 2003): 313–328.

Caruso, Denise. "A Tough Stance on Cyberspace Copyrights." *New York Times* (January 19, 1998). http://www.georgetown.edu/grad/CCT/courses/copytext.htm.

Castells, Manuel. *The Rise of the Network Society*. Oxford: Blackwell Publishers, 2000.

Cave, Damien. "Studio Technician." *Salon* (February 14, 2000). http://www.salon.com/tech/view/2000/02/14/valenti.

Cave, Damien. "Watermarks in Music?" *Salon* (July 31, 2000). http://archive.salon.com/tech/view/2000/07/31/sdmi/index.html.

"CD Crack: Magic Marker Indeed." *Wired News* (May 20, 2002). http://www.wired.com/news/technology/0,1282,52665,00.html.

Center for Democracy and Technology. "Implications of the Broadcast Flag: A Public Interest Primer." Washington, DC (December 2003).

Center for Democracy and Technology. "The Broadcast Flag: An Introduction." Online FAQ (May 23, 2004). http://www.cdt.org/copyright/broadcastflag/introduction.php.

Center for Democracy and Technology. "Mapping the Digital Video Copyright Landscape: Stakeholder Interests and the Internet." Washington, DC (March 2004). http://www.cdt.org/publications/copyright-matrix.shtml.

Chon, Margaret. "Paracopyright and the Digital Divide: Anti-Circumvention Provisions and Control Over Digital Information." Paper presented at Copyright's Balance in an Internet World, University of Dayton School of Law Symposium (2000).

Clark, Drew, and Bara Vaida. "Digital Divide: Hollywood vs. Silicon Valley." *National Journal's Technology Daily* (September 6, 2002). http://nationaljournal.com/about/njweekly/stories/2002/0906nj1.htm.

Clarke, Roger. "'Information Wants to Be Free . . .'" (2000). http://www.anu.edu.au/people/Roger.Clarke/II/IWtbF.html.

Coates, Tom. "(Weblogs and) the Mass Amateurisation of (Nearly) Everything . . ." *Plasticbag.org* (September 3, 2003). http://www.plasticbag.org/archives/2003/09/weblogs_and_the_mass_amateurisation_of_nearly_everything.shtml.

Cohen, Julie. "A Right to Read Anonymously: A Closer Look at 'Copyright Management' in Cyberspace." *Connecticut Law Review* 28 (Summer 1996): 981–1039.

Cohen, Julie. "Some Reflections on Copyright Management Systems and Laws Designed to Protect Them." *Berkeley Technology Law Journal* 12 (1997): 161–190. www.law.berkeley.edu/journals/btlj/articles/vol12/Cohen/html/text.html.

Cohen, Julie. "Lochner in Cyberspace: The New Economic Orthodoxy of 'Rights Management.'" *Michigan Law Review* 97.2 (1998): 462, 480–563. http://ssrn.com/abstract=128230.

Cohen, Julie. "Copyright and the Jurisprudence of Self-Help." *Berkeley Technology Law Journal* 13 (1998): 1089–1143. http://www.law.georgetown.edu/faculty/jec/self_help.pdf.

Cohen, Julie. "The Law and Technology of Digital Rights Management: DRM and Privacy." *Berkeley Technology Law Journal* 18 (2003): 575–617.

Cohen, Julie. "Pervasively Distributed Copyright Enforcement." *Georgetown Law Journal* 95.1 (2006): 1–48.

Cole, Michael. *Cultural Psychology: A Once and Future Discipline*. Cambridge, MA: Belknap Press of Harvard University Press, 1996.

Cole, Michael, and Yrjö Engeström. "A Cultural-Historical Approach to Distributed Cognition." In Gavriel Salomon, ed., *Distributed Cognitions: Psychological and Educational Considerations*, 1–46. Cambridge: Cambridge University Press, 1993.

Collins, Harry, and Trevor Pinch. *The Golem: What You Should Know about Science*. Cambridge: Cambridge University Press, 1998.

Commission of the European Communities. "Directive of the European Parliament and of the Council—On Measures and Procedures to Ensure the Enforcement of Intellectual Property Rights" (January 30, 2003). http://eur-lex.europa.eu/Lex UriServ/site/en/com/2003/com2003_0046en01.pdf.

Congressional Budget Office. "Copyright Issues in Digital Media" (August 2004).

Consumer Electronics Association. "Digital America" (2005). http://www.ce.org/Press/CEA_Pubs/819.asp.

Coombe, Rosemary J. *The Cultural Life of Intellectual Properties: Authorship, Appropriation, and the Law*. Durham, NC: Duke University Press, 1998.

Coral Consortium. "Entertainment, Technology and Consumer Electronics Leaders Unite for DRM Interoperability." Press release, Sunnyvale, CA (October 4, 2004). http://www.intertrust.com/main/news/2003_2005/041004_coral.html.

Corner, John. *Critical Ideas in Television Studies*. Oxford: Clarendon Press, 1999.

Craver, Scott, Min Wu, Bede Liu, Adam Stubblefield, Ben Swartlander, Dan Wallach, Drew Dean, and Edward Felten. "Reading between the Lines: Lessons from the SDMI Challenge." Paper presented at 10th USENIX Security Symposium, Washington, DC (August 13–17, 2001). http://www.usenix.org/events/sec01/craver.pdf.

Crawford, Susan. "The Biology of the Broadcast Flag." *Hastings Communications and Entertainment Law Journal* 25.2 (2004): 603–652. http://ssrn.com/abstract=500763.

Crichter, Chas. *Moral Panics and the Media*. Philadelphia: Open University Press, 2003.

Crichter, Chas. *Critical Readings: Moral Panics and the Media*. Maidenhead, UK: Open University Press, 2005.

Czitrom, Daniel. *Media and the American Mind: From Morse to McLuhan*. Chapel Hill: University of North Carolina Press, 1982.

Dam, Kenneth. "Self-Help in the Digital Jungle." *Journal of Legal Studies* 28.2 (1999): 393–412. http://ssrn.com/abstract=157448.

Danay, Robert. "Copyright vs. Free Expression: The Case of Peer-to-Peer File-Sharing of Music in the United Kingdom." *International Journal of Communications Law & Policy* 10 (2005). http://www.ijclp.org/10_2005/pdf/ijclp_02_10_2005.pdf.

David, Paul. "Clio and the Economics of QWERTY." *American Economic Review* 75.2 (May 1985): 332–337.

David, Paul, and Mark Shurmer. "Formal Standards-Setting for Global Telecommunications and Information Services." *Telecommunications Policy* 20.10 (1996): 789–815.

David, Shay. "Opening the Sources of Accountability." *First Monday* 9.11 (2004). http://www.firstmonday.org/issues/issue9_11/david/index.html.

Dick, Philip K. *The Philip K. Dick Reader.* New York: Pantheon Books, 2001.

"Digital Millennium Copyright Act." Vol. 17 U.S.C. 512, Chapter 12 of Title 17 of the U.S.C. (1998).

Doctorow, Cory. "Microsoft Research DRM Talk." Paper presented to Microsoft Research Group, Redmond, WA (June 17, 2004). http://www.craphound.com/msftdrm.txt.

Douglas, Susan. *Inventing American Broadcasting, 1899–1922.* Baltimore: Johns Hopkins University Press, 1987.

Drake, William. "The Internet Religious War." *Telecommunications Policy* 17.9 (December 1993): 643–649.

Duguid, Paul. "Material Matters: The Past and Futurology of the Book." In Geoffrey Nunberg, ed., *The Future of the Book,* 63–102. Berkeley: University of California Press, 1996. http://www.sociallifeofinformation.com/Material_Matters.htm.

"DVD-Cracking Teen Acquitted." *Wired News* (January 7, 2003). http://www.wired.com/news/politics/0,1283,57107,00.html.

"DVD Demystified." *DVD Frequently Asked Questions (and Answers).* Online FAQ (May 19, 2006). http://www.dvddemystified.com/dvdfaq.html.

Dyer, Richard. "Making 'White' People White." In Donald MacKenzie and Judy Wajcman, eds., *The Social Shaping of Technology,* 134–140. Buckingham, UK: Open University Press, 1999.

Dyson, Esther. "Intellectual Property on the Net." Electronic Frontier Foundation (1995). http://www.eff.org/Misc/Publications/Esther_Dyson/ip_on_the_net.article.

Dyson, Esther. "Intellectual Value." *Wired* 3.07 (July 1995): 136–141, 182–184.

Edwards, Paul. *The Closed World: Computers and the Politics of Discourse in Cold War America.* Cambridge, MA: MIT Press, 1996.

Eglash, Ron. "Appropriating Technology: An Introduction." In Ron Eglash, Jennifer Crossiant, Giovanna Di Chiro, and Rayvon Fouché, eds., *Appropriating Technology: Vernacular Science and Social Power*, vii–xxi. Minneapolis: University of Minnesota Press, 2004. http://www.rpi.edu/~eglash/eglash.dir/at/intro.htm.

Eisenstein, Elizabeth. *The Printing Revolution in Early Modern Europe.* Cambridge: Cambridge University Press, 1983.

Eisenstein, Elizabeth. "An Unacknowledged Revolution Revisited." *American Historical Review* 107.1 (2002): 87–105.

Eisenstein, Elizabeth. "Reply." *American Historical Review* 107.1 (2002): 126.

Electronic Frontier Foundation. "EFF Calls for Boycott of 'Hack SDMI Challenge.'" Press release, Washington, DC (September 18, 2000). http://www.eff .org/IP/Audio/SDMI/?f=20000918_eff_hacksdmi_boycott.html.

Electronic Frontier Foundation. "EFF Renews Its Call to Boycott the 'Hack SDMI' Challenge." Press release, Washington DC (September 29, 2000). http://www.eff .org/IP/Audio/SDMI/?f=20000929_eff_hacksdmi_revised_boycott.html.

Elkin-Koren, Niva. "It's All About Control: Rethinking Copyright in the New Information Landscape." In Niva Elkin-Koren and Neil Netanel, eds., *The Commodification of Information*, 79–106. Hague: Kluwer Law International, 2002.

Ellis, Rick. "Is 'Transitional Fair Use' The Wave of the Future?" *AllYourTV.com* (November 28, 2004). http://www.allyourtv.com/0405season/news/november/ 11282004transitional.html.

Engeström, Yrjö. "When Is a Tool? Multiple Meanings of Artifacts in Human Activity." In Yrjö Engeström, ed., *Learning, Working and Imagining: Twelve Studies in Activity Theory*, 171–195. Helsinki: Orienta-Konsultit, 1990.

Erickson, John. "Fair Use, DRM, and Trusted Computing." *Communications of the ACM* 46.4 (2003): 34–39.

Eschenfelder, Kristin, and Anuj Desai. "Software as Protest: The Unexpected Resiliency of U.S.-Based DeCSS Posting and Linking." *The Information Society* 20.2 (2004): 101–116.

Federal Communications Commission. "In the Matter of: Digital Broadcast Copy Protection—Notice of Proposed Rulemaking." MB Docket 02-230, #02-231 (August 8, 2002).

Federal Communications Commission. "In the Matter of: Digital Broadcast Content Protection—Report and Order and Further Notice of Proposed Rulemaking." MB Docket 02-230, #03-273 (November 4, 2003).

Federal Trade Commission and U.S. Department of Justice. "Antitrust Guidelines for Collaboration among Competitors" (2000). http://www.ftc.gov/os/2000/04/ftcdojguidelines.pdf.

Feist Enterprises, Inc. v. Rural Telephone Service Co. 499 340. U.S. S. Ct. 1991.

Felten, Edward. "A Skeptical View of DRM and Fair Use." *Communications of the ACM* 46.4 (2003): 57–59.

Fischer, Claude. *America Calling: A Social History of the Telephone to 1940.* Berkeley: University of California Press, 1992.

Fisher, William. "The Growth of Intellectual Property: A History of the Ownership of Ideas in the United States." In *Eigentum im Internationalen Vergleich,* 265–291. Göttingen, Germany: Vandenhoeck & Ruprecht, 1999. http://cyber.law.harvard.edu/people/tfisher/iphistory.pdf.

Fisher, William. "Theories of Intellectual Property." In Stephen Munzer, ed. *New Essays in the Legal and Political Theory of Property,* 168–200. Cambridge: Cambridge University Press, 2001.

Fisher, William. *Promises to Keep: Technology, Law, and the Future of Entertainment.* Stanford, CA: Stanford University Press, 2004.

Fiske, John. *Television Culture.* London: Methuen, 1987.

Fiss, Owen. *Liberalism Divided: Freedom of Speech and the Many Uses of State Power.* Boulder, CO: Westview Press, 1996.

Flanagan, Mary, Daniel Howe, and Helen Nissenbaum. "Embodying Values in Technology: Theory and Practice." Unpublished manuscript (August 31, 2005). http://www.nyu.edu/projects/nissenbaum/papers/Nissenbaum-VID.4-25.pdf.

Folsom v. Marsh. 9 9F Cas. 342. C.C.D. Mass. 1841.

Foucault, Michel. *Discipline and Punish: The Birth of the Prison.* New York: Pantheon, 1977.

Foucault, Michel. "What Is an Author?" In Josue Harari, ed., *Textual Strategies: Perspectives in Post-Structural Criticism,* 141–160. Ithaca, NY: Cornell University Press, 1979.

Friedman, Batya, and Helen Nissenbaum. "Bias in Computer Systems." *ACM Transactions on Information Systems* 14.3 (1996): 330–347.

Froomkin, Michael. "The Death of Privacy?" *Stanford Law Review* 52 (2000): 1461–1543. http://personal.law.miami.edu/~froomkin/articles/privacy-deathof.pdf.

Gaines, Jane. *Contested Culture: The Image, the Voice, and the Law.* Chapel Hill: University of North Carolina Press, 1991.

Galloway, Alexander. "Global Networks and the Effects on Culture." *The Annals of the American Academy of Political and Social Science* 597.1 (January 2005): 19–31.

Gandy, Oscar. "The Real Digital Divide: Citizens versus Consumers." In Leah Lievrouw and Sonia Livingstone, eds., *The Handbook of New Media: Social Shaping and Consequences of ICTs*, 448–460. London: Sage, 2002.

Garfinkel, Simson. "The Web's Unelected Government." *Technology Review* (November/December 1998): 38–47. http://www.technologyreview.com/read_article.aspx?id=11776&ch=infotech.

Garfinkel, Simson. *Database Nation: The Death of Privacy in the 21st Century*. Sebastopol, CA: O'Reilly & Associates, 2000.

Gates, Kelly. "Will Work for Copyrights: The Cultural Policy of Anti-Piracy Campaigns." *Social Semiotics* 16.1 (April 2006): 57–73.

Gaver, William. "Technology Affordances." *Proceedings of the SIGCHI Conference on Human Factors in Computing Systems: Reaching through Technology*, 79–84. New Orleans: ACM Press, 1991.

Gay, Geri, and Helene Hembrooke. *Activity-Centered Design: An Ecological Approach to Designing Smart Tools and Usable Systems*. Cambridge, MA: MIT Press, 2004.

Geertz, Clifford. *The Interpretation of Cultures: Selected Essays*. New York: Basic Books, 1973.

Gibson, James. "The Theory of Affordances." In Robert Shaw and John Bransford, eds., *Perceiving, Acting, and Knowing: Toward an Ecological Psychology*, 62–82. Hillsdale, NJ: Lawrence Erlbaum Associates, 1977.

Giddens, Anthony. *The Constitution of Society: Outline of the Theory of Structuration*. Cambridge: Polity Press, 1984.

Gieryn, Thomas. "Boundary-Work and the Demarcation of Science from Non-Science: Strains and Interests in Professional Ideologies of Scientists." *American Sociological Review* 48 (1983): 781–795.

Gieryn, Thomas. *Cultural Boundaries of Science: Credibility on the Line*. Chicago: University of Chicago Press, 1999.

Gieryn, Thomas. "What Buildings Do." *Theory and Society* 31 (2002): 35–74.

Gilchrist, Sue, and Sarah Strasser. "Full Federal Court Rules that PlayStation 'Mod-Chipping' Infringes Copyright Law." *FindLaw Australia* 53 (August 2003). http://www.findlaw.com.au/articles/default.asp?task=read&id=9574&site=GN.

Gillespie, Tarleton. "The Stories Digital Tools Tell." In John Caldwell and Anna Everett, eds., *New Media: Theses on Convergence, Media, and Digital Reproduction*, 107–126. London: Routledge, 2003.

Gillespie, Tarleton. "Copyright and Commerce: The DMCA, Trusted Systems, and the Stabilization of Distribution." *The Information Society* 24.4 (September 2004): 239–254.

Gillespie, Tarleton. "Engineering a Principle: 'End-to-End' in the Design of the Internet." *Social Studies of Science* 36.3 (June 2006): 427–457.

Gillespie, Tarleton. "Designed to 'Effectively Frustrate': Copyright, Technology, and the Agency of Users." *New Media & Society* 8.4 (2006): 651–669.

Gillespie, Tarleton. "Book Review: Steven Weber, 'The Success of Open Source.'" *Isis* 97.3 (September 2006): 592–593.

Gillespie, Tarleton. "Everything to Everyone." *Inside Higher Ed* (January 27, 2006). http://www.insidehighered.com/views/2006/01/27/gillespie.

Gillespie, Tarleton. "Price Discrimination, Regional Coding, and the Shape of the Digital Commodity." In Joe Karaganis and Natalie Jeremijenko, eds., *Structures of Participation in Digital Culture*. Durham, NC: Duke University Press, forthcoming.

Gilmore, John. "What's Wrong with Copy Protection" (February 16, 2001). http://www.toad.com/gnu/whatswrong.html.

Ginsburg, Jane. "A Tale of Two Copyrights: Literary Property in Revolutionary France and America." *Tulane Law Review* 64 (1990): 991–1031.

Ginsburg, Jane. "Copyright and Control over New Technologies of Dissemination." *Columbia Law Review* 101 (2001): 1613–1647.

Ginsburg, Jane. "From Having Copies to Experiencing Works: The Development of an Access Right in U.S. Copyright Law." *Journal of the Copyright Society of the USA* 50 (2003): 113–132. http://ssrn.com/abstract=222493.

Gitelman, Lisa. *Scripts, Grooves, and Writing Machines: Representing Technology in the Edison Era*. Stanford, CA: Stanford University Press, 1999.

Gitelman, Lisa. "Media, Materiality, and the Measure of the Digital, or, The Case of Sheet Music and the Problem of Piano Rolls." In Lauren Rabinovitz and Abraham Geil, eds., *Memory Bytes: History, Technology, and Digital Culture*, 237–262. Durham, NC: Duke University Press, 2004.

Gitelman, Lisa. *Always Already New: Media, History and the Data of Culture*. Cambridge, MA: MIT Press, 2006.

Gitelman, Lisa, and Geoffrey Pingree, eds. *New Media, 1740–1915*. Cambridge, MA: MIT Press, 2003.

Gitlin, Todd. *The Whole World Is Watching: Mass Media in the Making and Unmaking of the New Left*. Berkeley: University of California Press, 1980.

Gitlin, Todd. *Watching Television: a Pantheon Guide to Popular Culture*. New York: Pantheon Books, 1986.

Godwin, Mike. "Harry Potter and the Prisoners of the DTV Transition." Public Knowledge, Washington, DC (December 18, 2003). http://www.publicknowledge .org/news/analysis/harrypotter.

Godwin, Mike. "What Every Citizen Should Know about DRM, a.k.a. 'Digital Rights Management.'" Public Knowledge, Washington, DC (2004). http://www.public knowledge.org/pdf/citizens_guide_to_drm.pdf.

Goldstein, Paul. *Copyright's Highway: From Gutenberg to the Celestial Jukebox*, 1st ed. New York: Hill and Wang, 1994.

Goody, Jack. *The Domestication of the Savage Mind*. Cambridge: Cambridge University Press, 1977.

Graham, Stephen. "Beyond the 'Dazzling Light': From Dreams of Transcendence to the 'Remediation' of Urban Life—A Research Manifesto." *New Media & Society* 6.1 (February 2004): 16–25.

Grebb, Michael. "Uncle Sam Wants Your Airwaves." *Wired News* (September 22, 2004). http://www.wired.com/news/politics/0,1283,65041,00.html.

Greenberg, Josh. "Hackers and Tinkerers and Amateurs . . . Oh My!" Unpublished manuscript, George Mason University (2004).

Greenfeld, Karl. "You've Got Music!" *Time* (February 22, 1999): 58–59. http://www .time.com/time/archive/printout/0,23657,990272,00.html.

Greenfeld, Karl. "Meet the Napster." *Time* (October 2, 2000): 59–68.

Grint, Keith, and Steve Woolgar. "Computers, Guns, and Roses: What's Social about Being Shot?" *Science, Technology, & Human Values* 17.3 (1992): 366–380.

Gross, Robin. "World Summit to Create 'Pay-Per-Use' Society: Human Rights Ignored as Big Business Dominates Geneva." IP Justice, Geneva, Switzerland (December 21, 2003). http://www.ipjustice.org/WSIS/IPJ_WSIS_Report.html.

Hafner, Katie, and Matthew Lyon. *Where Wizards Stay Up Late: The Origins of the Internet*. New York: Simon & Schuster, 1996.

Halbert, Debora. "Weaving Webs of Ownership: Intellectual Property in an Information Age." Diss., Hawaii Research Center for Future Studies, University of Hawaii at Manoa (1996). http://www.futures.hawaii.edu/dissertation/TOC2.html.

Halbert, Debora. "Discourses of Danger and the Computer Hacker." *The Information Society* 13.4 (1997): 361–374.

Halbert, Debora. *Intellectual Property in the Information Age: The Politics of Expanding Ownership Rights*. Westport, CT: Quorum, 1999.

Halderman, J. Alex, and Edward Felten. "Lessons from the Sony CD DRM Episode" (2006). http://itpolicy.princeton.edu/pub/sonydrm-ext.pdf.

Hall, Stuart. "Encoding/Decoding." In Stuart Hall, ed., *Culture, Media, Language*, 128–138. London: Hutchinson Educational Ltd., 1980.

Haring, Bruce. *Beyond the Charts: MP3 and the Digital Music Revolution*. Los Angeles: JM Northern Media LLC, 2000.

Harmon, Amy. "Potent Software Escalates Music Industry's Jitters." *New York Times* (March 7, 2000): A1, C6.

Harvey, David. *The Condition of Postmodernity: An Enquiry into the Origins of Cultural Change*. Oxford: Blackwell, 1989.

Hawkins, Richard. "The Rise of Consortia in the Information and Communication Technology Industries: Emerging Implications for Policy." *Telecommunications Policy* 23.2 (1999): 159–173.

Hawkins, Richard, Robin Mansell, and Jim Skea, eds. *Standards, Innovation and Competitiveness: The Politics and Economics of Standards in Natural and Technical Environments*. Brookfield, VT: Edward Elgar, 1995.

Hebdige, Dick. *Subculture: The Meaning of Style*. London: Methuen, 1979.

Hemphill, Thomas, and Nicholas Vonortas. "U.S. Antitrust Policy, Interface Compatibility Standards, and Information Technology." *Knowledge, Technology, & Policy* 18.2 (Summer 2005): 126–147. http://www.gwu.edu/~elliott/faculty/vonortasantitrust05.pdf.

Herman, Andrew, and John Sloop. "The Politics of Authenticity in Postmodern Rock Culture: The Case of Negativland and the Letter 'U' and the Numeral '2.'" *Critical Studies in Mass Communication* 15.1 (March 1998): 1–20.

Hickman, Larry. *Technology as a Human Affair*. New York: McGraw-Hill, 1990.

Hong, Seung-Hyun. "The Effect of Napster on Recorded Music Sales: Evidence from the Consumer Expenditure Survey." Discussion paper #03–18, Stanford Institute for Economic Policy Research, Stanford, CA (January 30, 2004). http://siepr.stanford.edu/Papers/pdf/03-18.pdf.

Horwitz, Robert. *The Irony of Regulatory Reform: The Deregulation of American Telecommunications*. New York: Oxford University Press, 1989.

Horwitz, Robert. "The First Amendment Meets Some New Technologies: Broadcasting, Common Carriers, and Free Speech in the 1990s." *Theory and Society* 20.1 (February 1991): 21–72.

Howard-Spink, Sam. "Grey Tuesday, Online Cultural Activism and the Mash-up of Music and Politics." *First Monday* 9.10 (October 2004). http://firstmonday.dk/issues/issue9_10/howard/.

Howe, Jeff. "DVD Hackers Take a Hit in NY." *Wired News* (January 21, 2000). http://www.wired.com/news/print/0,1294,33816,00.html.

Howe, Jeff. "The Shadow Internet." *Wired* 13.01 (January 2005). http://www.wired.com/wired/archive/13.01/topsite_pr.html.

HR 105–551. "WIPO Copyright Treaties Implementation and Online Copyright Infringement Liability Limitation." U.S. House of Representatives (May 22, 1998).

Hughes, Thomas. "The Seamless Web: Technology, Science, Etcetera, Etcetera." *Social Studies of Science* 16.2 (May 1986): 281–292.

Hughes, Thomas. "The Evolution of Large Technological Systems." In Wiebe Bijker, Thomas Hughes, and Trevor Pinch, eds., *The Social Construction of Technical Systems: New Directions in the Sociology and History of Technology*, 51–82. Cambridge, MA: MIT Press, 1987.

Hunt, Arnold. "'Moral Panic' and Moral Language in the Media." *The British Journal of Sociology* 48.4 (December 1997): 629–648.

Hunter, Dan, and Gregory Lastowka. "Amateur-to-Amateur." *William and Mary Law Review* 46 (December 2004): 951–1030.

Hutchins, Edwin. *Cognition in the Wild*. Cambridge, MA: MIT Press, 1995.

Innis, Harold. *Empire and Communications*. Oxford: Clarendon Press, 1950.

Innis, Harold. *The Bias of Communication*. Toronto: University of Toronto Press, 1951.

Introna, Lucas, and Helen Nissenbaum. "Shaping the Web: Why the Politics of Search Engines Matters." *The Information Society* 16.3 (2000): 169–185. http://www.indiana.edu/~tisj/readers/full-text/16-3%20Introna.html.

Jackson, Matt. "Commerce Versus Art: The Transformation of Fair Use." *Journal of Broadcasting & Electronic Media* 39.2 (Spring 1995): 190–199.

Jackson, Matt. "Using Technology to Circumvent the Law: The DMCA's Push to Privatize Copyright." *Hastings Communications and Entertainment Law Journal* 23 (2001): 607–646.

Jackson, Matt. "From Private to Public: Reexamining the Technological Basis for Copyright." *Journal of Communication* 52.2 (June 2002): 416–433. http://joc.oxfordjournals.org/cgi/reprint/52/2/416.

Jain, Sanjay, and Yanfeng Zheng. "The Incumbent's Advantage? Charting the Institutional Response of Incumbent Firms to the Threat Posed by Emerging Technologies." Unpublished manuscript (2004).

Jaszi, Peter. "Toward a Theory of Copyright: The Metamorphoses of 'Authorship.'" *Duke Law Journal* 2 (April 1991): 455–502.

Jaszi, Peter. "Intellectual Property Legislative Update: Copyright, Paracopyright, and Pseudo-Copyright." Paper presented at Annual Meeting—The Future Network: Transforming Learning and Scholarship, Association of Research Libraries, Eugene, OR (May 13–15, 1998).

Jenkins, Henry. "Quentin Tarantino's Star Wars?: Digital Cinema, Media Convergence, and Participatory Culture." In David Thorburn and Henry Jenkins, eds., *Rethinking Media Change: The Aesthetics of Transition*, 281–312. Cambridge, MA: MIT Press, 2003. http://web.mit.edu/cms/People/henry3/starwars.html.

Jenkins, Henry, and David Thorburn. "Introduction: The Digital Revolution, the Informed Citizen, and the Culture of Democracy." In Henry Jenkins and David Thorburn, eds., *Democracy and New Media*, 1–20. Cambridge, MA: MIT Press, 2003.

Joerges, Bernward. "Do Politics Have Artefacts?" *Social Studies of Science* 29.3 (June 1999): 411–431.

Johns, Adrian. *The Nature of the Book: Print and Knowledge in the Making.* Chicago: University of Chicago Press, 1998.

Johns, Adrian. "Pop Music Pirate Hunters." *Daedalus* 131 (Spring 2002): 67–77.

Johns, Adrian. "How to Acknowledge a Revolution." *American Historical Review* 107.1 (2002): 106–125.

Johnson, Steven. *Interface Culture: How New Technology Transforms the Way We Create and Communicate.* San Francisco: HarperEdge, 1997.

Jones, Christopher. "Music Biz Builds a Time Bomb." *Wired News* (May 14, 1999). http://wired-vig.wired.com/news/technology/0,1282,19682,00.html.

Jones, Christopher. "SDMI: Shape Up or Ship Out." *Wired News* (April 28, 2000). http://www.wired.com/news/politics/0,1283,35966,00.html.

Jones, Steve. "Music That Moves: Popular Music, Distribution and Network Technologies." *Cultural Studies* 16.2 (2002): 213–232.

Kabushiki Kaisha Sony Computer Entertainment v. Stevens. 2003 FCAFC 157. Federal Court of Australia (2003). http://www.austlii.edu.au/au/cases/cth/FCAFC/2003/157.html.

Kahin, Brian, and Janet Abbate, eds. *Standards Policy for Information Infrastructure.* Cambridge, MA: MIT Press, 1995.

Karaganis, Joe, and Natalie Jeremijenko, eds. *Structures of Participation in Digital Culture.* Durham, NC: Duke University Press, forthcoming.

Katz, Jon. "Napster Aftermath: Fan vs. Corporate Rights." *Slashdot* (July 28, 2000). http://slashdot.org/features/00/07/27/154247.shtml.

Katz, Michael, and Carl Shapiro. "Network Externalities, Competition, and Compatibility." *The American Economic Review* 75.3 (June 1985): 424–440.

Kelly, Kevin. *Out of Control: The Rise of Neo-Biological Civilization*. Reading, MA: Addison-Wesley, 1994.

Kesan, Jay, and Rajiv Shah. "Fool Us Once Shame On You—Fool Us Twice Shame on Us: What We Can Learn from the Privatizations of the Internet Backbone Network and the Domain Name System." *Washington University Law Quarterly* 79.1 (Spring 2001): 89–220. http://ssrn.com/abstract=260834.

Klein, Hans, and Daniel Kleinman. "The Social Construction of Technology: Structural Considerations." *Science, Technology, & Human Values* 27.1 (2002): 28–52.

Kline, Ronald, and Trevor Pinch. "Users as Agents of Technological Change: The Social Construction of the Automobile in the Rural United States." *Technology and Culture* 37.4 (October 1996): 763–795.

Klinenberg, Eric, and Claudio Benzecry. "Introduction: Cultural Production in a Digital Age." *The Annals of the American Academy of Political and Social Science* 597.1 (January 2005): 6–18.

Kling, Rob. "Computerization and Social Transformations." *Science, Technology, & Human Values* 16.3 (1991): 342–367.

Kling, Rob. "Reply to Woolgar and Grint: A Preview." *Science, Technology, & Human Values* 16.3 (1991): 379–381.

Kling, Rob. "Audiences, Narratives, and Human Values in Social Studies of Technology." *Science, Technology, & Human Values* 17.3 (1992): 349–365.

Kling, Rob. "When Gunfire Shatters Bone: Reducing Socio-Technical Systems to Social Relationships." *Science, Technology, & Human Values* 17.3 (1992): 381–385.

Kling, Rob. "Hopes and Horrors: Technological Utopianism and Anti-Utopianism in Narratives of Computerization." In Rob Kling, ed., *Computerization and Controversy: Value Conflicts and Social Choices*, 2nd ed., 43–58. San Diego: Academic Press, 1996. http://rkcsi.indiana.edu/archive/kling/cc/2-HOPE4.html.

Kling, Rob, ed. *Computerization and Controversy: Value Conflicts and Social Choices*, 2nd ed. San Diego: Academic Press, 1996.

Kover, Amy. "Who's Afraid of This Kid?" *Fortune* (June 26, 2000): 129.

Ku, Raymond. "The Creative Destruction of Copyright: Napster and the New Economics of Digital Technology." *University of Chicago Law Review* 69.1 (2002): 263–324.

Labriola, Don. "Digital Content Protection: How Anti-Piracy Technologies Are Transforming Digital Media." *Extreme Tech* (May 16, 2002). http://www.extremetech.com/article2/0,1558,13923,00.asp.

Labriola, Don. "Digital Content Protection, Part II: How Anti-Piracy Technologies Are Transforming Digital Media." *Extreme Tech* (August 25, 2003). http://www.extremetech.com/article2/0,1697,1231582,00.asp.

Labriola, Don. "Digital Content Protection, Part III: How Anti-Piracy Technologies Are Transforming Digital Media." *Extreme Tech* (August 25, 2003). http://www.extremetech.com/article2/0,1697,1231583,00.asp.

Landes, William, and Richard Posner. "An Economic Analysis of Copyright Law." *Journal of Legal Studies* 18.2 (June 1995): 325–363.

"'Landmark' Accord on Copyrights." *Wired News* (January 14, 2003). http://www.wired.com/news/digiwood/0,1412,57211,00.html.

Lasica, J. D. *Darknet: Hollywood's War Against the Digital Generation.* Hoboken, NJ: Wiley, 2005.

Latour, Bruno. *Science in Action: How to Follow Scientists and Engineers through Society.* Cambridge, MA: Harvard University Press, 1987.

Latour, Bruno. "Where Are the Missing Masses? The Sociology of a Few Mundane Artifacts." "In Wiebe Bijker and John Law, eds., *Shaping Technology/Building Society: Studies in Sociotechnical Change*, 225–258. Cambridge, MA: MIT Press, 1994.

Latour, Bruno. *Aramis, or, The Love of Technology.* Cambridge, MA: Harvard University Press, 1996.

Latour, Bruno. "Which Politics for Which Artifacts?" *Domus* (June 2004). http://www.ensmp.fr/%7Elatour/presse/presse_art/GB-06%20DOMUS%2006-04.html.

Latour, Bruno (a.k.a. Jim Johnson). "Mixing Humans and Nonhumans Together: The Sociology of a Door-Closer." *Social Problems* 35 (1988): 298–310.

Laurel, Brenda. *The Art of Human-Computer Interface Design.* Reading, MA: Addison-Wesley, 1990.

Lave, Jean. *Cognition in Practice: Mind, Mathematics, and Culture in Everyday Life.* Cambridge: Cambridge University Press, 1988.

Law, John. ed. *Power, Action, and Belief: A New Sociology of Knowledge?* London: Routledge, 1986.

Law, John. "Technology and Heterogeneous Engineering: The Case of the Portuguese Expansion." In Wiebe Bijker, Thomas Hughes, and Trevor Pinch, eds., *The Social Construction of Technical Systems: New Directions in the Sociology and History of Technology*, 111–134. Cambridge, MA: MIT Press, 1987.

Lemley, Mark. "Beyond Preemption: The Law and Policy of Intellectual Property Licensing." *California Law Review* 87 (1999): 111–172.

Lemley, Mark. "Intellectual Property Rights and Standard-Setting Organizations." *California Law Review* 90 (April 2002): 1889–1990. http://ssrn.com/abstract=310122.

Lessig, Lawrence. *Code, and Other Laws of Cyberspace.* New York: Basic Books, 1999.

Lessig, Lawrence. "It's Still a Safe World for Microsoft." *New York Times* (November 9, 2001): A27.

Lessig, Lawrence. *The Future of Ideas: The Fate of the Commons in a Connected World.* New York: Random House, 2001.

Lessig, Lawrence. *Free Culture: How Big Media Uses Technology and the Law to Lock Down Culture and Control Creativity.* New York: Penguin Books, 2004.

Lessig, Lawrence. "Google's Tough Call." *Wired* 13.11 (November 2005). http://www.wired.com/wired/archive/13.11/posts.html?pg=8?tw=wn_tophead_4.

Levinson, Paul. *The Soft Edge: A Natural History and Future of the Information Revolution.* London: Routledge, 1997.

Levy, Nichelle. "Method to Their Madness: The Secure Digital Music Initiative, a Law and Economics Perspective." *Virginia Journal of Law and Technology* 5.3 (2000): 12.

Levy, Steven. "The Noisy War over Napster." *Newsweek* (June 5, 2000): 46–53.

Lewis, Justin. *The Ideological Octopus: An Exploration of Television and Its Audience.* New York: Routledge, 1991.

Lewis, Justin, and Toby Miller, eds. *Critical Cultural Policy Studies: A Reader.* Oxford: Blackwell, 2003.

Liebowitz, Stan. "Policing Pirates in the Networked Age." Policy Analysis, #438, Cato Institute (May 15, 2002). http://www.cato.org/pubs/pas/pa438.pdf.

Lievrouw, Leah. "Determination and Contingency in New Media Development: Diffusion of Innovations and Social Shaping of Technology Perspectives." In Leah Lievrouw and Sonia Livingstone, eds., *The Handbook of New Media: Social Shaping and Consequences of ICTs*, 181–199. London: Sage, 2002.

Lievrouw, Leah. "What's Changed about New Media? Introduction to the Fifth Anniversary of *New Media & Society*." *New Media & Society* 6.1 (February 2004): 9–15.

Lievrouw, Leah, and Sonia Livingstone, eds. *The Handbook of New Media: Social Shaping and Consequences of ICTs.* London: Sage, 2002.

Lipsitz, George. *Time Passages: Collective Memory and American Popular Culture.* Minneapolis: University of Minnesota Press, 1990.

Litman, Jessica. "The Public Domain." *Emory Law Journal* 39 (Fall 1990): 965–1023.

Litman, Jessica. "Revising Copyright Law for the Information Age." *Oregon Law Review* 75 (1996): 19–46. http://www.law.cornell.edu/commentary/intelpro/litrvtxt.htm.

Litman, Jessica. *Digital Copyright: Protecting Intellectual Property on the Internet.* Amherst, NY: Prometheus Books, 2001.

Litman, Jessica. "Sharing and Stealing." *Hastings Communication and Entertainment Law Journal* 27 (2004): 1–50.

Logie, John. "A Copyright Cold War? The Polarized Rhetoric of the Peer-to-Peer Debates." *First Monday* 8.7 (July 2003). http://www.firstmonday.org/issues/issue8_7/logie/.

Mackay, Hugh, Chris Carne, Paul Beynon-Davies, and Dough Tudhope. "Reconfiguring the User: Using Rapid Application Development." *Social Studies of Science* 30.5 (2000): 737–757.

Mackay, Hugh, and Gareth Gillespie. "Extending the Social Shaping of Technology Approach: Ideology and Appropriation." *Social Studies of Science* 22.4 (1992): 685–716.

Mackenzie, Dana. "The Code War." *Beyond Discovery* (February 12, 2003). http://www.beyonddiscovery.org/content/view.article.asp?a=3420.

MacKenzie, Donald, and Judy Wajcman, eds. *The Social Shaping of Technology*, 2nd ed. Buckingham, VC: Open University Press, 1999.

Mann, Charles. "The Heavenly Jukebox." *Atlantic Monthly* 3 (September 2000): 39–59. http://www.theatlantic.com/issues/2000/09/mann.htm.

Mann, Charles. "A Web-Only Primer on Public-Key Encryption." *Atlantic Monthly* (September 2002).

Manovich, Lev. "Cinema as a Cultural Interface." (1998). http://www.manovich.net/TEXT/cinema-cultural.html.

Manovich, Lev. *The Language of New Media.* Cambridge: MIT Press, 2001.

Mansell, Robin, and Roger Silverstone, eds. *Communication by Design: The Politics of Information and Communication Technologies.* Oxford: Oxford University Press, 1996.

Marks, Dean, and Bruce Turnbull. "Technical Protection Measures: The Intersection of Technology, Law and Commercial Licenses." Paper presented at Workshop on Implementation Issues of the WIPO Copyright Treaty (WCT) and the WIPO Performances and Phonograms Treaty (WPPT), Geneva, Switzerland (1999).

Marvin, Carolyn. *When Old Technologies Were New: Thinking about Electric Communication in the Late Nineteenth Century.* New York: Oxford University Press, 1988.

Marx, Leo. *The Machine in the Garden: Technology and the Pastoral Ideal in America.* New York: Oxford University Press, 1964.

Mattleart, Armand. *Mapping World Communication: War, Progress, Culture.* Minneapolis: University of Minnesota Press, 1994.

McCloud, Scott. "Misunderstanding Micropayments: BitPass, Shirky and The Good Idea that Refuses to Die." *ScottMcCloud.com* (September 11, 2003). http://www.scottmccloud.com/home/essays/2003-09-micros/micros.html.

McLuhan, Marshall. *Understanding Media: The Extensions of Man,* 1st ed. New York: McGraw-Hill, 1964.

McRobbie, Angela, and Sarah Thornton. "Rethinking Moral Panic for Multi-mediated Social Worlds." *British Journal of Sociology* 46.4 (1995): 559–574.

Merges, Robert. "From Medieval Guilds to Open Source Software: Informal Norms, Appropriability Institutions, and Innovation." Paper presented at Conference on the Legal History of Intellectual Property, Madison, WI (2004).

Metro-Goldwyn Mayer Studios, Inc. v. Grokster, Ltd. 123 2764. S. Ct. 2005.

Meyrowitz, Joshua. *No Sense of Place: The Impact of Electronic Media on Social Behavior.* New York: Oxford University Press, 1985.

Michel, Norbert. "Internet File Sharing: The Evidence So Far and What It Means for the Future." Policy Research & Analysis, #1790, The Heritage Foundation (August 23, 2004). http://www.heritage.org/Research/InternetandTechnology/bg1790.cfm.

Miles, Stephanie. "Infighting Threatens to Kill Net Music Antipiracy Standard." *CNet* (September 23, 1999). http://news.com.com/2100–1040–255669.html.

Miller, Toby, and George Yudice. *Cultural Policy.* London: Sage Publications, 2002.

Minar, Nelson, and Marc Hedlund. "A Network of Peers: Peer-to-Peer Models through the History of the Internet." In Andy Oram, ed., *Peer-to-Peer: Harnessing the Power of Disruptive Technologies,* 3–20. Sebastopol, CA: O'Reilly & Associates, 2001.

Montemagno, Marco. "P2P Manifesto" (January 15, 2005). http://rothko.hmdnsgroup.com/~montemag/p2pmanifesto_en.pdf.

Morley, David. *Family Television: Cultural Power and Domestic Leisure.* London: Comedia Publishing Group, 1986.

Morley, David. *Television, Audiences, and Cultural Studies.* London: Routledge, 1992.

Morley, David, and Charlotte Brunsdon. *The 'Nationwide' Television Studies.* London: Routledge, 1999.

Morton, David. *Off the Record: The Technology and Culture of Sound Recording in America.* New Brunswick, NJ: Rutgers University Press, 2000.

Mosco, Vincent. "Introduction: Information in the Pay-per Society." In Vincent Mosco and Janet Wasko, eds., *The Political Economy of Information,* 3–26. Madison: University of Wisconsin Press, 1988.

Mosco, Vincent. *The Digital Sublime: Myth, Power, and Cyberspace*. Cambridge, MA: MIT Press, 2004.

Mosco, Vincent, and Janet Wasko, eds. *The Political Economy of Information*. (Madison, WI: University of Wisconsin Press, 1988.

Motion Picture Association of America. "Motion Picture Association Vows Support of WIPO Treaty and Implementation Bill" (July 29, 1997).

Motion Picture Association of America. "Ratification of WIPO Treaties Caps Historical Congress for MPAA." Press release, Washington, DC (October 21, 1998).

Motion Picture Association of America. "Copyright Community Forms United 'Copyright Assembly.'" Press release, Washington, DC (February 14, 2000).

Motion Picture Association of America. "Valenti, Copyright Assembly Call on Congress to Protect and Support Copyright in Internet Age." Press release, Washington, DC (February 16, 2000).

Motion Picture Association of America. "Statement by Jack Valenti, on RIAA Announcement of Intention to Take Legal Action against Individuals Illegally Offering Music Online." Press release, Washington, DC (June 25, 2003).

Motion Picture Association of America. "Film/TV Industry Launches Public Service Announcements as Part of Nationwide Awareness Campaign on the Impact of Digital Piracy." Press release, Los Angeles. CA (July 22, 2003).

Motion Picture Association of America. "Protecting Movie Magic in the Digital Age." Press release, Washington, DC (June 15, 2004).

Motion Picture Association of America. "Jack Valenti Announces Resignation after 38 Years As Head of MPAA/MPA." Press release, Washington, DC (July 1, 2004).

Motion Picture Association of America. *Broadcast Flag: Frequently Asked Questions* Online FAQ (2005) http://www.mpaa.org/Broadcast_Flag_QA.asp.

Mukerji, Chandra. "Intelligent Uses of Engineering and the Legitimacy of State Power." *Technology and Culture* 44.4 (October 2003): 655–676.

Mukerji, Chandra, and Michael Schudson, eds. *Rethinking Popular Culture: Contemporary Perspectives in Cultural Studies*. Berkeley: University of California Press, 1991.

Mulgan, Geoff. *Communication and Control: Networks and the New Economies of Communication*. Cambridge: Polity Press, 1991.

Mulkay, Michael. "Norms and Ideology." *Social Science Information* 15 (1976): 637–656.

Mulkay, Michael, and Nigel Gilbert. "Replication and Mere Replication." *Philosophy of the Social Sciences* 16.1 (1986): 21–37.

Mulligan, Deirdre, John Han, and Aaron Bernstein. "How DRM-Based Content Delivery Systems Disrupt Expectations of 'Personal Use.'" In *Third ACM Workshop on Digital Rights Management*, 77–89. Washington, DC: ACM Press, 2003.

Naraine, Ryan. "Sony, Philips Snap Up Intertrust." *Internet News* (November 13, 2002). http://www.internetnews.com/bus-news/article.php/1499591.

National Research Council, Committee on Intellectual Property Rights in the Emerging Information Infrastructure. *The Digital Dilemma: Intellectual Property in the Information Age*. Washington, DC: National Academy Press, 2000.

National Telecommunications and Information Administration and The Benton Foundation. "Charting the Digital Broadcasting Future: Final Report of the Advisory Committee on Public Interest Obligations of Digital Television Broadcasters." Washington, DC (December 18, 1998).

Neilsen, Jakob. "The Case for Micropayments." *Alertbox: Current Issues in Web Usability* (January 25, 1998). http://www.useit.com/alertbox/980125.html.

Netanel, Neil. "From the Dead Sea Scrolls to the Digital Millennium; Recent Developments in Copyright Law." *Texas Intellectual Property Journal* 9 (Fall 2000): 19–63.

Nichols, David, and Michael Twidale. "The Usability of Open Source Software." *First Monday* 8.1 (2003). http://www.firstmonday.org/issues/issue8_1/nichols/index.html.

Nimmer, David. "A Riff on Fair Use in the Digital Millennium Copyright Act." *University of Pennsylvania Law Review* 148 (January 2000): 673–742.

Nimmer, David, Eliot Brown, and Gary Frischling. "The Metamorphosis of Contract into Expand." *California Law Review* 87 (January 1999): 17–77.

Nimmer, Melville. *Nimmer on Copyright: A Treatise on the Law of Literary, Musical, and Artistic Property, and the Protection of Ideas*. 1963. Reprint, New York: M. Bender, 1983.

Nisbet, Robert. *History of the Idea of Progress*. New Brunswick, NJ: Transaction Publishers, 1994.

Nissenbaum, Helen. "Protecting Privacy in an Information Age: The Problem of Privacy in Public." *Law and Philosophy* 17 (1998): 559–596. http://www.nyu.edu/projects/nissenbaum/papers/privacy.pdf.

Nissenbaum, Helen. "How Computer Systems Embody Values." *IEEE Computer* 34.3 (March 2001): 120, 118–119. www.nyu.edu/projects/nissenbaum/papers/embodyvalues.pdf.

Nissenbaum, Helen. "Hackers and the Contested Ontology of Cyberspace." *New Media and Society* 6.2 (2004): 195–217. http://www.nyu.edu/projects/nissenbaum/papers/hackers.pdf.

Nissenbaum, Helen. "Privacy as Contextual Integrity." *Washington Law Review* 79.1 (2004): 101–139. http://ssrn.com/abstract=534622.

Norman, Donald. *The Psychology of Everyday Things.* New York: Basic Books, 1988.

Nye, David. *American Technological Sublime.* Cambridge, MA: MIT Press, 1994.

Oberholzer-Gee, Felix, and Koleman Strumpf. "The Effect of File Sharing on Record Sales: An Empirical Analysis" (March 2004). http://www.unc.edu/~cigar/papers/FileSharing_March2004.pdf.

Okedji, Ruth. "Givers, Takers, and Other Kinds of Users: A Fair Use Doctrine for Cyberspace." *Florida Law Review* 53 (January 2001): 107–182.

Ong, Walter. *Orality and Literacy: The Technologizing of the Word.* London: Methuen, 1982.

Oram, Andy, ed. *Peer-to-Peer: Harnessing the Power of Disruptive Technologies.* Sebastopol, CA: O'Reilly & Associates, 2001.

Orlikowski, Wanda. "The Duality of Technology: Rethinking the Concept of Technology in Organizations." *Organization Science* 3.3 (August 1992): 398–427.

Orlowski, Andrew. "Apple De-Socializes iTunes." *The Register* (March 15, 2005). http://www.theregister.co.uk/2005/03/15/social_music/.

Oudshoorn, Nelly, and Trevor Pinch, eds. *How Users Matter: The Co-Construction of Users and Technologies.* Cambridge, MA: MIT Press, 2003.

Oudshoorn, Nelly, Els Rommes, and Marcelle Stiensra. "Configuring the User as Everybody: Gender and Design Cultures in Information and Communication Technologies." *Science, Technology, & Human Values* 29.1 (2004): 30–63.

Outwater, Edwin. "The History of Digital Copyright Management, or How the Cows Got on the Ice." *Medialine* (May 2000).

Parloff, Roger. "Copy This! Can 'Military' Technology Beat Digital Piracy?" *Inside.com* (March 12, 2001). No longer available online.

Patrizio, Andy. "DVD Piracy: It Can Be Done." *Wired News* (November 1, 1999). http://www.wirednews.com/news/print/0,1294,32249,00.html.

Patrizio, Andy. "Why the DVD Hack Was a Cinch." *Wired News* (November 2, 1999). http://www.wired.com/news/print/0,1294,32263,00.html.

Patry, William. *The Fair Use Privilege in Copyright Law,* 2nd ed. Washington, DC: Bureau of National Affairs, 1995.

Peitz, Martin, and Patrick Waelbroeck. "The Effect of Internet Piracy on CD Sales: Cross-Section Evidence." *CESifo* Working Paper Series #1122 (January 2004). http://ssrn.com/abstract=511763.

Pfaffenberger, Brian. "Technological Dramas." *Science, Technology, and Human Values* 17.3 (1992): 282–312.

Philips, Chuck. "Time Warner Tunes In New Delivery Channel (Interview with Richard Parsons)." *Los Angeles Times* (July 25, 2000): C1.

Philips Consumer Electronics. "Philips Consumer Electronics North America CEO Warns Congress that Plan Will Raise Costs, Complexity, and Confusion for Millions of Consumers in Digital TV Age." Press release, Washington, DC (April 25, 2002).

Phillips, David. "Cryptography, Secrets, and the Structuring of Trust." In Philip Agre and Marc Rotenberg, eds., *Technology and Privacy: The New Landscape*, 243–276. Cambridge, MA: MIT Press, 1997.

Pinch, Trevor, and Wiebe Bijker. "The Social Construction of Facts and Artefacts: Or How the Sociology of Science and the Sociology of Technology Might Benefit Each Other." *Social Studies of Science* 14.3 (August 1984): 399–441.

Pinch, Trevor, and Wiebe Bijker. "Science, Relativism and the New Sociology of Technology: Reply to Russell." *Social Studies of Science* 16.2 (May 1986): 347–360.

Piper, Fred, and Sean Murphy. *Cryptography: A Very Short Introduction*. Oxford: Oxford University Press, 2002.

Popper, Karl. *Conjectures and Refutations: The Growth of Scientific Knowledge*. London: Routledge, 1963.

Posner, Richard. "Antitrust in the New Economy." Olin Working Paper, #106, University of Chicago Law & Economics, Chicago, IL (November 2000). http://ssrn .com/abstract=249316.

ProCD Inc. v. Zeidenberg. 86 F. 3d 1447. 7th Cir. 1996.

Ratto, Matt. "The Pressure of Openness: The Hybrid Work of Linux Free/Open Source Software Developers." Diss., University of California, San Diego (2003).

Ratto, Matt. "Embedded Technical Expression: Code and the Leveraging of Functionality." *The Information Society* 21.3 (2005): 205–213.

Raymond, Eric. *The Cathedral and the Bazaar: Musings on Linux and Open Source by an Accidental Revolutionary*. Beijing: O'Reilly, 1999.

RealNetworks, Inc. v. Streambox, Inc. 2000 LEXIS 1889. U.S. Dist. 2000.

Recording Industry Association of America. "Worldwide Recording Industry Announces Precedent-Setting Initiative to Address New Digital Music Opportunities." Press release, New York (December 15, 1998). http://www.trinetcom.com/ riaa/release/.

Recording Industry Association of America v. Diamond Multimedia Systems, Inc. 180 F.3d 1072. 9th Cir. 1999.

Reidenberg, Joel. "Lex Informatica: The Formulation of Information Policy Rules through Technology." *Texas Law Review* 76.3 (1998): 553–584.

Rheingold, Howard. *The Virtual Community: Homesteading on the Electronic Frontier.* Reading, MA: Addison-Wesley, 1993.

Robin, Corey. *Fear: The History of a Political Idea.* Oxford: Oxford University Press, 2004.

Rose, Mark. *Authors and Owners: The Invention of Copyright.* Cambridge, MA: Harvard University Press, 1993.

Rosenblatt, Bill. "Blu-Ray Group Announces Content Protection Strategy." *DRM Watch* (August 11, 2005). http://www.drmwatch.com/drmtech/article.php/3526796.

Roush, Wade. "The Infinite Library: Does Google's Plan to Digitize Millions of Print Books Spell the Death of Libraries, or Their Rebirth?" *Technology Review* (May 2005). http://www.technologyreview.com/read_article.aspx?id=14408&ch=infotech.

Rubens, Paul. "Border Controls Crumble in DVD Land." *BBC News* (August 19, 2002). http://news.bbc.co.uk/1/hi/in_depth/sci_tech/2000/dot_life/2197548.stm.

Russell, Stewart. "The Social Construction of Artefacts: A Response to Pinch and Bijker." *Social Studies of Science* 16.2 (May 1986): 331–346.

S105-190. "The Digital Millennium Copyright Act." U.S. Senate (May 11, 1998).

Samarajiva, Rohan. "Surveillance by Design: Public Networks and the Control of Consumption." In Robin Mansell and Roger Silverstone, eds., *Communication by Design: The Politics of Information and Communication Technologies,* 129–156. Oxford: Oxford University Press, 1996.

Samuelson, Pamela. "Legally Speaking: The NII Intellectual Property Report." *Communications of the ACM* 37.12 (December 1994): 21–27. http://www.eff.org/Infrastructure/Govt_docs/HTML/ipwg_samuelson.html.

Samuelson, Pamela. "Questioning the Need for New International Rules on Author's Rights in Cyberspace." *First Monday* 1.4 (October 7, 1996). http://www.firstmonday.dk/issues/issue4/samuelson/index.html.

Samuelson, Pamela. "The Copyright Grab." *Wired* 4.01 (January 1996): 134–138, 188, 190–191. http://www.wired.com/wired/archive/4.01/white.paper_pr.html.

Samuelson, Pamela. "The U.S. Digital Agenda at the World Intellectual Property Organization." *Virginia Journal of International Law* 37 (1997): 369–439.

Samuelson, Pamela. "Intellectual Property and the Digital Economy: Why the Anti-Circumvention Regulations Need to Be Revised." *Berkeley Technology Law Journal* 14 (Spring 1999): 519–566.

Samuelson, Pamela. "DRM {and, or, vs.} the Law." *Communications of the ACM* 46.4 (2003): 41–45. www.sims.berkeley.edu/~pam/papers/acm_v46_p41.pdf.

Sandvig, Christian. "Shaping Infrastructure and Innovation on the Internet: The End-to-End Network that Isn't." In David Guston and Daniel Sarewitz, eds., *Shaping Science and Technology Policy: The Next Generation of Research* (Madison, WI: University of Wisconsin Press, 2006).

Schiller, Herbert. *Mass Communications and American Empire*. New York: A. M. Kelley, 1969.

Schiller, Herbert. "The Global Information Highway: Project for an Ungovernable World." In Iain Boal and James Brook, eds., *Resisting the Virtual Life: The Culture and Politics of Information*, 17–34. San Francisco: City Lights, 1995.

Schmandt-Besserat, Denise. *How Writing Came About*. Austin, TX: University of Texas Press, 1996.

Schneier, Bruce. *Secrets and Lies: Digital Security in a Networked World*. New York: John Wiley, 2000.

Schneier, Bruce. "Real Story of the Rogue Rootkit." *Wired News* (November 17, 2005). http://www.wired.com/news/politics/privacy/1,69601-0.html.

Schultz, Jason. "Meet the New iTunes, Less than the Old iTunes?" *LawGeek* (April 29, 2004). http://lawgeek.typepad.com/lawgeek/2004/04/meet_the_new_it.html.

Schumacher, Thomas. "'This Is a Sampling Sport': Digital Sampling, Rap Music, and the Law in Cultural Production." *Media, Culture and Society* 17.2 (April 1995): 253–274.

Schumpeter, Joseph. *Capitalism, Socialism, and Democracy*, 3rd ed. New York: Harper & Row, 1950.

Secure Digital Music Initiative. "SDMI Announces Standard for New Portable Devices: On-Time Specification Will Enable Creation of New Ways to Deliver Digital Music." Press release, Los Angeles, CA (June 28, 1999).

Secure Digital Music Initiative. "SDMI Portable Device Specification, Part 1: Version 1.0." Press release, Los Angeles, CA (July 8, 1999).

Secure Digital Music Initiative. "An Open Letter to the Digital Community." Press release, Los Angeles, CA (September 6, 2000). http://www.sdmi.org/pr/OL_Sept_6_2000.htm.

Secure Digital Music Initiative. "SDMI Reviews Screening Technology Needs." Press release, Amsterdam, Netherlands (May 18, 2001).

Shah, Rajiv, and Jay Kesan. "Manipulating the Governance Characteristics of Code." *Info* 5.4 (2003).

Shapiro, Carl, and Hal Varian. *Information Rules: A Strategic Guide to the Network Economy*. Cambridge, MA: Harvard Business School Press, 1999.

Sherman, Cary. "Presentation to the SDMI Organizing Plenary." Secure Digital Music Initiative, Los Angeles, CA (February 26, 1999).

Shirky, Clay. "The Case against Micropayments." *OpenP2P* (December 19, 2000). http://www.openp2p.com/lpt/a/515.

Shirky, Clay. "Weblogs and the Mass Amateurization of Publishing." *Clay Shirky's Writings about the Internet* (October 3, 2002). http://www.shirky.com/writings/weblogs_publishing.html.

Shirky, Clay. "Fame vs. Fortune: Micropayments and Free Content." *Clay Shirky's Writings about the Internet* (September 5, 2003). http://shirky.com/writings/fame_vs_fortune.html.

Silverstone, Roger. "The Tele-Technological System." In *Television and Everyday Life*, 78–103. New York: Routledge, 1994.

Silverstone, Roger, and Eric Hirsch. *Consuming Technologies: Media and Information in Domestic Spaces*. London; New York: Routledge, 1992.

Singh, Simon. *The Code Book: The Evolution of Secrecy from Mary, Queen of Scots, to Quantum Cryptography*. New York: Doubleday, 1999.

Sismondo, Sergio. "Some Social Constructions." *Social Studies of Science* 23.3 (August 1993): 515–553.

Slaton, Amy, and Janet Abbate. "The Hidden Lives of Standards: Technical Prescriptions and the Transformation of Work in America." In Michael Allen and Gabrielle Hecht, eds., *Technologies of Power: Essays in Honor of Thomas Parke Hughes and Agatha Chipley Hughes*, 95–144. Cambridge, MA: MIT Press, 2001.

Smith, Adam. *An Inquiry into the Nature and Causes of the Wealth of Nations*. New York: Modern Library Reprint, [1776] 1937.

Smith, Merritt Roe, and Leo Marx, eds. *Does Technology Drive History?: The Dilemma of Technological Determinism*. Cambridge, MA: MIT Press, 1994.

Smith, Richard. "Serious Privacy Problems in Windows Media Player for Windows XP." *ComputerBytesMan.com* (February 20, 2002). http://www.computerbytesman.com/privacy/wmp8dvd.htm.

Sony Corp. of America v. Universal City Studios, Inc. 464 U.S. 417. U.S. S. Ct. 1984.

Spector, Malcolm, and John Kitsuse, *Constructing Social Problems*. Menlo Park, CA: Benjamin Cummings, 1977.

Spigel, Lynn. *Make Room for TV: Television and the Family Ideal in Postwar America*. Chicago: University of Chicago Press, 1992.

Spigel, Lynn, and Denise Mann, eds. *Private Screenings: Television and the Female Consumer*. Minneapolis: University of Minnesota Press, 1992.

Spigel, Lynn, and Jan Olsson. *Television after TV: Essays on a Medium in Transition.* Durham, NC: Duke University Press, 2004.

Stallman, Richard. "Why Software Should Not Have Owners." In Richard Stallman, ed., *Free Software, Free Society: Selected Essays of Richard M. Stallman,* 45–50. Cambridge, MA: Free Software Foundation, 2002.

Standage, Tom. *The Victorian Internet: The Remarkable Story of the Telegraph and the Nineteenth Century's On-Line Pioneers.* New York: Walker and Company, 1998.

Starker, Steven. *Evil Influences: Crusades against the Mass Media.* New Brunswick, NJ: Transaction Publishers, 1989.

Starr, Paul. *The Creation of the Media: Political Origins of Modern Communications.* New York: Basic Books, 2004.

Stefik, Mark. "Letting Loose the Light: Igniting Commerce in Electronic Publication." In Mark Stefik, ed., *Internet Dreams: Archetypes, Myths, and Metaphors,* 219–254. Cambridge, MA: MIT Press, 1996.

Stefik, Mark. "Shifting the Possible: How Trusted Systems and Digital Property Rights Challenge Us to Rethink Digital Publishing." *Berkeley Technology Law Journal* 12.1 (1997): 137–159.

Sterne, Jonathan. *The Audible Past: Cultural Origins of Sound Reproduction.* Durham, NC: Duke University Press, 2003.

Sterne, Jonathan. "The MP3 as Cultural Artifact." *New Media & Society* 8.5 (2006): 825–842.

Stewart, Roy. "Digital Television Transition." Paper presented to Federal Communications Commission (April 19, 2001).

Strangelove, Michael. *The Empire of Mind: Digital Piracy and the Anti-Capitalist Movement.* Toronto: University of Toronto Press, 2005.

Streeter, Thomas. *Selling the Air: A Critique of the Policy of Commercial Broadcasting in the United States.* Chicago: University of Chicago Press, 1996.

Suchman, Lucy. *Plans and Situated Actions: The Problem of Human-Machine Communication.* Cambridge: Cambridge University Press, 1987.

Tanaka, Tatsuo. "Does File Sharing Reduce Music CD Sales? A Case of Japan." Working Paper #05-08, Institute of Innovation Research, Hitotsubashi University (December 13, 2004). http://www.iir.hit-u.ac.jp/file/WP05-08tanaka.pdf.

Tanner, Mike. "MP3 Music Pirates Avoid Legal Action." *Wired News* (May 23, 1997). http://www.wired.com/news/print/0,1294,4069,00.html.

Tassey, Gregory. "The Roles of Standards as Technology Infrastructure." In Richard Hawkins, Robin Mansell, and Jim Skea, eds., *Standards, Innovation and Competitive-*

ness: The Politics and Economics of Standards in Natural and Technical Environments, 161–171. Brookfield, VT: Edward Elgar, 1995.

Thorburn, David, and Henry Jenkins, eds. *Rethinking Media Change: The Aesthetics of Transition*. Cambridge, MA: MIT Press, 2003.

Tomlinson, John. *Cultural Imperialism: A Critical Introduction*. Baltimore: Johns Hopkins University Press, 1991.

Torvalds, Linus. "What Makes Hackers Tick? a.k.a. Linus' Law." In Pekka Himanen, ed., *The Hacker Ethic*, xiii–xvii. New York: Random House, 2001.

Turner, Frederick. "Cyberspace as the New Frontier? Mapping the Shifting Boundaries of the Network Society." Discussion group post, Red Rock News Eater Service (June 6, 1999). http://commons.somewhere.com/rre/1999/RRE.Cyberspace.as.the.N e.html?Search=cyberspace.

Turner, Fred. *From Counterculture to Cyberculture: Stewart Brand, the Whole Earth Network, and the Rise of Digital Utopianism*. Chicago: University of Chicago Press, 2006.

Turow, Joseph. "Audience Construction and Culture Production: Marketing Surveillance in the Digital Age." *The Annals of the American Academy of Political and Social Science* 597.1 (January 2005): 103–121.

Universal City Studios, Inc. et al. v. Eric Corley. 273 F.2d 429. 2d Cir. 2001.

Universal City Studios, Inc. v. Reimerdes. 111 F. Supp. 2d 294. S.D.N.Y. 2000.

U.S. Department of Commerce, Information Infrastructure Task Force. "Intellectual Property and the National Information Infrastructure: The Report of the Working Group on Intellectual Property Rights." Washington, DC (1995).

Vaidhyanathan, Siva. *Copyrights and Copywrongs: The Rise of Intellectual Property and How It Threatens Creativity*. New York: New York University Press, 2001.

Vaidhyanathan, Siva. *The Anarchist in the Library: How the Clash between Freedom and Control Is Hacking the Real World and Crashing the System*. New York: Basic Books, 2004.

Vaidhyanathan, Siva. "Remote Control: The Rise of Electronic Cultural Policy." *The Annals of the American Academy of Political and Social Science* 597.1 (January 2005): 122–133.

Vaidhyanathan, Siva. "A Risky Gamble with Google." *The Chronicle of Higher Education* 15 (December 2, 2005): B7. http://www.nyu.edu/classes/siva/archives/002445.html.

Vaidhyanathan, Siva. "Afterword: Critical Information Studies: A Bibliographic Manifesto." *Cultural Studies* 20.2–3 (March/May 2006): 292–315.

Valenti, Jack. "Home Recording of Copyright Works." U.S. House of Representatives, Committee on the Judiciary, Subcommittee on Courts, Civil Liberties, and the Administration of Justice (April 12, 13, 14, June 24, August 11, September 22, 23, 1982). http://cryptome.org/hrcw-hear.htm.

Valenti, Jack. "'. . . With a Wild Surmise, Silent, upon a Peak in Darien . . .' The Audiovisual Revolution in the Americas." Paper presented at Intellectual Property Conference of the Americas, Los Angeles, CA (July 15, 1996).

Valenti, Jack. "'There Is No Force under Heaven which Can Tear a Nation's Allegiance from Its Culture.' Some Testimony about the Endurance of a Country's National Culture as Well as Some Remarks and Cautionary Observations about the Audiovisual Future." Paper presented at Global Media Dialogue, Denmark (October 10, 1996).

Valenti, Jack. "'Quo Vadis?'" Paper presented to Consumer Electronic Manufacturers Association, Orlando, FL (May 23, 1996).

Valenti, Jack. "If You Can't Protect What You Own—You Don't Own Anything." U.S. House of Representatives, Subcommittee on Courts & Intellectual Property: On WIPO Copyright Treaties Implementation Act and the Online Copyright Liability Limitation Act (September 16, 1997).

Valenti, Jack. "Protecting America's Most Prized Export in the Digital World." Paper presented at Summer Internet World '98, Chicago, IL (July 16, 1998).

Valenti, Jack. "Protecting America's Grandest Trade Prize." U.S. Senate, Foreign Relations Committee: On WIPO Copyright Treaties Implementation Act and the Online Copyright Liability Limitation Act (September 10, 1998).

Valenti, Jack. "WIPO One Year Later: Assessing Consumer Access to Digital Entertainment on the Internet and Other Media." U.S. House of Representatives, Committee on Commerce, Subcommittee on Telecommunications, Trade, and Consumer Protection (October 28, 1999).

Valenti, Jack. "There's No Free Hollywood." Editorial. *New York Times* (June 21, 2000).

Valenti, Jack. "Copyright and Creativity—The Jewel in America's Trade Crown: A Call to Congress to Protect and Preserve the Fastest Growing Economic Asset of the United States." Paper presented at International Trademark Association, Santa Monica, CA (January 22, 2001).

Valenti, Jack. "A Clear Present and Future Danger: The Potential Undoing of America's Greatest Export Trade Prize. An Accounting of Movie Thievery in the Analog and Digital Format, in the U.S. and around the World." U.S. Senate, Committee on Foreign Relations (February 12, 2002).

Valenti, Jack. "If You Can't Protect What You Own, You Don't Own Anything! A Brief Report Concerning the Dark Underside of Internet Piracy as Well as the Possibility of a Cleansing Redemption to Benefit the American Consumer." U.S. Senate, Committee on Commerce, Science, and Transportation (February 28, 2002).

Valenti, Jack. "'Oh, To Have the Visionary Gifts of Ninon de Lenclos!' A Recital of Why Visual Entertainment, and in Particular the American Movie, Remains Immune to the Economic Blahs." Paper presented to Merrill Lynch Business Conference, Pasadena, CA (September 25, 2002).

Valenti, Jack. "'Let Us Build Together a Global Alliance Whose Mandate It Is to Protect Creative Works in the Digital World': A Call for Germany, the European Union and the United States to Forge Strong Barriers to Digital Piracy." Paper presented at DVD Entertainment Trade Forum, Munich (October 22, 2002).

Valenti, Jack. "'Man Is the Only Animal Who Both Laughs and Weeps, Because Man Is the Only Animal Who Understands the Difference between the Way Things Are and the Way They Ought to Be': Some Comments on the Moral Imperative." Paper presented at Duke University (February 24, 2003).

Valenti, Jack. "Emerson's Doctrine: The Very Good, the Not-So-Good, the Brooding Menace, and the Wonder and the Beauty of 'Human Behavior.'" Paper presented at ShoWest, Las Vegas, NV (March 4, 2003).

Valenti, Jack. "International Copyright Piracy: Links to Organized Crime and Terrorism." U.S. House of Representatives, Committee on the Judiciary, Subcommittee on Courts, the Internet, and Intellectual Property (March 13, 2003).

Valenti, Jack. "The Perils of Movie Piracy and Its Dark Effects on Consumers, the Million People Who Work in the Movie Industry, and the Nation's Economy: Some Facts, Worries and a Look at the Uncharted Future." U.S. Senate, Commerce Committee (September 17, 2003).

Valenti, Jack. "Thoughts on the Digital Future of Movies, the Threat of Piracy, the Hope of Redemption." U.S. Senate, Committee on Governmental Affairs, Permanent Subcommittee on Investigations on "Privacy & Piracy: The Paradox of Illegal File Sharing on Peer-to-Peer Networks and the Impact of Technology on the Entertainment Industry" (September 30, 2003).

Valenti, Jack. "International Intellectual Property Piracy: Stealing America's Secrets." U.S. Senate, Committee on Foreign Relations (June 9, 2004).

van Oost, Ellen. "Materialized Gender: How Shavers Configure the Users' Femininity and Masculinity." In Nelly Oudshoorn and Trevor Pinch, eds., *How Users Matter: The Co-Construction of Users and Technology*, 193–208. Cambridge, MA: MIT Press, 2003.

Varian, Hal, Joseph Farrell, and Carl Shapiro. *The Economics of Information Technology: An Introduction*. Cambridge: Cambridge University Press, 2004.

Venturelli, Shalini. "From the Information Economy to the Creative Economy: Moving Culture to the Center of International Public Policy." Discussion paper, Cultural Comment, Center for Arts and Culture, Washington, DC, 2001. http://www.culturalpolicy.org/pdf/venturelli.pdf.

Vogelstein, Fred. "Is It Sharing or Stealing?" *U.S. News and World Report* (June 12, 2000): 38–40.

von Lohmann, Fred. "Fair Use and Digital Rights Management: Preliminary Thoughts on the (Irreconcilable?) Tension between Them." Paper presented at Computers, Freedom, and Privacy (April 16, 2002): 3. http://www.eff.org/IP/DRM/fair_use_and_drm.html.

Vygotsky, Lev, and Michael Cole. *Mind in Society: The Development of Higher Psychological Processes*. Cambridge, MA: Harvard University Press, 1978.

Walterscheid, Edward. "Defining the Patent and Copyright Term: Term Limits and the Intellectual Property Clause." *Journal of Intellectual Property Law* 7 (Spring 2000): 315–394.

Walther, Joseph, Geri Gay, and Jeffrey Hancock. "How Do Communication and Technology Researchers Study the Internet?" *Journal of Communication* 55.3 (September 2005): 632–657. http://www.hci.cornell.edu/pubs/632.pdf.

Waterman, David. "The Political Economy of Audio-Visual Copyright Enforcement." Unpublished manuscript (June 2005). http://www.indiana.edu/~telecom/faculty/waterman/piracy_05.pdf.

Weber, Rachel. "Manufacturing Gender in Commercial and Military Cockpit Design." *Science, Technology, & Human Values* 22.2 (Spring 1997): 235–253.

Weber, Steve. *The Success of Open Source*. Cambridge, MA: Harvard University Press, 2004.

Weinberg, Alvin. "Can Technology Replace Social Engineering?" in Albert Teich, ed., *Technology and the Future*, 30–39. Boston: Bedford/St. Martin's, 2000.

Weiss, Martin, and Carl Cargill. "Consortia in the Standards Development Process." *Journal of the American Society for Information Science* 43.8 (1992): 559–565.

Wexler, Celia. "Channeling Influence: The Broadcast Lobby and the $70 Billion Free Ride." Report, Common Cause, Washington, DC (1997).

Williams, Raymond. *Television: Technology and Cultural Form*. London: Fontana, 1974.

Winner, Langdon. "Do Artifacts Have Politics?" *Daedalus* 109.1 (Winter 1980): 121–136.

Winner, Langdon. "Upon Opening the Black Box and Finding It Empty: Social Constructivism and the Philosophy of Technology." *Science, Technology, & Human Values* 18.3 (Summer 1993): 362–378.

"The Wired Scared Shitlist." *Wired* 3.1 (January 1995). http://www.wired.com/wired/archive/3.01/shitlist_pr.html.

Woolgar, Steve. "Configuring the User: The Case of Usability Trials." In John Law, ed., *A Sociology of Monsters: Essays on Power, Technology, and Domination*, 58–100. London: Routledge, 1991.

Woolgar, Steve. "The Turn to Technology in Social Studies of Science." *Science, Technology, & Human Values* 16.1 (Winter 1991): 20–50.

Woolgar, Steve. "Technologies as Cultural Artefacts." In William Dutton, ed., *Information and Communication Technologies—Visions and Realities*, 87–102. Oxford: Oxford University Press, 1996.

Woolgar, Steve, and Geoff Cooper. "Do Artefacts Have Ambivalences? Moses' Bridges, Winner's Bridges, and Other Urban Legends of STS." *Social Studies of Science* 29.3 (June 1999): 433–449.

Woolgar, Steve, and Keith Grint. "Computers and the Transformation of Social Analysis." *Science, Technology, & Human Values* 16.3 (1991): 368–378.

Wyatt, Sally. "Talking about the Future: Metaphors of the Internet." In Nik Brown, Brian Rappert, and Andrew Webster, eds., *Contested Futures: A Sociology of Prospective Techno-Science*, 109–126. Aldershot, UK: Ashgate Press, 2000.

Yamamoto, Lauren. "Copyright Protection and Internet Fan Sites: Entertainment Industry Finds Solace in Traditional Copyright Law." *Loyola of Los Angeles Entertainment Law Review* 20.1 (2000): 95–128. http://elr.lls.edu/issues/v20-issue1/yamamoto.pdf.

Zimmerman, Diane. "Adrift in the Digital Millennium Copyright Act: The Sequel." *Dayton Law Review* 26.2 (Winter 2001): 279–292.

About the Author

Tarleton Gillespie is an assistant professor in the Department of Communication at Cornell University, with affiliations in the Department of Science & Technology Studies and the Information Science program. He is also a non-residential fellow with the Center for Internet and Society at the Stanford University School of Law. His research, broadly examining the intersections of media, technology, law, and culture, has appeared in *The Information Society*, *Social Studies of Science*, and *New Media and Society*. He has chapters in two anthologies investigating the Internet and its implications: one in *New Media: Theses on Convergence, Media, and Digital Reproduction* (Anna Everett and John Caldwell, eds., Routledge, 2003) and *Structures of Participation in Digital Culture* (Joe Karaganis and Natalie Jeremijenko, eds., Duke University Press, 2007).

Gillespie was awarded his Ph.D. in Communication from the University of California, San Diego (2002); he also has a Masters in Communication from UCSD (1997) and a B.A. with honors in English from Amherst College (1994). In 2004, he was awarded a research fellowship by the Social Science Research Council, as part of its Digital Cultural Institutions Project, which helped support chapters 7 and 8 of this manuscript.

His work and most current information can be found at http://www.tarletongillespieorg/.

Index